Along These Lines

A Course for Developing Writers

Along These Lines

A Course for Developing Writers

John Sheridan Biays
Broward Community College

Carol Wershoven
Palm Beach Community College

PRENTICE HALL
Upper Saddle River, New Jersey 07458

Library of Congress Cataloging-in-Publication Data

Biays, John Sheridan.
    Along these lines / John Biays, Carol Wershoven.
        p.   cm.
    Includes index.
    ISBN 0-13-398447-8
    1. English language--Rhetoric--Problems, exercises, etc.
    2. English language--Grammar--Problems, exercises, etc.   3. Report
    writing--Problems, exercises, etc.   I. Wershoven, Carol.
    II. Title.
    PE1408.B4933   1997
    808'.042--dc21   97-26234
                                                                          CIP

Editor-in-Chief: Charlyce Jones Owen
Acquisitions Editor: Maggie Barbieri
Editorial Assistant: Joan Polk
Assistant Vice President of Humanities and Social Science: Barbara Kittle
Project Manager: Julie Sullivan
Manufacturing Manager: Nick Sklitsis
Prepress and Manufacturing Buyer: Mary Ann Gloriande
Creative Design Director: Leslie Osher
Interior Design: Circa 86
Cover Design: Circa 86
Supervisor of Production Services: John Jordan
Electronic Page Layout: Lori Clinton
Director of Marketing: Gina Sluss
Marketing Manager: Rob Mejia

This book was set in 11/13 Sabon by Prentice-Hall Production Services and was printed and
bound by Courier Companies, Inc. The cover was printed by The Lehigh Press, Inc.

Acknowledgments appear on page 434, which constitutes an extension of the copyright page.

 © 1998 by John Sheridan Biays and Carol Wershoven
Simon & Schuster/A Viacom Company
Upper Saddle River, New Jersey 07458

Printed in the United States of America
10 9 8 7 6 5 4 3 2 1

ISBN 0-13-398447-8

Prentice-Hall International (UK) Limited, *London*
Prentice-Hall of Australia Pty. Limited, *Sydney*
Prentice-Hall Canada Inc., *Toronto*
Prentice-Hall Hispanoamericana, S.A., *Mexico*
Prentice-Hall of India Private Limited, *New Delhi*
Prentice-Hall of Japan, Inc., *Tokyo*
Simon & Schuster Asia Pte. Ltd., *Singapore*
Editora Prentice-Hall do Brasil, Ltda., *Rio de Janeiro*

Contents

PREFACE XV

WRITING IN STEPS: *The Process Approach*

INTRODUCTION 1

CHAPTER ONE: *Writing a Paragraph: Illustration*   3

Beginning the Thoughtlines   3
   Freewriting, Brainstorming, Keeping a Journal   4
   Finding Specific Ideas   5
   Adding Details to an Idea   6
Focusing the Thoughtlines 12
   Listing Related Ideas 12
   Mapping 13
   Forming a Topic Sentence 13
Outlines for a Paragraph 19
   Checking Your Details 19
   Adding Details When There Aren't Enough 20
   Eliminating Details That Don't Relate to the Topic
     Sentence 20
   From List to Outline 21
   Determining the Order of Details 23
Roughlines for a Paragraph 28
Final Lines for a Paragraph 31
   Giving Your Paragraph a Title 32
   Reviewing the Writing Process 32
Lines of Detail: A Walk-Through Assignment 35
Writing Your Own Paragraph 36
Peer Review Form for a Paragraph 39

CHAPTER TWO: *Writing from Reading*   40

What Is Writing from Reading? 40
An Approach to Writing from Reading 40
   Attitude 40

Prereading 41
Why Preread? 41
Forming Questions before You Read 42
An Example of the Prereading Step 42
"A Ridiculous Addiction" by Gwinn Owens 42
Reading 44
An Example of the Reading Step 45
Answers to Prereading Questions 45
Rereading with Pen or Pencil 45
An Example of Rereading with Pen or Pencil 46
What the Notes Mean 49
Writing a Summary of a Reading 50
Thoughtlines: Marking a List of Ideas 50
Thoughtlines: Selecting a Main Idea 52
Outlines for a Summary 53
Roughlines: Attributing Ideas in a Summary 54
Final Lines for a Summary 55
Writing a Reaction to a Reading 56
Thoughtlines: Freewriting 56
Thoughtlines: Listing Ideas 57
Thoughtlines: Brainstorming 57
Thoughtlines: Developing Points of Agreement
   or Disagreement 58
Outlines for a Reaction to a Reading 58
Roughlines for a Reaction to a Reading 59
Final Lines for a Reaction to a Reading 59
Lines of Detail: A Walk-Through Assignment 60
Writing Your Own Paragraph on "A Ridiculous
   Addiction" 60
Peer Review Form for Writing from Reading 62
Writing from Reading 63
"Parental Discretion" by Dennis Hevesi 63
Writing from Reading "Parental Discretion" 66

CHAPTER THREE: *Description*   68

What Is Description? 68
Hints for Writing a Descriptive Paragraph 68
Writing the Descriptive Paragraph in Steps 75
Thoughtlines: Description 75
The Dominant Impression 76
Outlines: Description 79
Roughlines: Description 84
Transitions 87
Final Lines: Description 88
Lines of Detail: A Walk-Through Assignment 91
Writing Your Own Descriptive Paragraph 91
Peer Review Form for a Descriptive Paragraph 94

Writing from Reading: Description   95
  "A Present for Popo" by Elizabeth Wong   95
  Writing from Reading "A Present for Popo"   97

CHAPTER FOUR: *Narration*   98

What Is Narration?   98
  Giving the Narrative a Point   98
  Hints for Writing a Narrative Paragraph 103
  Using a Speaker's Exact Words in Narrative 105
Writing the Narrative Paragraph in Steps 105
  Thoughtlines: Narration 105
    Freewriting for a Narrative Topic 107
    Narrowing and Selecting a Suitable Narrative Topic 107
  Outlines: Narration 110
  Roughlines: Narration 114
    Revising for Sharper Details 114
    Checking the Topic Sentence 116
    Using Transitions Effectively in Narration 118
    The Revised Draft 118
  Final Lines: Narration 120
Lines of Detail: A Walk-Through Assignment 123
Writing Your Own Narrative Paragraph 123
Peer Review Form for a Narrative Paragraph 125
Writing from Reading: Narration 126
  "Rocky Rowf" by Edna Buchanan 126
  Writing from Reading "Rocky Rowf" 129

CHAPTER FIVE: *Process*   130

What Is Process? 130
  A Process Involves Steps in Time Order 130
  Hints for Writing a Process Paragraph 131
Writing the Process Paragraph in Steps 133
  Thoughtlines: Process 133
    Writing a Topic Sentence for a Process Paragraph 134
  Outlines: Process 136
  Roughlines: Process 140
    Using the Same Grammatical Person 141
    Using Transitions Effectively 142
    The Revised Draft 144
  Final Lines: Process 145
Lines of Detail: A Walk-Through Assignment 148
Writing Your Own Process Paragraph 149
Peer Review Form for a Process Paragraph 150
Writing from Reading: Process 151

"How to Land the Job You Want"
by Davidyne Mayleas 151
Writing from Reading "How to Land the Job
You Want" 154

CHAPTER SIX: *Comparison and Contrast*   155

What Is Comparison? What Is Contrast? 155
Hints for Writing a Comparison or Contrast
Paragraph 155
Writing the Topic Sentence for a Comparison
or Contrast Paragraph. 156
Organizing Your Comparison or Contrast Paragraph 156
Using Transitions Effectively for Comparison
or Contrast 162
Using Transitions in a Contrast Paragraph,
Point-by-Point Pattern 162
Using Transitions in a Contrast Paragraph,
Subject-by-Subject Pattern 163
Writing the Comparison or Contrast Paragraph in Steps 165
Thoughtlines: Comparison or Contrast 165
Getting Points of Comparison or Contrast 166
Adding Details to Your Points 168
Outlines: Comparison or Contrast 170
Roughlines: Comparison or Contrast 175
Revising the Draft 175
Final Lines: Comparison or Contrast 177
Contrast Paragraph: Point-by-Point Pattern 177
The Same Contrast Paragraph: Subject-by-Subject 180
Lines of Detail: A Walk-Through Assignment 183
Writing Your Own Comparison or Contrast Paragraph 184
Peer Review Form for a Comparison or Contrast Paragraph 186
Writing from Reading: Comparison or Contrast 187
"Against All Odds, I'm Just Fine" by Brad Wackerlin 187
Writing from Reading "Against All Odds,
I'm Just Fine" 188

CHAPTER SEVEN: *Classification*   189

What Is Classification? 189
Hints for Writing a Classification Paragraph 189
Writing the Classification Paragraph in Steps 194
Thoughtlines: Classification 194
Brainstorming a Basis for Classification 194
Matching the Points within the Types 195
Writing a Topic Sentence for a Classification
Paragraph 195

Outlines: Classification 197
Effective Order in Classifying 197
Roughlines: Classification 200
Final Lines: Classification 203
Lines of Detail: A Walk-Through Assignment 206
Writing Your Own Classification Paragraph 206
Peer Review Form for a Classification Paragraph 208
Writing from Reading: Classification 209
"Three Disciplines for Children" by John Holt 209
Writing from Reading "Three Disciplines for Children" 211

CHAPTER EIGHT: *Cause and Effect* 212

What Is Cause and Effect? 212
Hints for Writing a Cause or Effect Paragraph 212
Writing the Cause or Effect Paragraph in Steps 215
Thoughtlines: Cause or Effect 215
Freewriting on a Topic 215
Brainstorming and Interviewing for Ideas 216
Working with a List 216
Designing a Topic Sentence 217
Outlines: Cause or Effect 220
The Order of Causes or Effects 221
Roughlines: Cause or Effect 224
Linking Ideas in Cause or Effect 225
Making the Links Clear 225
Revising the Draft 226
Final Lines: Cause or Effect 229
Lines of Detail: A Walk-Through Assignment 231
Writing Your Own Cause or Effect Paragraph 232
Peer Review Form for a Cause or Effect Paragraph 233
Writing from Reading: Cause and Effect 234
"Students in Shock" by John Kellmayer 234
Writing from Reading "Students in Shock" 236

CHAPTER NINE: *Argument* 237

What Is Argument? 237
Hints for Writing an Argument Paragraph 237
Writing the Argument Paragraph in Steps 241
Thoughtlines: Argument 241
Grouping Your Ideas 242
Brainstorming for Clarity and Details 242
Outlines: Argument 245
The Order of Reasons in an Argument 245
Roughlines: Argument 249
Checking Your Reasons 250

Explaining the Problem or the Issue 250
Transitions That Emphasize 250
A Revised Draft 250
Final Lines: Argument. 253
Lines of Detail: A Walk-Through Assignment. 255
Writing Your Own Argument Paragraph 256
Peer Review Form for an Argument Paragraph. 257
Writing from Reading: Argument 258
"The Myth of Computer Literacy" by Douglas Noble 258
Writing from Reading "The Myth of Computer Literacy" 259
"Afrocentric Education Pointless if Girls Are Excluded"
by Julianne Malveaux. 260
Writing from Reading "Afrocentric Education
Pointless if Girls Are Excluded" 262

CHAPTER TEN: *Writing an Essay*   264

What Is an Essay? 264
Comparing the Single Paragraph and the Essay 264
Organizing an Essay 266
Writing the Thesis 266
Hints for Writing a Thesis 267
Writing the Essay in Steps 268
Thoughtlines: Essay. 269
Listing Ideas 269
Marking the Ideas on Your List 269
Clustering the Ideas 270
Outlines: Essay 273
Revising Your Draft Outline 274
Some Hints in Outlining 274
Revisiting the Thoughtlines Stage 276
Roughlines: Essay. 279
Writing the Introduction 279
Where Does the Thesis Go? 279
Hints for Writing the Introduction 280
Writing the Body of the Essay. 282
How Long Are the Body Paragraphs? 283
Developing the Body Paragraphs 283
Writing the Conclusion 285
Revising the Draft 287
Transitions within Paragraphs 288
Transitions between Paragraphs 288
A Revised Draft 289
Final Lines: Essay. 295
Creating a Title 295
Comparing the Stages of the Essay 295
Lines of Detail: A Walk-Through Assignment. 300
Writing Your Own Essay 302

Peer Review Form for an Essay 303
Writing from Reading: The Essay 304
    "Eleven" by Sandra Cisneros 304
    Writing from Reading "Eleven" 306
    "Just Walk on By: A Black Man Ponders His Power
      to Alter Public Space" by Brent Staples 306
    Writing from Reading "Just Walk on By: A Black
      Man Ponders His Power to Alter Public Space" 309

THE BOTTOM LINE: *Grammar for Writers*

INTRODUCTION 311

SECTION ONE: *The Simple Sentence* 315

Recognizing a Sentence 315
Recognizing Verbs 315
    More on Verbs 316
Recognizing Subjects 317
    More about Recognizing Subjects and Verbs 318
    Prepositions and Prepositional Phrases 319
Word Order 322
    More on Word Order 322
    Word Order in Questions 323
    Words That Can't Be Verbs 323
    Recognizing Main Verbs 324
    Verb Forms That Can't Be Main Verbs 324

SECTION TWO: *Beyond the Simple Sentence: Coordination* 329

Options for Combining Simple Sentences 329
Option 1: Using a Comma with a Coordinating Conjunction 330
    Where Does the Comma Go? 331
    Placing the Comma by Using S-V Patterns 331
Option 2: Using a Semicolon Between Two Simple
    Sentences 333
Option 3: Using a Semicolon and a Conjunctive Adverb 334
    Punctuating after a Conjunctive Adverb 335

SECTION THREE: *Beyond the Simple Sentence: Subordination* 340

More on Combining Simple Sentences 340
Option 4: Using a Dependent Clause to Begin a Sentence 340
Option 5: Using a Dependent Clause to End a Sentence 341

Using a Subordinating Conjunction 341
Punctuating Complex Sentences 342
Combining Sentences: A Review of Your Options 343

⑤ECTION FOUR: *Avoiding Sentence
                    Fragments*   348

Recognizing Fragments 348
Correcting Fragments 352

⑤ECTION FIVE: *Using Parallelism
                   in Sentences*   356

Achieving Parallelism 357

⑤ECTION SIX: *Correcting Problems
                  with Modifiers*   363

Correcting Modifier Problems 364
    Correcting Dangling Modifiers 366
Reviewing the Steps and the Solutions 368

⑤ECTION SEVEN: *Using Verbs Correctly*   371

Using Standard Verb Forms 371
The Past Tense 373
The Four Main Forms of a Verb 374
Irregular Verbs 375
    The Past Tense of *be, have, do* 376
    More Irregular Verb Forms 377

⑤ECTION EIGHT: *More on Verbs:
                     Consistency and Voice*   382

Consistent Verb Tenses 382
The Present Perfect and Past Perfect Tenses 385
The Past Perfect Tense 386
Passive and Active Voice 387
    Avoiding Unnecessary Shifts in Voice 389
    Small Reminders about Verbs 390

⑤ECTION NINE: *Making Subjects
                    and Verbs Agree*   393

Pronouns as Subjects 394
Special Problems with Agreement 394
    Finding the Subject 394

ALONG THESE LINES/Prentice-Hall, Inc.

Changed Word Order. 396
Compound Subjects 397
Indefinite Pronouns 398
Collective Nouns. 399
Making Subjects and Verbs Agree: The Bottom Line. 400

Ⓢ ECTION TEN: *Using Pronouns Correctly:*
Agreement and Reference 405

Agreement of a Pronoun and Its Antecedent 406
Indefinite Pronouns 406
Avoiding Sexism 407
Collective Nouns. 408
Pronouns and Their Antecedents: Being Clear 410

Ⓢ ECTION ELEVEN: *Using Pronouns Correctly:*
Consistency and Case 413

Choosing the Case of Pronouns 415
Problems Choosing Pronoun Case 416
Common Errors with Case of Pronouns 417

Ⓢ ECTION TWELVE: *Punctuation* 419

The Period 419
The Question Mark 419
The Semicolon 419
The Comma. 421
Other Ways to Use a Comma 422
The Apostrophe 425
The Colon. 426
The Exclamation Mark. 426
The Dash 427
Parentheses 427
The Hyphen. 427
Quotation Marks 428
Capital Letters 429
Numbers 431
Abbreviations 431

INDEX 435

ALONG THESE LINES/Prentice-Hall, Inc.

Preface

To Instructors

Along These Lines is a rhetoric/reader/grammar text designed for beginning writers. It is filled with exercises and activities, both individual and collaborative, because we believe that basic writing students are more motivated and learn more easily when they are actively involved with individual or collaborative tasks. The *Lines* in the title refer to the stages of the writing process:

    Thoughtlines: the time spent generating ideas,
    Outlines: the steps of planning and focusing,
    Roughlines: the steps of drafting and revising,
    Final Lines: the last step, proofreading.

The **rhetoric section** of *Along These Lines* is structured around these stages. After the first chapter explains and shows how these stages are parts of the process of writing a paragraph, subsequent chapters on writing a specific kind of paragraph or on writing an essay take the student through all the stages of writing that paragraph or essay, from the thoughtlines to the final lines. Each rhetorical chapter includes these distinctive features:

- Not much "talk" about writing; instead, no more than two pages of print are without a chart, box, list, example, or exercise;
- A lively, conversational tone, including Question-and-Answer formats, and dialogues;
- Checklists for each stage of the writing process;
- Exercises integrated throughout each chapter, so each concept is reinforced as soon as it is introduced;
- Collaborative exercises that have students writing with peers, interviewing classmates, reacting to others' suggestions, and building on others' ideas;
- Small, simple clusters of information surrounded by white space rather than intimidating expanses of small print;
- A recap of the stages of writing at the end of each chapter, where the outline, draft, and final version of the sample assignment are all in one place, for easy reference;
- Numerous writing topics and activities in each chapter, providing more flexibility for the instructor;
- A Peer Review Form in each chapter, so students can benefit from classmates' reactions to their drafts.

The **reading sections** of *Along These Lines* have these distinctive features:

- A separate and detailed chapter on Reading Critically and Writing from Reading, explaining and illustrating the steps of prereading, reading and rereading, annotating, summarizing, and reacting (in writing) to another's ideas;

- Prereading questions for each reading selection in the text, designed not only to anticipate key ideas but to spark interest and discussion;
- Vocabulary definitions for each reading selection;
- Grouping of selections by rhetorical pattern;
- Readings that appeal to these particular audiences: working students, returning students, students who are parents or spouses. The selections focus on such topics as **the workplace, getting an education, relationships, generational divisions and definitions, fitting in or feeling left out;**
- Readings that are accessible to this student audience—thus many of the selections come from newspapers or magazines students would flip through at a newsstand;
- Topics for Writing sparked by the content of the readings, designed to elicit thinking, not rote replication of a model.

The **grammar section** of *Along These Lines* includes these distinctive features:

- Numerous collaborative exercises, including, in many sections, exercises for students to devise their own examples to illustrate concepts they've just learned;
- Grammar concepts taught step-by-step, as in "Two Steps to Check for Fragments."

Along These Lines combines the traditional and the innovative; it stresses the planning stage of writing and proposes the outline as a useful tool. Instructors who do not stress outlining may skim the sections on outlining and prefer to spend more time on the sections on revision. **Both traditionalists and innovators will find something useful in the many activities, assignments, and exercises designed to get students thinking, reacting, and connecting ideas.** The text is designed to be a *menu*, and its goal is to provide enough options to accommodate a diversity of teaching strategies and student populations.

Instructors will find *Along These Lines* easy to use for several reasons:

- Its abundant exercises, activities, assignments, and readings enable teachers to select what they like and adapt their choices to the needs of different class sections.
- The perforated tear-out exercises reinforce every instructional concept and eliminate the pressure instructors face in preparing supplemental materials.
- The exercises provide an instant lesson plan for any class period or individualized work for students in a writing lab.
- Exercises that can be completed in class are marked with a bar for easy reference. Similarly, each Peer Review Form has a clearly marked tab at the end of a chapter.

Along These Lines has many unique features, but the book's most distinguishing feature is its assumption that a basic writing text does not have to be tedious or patronizing. In contrast, *Along These Lines* is written with the philosophy that students deserve a book as stimulating and challenging as the lives they lead.

Note on Ancillary Materials

Instructors who adopt *Along These Lines* may order the following materials to supplement their instruction:

- Instructor's Manual (ISBN 0-13-759853-X), containing answers to exercises, sample syllabi, and suggestions for using *Along These Lines;*
- Exercise booklet (ISBN 0-13-759879-3), containing additional exercises for all parts of *Along These Lines*: the rhetoric, reading, and grammar sections;
- *The Writer's Solution,* an interactive writing program containing two CDs. One, Language Lab, an interactive grammar tutorial while the other, Writing Lab, offers practice in the development of writing skills through each of the rhetorical modes.
- *The Writer's Toolkit,* a disk-based program based on *The Writer's Solution* Writing Lab CD. It contains a multitude of writing exercises designed to help students become better writers.
- *PH Diagnostic Tests for Developmental Writing,* a testing program available in MAC (ISBN 0-13-616426-9), WIN (ISBN 0-13-621640-4), and DOS (ISBN 0-13-616434-X) formats, and in a booklet format (ISBN 0-13-621657-9). It is designed to allow instructors to create their own tests based on level or geared toward testing a specific skill or set of skills. It is free to instructors upon adoption of *Along These Lines.*
- *Prentice Hall's Blue Pencil Software* (ISBN 0-13-759861-0), an interactive editing program allowing students to practice their writing by making revisions in paragraph-length passages on their computer screen;
- *Prentice Hall/Simon and Schuster's Transparencies for Writers* (ISBN 0-13-703209-9), which covers grammar, punctuation, and mechanics via overlays that show how sentence and paragraph errors can be corrected more effectively.

Contact your Prentice Hall sales representative for further details, or call Prentice Hall Faculty Services at 1-800-526-0485.

Acknowledgments

We've always known that collaborative learning methods can enhance instruction for students, but we're now convinced that ongoing collaboration between caring editors and authors is essential for producing an aesthetically pleasing and pedagogically sound text. *Along These Lines* reflects the collective efforts of many talented, dedicated individuals along *all* lines.

We are indeed grateful to Maggie Barbieri, senior editor, for enthusiastically endorsing our vision and for providing comprehensive updates during the development process. We are further indebted to Bobbie Lewis and Julie Sullivan, whose superb editing talents helped us shape, reorganize, and ultimately increase our book's scope and accessibility. Thanks also to Leslie Osher, Maureen Richardson, Susanna Lesan, Shelley Kupperman, and Bonnie Biller for their careful attention to detail during the design stages and for keeping the project on schedule.

Several reviewers were kind enough to provide detailed critiques of the manuscript in various stages of development. Joan Polk coordinated these reviews and provided us with timely feedback. We deeply appreciate the collegial suggestions of Jeanne Ali, Miami-Dade Community College; Kathleen Beauchene, Community College of Rhode Island; Stanley Coberly, West Virginia University at Parkersburg; Carin Halper, Fresno City College; Jim Harcharik, Rock Valley College; Patricia Illing, Longview Community College; Ken McLaurin, Central Piedmont Community College; Roberta Panish, Rockland Community College; Bonnie Ronson, Hillsborough Community College; Elizabeth Semtner, Rose State University; Karen Standridge, Pikes Peak Community College; Kathleen Tickner, Brevard Community College, and Ted Walkup, Clayton College and State University. Additionally, friends and colleagues at Broward Community College offered valuable design suggestions and ongoing support, especially Mary Ellen Grasso, Phyllis Luck, Tony De Los Santos, Susan Heslekrants, and Flora Cohen.

Finally, we offer sincere thanks to two individuals instrumental in launching our project. James Dawsey worked diligently to produce a sample typeset chapter that mirrored the objectives in our original proposal, while Mark Cohen, former sales representative and current acquisitions editor, championed our cause by serving as an energetic and thoroughly professional liaison to Prentice Hall headquarters in New Jersey.

John Sheridan Biays
Carol Wershoven

Along These Lines

A Course for Developing Writers

WRITING IN STEPS

The Process Approach

ALONG THESE LINES/Prentice-Hall, Inc.

INTRODUCTION

Learning By Doing

Writing is a skill, and like any skill, writing improves with practice. Through a menu of activities, this book gives you the opportunity to improve your writing. Some activities can be done alone; some ask that you work with a partner or with a group. You can do some in the classroom; some can be done at home. The important thing to remember is that *good writing takes practice*; you can learn to write well by writing.

Steps Make Writing Easier

Writing is easier if you *don't try to do everything at once*. Producing a piece of effective writing demands that you think, plan, focus, and draft, then re-think, revise, edit, and proofread. You can become frustrated if you try to do all these things at the same time.

To make the task of writing easier, *Along These Lines* breaks the process into four major parts:

THOUGHTLINES

In this step, you *think* about your topic, and you gather ideas. You *react* to your own ideas and add more ideas to your first thoughts. Or you react to other people's ideas as a way of generating your own writing material.

OUTLINES

In this step, you begin to *plan* your writing. You examine your ideas and begin to *focus* them around one main idea. Planning involves combining, dividing, and even discarding the ideas you started with. It involves more thinking about the point you want to make and devising the best way to express it.

1

ROUGHLINES

In this step, the thinking and planning begin to shape themselves into a piece of writing. You complete a *draft* of your work, a rough version of the finished product. And then you think again, as you examine the draft and check it. Checking it begins the process of *revision*, "fixing" the draft so that it takes the shape you want and expresses your ideas clearly.

FINAL LINES

In this step, the final draft of your writing gets one last, careful *review*. When you prepare the final copy of your work, you *proofread* and concentrate on identifying and correcting any mistakes in spelling, mechanics, or punctuation you may have overlooked. This step is the *final check* of your work to make sure your writing is the best that it can be.

These four steps in the writing process—*thoughtlines*, *outlines*, *roughlines*, and *final lines*—always overlap. You may be changing your plan (the *outlines* stage) even as you work on the *roughlines* of your paper. And there's no rule that says you can't move back to an earlier step when necessary. Thinking of writing as a series of steps helps you to see the process as a *manageable task*. You can avoid doing everything at once and becoming overwhelmed by the challenge.

Once you learn these four steps, you can put them to use. As you work through the chapters of this book, you will work with examples of each of the four steps and practice them.

ALONG THESE LINES/Prentice-Hall, Inc.

Usually, students write because they have an assignment that requires them to write on a particular topic or choice of topics, and the writing is due by a certain day. If you get such an assignment and it calls for one paragraph, you might wonder, "Why a paragraph? Why not something large, like a two- or three-page paper? After all, many teachers will ask for papers, not just paragraphs."

For one thing, all essays are a series of paragraphs. If you can write one good paragraph, you can write more than one. *The paragraph is the basic building block of any essay.* It is a group of sentences focusing on one idea or one point. Keep this concept in mind: *one idea for each paragraph.* Focusing on one idea or one point gives a paragraph *unity.* If you have a new point, start a new paragraph.

You may ask, "Doesn't this mean a paragraph will be short? How long should a paragraph be, anyway?" To convince a reader of one main point, you need to make it, support it, develop it, explain it, and describe it. There will be shorter and longer paragraphs, but for now, you can assume your paragraph will be somewhere between seven and twelve sentences long.

This chapter will guide you through each stage of the writing process:

- Thoughtlines—how to generate ideas for your paragraph
- Outlines—how to organize your ideas
- Roughlines—how to make and revise rough drafts
- Final Lines—how to edit and refine your ideas

We give extra emphasis to the thoughtlines in this chapter, to give you that extra help in getting started.

BEGINNING THE THOUGHTLINES

Suppose your instructor asks you to write a paragraph about clothes. To write effectively, you need to know your purpose and your audience. In this case, you already know your *purpose,* to write a paragraph that makes some point about clothes. And you know your *audience,* since you are writing this paragraph for your instructor and classmates. Often, your purpose is to write a specific type of paper for a class. But sometimes you may have to write with a different purpose or for a particular audience. Writing instructions for a new employee at your workplace, or writing a letter of complaint to a manufacturer, or composing a short biographical essay for a scholarship application are examples of different purposes and audiences.

Freewriting, Brainstorming, Keeping a Journal

Once you have identified your purpose and audience, you can begin by finding some way to *think on paper*. You can use the techniques of freewriting, brainstorming, or keeping a journal to gather ideas.

Freewriting   Give yourself fifteen minutes to write whatever comes into your mind on your subject. If your mind is a blank, write, "My mind's a blank. My mind's a blank," over and over until you think of something else. The main goal of *freewriting* is to *write without stopping*. Don't stop to tell yourself, "This is stupid," or "I can't use any of this in a paper." Don't stop to correct your spelling or punctuation. Just write. Let your ideas flow. Write freely. Here's an example:

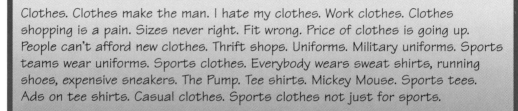

Freewriting about Clothes

Clothes. Clothes make the man. I hate my clothes. Work clothes. Clothes shopping is a pain. Sizes never right. Fit wrong. Price of clothes is going up. People can't afford new clothes. Thrift shops. Uniforms. Military uniforms. Sports teams wear uniforms. Sports clothes. Everybody wears sweat shirts, running shoes, expensive sneakers. The Pump. Tee shirts. Mickey Mouse. Sports tees. Ads on tee shirts. Casual clothes. Sports clothes not just for sports.

Brainstorming   *Brainstorming* is like freewriting because you write whatever comes into your head, but it is a little different because you can pause *to ask yourself questions* that will lead to new ideas. When you brainstorm alone, you "interview" yourself about a subject. Or you can brainstorm, and ask questions, within a group.

   If you are brainstorming about clothes, alone or with a partner or group, you might begin by listing ideas and then add to the ideas by asking and answering questions. Here's an example:

Brainstorming about Clothes

Clothes.
Clothes shopping.

What kind of clothes?
Work clothes. Sports clothes. Sports teams wear uniforms. Insignias of teams.

Who else wears uniforms?
The military wear uniforms. Some schools wear uniforms.

Are there special clothes for certain times and places?
The workplace requires certain clothes. Sports clothes—basketball, tennis, running shoes. Casual clothes are for any time.

What's casual?
Shorts, sweats, jeans, sneakers, tee shirts.

When do you wear tee shirts?
Weekends, evenings. Some people wear casual clothes to work or to shop. Tee shirts are everywhere. All ages wear them. In all places.

If you feel like you are running out of ideas in brainstorming, try to form a question out of what you've just written. Go where your questions and answers lead you. For example, if you write, "Some students wear school uniforms," you could form these questions:

Which students? What kind of schools? What grades? Are school uniforms a good idea? Why? Why not?

You could also make a list of your brainstorming ideas, but remember to *do only one step at a time.*

Keeping a Journal   A *journal* is a notebook of your personal writing, a notebook in which you write regularly and often. *It is not a diary, but it is a place to record your experiences, reactions, and observations.* In it, you can write about what you've done, heard, seen, read, or remembered. You can include sayings that you'd like to remember, news clippings, snapshots—anything that you'd like to recall or consider. Journals are a great way to practice your writing and a great source of ideas for writing.

If you were asked to write about clothes, you might look through entries in your journal, in search of ideas, and might see something like this:

Journal Entry about Clothes

I went to the mall yesterday to look for some good shoes. What a crowd! Some big sale was going on, and the stores were packed. Everybody was pushing and shoving. I just left. I'll go when it's not so crowded. I hate buying clothes and shoes. Wish I could just wear jeans and tee shirts all the time. But even then, the jeans have to have the right label, or you're looked down on. There are status labels on the tee shirts, too. Not to mention expensive athletic shoes.

Finding Specific Ideas

Whether you freewrite, brainstorm, or consult your journal, you end up with something on paper. Follow these first ideas; see where they can take you. You're looking for specific ideas, each of which can focus the general one you started with. At this point, you don't have to decide which specific idea you want to write about. You just want to narrow your range of ideas.

You might think, "Why should I narrow my ideas? Won't I have more to say if I keep my topic big?" But remember that a paragraph has one idea. You want to say one thing clearly, and with convincing details that support it. If you try to write one paragraph on the broad topic of clothes, for example, you'll probably make only general statements that say little. And the big, sweeping statements will bore your reader.

General ideas are big, broad ones. Specific ideas are smaller and narrower. If you scanned the **freewriting** example on clothes, you might underline many specific ideas that could be topics:

Clothes. Clothes make the man. I hate my clothes. <u>Work clothes. Clothes</u>

<u>shopping</u> is a pain. <u>Sizes</u> never right. Fit wrong. <u>Price</u> of clothes is going up.

People can't afford new clothes. <u>Thrift shops. Uniforms. Military uniforms. Sports</u>

teams wear <u>uniforms. Sports clothes.</u> Everybody wears <u>sweatshirts. Running</u>

<u>shoes</u>, sneakers, <u>expensive sneakers.</u> The Pump. <u>Tee shirts.</u> Mickey Mouse. <u>Sports</u>

<u>tees. Ads on tees. Casual clothes.</u> Sports clothes not just for sports.

Consider the underlined terms. Many of them are specific ideas about clothes. You could write a paragraph about one item on the list or about several related items.

Or you could make a list after **brainstorming,** and you could underline specific ideas about clothes:

clothes	clothes for a certain time
<u>work clothes</u>	clothes for a certain place
<u>sports uniforms</u>	<u>clothes shopping</u>
<u>military uniforms</u>	<u>sports clothes</u>
<u>basketball clothes</u>	<u>team insignia</u>
<u>running shoes</u>	<u>school uniforms</u>
<u>casual clothes at work</u>	<u>tennis clothes</u>
<u>tee shirts everywhere</u>	<u>casual clothes</u>
<u>ages of people who wear tee shirts</u>	

These specific ideas could lead you to a specific topic.

If you reviewed the **journal entry** on clothes, you would be able to underline many specific ideas:

I went to the mall yesterday to look for some <u>good shoes.</u> What a crowd! Some big sale was going on, and the stores were packed. Everybody was pushing and shoving. I just left. I'll go when it's not so crowded. I hate <u>buying clothes and shoes.</u> Wish I could just wear <u>jeans and tee shirts</u> all the time. But even then, the jeans have to have the <u>right label,</u> or you're looked down on. There are <u>status labels</u> on the <u>tee shirts,</u> too. Not to mention <u>expensive athletic shoes.</u>

Remember, following the steps can lead you to specific ideas. Then, after you have a list of specific ideas, pick one and try to develop it by adding details.

Adding Details to an Idea

You can develop the one idea you picked in a number of ways:

1. *Check your list* for other ideas that seem to fit with the one you've picked.
2. *Brainstorm*—ask yourself more questions about your topic, and use the answers as details.
3. *List any new ideas* you have that may be connected to your first idea.

For instance, you may decide to work with the list gathered through freewriting:

sports clothes	casual clothes
work clothes	clothes shopping
sizes	price

thrift shops   uniforms
military uniforms   running shoes
sweat shirts   tee shirts
expensive sneakers   ads on tees
sports tees

Looking at this list, you might decide you want to write something about this topic: tee shirts.

One way to add details is to go back and check your list for other ideas that seem to fit with the topic of tee shirts. You find

sports clothes, ads on tees, sports tees

Another way to add details is to brainstorm some questions that will lead you to more details. The questions do not have to be connected to each other; they are just questions that could lead you to ideas and details:

Q A

Question: Who wears tee shirts?
Answer: Athletes, children, teens, movie stars, musicians, parents, old people,
          restaurant workers.

Question: How much do they cost?
Answer: Some are cheap, but some are expensive.

Question: What kinds of tees are there?
Answer: Sports tees, concert tees, college names on tees, designer tees.

Question: Why do people wear them?
Answer: They're comfortable and fashionable.

Question: What ads are on tees?
Answer: Beer, sporting goods.

Another way to add details is to list any ideas that may be connected to your first idea, tee shirts. The list might give you more specific details:

Mickey Mouse shirts
surfer tee shirts
souvenir tee shirts
political slogans on tees
tee shirts under suit jackets

If you tried all three ways of adding details, you would end up with this list of details connected to the topic of tee shirts:

sports clothes	parents	beer ads on tees
sports tees	old people	sporting goods on tees
ads on tees	restaurant workers	Mickey Mouse shirts
athletes	some cheap	surfer tees
children	some expensive	souvenir tees
teens	concert tees	political slogans on tees
movie stars	college names on tees	tees under suit jackets
musicians	designer tees	

EXERCISE

ALONG THESE LINES/Prentice-Hall, Inc.

Beginning the Thoughtlines: A Summary

The thoughtlines stage of writing a paragraph enables you to gather ideas. This process begins with three steps:

1. *Think on paper and write down any ideas that you have about a general topic.* You can do this by freewriting, brainstorming, or by keeping a journal.

2. *Scan your writing for specific ideas that have come from your first efforts.* List these specific ideas.

3. *Pick one specific idea.* Then, by reviewing your early writing, by questioning, and by thinking further, you can add details to the one specific idea.

This process may seem long, but once you've worked through it several times, it will become nearly automatic. When you think about ideas before you try to shape them into a paragraph, you are off to a good start. Confidence comes from having something to say, and once you have a specific idea, you will be ready to begin shaping and developing details that support it.

▶ **EXERCISE 1: Creating Questions for Brainstorming**

You can do this exercise alone, with a partner, or with a group. Following are several topics. For each one, brainstorm by writing at least six questions related to the topic that could lead you to further details. The first topic is done for you:

   a. topic: dogs

   Question 1. Why are dogs such popular pets?

   Question 2. What kind of dog is a favorite pet in America?

   Question 3. Are dogs hard to train?

   Question 4. What dog, in your life, do you remember best?

   Question 5. What's the most famous dog on television?

   Question 6. Are there dogs as cartoon characters?

   b. topic: exercise

   Question 1. _____

   Question 2. _____

   Question 3. _____

   Question 4. _____

   Question 5. _____

   Question 6. _____

   c. topic: driving

   Question 1. _____

Question 2. _____

Question 3. _____

Question 4. _____

Question 5. _____

Question 6. _____

d. topic: shopping

Question 1. _____

Question 2. _____

Question 3. _____

Question 4. _____

Question 5. _____

Question 6. _____

e. topic: sports

Question 1. _____

Question 2. _____

Question 3. _____

Question 4. _____

Question 5. _____

Question 6. _____

▶ **E X E R C I S E 2 : Finding Specific Details in Freewriting**

You can do this exercise alone, with a partner, or with a group. Following are two samples of freewriting. Each is a written response to a different topic. Read each sample, and then underline any words and phrases that could become the focus of a paragraph.

Freewriting Reaction to the Topic of Getting Up in the Morning

I hate to get up. Night owl. Night owls stay up late, get up late. Not a morning person. Alarm clock screams at me. But if I use a clock radio, I fall asleep again. Bed feels so warm. Getting up in the dark is the worst. Morning people just spring up out of bed. They love to get up. They talk. They eat big breakfasts. I swig a diet cola. Ugh! No cereal or toast. Breakfast food is disgusting!

Freewriting Reaction to the Topic of Recycling

Recycling. Save the planet. Throwing away what's still good is wrong. Save old clothes. They can be mended. Shoe repair instead of new shoes. Recycled paper is another way to save. Lots of paper is wasted at work. Memos. Announcements. Styrofoam cups at work. Why not mugs? Greeting cards on recycled paper. I put old newspapers in a recycling bin at home. Recycling glass containers is another way to save and re-use. But washing out glass jars and bottles is a hassle. Where is the recycling center?

▶ E X E R C I S E   3 :   **Finding Specific Details in a List**

You can do this exercise alone, with a partner, or with a group. Following are several lists of words or phrases. In each list, one item is a general term; the others are more specific. Underline the words or phrases that are more specific. The first list is done for you:

a. <u>apple pie</u>
   <u>ice cream</u>
   desserts
   <u>butterscotch pudding</u>
   <u>jello</u>
   <u>chocolate brownies</u>

d. late registration
   closed classes
   going to college
   finding an advisor
   buying the right textbooks
   selecting the right courses

b. children and television
   Saturday morning cartoons
   toy commercials
   child actors
   frightening fairy tales

e. baseball caps
   bandanna
   covering for the head
   scarf
   beret

c. tennis commentators
   sports
   half-time shows
   instant replay
   Monday night football
   artificial turf

f. uniforms
   military stripes
   football numbers
   school colors
   regulation boots
   team insignia

▶ E X E R C I S E   4 :   **Collaborative Exercise: Finding Specific Words to Match General Terms**

Following are some general terms. On the numbered lines, list four specific words or phrases connected to each general term. After you have completed your lists, tear out your answers. Exchange your paper with a partner. You should add two more specific items to your partner's list. Be prepared to read your list aloud to the class, and add all the new items you hear from other lists. The first question is done for you.

a. general term: furniture

specific words or phrases:

1. _____*chair*_____   4. _____*table*_____

2. _____desk_____   5. _____sofa_____

3. _____bureau_____   6. _____stool_____

extras: _____recliner, bed_____

b. general term: trees

specific words or phrases:

1. _____   4. _____

2. _____   5. _____

3. _____   6. _____

extras: _____

c. general term: relatives

specific words or phrases:

1. _____   4. _____

2. _____   5. _____

3. _____   6. _____

extras: _____

d. general term: greeting cards

specific words or phrases:

1. _____   4. _____

2. _____   5. _____

3. _____   6. _____

extras: _____

e. general term: insects

specific words or phrases:

1. _____   4. _____

2. _____   5. _____

3. _____   6. _____

extras: _____

▶ **EXERCISE 5: Collaborative Exercise on Finding Topics Through Freewriting**

The following exercise must be completed with a partner or with a group. Pick one of the topics and freewrite on it for ten minutes. Then read your freewriting to your partner or your group. Ask your listener(s) to jot down any words or phrases that could lead to a specific topic for a paragraph.

Your listener(s) should read the jotted down words or phrases to you. You will be hearing a collection of specific ideas that came from *your* writing. As you listen, underline the words in your freewriting.

Freewriting topics (pick one):
a. telephone calls
b. chores
c. friends

Freewriting on (name of topic chosen):_____

_____

_____

_____

_____

_____

_____

FOCUSING THE THOUGHTLINES

The next step of writing is to *focus* your ideas *around some point*. Your ideas will begin to take a focus if you reexamine them and look for related ideas. Two techniques that you can use are to

- mark a list of related ideas, or
- map related ideas.

Listing Related Ideas

To develop a marked list, take another look at the list developed under the topic of tee shirts. In this list, you'll notice some of the items have been marked with letters that represent categories for related ideas:

K   marks ideas about the kinds of people who wear tee shirts
C   marks ideas about the cost of tee shirts
P   marks ideas about what is pictured or written on tee shirts

Following is the marked list of ideas related to the topic of tee shirts:

	sports clothes	C	some expensive
	sports tees	P	concert tees
P	ads on tees	P	college names on tees
K	athletes		designer tees
K	children	P	beer ads on tees
K	teens	P	sporting goods on tees
K	movie stars	P	Mickey Mouse shirts
K	musicians	P	surfer tees
K	parents	P	souvenir tees
K	old people	P	political slogans on tees
K	restaurant workers		tees under suit jackets
C	cheap		

You have probably noticed that some items are not marked: sports clothes, sports tees, designer tees, and tees under suit jackets. Perhaps you can come back to them later, or you may decide you don't need them in your paragraph.

To make it easier to see what ideas you have, and how they are related, try *grouping related ideas*, giving each list a title, like this:

kinds of people who wear tee shirts

athletes	movie stars	old people
children	musicians	restaurant workers
teens	parents	

the cost of tee shirts

cheap   some expensive

what is pictured or written on tee shirts

ads on tees	beer ads	souvenir tees
concert tees	sporting goods	political slogans
college names	Mickey Mouse	

Mapping

Another way to focus your ideas is to mark your first list of ideas, and then cluster the related ideas into separate lists. You can *map* your ideas, like this:

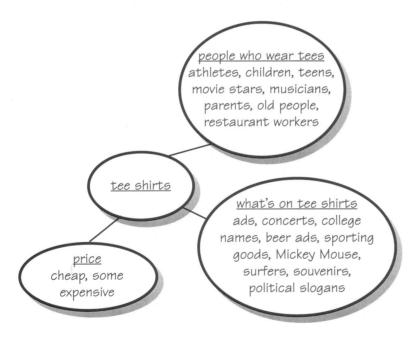

Whatever way you choose to examine and group your details, you are working toward a focus, a point. You are asking and beginning to answer the question, "Where do the details lead?" The answer will be the main idea of your paragraph, which will be stated in the topic sentence.

Forming a Topic Sentence

To form a topic sentence, do the following:

1. Review your detail and see if you can form some general idea that will summarize the detail.
2. Write that general idea as one sentence.

The sentence that summarizes the detail is the *topic sentence*. It makes a general point, and the more specific details you have gathered will support this point.

To form a topic sentence about tee shirts, you can ask yourself questions about the details. First, there is much detail about tee shirts. You could ask yourself, "What kind of details do I have? Can I summarize them?" You might then summarize the details to get the topic sentence:

People of various backgrounds and ages wear all kinds of tee shirts.

Check the sentence against your details. Does it cover the people who wear tees? Does it cover what's on the shirts? Yes. The topic sentence says, "*People of various backgrounds and ages* wear *all kinds* of tee shirts."

Be careful. *Topics are not the same as topic sentences. Topics are the subjects you will write about.* A topic sentence states the *main idea* you have developed on a topic. Consider the differences between the topics and the topic sentences below:

topic: Why courtesy is important
topic sentence: Courtesy takes the conflict out of unpleasant encounters.

topic: Dogs and their owners
topic sentence: Many dog owners begin to look like their pets.

Topic sentences *do not announce; they make a point*. Look at the following sentences, and notice the differences between the sentences that announce and the topic sentences.

announcement: I will discuss the process of changing a tire.
topic sentence: Changing a tire is easy if you have the right tools and follow a simple process.

announcement: An analysis of why recycling paper is important will be the subject of this paper.
topic sentence: Recycling paper is important because it saves trees, money, and even certain animals.

Topic sentences can be too big to develop in one paragraph. A topic sentence that is *too broad* may take many paragraphs, even pages of writing, to develop. Look at the following broad sentences, and then notice how they can be narrowed.

too broad: Athletes get paid too much money. (This sentence is too broad because the term "athletes" could mean anything from professional boxers to college football players to neighborhood softball teams; "too much money" could mean any fee that basketball players receive for endorsing products to bonuses that professional football players get if they make the Super Bowl. The sentence could also refer to all athletes in the world at any time in history.)
a narrower, better topic sentence: Last year, several professional baseball players negotiated high but fair salaries.

too broad: I changed a great deal in my last year of high school. (The phrase "changed a great deal" could refer to physical changes, intellectual changes, emotional changes, or to changes in attitude, changes in goals, or just about any other change you can think of.)
a narrower, better topic sentence: In my last year of high school, I overcame my shyness.

ALONG THESE LINES/Prentice-Hall, Inc.

Topic sentences can be too small to develop in one paragraph. A topic sentence that is *too narrow* can't be supported by details. It may be a fact, which can't be developed. A topic sentence that is too narrow leaves you with nothing more to say.

too narrow: I hate broccoli.
an expanded topic sentence: I hate broccoli for two reasons.

too narrow: It takes twenty minutes to get out of the airport parking lot.
an expanded topic sentence: Congestion at the airport parking lot is causing problems for travelers.

The thoughtlines stage should begin with free, unstructured thinking and writing. As you work through the thoughtlines process, your thinking and writing will become more focused.

Focusing the Thoughtlines: A Summary

The thoughtlines stage of writing a paragraph enables you to develop an idea into a topic sentence and related details. You can focus your thinking by working in steps.

1. Try marking a list of related details or try mapping to group your ideas.

2. Write a topic sentence that summarizes your details.

3. Check that your topic sentence is a sentence (not a topic), is not too broad or too narrow, and is not an announcement. Check that it makes a point and focuses the details you have developed.

▶ **E X E R C I S E 1 :** **Grouping Related Items in Lists of Details**

Following are lists of details. In each list, circle the items that seem to fit into one group; then underline the items that seem to belong to a second group. Some items may not belong in either group. The first list is done for you.

a. topic: rainy weekends

(no sports activities)   (can't jog in neighborhood)

(picnics cancelled)   rains most in autumn

catch up on chores   read a book

not forecast by weathermen   (park too wet to visit)

go to a mall   watch a movie

b. topic: diets

diet soda   frozen yogurt

crash diet   junk foods

EXERCISE

ice cream	fresh fruit
pizza with everything	desired weight
potato chips	rich desserts

c. **topic:** living away from home for the first time

an apartment	doing your own laundry
no curfew	cleaning up the mess
can set your own schedule	unlimited parties
paying the rent	phone bill
electric bill	

▶ **EXERCISE 2:** **Writing Topic Sentences for Lists of Details**

Following are lists of details that have no point or topic sentence. Write an appropriate topic sentence for each one.

a. topic sentence: _____

_____

Can watch a movie in the comfort of your own room
Renting a movie costs little
No need to dress up
No crowds to fight
Don't have to wait in line
Can watch it when convenient
Can watch it several times over rental period

b. topic sentence: _____

_____

birthday cakes
wedding cakes
Super Bowl cakes shaped like a football
fruitcakes
pound cakes
angel food cakes
devil's food cakes
heart-shaped cakes for Valentine's Day

c. topic sentence: _____

_____

Reese scored the most points on the court.
He never tried to be the center of attention.
He was modest.
He was a team player.
Reese got along well with the coaches.
Reese came to all the practices.

EXERCISE

d. topic sentence: _____

_____

Tamara spoke clearly in speech class.
Her presentations were well organized.
She critiqued classmates' speeches tactfully.
She volunteered to be a speech team leader.
In communicating, Tamara maintained her sense of humor.
She motivated others to complete their speech research.

▶ **EXERCISE 3:** **Collaborative Exercise on Turning Topics into Topic Sentences**

Following is a list. Some of the items in the list are topic sentences, but some are topics. Working with a partner or with a group, put an *X* by the items that are topics. On the lines following the list, rewrite the topics into topic sentences.

a. _____ Three characteristics of a good friend

b. _____ Learning to drive takes practice

c. _____ The most frightening experience of my life

d. _____ Many snakes make good pets

e. _____ Why I hate giving oral reports

f. _____ I learned to be punctual on my first job

g. _____ A younger brother can be a good buddy

h. _____ How to meet the person of your dreams

i. _____ I got the job I wanted through planning and persistence

j. _____ My twenty-first birthday was the happiest day of my life

Rewrite the topics. Make each one into a topic sentence:

_____

_____

_____

_____

_____

_____

▶ **EXERCISE 4:** **Collaborative Exercise on Revising Topic Sentences That Are Too Broad**

Following is a list of topic sentences. Some of them are too broad to support in one paragraph. Working with a partner or with a group, put an *X* by the ones that are too broad. Then, on the lines following the list, rewrite those sentences, focusing on a limited idea—a topic sentence—that could be supported in one paragraph.

a. _____ Being a parent is not easy.

b. _____ The toughest part of training my puppy was getting him to walk on a leash.

c. _____ The economy makes life difficult for many Americans.

d. _____ My habit of gossiping can get me into trouble.

e. _____ Putting my five-year-old to bed at night is a challenge.

f. _____ Ramon wants to be a success and achieve the American Dream.

g. _____ People have a right to privacy.

h. _____ Amy dreams of owning her own restaurant.

Rewrite the broad sentences. Make each one more limited.

_____

_____

_____

_____

_____

_____

_____

_____

▶ **EXERCISE 5:** **Collaborative Exercise for Making Announcements into Topic Sentences**

Following is a list of sentences. Some are topic sentences. Some are announcements. Working with a partner or with a group, put an X by the announcements. Then on the lines following the list, rewrite the announcements, making them into topic sentences.

a. _____ Hunting too near a populated area can be dangerous.

b. _____ The consequences of telling a white lie will be the subject of this paper.

c. _____ The emotional benefits of exercise are going to be explained.

d. _____ Marrying too young often presents financial challenges.

e. _____ Our town needs a better bus system.

f. _____ A network of bike paths through our community would encourage people to leave their cars at home.

g. _____ Why more day care centers are needed in this town is the area to be discussed.

Rewrite the announcements. Make each one a topic sentence.

_____

_____

_____

_____

_____

_____

_____

_____

▶ **E X E R C I S E   6 :   Collaborative Exercise for Revising Topic Sentences That Are Too Narrow**

Following is a list of topic sentences. Some of them are topics that are too narrow; they cannot be developed with details. Working with a partner or with a group, put an *X* by the ones that are too narrow. Then, on the lines following, rewrite those sentences as broader topic sentences that could be developed in one paragraph.

a. _____ It rained all day yesterday.

b. _____ On rainy days, I have to pay careful attention to the way I drive.

c. _____ My dog is a mixed breed.

d. _____ A stray cat turned out to be a wonderful pet.

e. _____ I love bargain hunting.

f. _____ I like working the night shift for several reasons.

g. _____ My brother failed the written part of his driving test.

h. _____ Inez is a good tennis player because she devotes all her free time to the sport.

Rewrite the narrow sentences. Make each one broader.

_____

_____

_____

_____

_____

_____

_____

_____

OUTLINES FOR A PARAGRAPH

Checking Your Details

Once you have a topic sentence, you can begin working on an *outline* for your paragraph. The outline is a plan that helps you stay focused in your writing. The outline begins to form when you write your topic sentence and list details beneath it. You can now look at your list and ask yourself an important question: "Do I have enough details to support my topic sentence?" Remember, your goal is to write a paragraph of seven to twelve sentences.

Consider this topic sentence and list of details:

topic sentence: People can be very rude when they shop in supermarkets.

details: push in line
express lane
too many items

Does the list contain enough detail for a paragraph of seven to twelve sentences? Probably not.

Adding Details When There Aren't Enough

To add details, try brainstorming. Ask yourself some questions:

Where else in supermarkets are people rude?
Are they rude in other lanes besides the express lane?
Are they rude in the aisles? How?
Is there crowding anywhere? Where?

By brainstorming, you might come up with these details:

topic sentence: People can be very rude when they shop in supermarkets.

details: push in line
express lane
too many items
hit my cart with theirs in aisles
block aisles while they decide
push ahead in deli area
will not take a number
argue with cashier over prices
yell at the bag boy

Keep brainstorming until you feel you have sufficient details for a seven- to twelve-sentence paragraph. Remember, it is better to have too much detail than too little, for you can always edit the extra details later.

If you try brainstorming and still don't have many details, you can refer to your original ideas—your freewriting or journal—for other details.

Eliminating Details That Don't Relate to the Topic Sentence

Sometimes, what you thought were good details don't relate to the topic sentence because they don't fit or support your point. Eliminate details that don't relate to the topic sentence. For example, the following list contains details that really don't relate to the topic sentence. Those details are crossed out.

topic sentence: Waiters have to be very patient in dealing with their customers.

details: customers take a long time ordering
~~waiter's salary is low~~
waiters have to explain specials twice
customers send orders back
customers blame waiters for any delays

```
                    customers want food instantly
                    waiters can't react to sarcasm from
                    customers
                    waiters can't get angry if customer
                    does
                    waiters work long shifts
                    customers change their minds after
                    ordering
```

From List to Outline

Take another look at the topic sentence and the list of details on tee shirts:

```
topic sentence: People of various backgrounds and ages
                wear all kinds of tee shirts.

       details: athletes
                children
                teens
                movie stars
                musicians
                parents
                old people
                restaurant workers
                ads on tees
                concert tees
                college names
                beer ads
                sporting goods
                Mickey Mouse shirts
                surfer tees
                souvenir tees
                political slogans
```

After you scan that list, you're ready to develop the outline of the paragraph.

An *outline* is a plan for writing. It is a kind of draft in list form. It sketches what you want to write and the order in which you want to present it. An organized, logical list will make your writing unified because each item on the list will relate to your topic sentence.

When you plan, keep your topic sentence in mind:

```
People of various backgrounds and ages wear all kinds
of tee shirts.
```

Notice that the key words are underlined and lead to three key phrases:

```
people of various backgrounds
people of various ages
all kinds of tee shirts
```

Can you put the details together, so that they connect to one of these key phrases?

people of various backgrounds

```
athletes, movie stars, musicians, restaurant workers
```

people of various ages

children, teens, parents, old people

all kinds of tee shirts

concert tees, college names on tees, beer ads, sporting goods, Mickey Mouse shirts, surfer tees, souvenir tees, political slogans

With this kind of grouping, you have a clearer idea of how to organize a paragraph. You may have noticed that the details grouped under each phrase give *examples* that are connected to the topic sentence. That is, the details—athletes, movie stars, musicians, and restaurant workers—are all examples of people of various backgrounds who wear tee shirts. *When you use examples to support a point, you use a form of writing called illustration.* In your writing, you often use illustration because you frequently want to explain a general point with a specific example.

Now that you have grouped your ideas with key phrases and examples, you can write an outline:

An Outline for a Paragraph

topic sentence: People of various backgrounds and ages wear all kinds of tee shirts.

details:

various backgrounds
{
Athletes wear tee shirts.
Movie stars are seen in them.
Musicians perform in tee shirts.
Restaurant workers wear tee shirts.

various ages
{
Children and teens wear tee shirts.
Parents and old people wear them.

kinds of tees
{
There are tee shirts sold at concerts.
Some shirts have the names of colleges on them.
Others advertise a brand of beer or sporting goods.
Mickey Mouse is a favorite character on them.
Surfers' tee shirts have seascapes on them.
Some shirts are souvenirs.
Others have political slogans.

As you can see, the outline combined some details from the list. Even with these combinations, the details are very rough in style. As you reread the lists of detail, you'll notice places that need more combination, places where ideas need more explaining, and places that are repetitive. Keep in mind that an outline is merely a rough organization of your paragraph.

As you work through the steps of designing an outline, you can check for the following:

A Checklist for an Outline

✔ **Unity:** Do all the details relate to the topic sentence? If they do, the paragraph will be unified.

✔ **Support:** Do I have enough supporting ideas? Can I add to these ideas with more specific details?

✔ **Coherence:** Are the details listed in the right order? If the order of points is logical, the paragraph will be coherent.

Check the sample outlines again, and you'll notice that the details are grouped in the same order as the topic sentence: first, details about kinds of people; then, details about the ages of people; and next, details about kinds of tee shirts. Putting details in an order that matches the topic sentence is a logical order for this paragraph.

Determining the Order of Details

Putting the details in logical order makes the ideas in your paragraph easy to follow. The most logical order for a paragraph depends on the subject of the paragraph. If you are writing about an event, you might use *time order* (such as telling what happened first, second, and so forth); if you are arguing some point, you might use *emphatic order* (such as saving your most convincing idea for last); if you are describing a room, you might use *space order* (such as from left to right, or from top to bottom).

The format of the outline helps to organize your ideas. The topic sentence is written above the list of details. This position helps you remember that the topic sentence is the main idea, and the detail that supports it is written under it. The topic sentence is the most important sentence of the paragraph. You can easily check each item on your list against your main idea. You can also develop the unity (relevance) and coherence (logical order) of your details.

When you actually write a paragraph, the topic sentence does not necessarily have to be the first sentence in the paragraph. Read the following paragraphs, and notice where each topic sentence is placed.

Topic Sentence at the Beginning of the Paragraph

Watching a horror movie on the late show can keep me up all night. The movie itself scares me to death, especially if it involves a creepy character sneaking up on someone in the dark. After the movie, I'm afraid to turn out all the lights and be alone in the dark. Then every little noise seems like the sound of a sinister intruder. Strange shapes seem to appear in the shadows. My closet becomes a place where someone could be hiding. There might even be a creature under the bed! And if I go to sleep, these strange invaders might appear from under the bed or inside the closet.

Topic Sentence in the Middle of the Paragraph

The kitchen counters gleamed. In the spice rack, every jar was organized neatly. The sink was polished, and not one spot marred its surface. The stove burners were surrounded by dazzling stainless steel rings. <u>The chef kept an immaculate kitchen.</u> There were no finger marks on the refrigerator door. No sticky spots dirtied the floor. No crumbs hid behind the toaster.

Topic Sentence at the End of the Paragraph

On long summer evenings, we would play softball in the street. Sometimes we'd play until it was so dark we could barely see the ball. Then our mothers would come to the front steps of the row houses and call us in, telling us to stop our play. But we'd pretend we couldn't hear them. If they insisted, we'd beg for a few minutes more, or for just one more game. It was so good to be outdoors with our friends. It was warm, and we knew we had weeks of summer vacation ahead. There was no school in the morning; there would be more games to play. <u>We loved those street games on summer nights.</u>

ALONG THESE LINES/Prentice-Hall, Inc.

Be sure to follow your own instructor's direction about placement of the topic sentence.

▶ **E X E R C I S E   1 :   Adding Details to Support a Topic Sentence**

The following topic sentences have some—but not enough—details. Write sentences to add details to the list following each topic sentence. If your instructor agrees, you may want to work with a writing partner or with a group.

a. topic sentence: My closet is full of items I have saved because of the memories they bring.

1. I have an old high school year book.
2. It reminds me of my senior year.
3. There is an old ragged sweatshirt.
4. _____
5. _____
6. _____
7. _____
8. _____
9. _____

b. topic sentence: Owning a car costs more money than just the cost of the car itself.

1. Gas is a regular expense.
2. _____
3. _____
4. _____
5. _____
6. _____
7. _____

c. topic sentence: When I have a day off, I can find several inexpensive ways to enjoy the time.

1. I often take a long walk.
2. _____
3. _____
4. _____
5. _____
6. _____
7. _____

d. topic sentence: The first day of college can be confusing and tense.

1. A student may not know how to find the classroom for his or her first class.
2. So the student rushes around, terrified of being late to class.
3. A new student worries about how hard the classes will be.

4. _____

5. _____

6. _____

7. _____

▶ **EXERCISE 2: Eliminating Details That Don't Fit**

Following are topic sentences and lists of supporting details. Cross out the details that don't fit the topic sentence.

a. topic sentence: Toy commercials on TV can be deceiving to little children.

details: They show happy, excited groups of youngsters playing with a toy.
Children viewing may think the toy will make them happy.
They may think the toy will bring them friends.
The commercials show dolls or robots or action figures in motion.
In reality, the figures don't move.
They often show cars or trucks racing around.
As a child, I had a collection of model trucks.
In small print, the toy car or truck ad says, "Batteries not included."
Small children can't read and don't know about the batteries needed.

b. topic sentence: Everywhere I look, I see how sports can influence fashion.

details: Both sexes wear surfer clothes.
Children and adults wear athletic shoes.
The NBA playoffs are on prime time TV.
Older men wear golf shirts.
People wear sweat pants to the store or to visit friends.
Sweat bands are common headgear.
Baseball caps are seen in many places.
Athletes are used to sell soft drinks.

c. topic sentence: People give many excuses for not voting.

details: Some people say their vote doesn't count.
Others say they don't know where their precinct is.
Some people admit they forget to vote.
There are local elections next week.
Some people haven't registered to vote.
Some people say all the candidates are unacceptable.
A few people claim they don't have time to vote.
People who vote get a sticker that says, "I voted."

▶ **E X E R C I S E 3 : Coherence: Putting Details in the Right Order**

You can do this exercise alone, with a partner, or with a group. These outlines have details that are in the wrong order. In the space provided, number the sentences in the right order: 1 would be the number for the first sentence, and so forth.

a. topic sentence: My first babysitting job was a disaster from start to finish.

_____ Six-year-old Tyrone cried when his mother said good-bye.

_____ I tried to distract him from his crying by reading him a story.

_____ He threw the storybook across the room.

_____ He pulled the storybook from my hands.

_____ He wouldn't eat at dinner.

_____ When it was time for dinner, I made him his favorite food.

_____ He refused to go to bed.

_____ I tried to get him to take a bath before bedtime.

_____ When I got him into the tub, he splashed water all over me.

_____ His mother came home.

_____ I was asleep, exhausted.

_____ His mother found Tyrone awake, watching late-night TV.

b. topic sentence: I have a hard time wrapping a gift.

_____ I can never find a box.

_____ The tissue paper is crumpled.

_____ I can't get the ribbon to lie flat on the box.

_____ The bows never turn out nicely.

_____ The wrapping paper gets wrinkled and lumpy at the ends of the box.

_____ I use too much Scotch tape as I seal the ends of the wrapping paper.

_____ I always cut too much wrapping paper.

_____ The Scotch tape shines all over the wrapped box.

c. topic sentence: Losing my credit cards was a stressful experience.

_____ I notified the credit card companies immediately.

_____ I looked in my wallet and saw my Visa and Discover cards were missing from their slots.

_____ I had to look all over the house for the credit card companies' phone numbers.

_____ I panicked when I saw the cards weren't anywhere in my wallet.

_____ Even after I called the card companies, I was worried about strangers charging things on my cards.

ROUGHLINES FOR A PARAGRAPH

The outline is a draft of your paragraph in list form. You are now ready to write the list in paragraph form, to "rough out" a draft of your assignment. The *roughlines* stage of writing is the time to draft, revise, edit, and draft again. You may write several *drafts* or versions of the paragraph in this stage. Writing several drafts is not an unnecessary chore or a punishment. It is a way of taking pressure off yourself. By revising in steps, you are telling yourself, "The first try doesn't have to be perfect."

Review the outline on tee shirts. You can create a first draft of this outline in the form of a paragraph. (*Remember that the first line of each paragraph is indented.*) In the draft of the following paragraph, the first sentence of the paragraph is the topic sentence.

A Roughlines First Draft of a Paragraph

```
     People of various backgrounds and ages wear all
kinds of tee shirts. Athletes wear tee shirts. Movie
stars are seen in them. Musicians perform in tee
shirts. Restaurant workers wear tee shirts. Children
and teens wear tee shirts. Parents and older people
wear them. There are tee shirts that are sold at
concerts. Some shirts have the names of colleges on
them. Others advertise a brand of beer or sporting
goods. Mickey Mouse is a favorite character on them.
Surfer tee shirts have seascapes on them. Some
shirts are souvenirs. Others have political slogans.
```

Once you have a first draft, you can begin to think about revising and editing it. *Revising* means rewriting the draft to change the structure, the order of the sentences, and the content. *Editing* includes making changes in the choice of words, in the selection of details, in the punctuation, and in the pattern and kinds of sentences. It may also include *adding transitions*, which are words, phrases, or sentences that link ideas.

One easy way to begin the revising and editing process is to read your work aloud to yourself. As you do so, listen carefully to your words, and concentrate on their meaning. Each question in the following checklist will help you focus on a specific part of revising and editing. The name (or key term) for each part is in parentheses.

A Checklist for Revising the Draft of a Paragraph (with key terms)

✔ Am I sticking to my point? (unity)

✔ Should I take out any ideas that don't fit? (unity)

ALONG THESE LINES/Prentice-Hall, Inc.

✔ Do I have enough to say about my point? (support)

✔ Should I add any details? (support)

✔ Should I change the order of my sentences? (coherence)

✔ Is my choice of words appropriate? (style)

✔ Is my choice of words repetitive? (style)

✔ Are my sentences too long? Too short? (style)

✔ Should I combine any sentences? (style)

✔ Am I running sentences together? (grammar)

✔ Am I writing complete sentences? (grammar)

✔ Can I link my ideas more smoothly? (transitions)

If you apply the checklist to the draft of the paragraph on tee shirts, you will probably find these rough spots:

- The sentences are very short and choppy.
- Some sentences could be combined.
- Some words are repeated often.
- Some ideas would be more effective if they were supported by more details.
- The paragraph could use a few transitions.

Consider the following revised draft of the paragraph, and notice the changes, underlined, that have been made in the draft:

A Roughlines Revised Draft of a Paragraph

topic sentence:	People of various backgrounds and ages wear all kinds of tee shirts.
sentences combined	<u>Athletes and movie stars are seen in them.</u> <u>Musicians often perform</u>
sentences combined	<u>in them, and restaurant workers</u>
details added	<u>sometimes work in tee shirts printed with the name of the restaurant.</u>
sentences combined	<u>Children, teens, their parents, and older people all wear tee shirts.</u>
transition	<u>Almost anything can be printed or</u>
sentence added	<u>pictured on a tee shirt.</u> <u>At concerts, fans can buy tee shirts stamped with the name of the group on stage.</u> College students can wear the name of their college on a shirt. Some shirts advertise a brand of beer,
details added	<u>like Budweiser,</u> or a sporting goods
details added	company, <u>like Nike.</u> Mickey Mouse is

	a favorite character on tee shirts.
transition added	<u>Other kinds of shirts include shirts</u>
sentences combined	<u>with seascapes on them, and souvenir</u>
	<u>shirts, like the ones that say, "My</u>
details added	<u>folks visited Philadelphia, and all</u>
	<u>I got was this lousy tee shirt."</u>
transition added	<u>Other shirts</u> have political slogans,
details added	<u>like "Save the Whales."</u>

When you are revising your own paragraph, you can use the checklist to help you. Read the checklist several times; then reread your draft, looking for answers to the questions on the list. If your instructor agrees, you can work with your classmates. You can read your draft to a partner or to a group. Your listener(s) can react to your draft by applying the questions on the checklist and by making notes about your draft as you read. When you are finished reading aloud, your partner(s) can discuss their notes about your work.

► **EXERCISE 1: Revising a Draft by Combining Sentences**

The paragraph below has many short, choppy sentences that are underlined. Wherever you see two or more underlined sentences clustered next to each other, combine them into one clear, smooth sentence. Write your revised version of the paragraph in the spaces above the lines.

Paragraph to Be Revised

My brother is a baseball fanatic. He wakes up in the morning thinking about the game. <u>He reaches for the newspaper. He checks out all the base-ball scores.</u> He talks about baseball during breakfast. He can't stop talking and thinking about baseball during work. <u>He talks about his favorite teams during his break. He has baseball conversations during lunch. With customers, he argues about the sport.</u> My brother's clothes reflect his obsession. <u>He has seven baseball caps. There are three baseball jackets in his closet. He owns at least twelve shirts marked with team insignia.</u> For him, it's always baseball season.

► **EXERCISE 2: Collaborative Exercise for Adding Details to a Draft**

Complete this exercise with a partner or with a group. The following paragraph lacks the kind of details that would make it more interesting. Working with a partner or with a group, add the details in the blank spaces provided. When you are finished with the additions, read the revised paragraph to the class.

Paragraph to Be Revised

Radio stations offer something for almost everyone. For teenagers, there are stations like _____ that play the top forty hits of the day. Other stations for teens ignore the current top forty selections, and play different kinds of music. For example, teens can listen to _____ or _____ music instead of the same forty hits played over and over. Older listeners also have a wide selection of music stations, from those that play _____ music to those that play _____ tunes. And for those radio listeners who aren't interested in music at all, other stations offer other kinds of programming. Some stations broadcast _____, _____, or _____ instead of music.

FINAL LINES FOR A PARAGRAPH

The final lines of your paragraph are the result of careful thinking, planning, and revising. After many drafts, and when you are satisfied with the result, you read the final draft to polish and proofread. You can avoid too many last-minute corrections if you check your last draft carefully for the following:

- spelling errors
- punctuation errors
- mechanical errors
- word choice
- a final statement

Take a look at the following final draft of the tee shirt paragraph. The draft has been corrected directly above the crossed out material. At the end, you'll notice a concluding statement has been added to unify the paragraph.

Correcting the Final Draft of a Paragraph

People of various backgrounds and ages wear all kinds

of tee shirts. *Athletes* ~~Atheletes~~ and movie *stars* ~~star's~~ are seen in

them, musicians often perform in them, and *restaurant* ~~restraunt~~

workers sometimes work in tee shirts printed with the

name of the restaurant. Children, teens, their parents,

and *elderly* ~~older~~ people all wear tee shirts. Almost anything

can be painted or pictured on a tee shirt. At concerts,

fans can buy tee shirts stamped with the name of the

on

College students

group ~~of~~ stage. ~~Collegestudents~~ can wear the name of

their

~~there~~ college on a shirt. Some shirts advertise a brand

of beer, like Budweiser, or a sporting goods company,

like Nike. Mickey Mouse is a favorite character on tee

shirts. Other kinds of tee shirts include surfer shirts

with seascapes on them and souvenir shirts, like the

My folks

ones that say, "~~my folk's~~ visited Philadelphia, and all

I got was this lousy tee shirt." Other shirts have

political slogans, like "Save the Whales." What is writ-

ten or pictured on tee shirts is as varied as the people

who wear them.

Giving Your Paragraph a Title

When you prepare the final copy of your paragraph, you may be asked to give it a title. The title should be short and should fit the subject of the paragraph. For example, an appropriate title for the paragraph on tee shirts could be "Tee Shirts," or "The Variety of Tee Shirts." Check with your instructor to see if your paragraph needs a title. (In this book, the paragraphs do not have titles.)

Reviewing the Writing Process

This chapter has taken you through *four important steps* in writing. As you become more familiar with the steps and more comfortable with working through them, you will be able to work more quickly. For now, try to remember the four steps:

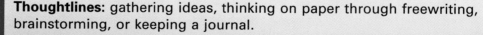

The Steps of the Writing Process

Thoughtlines: gathering ideas, thinking on paper through freewriting, brainstorming, or keeping a journal.

Outlines: planning the paragraph by grouping details, focusing the details with a topic sentence, listing the support, and devising an outline.

Roughlines: drafting of the paragraph, then revising and editing it.

Final Lines: preparing the final version of the paragraph, with one last proofreading check for errors in preparation, punctuation, and mechanics.

ALONG THESE LINES/Prentice-Hall, Inc.

Here and on the next page you will find outlines, roughlines, and final lines versions of the paragraph on tee shirts. Can you spot the changes?

**An Outlines Version
of a Paragraph**

topic sentence:	People of various backgrounds and ages wear all kinds of tee shirts.
details:	Athletes wear tee shirts.
Movie stars are seen in them.
Musicians perform in them.
Restaurant workers wear tee shirts.
Children and teens wear tee shirts.
Parents and old people wear them.
There are tee shirts that are sold at concerts.
Some shirts have the names of colleges on them.
Others advertise a brand of beer or sporting goods.
Mickey Mouse is a favorite character on them.
Surfer tee shirts have seascapes on them.
Some shirts are souvenirs.
Others have political slogans.

**A Roughlines Version
of a Paragraph**

People of various backgrounds and ages wear all kinds of tee shirts. Athletes and movie stars are seen in them. Musicians often perform in them, and restaurant workers sometimes work in tee shirts marked with the name of the restaurant. Children, teens, their parents, and older people all wear tee shirts. Almost anything can be printed or pictured on a tee shirt. At concerts, fans can buy tee shirts stamped with the name of the group on stage. College students can wear the name of their college on a shirt. Some shirts advertise a brand of beer, like Bud, or a sporting goods company, like Nike. Mickey Mouse is a favorite character on tee shirts. Other kinds of shirts include shirts with seascapes on them, and souvenir shirts, like the ones that say, "My folks went to Philadelphia, and all I got was this lousy tee shirt." Other shirts have political slogans, like "Save the Whales."

> ### A Final Lines Version of a Paragraph
> (Changes from the roughlines version are underlined.)
>
>   People of various backgrounds and ages wear
> all kinds of tee shirts. Athletes and movie stars
> are seen in them. Musicians often perform in <u>ragged
> tees</u>, and restaurant workers sometimes work in tee
> shirts printed with the name of the restaurant.
> Children, teens, their parents, and <u>elderly</u> people
> all wear tee shirts. Almost anything can be printed
> or pictured on a tee shirt. At concerts, <u>for
> example</u>, fans can buy tee shirts stamped with the
> name of the group on stage. College students can
> wear the name of their college on a shirt. Some
> <u>popular</u> shirts advertise a brand of beer, like Bud,
> or a sporting goods company, like Nike. Mickey Mouse
> is a favorite character on tee shirts. Other kinds
> of tee shirts include <u>surfer</u> shirts with seascapes
> on them and souvenir shirts, like the <u>surly</u> ones
> that say, "My folks visited Philadelphia, and all I
> got was this lousy tee shirt." Other shirts have
> political slogans, like "Save the Whales." <u>What is
> written or pictured on tee shirts is as varied as
> the people who wear them.</u>

▶ **E X E R C I S E 1 :** **Correcting the Errors in the Final Lines of a Paragraph**

Proofread the following paragraph, looking for errors in word choice, spelling, punctuation, and mechanics. Correct the errors by crossing out each mistake and writing the correction above it.

Every time I am on the telephone and I need to write something down, I

am caught in a terible dilemma. First of all, their is never any paper nearby.

Even thou I live in an apartment full of schoolbooks notebooks pads and

typing paper, they're is never any papper near the telephone. I wind up des-

perately looking for anything I can write on. Sometimes i write on coupons

my mother has saved in the kitchen, but coupons are shiny and don't take

writing well. If I do manage to find some better paper, I can't find a pen or

pencil! Our home is full of pen's and pencil's, but I can never find even a stubbby old pencil or a leaky old ballpoint when I need it. In emergencies, I

have taken telephone messages with a crayon and a lipstick.

Lines of Detail: A Walk-Through Assignment

This assignment involves working within a group to write a paragraph.

Step 1: Read the following three sentences. Pick the one sentence you'd prefer
as a possible topic sentence for a paragraph. Fill in the blank for the
sentence you choose.

Pick one sentence and fill in the blank:

a. The most frightening movie I've ever seen was _____ (fill

in the title).

b. If money were no problem, the car I'd buy is _____ (fill in

the name of the car).

c. The one food I refuse to eat is _____ (fill in the name of

the food).

Step 2: Join a group composed of other students who picked the same topic
sentence as you. In your class, you'll have "movie" people, "car"
people, and "food" people. Brainstorm in a group. Discuss questions
that could be used to get ideas for your paragraph.

For the movie topic, sample questions could include, "What was
the most frightening part of the movie?" or "What kind of movie was
it?—a ghost story, a horror movie, and so forth."

For the car topic, sample questions could include, "Have you
ever driven this kind of car?" or "Do you know anyone who has a
car like this one?"

For the food topic, sample questions could include, "Did you
hate this food when you were a child?" or "Where has this food been
served to you?" As you discuss, write the questions, not the answers,
in the following blanks. Keep the questions flowing. Don't stop to
say, "That's silly," or "I can't answer that." Try to gather at least fifteen questions.

Fifteen Brainstorming Questions:

1. _____

2. _____

3. _____

4. _____

5. _____

6. _____

7. _____

8. _____

ALONG THESE LINES/Prentice-Hall, Inc.

9. _____

10. _____

11. _____

12. _____

13. _____

14. _____

15. _____

Step 3: Split up. Alone, begin to think on paper. Answer as many questions as you can, or add more questions and answers, or freewrite.

Step 4: Draft an outline of the paragraph. You will probably have to change the topic sentence to fit the details you've gathered. For example, your new topic sentence might be something like:

_____ was the most frightening movie I've ever seen; it

creates fear by using _____, _____, and

_____.

                                     or

If money were no problem, I'd buy a _____ for its

performance, _____, and _____.

                                     or

I refuse to eat _____ because _____.

Remember to look at your details to see where they lead you. The details will help you refine your topic sentence.

Step 5: Prepare the first draft of the paragraph.

Step 6: Read the draft aloud to your writing group, the same people who met to brainstorm. Ask each member of your group to make at least one positive comment and one suggestion for revision.

Step 7: Revise and edit your draft, considering the group's ideas and your own ideas for improvement.

Step 8: Prepare a final copy of the paragraph.

Writing Your Own Paragraph

When you write on any of these topics, follow the stages of thoughtlines, outlines, roughlines, and final lines in preparing your paragraph.

1. This assignment requires you to interview a partner. Your final goal is to write a paragraph that will introduce your partner to the rest of the class. In the final paragraph, you may design your own topic sentence or use one of the following topic sentences, filling in the blanks with the material you've discovered:

There are several things you should know about _____ (fill

in your partner's name).

ALONG THESE LINES/Prentice-Hall, Inc.

or

Three unusual things have happened to _____ (fill in your

partner's name).

Before you write the paragraph, follow these steps:

Step 1: Prepare to interview a classmate. Make a list of six questions you
might want to ask. They can be questions such as, "Where are you
from?" or "Have you ever done anything unusual?" Write *at least six
questions* before you start the interview. List the questions on the
following interview form, leaving room to fill in short answers later.

Interview Form

Question 1: _____

Answer: _____

Question 2: _____

Answer: _____

Question 3: _____

Answer: _____

Question 4: _____

Answer: _____

Question 5: _____

Answer: _____

Question 6: _____

Answer: _____

Additional questions and answers: _____

_____

_____

_____

Step 2: Meet and interview your partner. Ask the questions on your list. Jot
down brief answers. Ask *any other questions* you think of as you are
talking; write down the answers on the additional lines at the end of
the interview form.

Step 3: Change places. Let your partner interview you.

Step 4: Split up. Use the list of questions and answers about your partner as
the thoughtlines part of your assignment. Work on the outlines and
the roughlines steps.

Step 5: Ask your partner to read the roughlines version of your paragraph,
to write any comments or suggestions for improvement below the
paragraph, and to mark any spelling or grammar errors in the paragraph itself.

ALONG THESE LINES/Prentice-Hall, Inc.

Step 6: When you have completed a final lines version of the paragraph, read
         the paragraph to the class.

2. Following are some topic sentences. Select one and use it to write a
   paragraph.

Many kinds of people wear _____ for a variety of reasons.

My daily life provides several irritations.

High school students should never forget that _____ .

College is a good place to _____ and

_____ .

3. Select one of the following topics listed. Narrow an aspect of the topic
   and write a paragraph on it. If you choose the topic of exams, for example, you might narrow it by writing about your experiences with the
   SAT test.

List of Topics for a Paragraph

a part-time job	a way to reduce stress	music
single parents	voice mail	toys
exams	boyfriends/girlfriends	cars
old songs	saving money	gossip

Name: _____   **Section:** _____

Peer Review Form for a Paragraph

After you've written a roughlines version of your paragraph, let a writing partner read it. When your partner has completed the following form, discuss the comments. Then repeat the same process for your partner's paragraph.

The topic sentence of this paragraph is

_____

_____

_____

The detail that I liked best begins with the words

_____

_____

_____

The paragraph has _____ (enough, too many, too few)

details to support the topic sentence.

A particularly good part of the paragraph begins with the words

_____

_____

_____

I have questions about

_____

_____

_____

Other comments on the paragraph:

_____

_____

_____

_____

_____

_____

Reviewer's name: _____

WHAT IS WRITING FROM READING?

One way to find topics for writing is to draw from your ideas, memories, and observations. Another way is to write from reading you've done. You can react to it; you can agree or disagree with something you've read. In fact, many college assignments ask you to write about assigned reading: an essay, a chapter in a textbook, an article in a journal. This kind of writing requires an active, involved attitude toward your reading. Such reading is done in steps:

1. preread
2. read
3. reread with a pen or pencil

After you've completed these three steps, you can write from your reading. You can write about what you've read or react to it.

AN APPROACH TO WRITING FROM READING

Attitude

Before you begin the first step of this reading process, you have to have a certain *attitude*. That attitude involves thinking of what you read as half of a conversation. The writer has opinions and ideas; he or she makes points just as you do when you write or speak. The writer supports his or her points with specific details. If the writer were speaking to you in a conversation, you would respond to his or her opinions or ideas. You would agree, disagree, or question. You would jump into the conversation, linking or contrasting your ideas with those of the other speaker.

The right attitude toward reading demands that you read the same way you converse: you *become involved*. In doing this, you talk back as you read, and later, you react in your own writing. Reacting as you read will keep you focused on

ALONG THESE LINES/Prentice-Hall, Inc.

what you are reading. If you are focused, you'll remember more of what you read. With an active, involved attitude, you can begin the step of prereading.

Prereading

Before you actually read an assigned essay, a chapter in a textbook, or an article in a journal, magazine, or newspaper, take a few minutes to look it over, and be ready to answer the following questions:

A Prereading Checklist

✔ How long is this reading?

✔ Will I be able to read it in one sitting, or will I have to schedule several time periods to finish it?

✔ Are there any subheadings in the reading? Do they give any hints about the reading?

✔ Are there any charts? Graphs? Boxed information?

✔ Are there any photographs or illustrations with captions? Do the photos or captions give me any hints about the reading?

✔ Is there any introductory material about the reading or its author? Does the introductory material give me any hints about the reading?

✔ What is the title of the reading? Does the title hint at the point of the reading?

✔ Are any parts of the reading underlined, italicized, or emphasized in some other way? Do the emphasized parts hint at the point of the reading?

Why Preread?

Prereading takes very little time, but it helps you immensely. Some students believe it's a waste of time to scan an assignment; they think they should jump right in and get the reading over with. However, spending just a few minutes on preliminaries can save hours later. And most important, prereading helps you to become a *focused* reader.

If you scan the length of an assignment, you can pace yourself. And if you know how long a reading is, you can alert yourself to its plan. A short reading, for example, has to come to its point fairly soon. A longer essay may take more time to develop its point and may use more details and examples.

Subheadings, charts, graphs, illustrations, boxed or other highlighted materials are important enough that the author wants to emphasize them. Looking over that material *before* you read gives you an overview of the important points the reading will contain.

Introductory material or introductory questions will also help you know what to look for as you read. Background on the author or on the subject may hint at ideas that will come up in the reading. Sometimes even the title of the reading will give you the main idea.

You should preread so that you can start reading the entire assignment with as much *knowledge* about the writer and the subject as you can get. When you then read the entire assignment, you will be reading *actively*, for more knowledge.

Forming Questions before You Read

If you want to read with a focus, it helps to ask questions before you read. Form questions by using the information you gain from prereading.

Start by noting the title and turning it into a question. If the title of your assigned reading is "Reasons for the Alien and Sedition Acts," you can ask the question, "What were the reasons for the Alien and Sedition Acts?"

You can turn subheadings into questions. If you are reading an article on beach erosion, and one subheading is "Artificial Reefs," you can ask, "How are artificial reefs connected to beach erosion?"

You can also form questions from graphs and illustrations. If a chapter in your history book includes a photograph of a Gothic cathedral, you could ask, "How are Gothic cathedrals connected to this period in history?" or "Why are Gothic cathedrals important?" or "What is Gothic architecture?"

You can write down these questions, but it's not necessary. Just forming questions and keeping them in the back of your mind helps you read actively and stay focused.

An Example of the Prereading Step

Take a look at the article that follows. Don't read it; *preread* it.

A RIDICULOUS ADDICTION
Gwinn Owens

Gwinn Owens, a retired editor and columnist for the Baltimore Evening Sun, *writes this essay about his experience in parking lots, noting that the American search for a good parking space "transcends logic and common sense."*

Words You May Need to Know

addiction: a compulsive habit
transcends: rises above, goes beyond the limits of
stymied: hindered, blocked, defeated
preening: primping, making yourself appear elegant
perusing: reading
coveted: desired, eagerly wished for

atavistically: primitively
acrimonious: bitter, harsh
ensconced: securely sheltered
idiocy: foolish behavior
emporium: store
contempt: scorn, lack of respect
holy grail: a sacred object that the Knights of the Round Table devoted years to finding

A RIDICULOUS ADDICTION
Gwinn Owens

Let us follow my friend Frank Bogley as, on the way home from work, he swings into the shopping mall to pick up a liter of Johnny Walker, on sale at the Bottle and Cork. In the vast, herringboned parking area there are, literally, hundreds of empty spaces, but some are perhaps as much as a 40-second walk from the door of the liquor store. So Bogley, a typical American motorist, feels compelled to park as close as possible.

He eases down between the rows of parked cars until he notices a blue-haired matron getting into her Mercedes. This is a prime location, not more than 25 steps from the Bottle and Cork. Bogley stops to await her departure so as to slip quickly into the vacated slot. She shuts the door of her car as Bogley's engine surges nervously. But she does not move. She is, in fact, preening her hair and perusing a magazine she just bought.

The stymied Bogley is now tying up traffic in that lane. Two more cars with impatient drivers assemble behind him. One driver hits his horn lightly, then angrily. Bogley opens his window and gives him the finger, but reluctantly realizes that the Mercedes isn't about to leave. His arteries harden a little more as, exasperated, he gives up and starts circling the lot in search of another space, passing scores of empty ones which he deems too far from his destination. Predictably, he slips into the space for the handicapped. "Just for a moment," he says to his conscience.

The elapsed time of Bogley's search for a convenient parking space is seven minutes. Had he chosen one of the abundant spaces only a few steps farther away, he could have accomplished his mission in less than two minutes, without frazzled nerves or skyrocketing blood pressure—his as well as those who were backed up behind him. He could have enjoyed a little healthful walking to reduce the paunch that is gestating in his middle.

Frank Bogley suffers an acute case of parking addiction, which afflicts more Americans than the common cold. We are obsessed with the idea that it is our constitutional right not to have to park more than 10 steps from our destination.

Like all addictions, this quest for the coveted spot transcends logic and common sense. Motorists will pursue it without concern over the time it takes, as if a close-in parking space were its own sweet fulfillment. They will park in the fire lane, in the handicapped space or leave the car at the curb, where space is reserved for loading.

The quest atavistically transcends politeness and civility. My local paper recently carried a story about two motorists who, seeing a third car about to exit a spot, both lusted for the vacancy. As soon as the departing vehicle was gone, one of the standbys was a little faster and grabbed the coveted prize. The defeated motorist leaped from his car, threw open his rival's door and punched him in the snoot. He was charged with assault. Hell hath no fury like a motorist who loses the battle for a close-in parking space.

The daily obsession to possess the coveted slot probably shortens the life of most Americans by at least 4.2 years. This acrimonious jockeying, waiting, backing, maneuvering for the holy grail of nearness jangles the nerves, constricts the arteries and turns puppylike personalities into snarling mad dogs.

I know a few Americans who have actually kicked the habit, and they are extraordinarily happy people. I am one, and I owe my cure to my friend Lou, who is the antithesis of Frank Bogley. One day I recognized Lou's red Escort in the wallflower space of the parking lot at our local supermarket. There was not another vehicle within 80 feet.

In the store I asked him why he had ensconced his car in lonely splendor. His answer made perfect sense: "I pull in and out quickly, nobody else's doors scratch my paint and I get a short walk, which I need." Lou, I might point out, is in his 60s and is built like 25—lean and fit.

These days, I do as Lou does, and a great weight has been lifted. Free of the hassle, I am suddenly aware of the collective idiocy of the parking obsession—angry people battling for what is utterly without value. I acquire what does have value: saving of time, fresh air, peace of mind, healthful exercise.

The only time I feel the stress now is when I am a passenger with a driver who has not yet taken the cure. On one recent occasion I accepted a ride with my friend Andy to a large banquet at which I was a head-table guest. The banquet hall had its own commodious parking lot, but Andy is another Frank Bogley.

He insisted on trying to park near the door "because it is late." He was right, it *was* late, and there being no slots near the door, he then proceeded to thread his way through the labyrinth of the close-in lot, as I pleaded that I didn't mind walking from out where there was plenty of space. He finally used five minutes jockeying his big Lincoln into a Honda-size niche. Thanks to Andy's addiction, I walked late into the banquet hall and stumbled into my conspicuous seat in the midst of the solemn convocation. My attitude toward him was a mixture of pity and contempt, like a recovering alcoholic must feel toward an incipient drunk.

These silly parking duels, fought over the right not to walk 15 more steps, can be found almost anywhere in the 50 states. They reach their ultimate absurdity, however, at my local racquet and fitness club. The battle to park close to the door of the athletic emporium is fought as aggressively as at the shopping mall. Everyone who parks there is intending to engage in tennis, squash, aerobic dancing, muscle building or some other kind of athletic constitutional. But to have to exercise ahead of time by walking from the lot to the door is clearly regarded by most Americans as unconstitutional.

By prereading the article, you might notice the following:

The title is "A Ridiculous Addiction."
The author is a retired newspaper writer from Baltimore.
There are many vocabulary words you may need to know.
The essay is about parking lots.
The introductory material says that the American habit of searching for a desirable parking space goes beyond the limits of common sense.

You might begin reading the article with these questions in mind:

What is the addiction?
How can an addiction be ridiculous? An addiction is usually considered something very serious, like an addiction to drugs.
What do parking spaces have to do with addiction?
What's so illogical about looking for a good parking space?

Reading

The first time you read, try to *get a sense of the whole piece* you are reading. Reading with questions in mind can help you do this. If you find that you are confused by a certain part of the reading selection, go back and reread that part. If you do not know the meaning of a word, check the vocabulary list to see if the word is defined for you. If it isn't defined, try to figure out the meaning from the way the word is used in the sentence.

ALONG THESE LINES/Prentice-Hall, Inc.

If you find that you have to read more slowly than usual, don't worry. People vary their reading speed according to what they read and why they are reading it. If you are reading for entertainment, for example, you can read quickly; if you are reading a chapter in a textbook, you must read more slowly. The more complicated the reading selection, the more slowly you will read it.

An Example of the Reading Step

Now read "A Ridiculous Addiction." When you've completed your first reading, you will probably have some answers to the following prereading questions that you formed.

Answers to Prereading Questions

The author says that the ridiculous addiction is the need to find the best parking space.
He means it's ridiculous because it makes parking a serious issue, and because people do silly things to get good parking spots.
People are illogical about getting parking spaces because they'll even be late for an event in order to get a good one. Or they often get upset.

Rereading with Pen or Pencil

The second reading is the crucial one. At this point, you begin to think on paper, as you read. In this step, you make notes or write about what you read. Some students are reluctant to do this, for they are not sure what to note or write. Think of *making these notes as a way of learning, thinking, reviewing, and reacting*. Reading with a pen or pencil in your hand keeps you alert. With that pen or pencil, you can

mark the main point of the reading
mark other points
define words you don't know, in the margin
question parts of the reading you're not sure of
evaluate the writer's ideas
react to the writer's opinions or examples
add ideas, opinions, or examples of your own

There is no single system for marking or writing as you read. Some readers like to underline the main idea with two lines and to underline other important ideas with one line. Some students like to put an asterisk, a star, next to important ideas, while others like to circle key words.

Some people use the margins to write comments like, "I agree!" or "Not true!" or "That's happened to me." Sometimes readers put questions in the margin; sometimes they summarize a point in the margin, next to its location in the essay. Some people make notes in the white space above the reading and list important points, while others use the space at the end of the reading. Every reader who writes as he or she reads has a personal system; what these systems share is an attitude. *If you write as you read, you concentrate on the reading selection, get to know the writer's ideas, and develop ideas of your own.*

As you reread and write notes, don't worry too much about noticing the "right" ideas. Think of rereading as the time to jump into a *conversation* with the writer.

An Example of Rereading with Pen or Pencil

For "A Ridiculous Addiction," your marked article might look like the following:

A Ridiculous Addiction
by Gwinn Owens

Let us follow my friend Frank Bogley as, on the way home from work, he swings into the shopping mall to pick up a liter of Johnny Walker, on sale at the Bottle and Cork. In the vast, herringboned parking area there are, literally, hundreds of empty spaces, but some are perhaps as much as a 40-second walk from the door of the liquor store.

the bad habit So Bogley, <u>a typical American motorist, feels compelled to park as close as possible.</u>

He eases down between the rows of parked cars until he notices a blue-haired matron getting into her Mercedes. This is a prime location, not more than 25 steps from the Bottle and Cork. Bogley stops to await her departure so as to slip quickly into the vacated slot. She shuts the door of her car as Bogley's engine surges nervously. But she does not move. She is, in fact, preening her hair and perusing a magazine she just bought.

The stymied Bogley is now tying up traffic in that lane. Two more cars with impatient drivers assemble behind him. One driver hits his horn lightly, then angrily. Bogley opens his window and gives him the finger, but reluctantly realizes that the Mercedes isn't about to leave. His arteries harden a little more as, exasperated, he gives up and starts circling the lot in search of another space, passing scores of empty ones which he deems too far from his destination. <u>Predictably, he slips into the space for</u> *I hate this!* <u>the handicapped.</u> "Just for a moment," he says to his conscience.

<u>The elapsed time of Bogley's search for a convenient parking space</u> *wasted time* <u>is seven minutes.</u> Had he chosen one of the abundant spaces only a few

ALONG THESE LINES/Prentice-Hall, Inc.

steps farther away, <u>he could have accomplished his mission in less than</u>

irritation

<u>two minutes</u>, without <u>frazzled nerves</u> or <u>skyrocketing blood pressure</u>—

<u>his as well as those who were backed up behind him</u>. He could have

enjoyed a little healthful walking to reduce the paunch that is gestating

in his middle.

Frank Bogley suffers an acute case of parking addiction, which afflicts

more Americans than the common cold. <u>We are obsessed with the idea</u>   *

<u>that it is our constitutional right not to have to park more than 10 steps</u>   *

<u>from our destination.</u>

<u>Like all addictions, this quest for the coveted spot transcends logic</u> *

<u>and common sense.</u> Motorists will pursue it without concern over <u>the</u>

<u>time it takes</u>, as if a close-in parking space were its own sweet fulfillment.

They will <u>park in the fire lane</u>, <u>in the handicapped space</u> or <u>leave the car</u>

<u>at the curb, where space is reserved for loading.</u>

The quest atavistically <u>transcends politeness and civility</u>. My local

paper recently carried a story about two motorists who, seeing a third car

example

about to exit a spot, both lusted for the vacancy. As soon as the depart-

ing vehicle was gone, one of the standbys was a little faster and grabbed

the coveted prize. The defeated motorist leaped from his car, threw open

his rival's door and punched him in the snoot. He was charged with

<u>assault.</u> Hell hath no fury like a motorist who loses the battle for a close-

in parking space.

The daily obsession to possess the coveted slot probably shortens the

life of most Americans by at least 4.2 years. This acrimonious jockeying,

waiting, backing, maneuvering for the holy grail of nearness <u>jangles the</u>

<u>nerves,</u> <u>constricts the arteries</u> and <u>turns puppylike personalities into</u>

<u>snarling mad dogs.</u>

I know a few Americans who have actually kicked the habit, and they

are extraordinarily happy people. I am one, and I owe my cure to my

opposite ◄────────────────

friend Lou, who is the (antithesis) of Frank Bogley. One day I recognized

Lou's red Escort in the wallflower space of the parking lot of our local

supermarket. There was not another vehicle within 80 feet.

In the store I asked him why he had ensconced his car in lonely splen-

dor. His answer made perfect sense: "I pull in and out quickly, nobody

breaking the habit: advantages

else's doors scratch my paint and I get a short walk, which I need." Lou,

I might point out, is in his 60s and is built like 25—lean and fit.

These days, I do as Lou does, and a great weight has been lifted. Free

of the hassle, I am suddenly aware of the collective idiocy of the parking

obsession—angry people battling for what is utterly without value. I

acquire what does have value: saving of time, fresh air, peace of mind,

more advantages

healthful exercise.

The only time I feel the stress now is when I am a passenger with a

back to bad habit

driver who has not yet taken the cure. On one recent occasion I accepted

a ride with my friend Andy to a large banquet at which I was a head-table

guest. The banquet hall had its own commodious parking lot, but Andy

is another Frank Bogley.

He insisted on trying to park near the door "because it is late."

He was right, it *was* late, and there being no slots near the door, he then

proceeded to thread his way through the labyrinth of the close-in lot,

as I pleaded that I didn't mind walking from out where there was

plenty of space. He finally used five minutes jockeying his big Lincoln

How true!

into a Honda-size niche. Thanks to Andy's addiction, I walked late into

the banquet hall and stumbled into my conspicuous seat in the midst of

the solemn convocation. My attitude toward him was a mixture of pity

ALONG THESE LINES/Prentice-Hall, Inc.

and contempt, like a recovering alcoholic must feel toward an incipient drunk.

<u>These silly parking duels, fought over the right not to walk more than</u> <u>15 steps, can be found almost anywhere in the 50 states.</u> They reach their ultimate absurdity, however, at my local racquet and fitness club. The battle to park close to the door of the athletic emporium is fought as aggressively as at the shopping mall. Everyone who parks there is intending to engage in tennis, squash, aerobic dancing, muscle building or some other kind of athletic constitutional. But to have to exercise ahead of time by walking from the lot to the door is clearly regarded by most Americans as unconstitutional.

more on bad habit

What the Notes Mean

In the sample above, the underlining indicates sentences or phrases that seem important. The words in the margin are often summaries of what is underlined. The words "wasted time," "irritation," and "effects," for instance, are like subtitles or labels in the margin. The asterisks refer to very important ideas.

Some words in the margin are reactions. When Owens describes a man who parked illegally in a handicapped spot, the reader notes, "I hate this!" When the writer talks about a Lincoln trying to fit into a Honda-sized spot, the reader writes, "How true!" One word in the margin is a definition. The word "antithesis" in the selection is defined as "opposite" in the margin.

The marked-up article is a flexible tool. You can go back and mark it further. You may change your mind about your notes and comments and find other, better or more important points in the article.

You write as you read to involve yourself in the reading process. Marking what you read can help you in other ways, too. If you are to be tested on the reading selection or asked to discuss it, you can scan your markings and notations at a later time for a quick review.

▶ **EXERCISE 1:** **Reading and Making Notes**
for a Selection

Following is the last paragraph of "A Ridiculous Addiction." First, read it. Then reread it and make notes on the following:

1. Underline the sentence that begins the long example in the paragraph.
2. Circle a word you don't know and define it in the margin.
3. In the margin, add your own example of a place where people fight for parking spaces.
4. At the end of the paragraph, summarize the point of the paragraph.

Paragraph from "A Ridiculous Addiction"

These silly parking duels, fought over the right not to walk more than 15 steps, can be found almost anywhere in the 50 states. They reach their ultimate absurdity, however, at my local racquet and fitness club. The battle to park close to the door of the athletic emporium is fought as aggressively as at the shopping mall. Everyone who parks there is intending to engage in tennis, squash, aerobic dancing, muscle building, or some other kind of athletic constitutional. But to have to exercise ahead of time by walking from the lot to the door is clearly regarded by most Americans as unconstitutional.

Main point of the paragraph: _____

_____

WRITING A SUMMARY OF A READING

There are a number of ways you can write about what you've read. You may be asked for a summary of an article or chapter, or for a reaction to it, or to agree or disagree with it. For each of these, this chapter will give you guidelines, so you can *follow the steps* of thoughtlines, outlines, roughlines, and final lines.

A *summary* of a reading tells the important ideas in brief form. It includes (1) the writer's main idea, (2) the ideas used to explain the main idea, and (3) some examples used to support the ideas.

When you preread, read, and make notes on the reading selection, you have already begun the thoughtlines stage for a summary. You can think further, on paper, by *listing the points* (words, phrases, sentences) you've already marked on the reading selection.

Thoughtlines: Marking a List of Ideas

To find the main idea for your summary and the ideas and examples connected to the main idea, you can *mark related items on your list*. For example, the expanded list below was made from "A Ridiculous Addiction." Four symbols are used to mark the following:

    k   the kinds of close spots people will take
    ×   all examples of what can happen when people want a good spot
    −   the negative effects of the close-parking habit
    +   the advantages of breaking the habit

Items without a mark do not fit any of the categories.

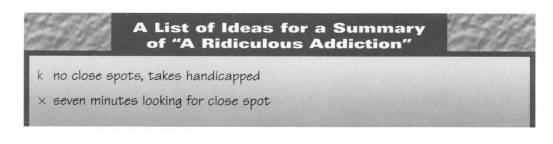

A List of Ideas for a Summary of "A Ridiculous Addiction"

k no close spots, takes handicapped

× seven minutes looking for close spot

  − wasted time, could have found another in two minutes

× got mad

× made others wait

× they got angry

Americans obsessed with right to good spot

transcends logic

no common sense

k park in fire lane

k leave car at curb

k loading zone

− impolite

× an assault over a spot

− jangles nerves, constricts arteries, makes people mad dogs

kicking the habit

+ get in and out fast

+ no scratched car doors

+ good exercise

+ saving time

+ fresh air

+ peace of mind

+ healthful exercise

× late for big dinner

× fitness clubs the silliest—won't walk

The marked list could then be reorganized, like this:

kinds of close spots people will take

handicapped
fire lane
curb
loading zone

examples of what can happen when people want a good spot

seven minutes of wasted time
others, waiting behind, get mad
an assault over a spot
late for a big dinner
members of the fitness club won't walk

negative effects of the close-parking habit

wasted time
impolite
jangles nerves, constricts arteries
makes people mad dogs

advantages of breaking the habit

get in and out fast
no scratched car doors
good exercise
saving time
fresh air
peace of mind
healthful exercise

Thoughtlines: Selecting a Main Idea

The next step in the process is to select the idea you think is the writer's *main point*. If you look again at the list of ideas, you'll note a cluster of ideas that are unmarked:

Americans obsessed with the right to a good spot
transcends logic
no common sense

You might guess that they are unmarked because they are more general than the other ideas. In fact, these ideas are connected to the title of the essay: "A Ridiculous Addiction," and they are connected to some of the questions in the prereading step of reading: "What's the addiction?" and "How can an addiction be ridiculous?"

Linking the ideas may lead you to a *main idea* for the summary of the reading selection:

Americans' obsession with finding a good parking spot makes no sense.

Once you have a main idea, check it to see if it fits with the other ideas in your organized list. *Do the ideas in the list connect to the main idea?* Yes. "Kinds of close spots people take" explains how silly it is to break the law. "Examples of what can happen" and "negative effects" show why the habit makes no sense, and "advantages of breaking the habit" shows the reasons to conquer the addiction.

Once you have a main point that fits an organized list, you can move to the *outlines stage* of a summary.

▶ **E X E R C I S E   1 :   Marking a List of Ideas and Finding the Main Idea for a Summary**

Following is a list of ideas from an article called "How to Land the Job You Want." Read the list, and then mark it with one of these symbols:

X = examples of people looking for or getting jobs
S = steps in getting a job
A = advice from employers

After you've marked all the ideas, survey them, and think of one main idea. Try to focus on an idea that connects to the title, "How to Land the Job You Want."

List of Ideas

_____ Six-year-old Tyrone cried when his mother said good-bye.

_____ Laid-off engineer used his personality to get a sales job.

_____ Insurance company manager says applicants can walk in without appointment.

_____ Find the hidden job market.

_____ Unemployed teacher found a job through his insurance agent.

_____ Bank worker got a job through his club.

_____ Prepare specifically for each interview.

_____ Locate hidden openings.

_____ Company director says a good letter of application is crucial.

_____ Make resume strong and polished.

_____ Put yourself in employer's place in writing a resume.

_____ Cabinet maker checked phone books of nine cities for companies in his field.

_____ Use the library to research job opportunities.

Main idea: _____

_____

Outlines for a Summary

Below is a sample of the kind of outline you could do for a summary of "A Ridiculous Addiction." As you read it, you'll notice that the main idea of the thoughtlines stage has become the topic sentence of the outline, and the other ideas have become the details.

```
        Outline for a Summary
      of "A Ridiculous Addiction"

topic sentence: Americans' obsession with finding a
                good parking spot makes no sense.

details:
                Many bad or silly things can happen
                when people try for a good spot.
                One person wasted seven minutes.
                He made other drivers angry.
                Someone else got involved in an
   examples    assault.
                Someone else was late for a big
                dinner.
                Silly people, on their way to a
                fitness club, will avoid the walk
                in the fitness club parking lot.
```

negative effects	{	Looking for a close spot can make people impolite or turn them into mad dogs.
		It can jangle drivers' nerves or constrict arteries.
		Some people will even break the law and take handicapped spots or park in a fire lane or loading zone.
advantages of kicking the habit	{	If people can give up the habit, they can gain advantages.
		A far-away spot is not popular, so they can get in and out of it fast.
		Their cars won't be scratched.
		They get exercise and fresh air by walking.

In the preceding outline, some ideas from the original list have been left out (they were repetitive) and the order of some points has been re-arranged. That kind of selecting and re-arranging is what you do in the outlines stage of writing a summary.

Roughlines: Attributing Ideas in a Summary

The first draft of your summary paragraph is your first try at *combining* all the material into one paragraph. This draft is much like the draft of any other paragraph, with one exception: *When you summarize another person's ideas, be sure to say whose ideas you are writing.* That is, *attribute* the ideas to the writer. Let the reader of your paragraph know

1. the author of the selection you are summarizing
2. the title of the selection you are summarizing

You may wish to do this by giving your summary paragraph a *title*, such as

    A Summary of "A Ridiculous Addiction," by Gwinn Owens

(Note that you put the title of Owens' essay in quotation marks.)

Or you may want to *put the title and author into the paragraph itself.* Below is a roughlines version of a summary of "A Ridiculous Addiction" with the title and author incorporated into the paragraph.

A Roughlines Draft for a Summary of "A Ridiculous Addiction"

"A Ridiculous Addiction" by Gwinn Owens says that Americans' obsession with finding a good parking spot makes no sense. Many bad or silly things can happen when people try for a good spot. One person wasted seven minutes. He made other drivers angry.

ALONG THESE LINES/Prentice-Hall, Inc.

> Someone else got involved in an assault. Someone
> else was late for a big dinner. Silly people, on
> their way to a fitness club, will avoid the walk in
> the fitness parking lot. Looking for a close spot
> can make people impolite or turn them into mad dogs.
> It can be stressful. Some people even break the law
> and take handicapped spots or park in a fire lane or
> loading zone. If people can give up the habit, they
> can gain advantages. A far-away spot is not popular,
> so they can get in and out of it fast. Their cars
> won't be scratched. They get exercise and fresh air
> by walking.

When you look this draft over and read it aloud, you may notice a few problems:

1. It is wordy.
2. In some places, the word choice could be better.
3. Some of the sentences are choppy.
4. It might be a good idea to mention that the examples in the summary were Gwinn Owens'.

Revising the draft would mean rewriting to eliminate some of the wordiness, to combine sentences or smooth out ideas, and to insert the point that the author, Gwinn Owens, gave the examples used in the summary. When you state that Owens created the examples, you are clearly giving the author credit for his ideas. Giving credit is a way of attributing ideas to the author.

Note: When you refer to an author in something that you write, use the author's first and last name the first time you make a reference. For example, you write "Gwinn Owens" the first time you refer to this author. Later in the paragraph, if you want to refer to the same author, use only his or her last name. Thus, a second reference would be to "Owens."

Final Lines for a Summary

Look carefully at the final version, the final lines copy of the summary. Notice how the sentences have been changed, words added or taken out, and how "Owens" is used to show that the examples given came from the essay.

> **Final Lines for a Summary**
> **of "A Ridiculous Addiction"**

> "A Ridiculous Addiction" by Gwinn Owens says that
> Americans' obsession with finding a good parking
> spot makes no sense. Owens gives many examples of
> the unpleasant or silly things that can happen when
> people try for a good spot. One person wasted seven
> minutes and made the other drivers angry. Someone
> else got involved in an assault; another person was
> late for an important dinner. At fitness club

> parking lots, people coming to exercise are missing
> out on the exercise of walking through the parking
> lot. Looking for a good spot can turn polite people
> into impolite ones or even into mad dogs. The search
> is not only stressful; it can also lead people to
> break the law by taking handicapped, fire lane, or
> loading zone spots. If people broke the habit and
> took spots farther away from buildings, they would
> have several advantages. No one wants the far-away
> spots, so drivers can get in and out fast, without
> any scratches on their cars. In addition, people who
> break the habit get exercise and fresh air.

Writing summaries is good writing practice, and it also helps you develop your reading skills. Even if your instructor does not require you to turn in a polished summary of an assigned reading, you may find it helpful to summarize what you have read. In many classes, midterms or other exams cover many assigned readings. If you make short summaries of each reading, as it is assigned, you will have a helpful collection of focused, organized material to review.

WRITING A REACTION TO A READING

A summary is one kind of writing you can do after reading, but there are other kinds. Your instructor might ask you to *react* by writing about some idea you got from your reading. If you read "A Ridiculous Addiction," for example, your instructor might have asked you to react to it by writing about some practice or habit that irritates you. You can begin to gather ideas by freewriting.

Thoughtlines: Freewriting

You can freewrite in a reading journal, if you wish. To freewrite, you can

- write key points made by the author
- write about whatever you remember from the reading selection
- write down any of the author's ideas that you think you might want to write about someday
- list questions raised by what you've read
- connect the reading selection to other things you've read, heard, or experienced.

A freewriting that reacts to "A Ridiculous Addiction" might look like this:

Freewriting for a Reaction to a Reading

"A Ridiculous Addiction"—Gwinn Owens

People are silly in fighting for parking spaces. Spot has to be close by. Never more than 10 steps away. They get mean. Angry. Take handicapped spots. How selfish! Fire lane! Dangerous! Really waste time looking and waiting for

> good spot. Health club parkers there to get exercise but don't want to walk far in parking lot. <u>Why</u> is it such a big deal? Yesterday a guy cut in front of me, from opposite direction, to grab a parking space. Some spots are too small for big cars. What about people who back into spots? Why? To make a quick getaway?

Freewriting helps you review what you've read, and it can give you topics for a paragraph that is different from a summary.

Thoughtlines: Listing Ideas

Instead of freewriting about "A Ridiculous Addiction," you might *review* the essay, and *list* ideas from it that you might want to write more about. Here is a list of some ideas from "A Ridiculous Addiction." The exact words used from the essay are enclosed in quotation marks.

Listing Ideas for a Reaction to a Reading

taking handicapped spaces
fights in parking lots over spaces
people who get in their cars and don't pull out of a spot
big cars in small spaces
damage to cars
"silly parking duels"
"angry people battling for what is utterly without value"

Thoughtlines: Brainstorming

After you get a list, you can *brainstorm* about the whole list or about a part of it. You can ask yourself questions to lead you towards a topic for your own paragraph. For instance, brainstorming on the idea, "angry people battling for what is utterly without value" could look like this:

Brainstorming from a List

Owens says people fighting for spaces are "battling for what is utterly without value." So why do they do it? Is there any other time drivers battle for what has no value?
Sure. On the highway. All the time.

How?
They weave in and out. They cut me off. They tailgate. They speed.

What are they fighting for?
They want to gain a few minutes. They want to get ahead. Driving is some kind of contest for them.

Then, don't they get some kind of satisfaction from the battle?
Not really. I often see them at the same red light I've stopped at. And their driving is very stressful for them. It raises their blood pressure, makes them angry and unhappy. They can't really win.

Could you write a paragraph on drivers who think of driving as a contest? If so, your brainstorming, based on your reading, might lead you to a topic.

Thoughtlines: Developing Points of Agreement or Disagreement

Another way to use a reading selection to lead you to a topic is to review the selection and jot down any statements that provoke a strong reaction in you. You are looking for sentences with which you can agree or disagree. If you already marked "A Ridiculous Addiction" as you read, you might list these statements as points of agreement or disagreement:

Points of Agreement or Disagreement from a Reading

"Hell hath no fury like a motorist who loses the battle for a close-in parking space." —agree

"This quest for the coveted spot transcends logic and common sense." —disagree

---

Then you might *pick one of the statements and react to it, in writing*. If you disagreed with the second statement that "this quest for the coveted spot transcends logic and common sense," you might develop the thoughtlines part of writing by listing your own ideas. You might focus on why a close parking space is important to you. With a focus and a list of reasons, you could move to the outlines part of writing from reading.

Outlines for a Reaction to a Reading

An outline might look like the one following. As you read it, notice that the topic sentence and ideas are *your opinions*, not the ideas of the author of "A Ridiculous Addiction." You used his ideas to come up with your own thoughts.

Outline for a Reaction to a Reading

topic sentence: Sometimes a close parking spot is important.

details:

convenience { I may have heavy bags to carry from the store.
Cars can be vandalized.

car safety { Vandalism and burglary are more likely if the car is parked at a distance.

personal safety { I can be attacked in a parking lot.
Attacks are more likely at night.
Muggings are more likely if I am parked far away.

Roughlines for a Reaction to a Reading

If your written reaction gives you enough good points to develop, you are on your way to a paragraph. If you began with the ideas above, for example, you could develop them into a paragraph like this:

> ## A Roughlines Draft for a Reaction to a Reading
>
> Sometimes a close parking spot is important. The short distance to a store can make a difference if I have heavy bags or boxes to carry from the store to my car. Convenience is one reason for parking close. A more important reason is safety. In my neighborhood, cars are often vandalized. Sometimes, cars get broken into. Cars are more likely to get vandalized or burglarized if they are parked far from stores. Most of all, I am afraid to park far from stores or restaurants because I am afraid of being attacked in a parking lot, especially at night. If I am far away from buildings and other people, I am more likely to be mugged.

Final Lines for a Reaction to a Reading

When you read the preceding paragraph, you probably noticed some places where it could be revised:

- It could use more specific details.
- It should attribute the original idea about parking to Gwinn Owens, probably in the beginning.
- Some sentences could be combined.

Following is the final lines version of the same paragraph. As you read it, notice how a new beginning, added details, and combined sentences make it a smoother, clearer, and more developed paragraph.

> ## Final Lines for a Reaction to a Reading
>
> Gwinn Owens says that people who look for close parking spaces are foolish, but I think that sometimes a close parking spot is important. The short distance to a store can make a difference if I have heavy bags or boxes to carry from the store to my car. Convenience is one reason for parking close, but the more important reason is safety. In my neighborhood, cars are often vandalized. Antennas get broken off; the paint gets deliberately scratched. Sometimes, cars get broken into. Radios and tape players are stolen. Cars are more likely to get

vandalized or burglarized if they are parked far
from stores. Most of all, I am afraid to park far
from stores or restaurants because I am afraid of
being attacked in a parking lot, especially at
night. If I am far away from buildings or other
people, I am more likely to be mugged.

Reading can give you many ideas for your own writing. Developing those ideas into a polished paragraph requires the same writing process as any good writing, a process that takes you through the steps of thoughtlines, roughlines, outlines, and final lines.

Lines of Detail: A Walk-Through Assignment

Here are two ideas from "A Ridiculous Addiction":

a. People who want a good parking space often break the parking laws.
b. People who search for good parking spots become mean and nasty.

Pick *one* of these ideas, with which you agree or disagree. Write a paragraph explaining why you agree or disagree. To write your paragraph, follow these steps:

Step 1: Begin the thoughtlines by listing at least four reasons why you agree or disagree.

Step 2: Read your list to a partner or to a group. With the help of your listener(s), add reasons or details to explain the reasons.

Step 3: Once you have enough ideas, transform the statement you agreed or disagreed with into a topic sentence.

Step 4: Write an outline by listing your reasons and details below the topic sentence. Check that your list is in a clear and logical order.

Step 5: Write a roughlines draft of your paragraph. Check that you have attributed Gwinn Owens' statement, that you have enough details, and that you have combined any choppy sentences. Revise your draft until the paragraph is smooth and clear.

Step 6: Before you prepare the final copy, check your last draft for errors in spelling, punctuation, and word choice.

Writing Your Own Paragraph on "A Ridiculous Addiction"

When you write on one of these topics, be sure to work through the stages of thoughtlines, outlines, roughlines, and final lines in preparing your paragraph.

1. Gwinn Owens writes about Americans' addiction to the close parking space. Write about another addiction that Americans have. Instead of writing about a topic like drug or alcohol addiction, follow Owens' example and write about a social habit that is hard to break. You might, for instance, write about people's habit of

   driving while talking on a phone   tailgating
   weaving in and out of traffic   speeding

ALONG THESE LINES/Prentice-Hall, Inc.

driving too slowly					pushing in line
running yellow traffic lights			littering

Once you've chosen a habit, brainstorm, alone or with a partner, for details. Think about details that could fit these categories:

why the habit is foolish
why the habit is dangerous
when and where people act this way
advantages of breaking the habit

Ask yourself questions, answer them, and let the answers lead to more questions. Once you've collected some good details, work through the stages of writing a paragraph.

2. Gwinn Owens writes about a great invention, the car, and about the parking problems caused by cars. Following are several other, recent inventions that can cause problems. Your goal is to write a paragraph about the problems one of these inventions can cause.

To start, pick two of the following inventions. Alone, or with a partner or a group, brainstorm both topics: ask questions, answer them, add details, so that each topic can lead you to enough ideas for a paragraph.

After you've brainstormed, pick the topic you like better and work through the stages of preparing a paragraph.

Topics to brainstorm: problems that could be caused by telephone answering machines, car alarms, automatic teller machines, cell phones, or beepers.

Brainstorm for Topic 1: _____

_____

_____

_____

_____

Brainstorm for Topic 2: _____

_____

_____

_____

_____

PEER REVIEW

Name: _____   **Section:** _____

Peer Review Form for Writing from Reading

After you've written a roughlines version of your paragraph, read it to a writing partner. Then let your partner read it silently, looking for the answers to the following questions. After your partner has completed the following form, discuss it.

   Repeat the same process for your partner's paragraph.

This paragraph (pick one) (1) summarizes, (2) agrees or disagrees, or (3) writes about an idea connected to a reading selection.

I think this paragraph needs/does not need to include the title and author of the reading selection.

The topic sentence of this paragraph is:

_____

_____

The best part of this paragraph started with the words

_____

_____

One suggestion to improve this paragraph is to

_____

_____

_____

Other comments on the paragraph:

_____

_____

_____

_____

_____

_____

_____

_____

_____

Reviewer's name:_____

Writing from Reading

To practice the skills you've learned in this chapter, follow the steps of prereading, reading, and rereading with a pen or pencil as you read the following selection.

PARENTAL DISCRETION
Dennis Hevesi

Dennis Hevesi is a writer for the New York Times. *In this essay, he writes about how the family structure changes when a parent goes back to school.*

Before you read this selection, consider these questions:

How would you feel if one of your parents went to the same college you attended?
Is there an age that is "too old" to go to college?
At your college, do younger and older students mix?
Do older students have special problems with attending college?
Can a family help (or hurt) a student's chances of succeeding in college?

Words You May Need To Know

discretion: the right to make your own decision
wrought: inflicted
havoc: disorder, confusion
diehard: stubbornly committed, dedicated
feminists: people who fight for women's rights
limelight: attention
genes: a unit in the body that con-

trols the development of hereditary traits
maternal: motherly
anthropology: a study of the origins, physical and cultural development of mankind
Renaissance: a period of history, roughly from the late 1300s to 1600, in Europe

PARENTAL DISCRETION
Dennis Hevesi

When the letter came saying that Pamela Stafford, after all her part-time study at night, had been accepted at the age of 34 as a full-time student by the University of California at Berkeley, her two teen-age sons leaped into the air, slapped palms in a high-five and shouted: "We did it! We did it!"

"I'm not sure they included me," she said.

Several months ago, when Gary Hatfield, also 34, and a sophomore at the Ohio State University, in Columbus, was telling his son, Seth, 11, why he was spending so much time studying, "He patted me on the shoulder and said: 'Dad, I understand. You want to finish school,'" Mr. Hatfield recalled, adding, "Blessed is the child's forgiving nature."

In hundreds of homes throughout the nation, as the rolls of those signing up for continuing education courses grow, getting mom or pop off to school has often wrought a kind of joyous havoc on family life and forced the sort of realignment of expectations that would warm the hearts of diehard feminists.

A Switch of Family Roles   Dads or children are doing the shopping, the cooking, the cleaning, the laundry. Teen-agers have become the family chauffeur, or at least make sure the car is available when a parent has to get to class. Schedules have been turned on end. Children have even adopted parental roles—nagging when homework hasn't been done.

Mr. Hatfield, an English major, wants to teach high school or college English. "I'll sometimes get jabbed if I make a spelling or grammatical mistake," he said. "Seth will say, 'Hey, English teacher . . .'"

What can come through the difficulties and the role reversals is a shared commitment, a strengthened bond and a deepened appreciation for education. "When I went back to school, my older son went from being a C and D student to making honor roll," said Ms. Stafford, who is divorced and lives in Albany, near the university. "The younger guy, well, not as much improvement. But he did develop a more serious attitude toward school. Now, it's sort of a given that what you really do in life is finish school first."

And when the boys—Joseph, 18, and Christopher, 14—run into what Ms. Stafford called "the geek mentality" of friends who think doing well in school is totally lame, they are equipped to respond. "Joseph once told his friend," Ms. Stafford said, " 'Hey, my mom is smart. It's in the genes. I can't help being smart.' "

Mom is indeed smart. Out of a possible 4.0, Ms. Stafford is maintaining a 3.9 grade-point average as an English major at Berkeley, where she is also on staff as an administrative assistant.

"I felt really guilty about taking night courses," she said. "Then, at the end of that first semester, I got an A in ancient Mediterranean literature, and my sons developed an investment in my education. They sort of fired me as a mother and recreated me as a student."

Joseph, now a freshman at St. Mary's College in nearby Moraga, said: "I had to cook, wash dishes, pretty much take care of myself and my brother, too. There were times when I wished she was around; when things would happen that I couldn't handle."

Joseph said Christopher "was always a hyper kid. So I just had to be real patient. I talked to him about girls, about drugs. He doesn't do the silly stuff he used to do to get attention, like kitchen gymnastics—you know, dancing and flipping around the house like an idiot. Sometimes we fought. But he and I loved each other enough to punch each other and then hug."

Mysterious Disappearances During Finals   During midterms and finals, Ms. Stafford said, the boys "would mysteriously disappear" so that she could study. "I like to deejay," Joseph said, "you know, sound-mixing in my room. I had to do this with headphones the entire time. There could be no noise."

Between classes, Ms. Stafford would call home "and try to at least bring a maternal presence into the conversation: 'Have you done your homework? Have you done your chores?' But they would say, 'Hey, we don't need you. Goodness, the things we go through putting a parent through school.' "

Sometimes it seemed that Seth Hatfield wasn't so much putting his father through school as accompanying him. "Last quarter, I was taking an anthropology course," Mr. Hatfield said, "and one of the evenings I would take Seth to that class. He would sit and do his homework at the table with me. And the teacher was so nearsighted that she would walk by and give him handouts, just like one of the students."

Mr. Hatfield, who is divorced and lives in Columbus, has worked as a landscaper, a salesman, a counselor to juvenile delinquents, and a social

ALONG THESE LINES/Prentice-Hall, Inc.

worker at a home for the mentally retarded. With a part-time job, a little money in the bank and a grant from Ohio State, he returned to college in 1987 and is maintaining a grade-point average of 3.2.

"I get hit with anxiety attacks," he said, "because here I am plowing through Renaissance literature and wishing I was sitting with my son playing a game."

Getting Early Exposure to College   But Seth doesn't complain, and his exposure to college has had benefits. "I found out from his teachers that he speaks proudly of going to Ohio State with his dad," Mr. Hatfield said. "Just walking across campus, with him wearing his Ohio State sweatshirt, gives me the opportunity to familiarize him with what the place really is. We go plunder through the library. He knows that the computer catalogue search system can lead him to information on Superman."

"I might go there when I grow up," Seth said. "When my dad gets his education, if he becomes a teacher, he'll have a larger income and I might even have him as a teacher. Maybe I'll borrow money from him for lunch."

Mr. Hatfield realizes that Seth, who lives with his mother about a mile away, is his first priority. "I will cut class to go to his band concert," he said. "Those things are too precious. I can take an incomplete in a course and make it up. I can't take an incomplete as a parent and ever make that up."

▶ **EXERCISE 1:**   **Understanding the Examples in "Parental Discretion"**

Hevesi uses examples to illustrate what happens to families when parents go to college. He uses the same families over and over in his examples, to make different points. Following are lists of the parents attending college in each family. Add the names and ages of the children connected to each family.

Family #1: mother: Pamela Stafford, age 34

child (or children) and age(s) _____

_____

Family #2: father: Gary Hatfield, age 34

child (or children) and age(s) _____

_____

Hevesi uses these families to illustrate a number of good and bad things that can happen when parents return to college. Reread his essay. Then find one example that illustrates each of the following points. Be specific, using the names of the parents and children.

a. Children get exposed to college on visits.

example: _____

_____

b. Children do better at school.

example: _____

_____

c. Parents feel guilty about spending so much time away from children.

example: _____

_____

d. Children get anxious about taking on too much responsibility for the household.

example: _____

_____

e. Parents get praise from their children.

example: _____

_____

f. Parents and children grow closer.

example: _____

_____

Writing from Reading "Parental Discretion"

When you write on any of the following topics, be sure to work through the stages of thoughtlines, outlines, roughlines, and final lines in preparing your paragraph.

1. Using the ideas and examples you gathered in Exercise 1, write a summary paragraph of Hevesi's article.

2. No matter how old you are, attending college presents certain challenges. If you are the "traditional" college age of eighteen or nineteen, you may face the challenge of adjusting to a place that is not like high school. If you are in your twenties, you may be facing other challenges: earning money for college, living at home and going to college, balancing the demands of a family, work, and school. Students in their thirties, forties, fifties, sixties, and seventies all have different problems when they go to college. Write a paragraph about the problems one age group faces while attending college. You may use a topic sentence like this one:

   It's not easy being eighteen (or twenty-five, or thirty, or sixty—you fill in the age) and going to college.

   If your instructor permits, you might interview a writing partner about the difficulties that his or her age group faces in going to college. Then your partner can interview you. By interviewing, each of you can help the other gather details.

3. As an alternative to topic 2, choose a topic sentence that is closer to your experience, like one of these:

   It's not easy working full time and going to college.
   It's not easy being in a wheelchair and going to college.
   It's not easy being a single parent and going to college.

ALONG THESE LINES/Prentice-Hall, Inc.

4. Begin this assignment by working with a group. Plan a paragraph with this topic sentence:

Today, the term "college student" can include many kinds of people.

In your group, have each member support the topic sentence by talking about himself or herself. You might mention age, reason for going to college, ethnic background, college major, hobbies, special talents, family background, and so forth. As each member describes himself or herself, write down the details. Ask follow-up questions and write down the answers. After you have gathered enough specific examples, write your paragraph.

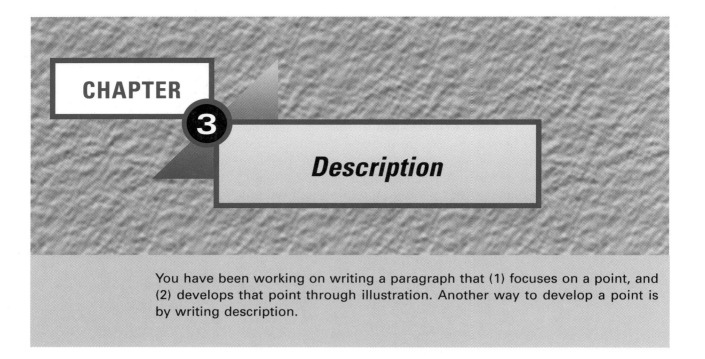

CHAPTER 3

Description

You have been working on writing a paragraph that (1) focuses on a point, and (2) develops that point through illustration. Another way to develop a point is by writing description.

WHAT IS DESCRIPTION?

Description shows a reader what a person, place, thing, or situation is like. When you write description, you try to show, not tell, about something. You want to make the reader see that person, place, or situation, and then, perhaps, to make the reader think about or act on what you've shown.

Hints for Writing a Descriptive Paragraph

Using Specific Words and Phrases   The reader will see what you are describing if you use specific words and phrases. When a word or phrase is *specific*, it is exact and precise. The opposite of specific language is *general* language, which is vague or fuzzy. Think of the difference between specific and general in this way:

Imagine that you are browsing through a used car lot. A salesman approaches you.

"Can I help you?" the salesman asks.
"I'm looking for a good, reliable car," you say.
"Well, what kind of car did you have in mind?" asks the salesman.
"Not too old," you say.
"A sports car?" asks the salesman.
"Maybe," you say.

The conversation could go on and on. You are being general in saying that you want a "good, reliable" car. The salesman, however, is looking for specific details: How old a car do you want? What model of car?

In writing, if you use words like "good" or "nice" or "bad" or "interesting," you will have neither a specific description nor an effective piece of writing. Whenever you can, try to use the more explicit word instead of the general term. To find a more explicit term, ask yourself such questions as, "What type?" or "How?" The examples below show how a general term can be replaced by a more specific one.

general word: hat (Ask "What type?")
more specific words: beret, fedora, baseball cap

ALONG THESE LINES/Prentice-Hall, Inc.

general word: lettuce (Ask "What type?")
more specific words: iceberg lettuce, Romaine, arugula

general word: ran (Ask "How?")
more specific words: raced, sprinted, loped

general word: nice (Ask "How?")
more specific words: friendly, outgoing, courteous

general word: cleaned (Ask "How?")
more specific words: swept, scoured, scrubbed

▶ **EXERCISE 1:** Identifying General and Specific Words

Following are lists of words. Put an X by the most general term in each list. The first one is done for you.

List a

_____ waiter

_X_ restaurant employee

_____ cook

_____ cashier

_____ dishwasher

List b

_____ toaster

_____ electric can opener

_____ coffee maker

_____ kitchen appliances

_____ blender

List c

_____ fiesta

_____ luau

_____ barbeque

_____ party

_____ clambake

List d

_____ weather forecaster

_____ news reporter

_____ news anchor

_____ sports reporter

_____ TV newsperson

List e

_____ watch

_____ pin

_____ ring

_____ cuff links

_____ jewelry

List f

_____ science

_____ biology

_____ chemistry

_____ astronomy

_____ physics

▶ **EXERCISE 2:** Ranking General and Specific Items

Following are lists of items. In each list, rank the items from the most general (1) to the most specific (4).

List a

_____ reading material

_____ magazine

List d

_____ government programs

_____ college loan

_____ weekly magazine   _____ money for students

_____ *Time*   _____ financial aid

List b   **List e**

_____ dairy products   _____ stinging insect

_____ low-fat cottage cheese   _____ insect

_____ cheese   _____ dangerous insect

_____ source of calcium   _____ killer bee

List c   **List f**

_____ toys for toddlers   _____ car phone

_____ stuffed animals   _____ telephone

_____ toys   _____ invention

_____ teddy bear   _____ recent invention

► **E X E R C I S E   3 :   Collaborative Exercise in Interviewing
                                          for Specific Answers**

To practice being specific, interview a partner. Ask your partner to answer the
questions below. Write his or her answers in the spaces provided. When you have
finished, change places. In both interviews, your goal is to find specific answers,
so you should both be as explicit as you can in your answers.

Interview Questions

1. What is your favorite flavor of ice cream? _____

2. What did you eat and drink for breakfast this morning? _____
_____

3. What is your favorite football team? _____

4. What TV personality do you most dislike? _____

5. If you were painting your room, what color would you choose?
_____

6. What fabric do you think is the softest? _____

7. When you think of a fierce dog, what breed comes to mind? _____
_____

8. When you think of a fast car, what car do you picture? _____
_____

9. What specific items of your clothing are the most comfortable?
_____
_____

▶ **E X E R C I S E   4 :   Collaborating to Find Specific Words or Phrases**

With a partner or group, list four specific words or phrases beneath each general one. You may use brand names where they are appropriate. The first word on List a is done for you.

List a

general word: blue

specific word or phrase: _aquamarine_ _____

_____

_____

_____

List b

general word: walked

specific word or phrase: _____

_____

_____

_____

List c

general word: athletic shoes

specific word or phrase: _____

_____

_____

_____

List d

general word: hungry

specific word or phrase: _____

_____

_____

_____

List e

general word: musician

specific word or phrase: _____

_____

_____

_____

E X E R C I S E

List f

general word: cried

specific word or phrase: _____

_____

_____

_____

▶ **EXERCISE 5:** **Identifying Sentences That Are Too General**

Below are lists of sentences. Put an *X* by one sentence in each group that is general and vague.

a. 1. _____ Jose is an easygoing person.

2. _____ Jose will smile at an insult.

3. _____ Jose's most typical remark is, "No problem."

b. 1. _____ Her eyes were red and swollen.

2. _____ Her mouth was turned down at the corners.

3. _____ She looked unhappy.

c. 1. _____ The dress was pretty.

2. _____ The dress had peach and yellow flowers on it.

3. _____ The dress was pale green silk.

d. 1. _____ Children pushed in line for the swings at the park.

2. _____ The park was swarming with joggers.

3. _____ The park was busy.

e. 1. _____ He will always be there for me.

2. _____ When I was sick, he took care of my daughter.

3. _____ He lent me money when I lost my job.

Using Sense Words in Your Descriptions One way to make your description specific and vivid is to use *sense words* or words that relate to the five senses. As you plan a description, ask yourself:

What does it *look* like?
What does it *sound* like?
What does it *smell* like?
What does it *taste* like?
What does it *feel* like?

Of course, you can't make use of all of the five senses in every description, but *brainstorming by asking questions* about the five senses can help you to find specific detail. For example, if you were thinking about describing a particularly good meal you had eaten, you might *brainstorm for detail*, like this:

Q A

Question: What was the meal?
Answer: Lasagna.
Question: What else?
Answer: Garlic Bread. Salad.

Question: What did the lasagna look like?
Answer: The lasagna was thick layers of red and white. It was stuffed into a huge glass pan, pouring over the sides.

Question: What did it smell like?
Answer: Garlic, oregano, spicy tomatoes.
Question: How did it taste?
Answer: Delicious.
Question: Can you be specific?
Answer: The lasagna was rich, full of tomatoes and cheese. The salad was crisp, and it tasted of an olive oil and wine vinegar dressing and of parmesan cheese.

Question: Any textures?
Answer: The outer noodles were crackly. The ricotta cheese was as creamy as butter. The croutons on the salad were crunchy. The lettuce was crisp but slick with the dressing. The bread was toasty on the outside, but inside it was spongy and saturated with garlic butter.

Sense details make a description vivid. Try to include details about the five senses in your descriptions. Often you can brainstorm sense details more easily if you focus your thinking.

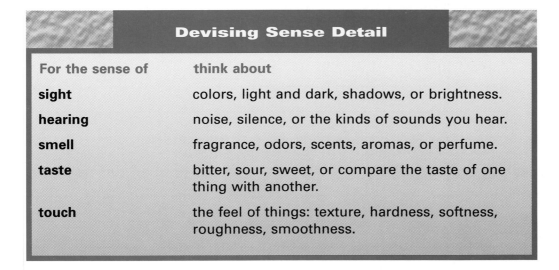

Devising Sense Detail

For the sense of	think about
sight	colors, light and dark, shadows, or brightness.
hearing	noise, silence, or the kinds of sounds you hear.
smell	fragrance, odors, scents, aromas, or perfume.
taste	bitter, sour, sweet, or compare the taste of one thing with another.
touch	the feel of things: texture, hardness, softness, roughness, smoothness.

EXERCISE

EXERCISE 1: Collaborative Exercise: Brainstorming Sense Detail for a Descriptive Paragraph

With a partner or a group, brainstorm the following ideas for a paragraph. That is, for each topic, list at least ten questions and answers that could help you create sense detail. Be prepared to read your completed exercise to another group or to the class.

ALONG THESE LINES/Prentice-Hall, Inc.

a. topic: The kitchen was the messiest I have ever seen.

Brainstorm questions and answers: _____

_____

_____

_____

_____

_____

_____

_____

_____

_____

_____

b. topic: The beach provided a soothing environment.

Brainstorm questions and answers: _____

_____

_____

_____

_____

_____

_____

_____

_____

_____

_____

c. topic: The Halloween party thrilled the kindergartners.

Brainstorm questions and answers: _____

_____

_____

_____

_____

_____

_____

_____

_____

ALONG THESE LINES/Prentice-Hall, Inc.

▶ **E X E R C I S E   2 :   Writing Sense Words**

Alone, with a partner, or with a group, write sense descriptions for the items following. When you've completed the exercise, be prepared to share your descriptions with the class.

a. Write four words or phrases to describe the texture of a blanket:

_____

_____

b. Write four words or phrases to describe what a silver ring looks like:

_____

_____

c. Write four words or phrases to describe the sounds of a nightclub:

_____

_____

d. Write four words or phrases to describe the taste of burned toast:

_____

_____

WRITING THE DESCRIPTIVE PARAGRAPH IN STEPS

T HOUGHTLINES: DESCRIPTION

Writing a description paragraph begins with thinking on paper, looking for specific details and sense descriptions. You can think by brainstorming, freewriting, or writing in a journal. For example, you might decide to write about your first apartment. Brainstorming might lead you to something like the following questions and answers:

Q A

Brainstorming for a Description

Topic: My First Apartment

Question: What did the apartment look like?
Answer: One room and a kitchenette.

Question: What do you remember about it?
Answer: I was broke after paying my first and last month's rent and a security deposit.

Question: But what did the apartment look like?
Answer: Well, I was broke, so it looked thrown together.

Question: What do you mean?
Answer: Thrift shop furniture. An old bed, an armchair with plastic cushions. I used the bed as a couch.

Question:	What else was in there?
Answer:	A bookcase I made. My old cassette player and speakers.

Question:	What else? Curtains on the windows? Or shades?
Answer:	I made curtains out of printed sheets. I was so proud of them. I hung them with brass rings on rods. I had posters taped to the wall.

Question:	Posters of what?
Answer:	Old movie posters.

Question:	Do you remember any smells?
Answer:	No.

Question:	How about sounds?
Answer:	My cassette player. And a wheezy old fan.

You might list your answers and then decide that you could add more detail by asking more questions:

What was the bed like? Describe it. Tell more about the plastic armchair. How did you make the curtains? What color were they? Why were you proud of them? How did you make the bookcase? What movies were advertised on the posters? What kind of fan did you have? What else was in the room? What about the kitchenette?

By answering the questions, you could add detail, so that you might have a list that looks like this:

- small apartment—one room and a kitchenette
- kitchenette was old but had working refrigerator, stove and sink
- looked thrown together
- an old bed from a thrift shop
- took off the headboard, covered the bed with a blue tablecloth to look like a couch—covered the wall beside the bed with blue and red pillows
- thrift shop armchair with plastic cushions. Camouflaged the yellow plastic with lots of blue pillows.
- a bookcase I made out of bricks and lumber. 5 feet high, looked like a wall unit.
- my cassette player and speakers on the bookcase
- also had books, framed photos, a candle in a wine bottle dripped with wax
- curtains out of blue and red striped sheets
- proud of them—hung them on brass rods
- movie posters of 2001: A Space Odyssey and Close Encounters of the Third Kind. Lots of blue colors in them.
- wheezy old fan, round, with wires around blades
- also a coffee table I got at a garage sale
- one table leg shorter than the others

The Dominant Impression

When you think you have enough detail, you can begin to think about focusing that detail. Review your detail and consider where it is taking you. If you were to look at the previous list, you might identify ideas that keep showing up through the detail:

I didn't have much money to furnish my first apartment.
I was creative.

I was proud of some of my ideas.
I had to rely on thrift shops and garage sales.
I had to be resourceful.

If you wanted to use one main idea from the list above, you could. It would be the dominant impression, or the main point of the description. Or you could combine ideas to create a dominant impression. For example, your dominant impression could be

My first apartment showed what I could do with little cash and plenty of ideas.

Once you have a dominant impression, you are ready to add more ideas to explain and support it. You should try to make the added details specific by using sense description where appropriate.

▶ **E X E R C I S E 1: Adding Details to a Dominant Impression**

Do this exercise alone, with a partner, or with a group. Following are sentences that could be used as a dominant impression in a descriptive paragraph. Add more details. Some details, to explain and support the dominant impression, are already given.

a. **dominant impression:** The teenager looked like he had dressed in a
                                             hurry.

details: 1. His shirt was hanging out of his jeans. _____

2. The laces of his sneakers were untied. _____

3. _____

4. _____

5. _____

b. **dominant impression:** The hallway of the apartment was cluttered.

details: 1. A bicycle leaned against one wall. _____

2. A skateboard was shoved under the bike. _____

3. _____

4. _____

5. _____

c. **dominant impression:** The bakery invited me to come in and buy
                                             something.

details: 1. The display window was filled with freshly baked sticky cinnamon rolls.

2. Next to the rolls was a pyramid of dark chocolate brownies. _____

3. _____

4. _____

5. _____

d. dominant impression: The teddy bear was worn from much handling
                         and love.

details: 1. _One glass eye was missing._

          2. _A brown ear had been mended with white thread._

          3. _____

          4. _____

          5. _____

▶ **EXERCISE 2: Creating a Dominant Impression
                 from a List of Details**

Do this exercise alone, with a partner, or with a group. Following are lists of
details. For each list, write one sentence that could be used as the dominant
impression created by the details.

a. dominant impression: _____

_____

_____

details: People were pushed together behind the cash register, waiting for
          tables.
          The waiters raced from the tables to the kitchen, carrying plates of
          fajitas, burritos, and tacos.
          Every table was filled with people.
          The hostess zigzagged between tables, trying to give menus to
          newcomers.
          The tables were so close together that strangers elbowed each other.

b. dominant impression: _____

_____

_____

details: Thirty students sat at thirty desks, looking at the tests before them.
          Their eyes never strayed to the left or right.
          A few students tapped nervously with their pencils.
          The only sounds came from the pacing of the instructors and the
          turning of the test pages.
          One instructor held a watch in his hand.
          One student's knees were shaking.

c. dominant impression: _____

_____

_____

details: The paint on the old car had been buffed to a deep shine.
          The chrome dazzled.
          Every spoke of the hubcaps reflected light.
          The hood ornament was bright silver.
          The finish on the car's paint was as smooth as porcelain.

OUTLINES: DESCRIPTION

You can use the sentence you created as the dominant impression for the topic sentence of your outline. Beneath the topic sentence, list the details you have collected. Once you have this rough list, check the details, and ask:

Do all the details fit the topic sentence?
Are the details in logical order?

Following is the topic sentence and a list of details for the paragraph describing an apartment. The details are written in short sentences. The sentences that are crossed out *don't fit* the topic sentence.

topic sentence: My first apartment showed what I could do with little cash and plenty of ideas.

details: It was a small apartment.
~~It was one room and a kitchenette.~~
~~The kitchen was old but had a working refrigerator, stove, and sink.~~
~~The apartment looked thrown together.~~
I got an old bed from a thrift shop.
I took off the headboard.
I covered the bed with a blue tablecloth to look like a couch.
I got an armchair from the thrift shop.
It had plastic cushions.
I camouflaged the yellow plastic cushions with lots of blue pillows.
I made a bookcase out of bricks and lumber.
It was five feet high, like a wall unit.

I put my cassette player and speakers on the bookcase.

I also put some books, framed photos, a candle in a wine bottle dripped with wax.

I made curtains out of blue and red striped sheets.

I was proud of them.

I hung them on brass rods.

On the wall I had movie posters of *2001: A Space Odyssey* and *Close Encounters of the Third Kind.*

The posters had lots of blue in them.

~~I also had a wheezy old, round, table fan with wire around the blades.~~

~~I had a coffee table I got at a garage sale.~~

~~One leg was shorter than the others.~~

Notice what is crossed out. The details about the kitchen, the fan, and the coffee table don't relate much to the topic sentence. The topic sentence is about decorating with little money and plenty of ideas. Because the kitchen isn't really discussed in the rest of the details, and since the fan isn't part of the decorating, the sentences about the kitchen and the fan don't fit. And, if you want the paragraph to make a point about your clever decorating skills, you don't want a detail that says the apartment "looked thrown together," so that detail is eliminated, too.

Keep in mind that, as you write and revise, you may decide to eliminate other ideas, or to re-insert ideas you once rejected, or to add new ideas. Changing your mind is a natural part of revising.

Once you've firmed up your list of details, check the *order*. Remember, when you write a description, you are trying to make the reader *see*. It will be easier for the reader to visualize what you see if you put your description in a simple, logical order. You might want to put descriptions in order by time sequence (first to last) or by spatial position (top to bottom, or right to left). You might also group by similar types or categories (for example, all about the flowers, then all about the trees in a park).

If you are describing a house, for instance, you may want to start with the outside of the house and then describe the inside. You don't want the details to shift back and forth, from outside to inside and back to outside. If you are describing a person, you might want to group together all the details about his or her face before you describe the body. You might describe a meal from first course to dessert.

Look again at the details of the outline describing the apartment. It is logical to use three categories to create a simple order: furniture in general, furniture against the wall, and decorations for windows and walls.

An Outline for a Descriptive Paragraph

topic sentence: My first apartment showed what I could do with a little cash and plenty of ideas.

details:

furniture
> It was a small apartment.
> I got an old bed from a thrift shop.
> I took off the headboard.
> I covered the bed with a blue tablecloth to make the bed look like a couch.
> I covered the wall side with red and blue pillows.
> I got an arm chair from a thrift shop.
> It had plastic cushions.
> I camouflaged the yellow plastic cushions with lots of blue pillows.

furniture against the wall
> I made a bookcase out of bricks and lumber.
> It was five feet high, like a wall unit.
> I put my cassette player and speakers on the bookcase.
> I also put some books, framed photos, a candle in a wine bottle dripped with wax.

windows and walls
> I made curtains out of blue and red striped sheets.
> I hung them on brass rods.
> I was proud of them.
> On the wall I had movie posters of 2001: A Space Odyssey and Close Encounters of the Third Kind.
> They had lots of blue in them.

Once you have a list of details that are focused on the topic sentence and arranged in some logical order, you can begin the roughlines stage of writing the descriptive paragraph.

▶ E X E R C I S E 1 : **Finding Details That Don't Fit**

Alone, with a partner, or with a group, survey the following lists. Each list includes a topic sentence and several details. In each list cross out the details that don't fit the topic sentence.

a. topic sentence: My brother's garden was neglected.

details: Weeds cluttered the flower beds.
Grass peeped through the cracks in the sidewalks.
Yellow dandelions bloomed in the lawn.
The apple tree had many apples.
The yard was bordered by a fence.
The long, uncut grass tickled my ankles.
An overgrown vine strangled a small tree.
Ants swarmed from anthills and stung me.
Some flowers wilted from lack of water.

b. topic sentence: My Aunt Maria was a motherly woman.

details: She always greeted me with a big hug.
She crushed me against her plump body.
She smelled like the gingerbread cookies she always made for me.
She was born in Guatemala.
She always checked to see if I was dressed warmly enough to go outside.
She carried small treats in her apron.
She made me wash my hands before meals.
She had deep brown eyes.

c. topic sentence: Levar was a very spoiled child.

details: He would interrupt his mother when she was talking to people.
He'd pull at her sleeve or the hem of her dress.
He'd whine, "Mom, Mom, I want to go now," or "Mom, can I have a dollar?"
He had about a hundred toys.
Whenever he broke a toy, he got a new one right away.
Levar wore designer clothes, even to play in.
Levar had no set bedtime; he was allowed to stay up as long as he wanted.
Levar had a little sister, Denise.
Levar had big, black eyes with long, soft lashes.

▶ E X E R C I S E 2 : **Putting Details in Order**

Do this exercise alone, with a partner, or with a group. Following are lists that start with a topic sentence. The details under each topic sentence are not in the right order. Put each detail in logical order by labelling it, with 1 being the first detail, 2 the second, and so forth, after the topic sentence.

a. topic sentence: The picnic turned out to be a disaster.

details: _____ We got lost on the way to the picnic.

_____ The ice in the ice chest melted.

_____ The lemonade was warm.

_____ Back home, we didn't close the lid on the cooler when we were packing it.

b. topic sentence: The Jackson house looked haunted.
               (Arrange the details from outside to inside.)

details: _____ The tall, iron fence around the house was rusted and crumbling.

           _____ The front hall smelled like a dead rat.

           _____ The house was covered by a dark green vine.

           _____ The front door creaked and groaned.

           _____ A long, twisting staircase loomed at the end of the hall.

c. topic sentence: The bodyguard was a frightening person.
               (Arrange the details from head to foot.)

details: _____ His cold eyes stared straight ahead.

           _____ His mouth never moved.

           _____ He stood poised on the balls of his feet, ready to spring.

           _____ His wide shoulders strained against the fabric of his shirt.

           _____ His neck was as thick as a tree.

           _____ His fists were half clenched.

▶ **E X E R C I S E   3 :**   **Collaborative Exercise in Creating Detail Using a Logical Order**

The following lists include a topic sentence and indicate a required order for the details. Working with a partner or group, write five sentences of detail in the required order.

a. topic sentence: Her new truck dazzled my eyes.
               (Describe the truck from inside to outside.)

1. _____

2. _____

3. _____

4. _____

5. _____

b. topic sentence: The movie was full of exciting moments.
               (Describe the movie from beginning to end.)

1. _____

2. _____

3. _____

4. _____

5. _____

c. topic sentence: The traffic jam showed people at their worst.
(First describe the scene; then describe the drivers' behavior.)

1. _____
2. _____
3. _____
4. _____
5. _____

d. topic sentence: His clothes showed a lack of style.
(Describe him from head to foot.)

1. _____
2. _____
3. _____
4. _____
5. _____

e. topic sentence: The tornado wrecked my back yard.
(First describe what it did to plants and trees, then what it did to the patio.)

1. _____
2. _____
3. _____
4. _____
5. _____

Ⓡ OUGHLINES: DESCRIPTION

After you have an outline, the next step is creating a draft of the paragraph. At this point, you can begin combining some of the ideas in your outline, making two or more short sentences into one longer one. Or you can write your first draft in short sentences and combine the sentences later. Your goal is simply to put your ideas into paragraph form. Then you can see how they look and check them to see what needs to be improved.

The first draft of a paragraph won't be perfect. If it were perfect, it wouldn't be a first draft. Once you have the first draft, check it, using the following list:

A Checklist for Revising a Descriptive Paragraph

✔ Are there enough details?

✔ Are the details specific?

ALONG THESE LINES/Prentice-Hall, Inc.

> ✔ Do the details use sense words?
>
> ✔ Are the details in order?
>
> ✔ Is there a dominant impression?
>
> ✔ Do the details connect to the dominant impression?
>
> ✔ Have I made my point?

A common problem in writing description is creating a fuzzy, vague description. Take a look at the following fuzzy description:

> The football fans were rowdy and excited. They shouted when their team scored. Some people jumped up. The fans showed their support by cheering and stomping. They were enjoying every minute of the game.

The description could be revised so that it is more specific and vivid:

> The football fans were rowdy and excited. When their team scored, they yelled, "Way to go!" or "Stomp 'em! Crush 'em!" until they were hoarse. Three fans, wearing the team colors of blue and white on their shirts, shorts, and socks, jumped up, spilling their drinks on the teenagers seated below them. During timeouts, the fans chanted rhythmically, and throughout the game they stomped their feet in a steady beat against the wooden bleachers. As people chanted, whooped, and woofed, they turned to grin at each other and thrust their clenched fists into the air.

The vivid description meets the requirements of the checklist. It has enough specific details in logical order. The details use sense words to describe what the fans looked and sounded like, and they also support a dominant impression of rowdy, excited fans. The vivid, specific details make the point.

ALONG THESE LINES/Prentice-Hall, Inc.

▶ **E X E R C I S E   1 :** **Revising a Paragraph by Eliminating Irrelevant Sentences**

Following are two descriptive paragraphs. In each, there are sentences that are irrelevant, meaning that they don't have anything to do with the first sentence, the topic sentence. Cross out the irrelevant sentences in the following paragraphs.

a. John looked and sounded like he had a bad cold. His voice was hoarse and raspy, and it sounded like it hurt him to talk. His nostrils were red and chafed around the edges, as if he had wiped his nose with hundreds of Kleenex. His cheeks looked flushed and feverish. His eyes had a watery sheen. Sometimes my eyes get like that when I have an allergy. I am allergic to cats. John sneezed four times in thirty seconds. There's nothing worse than sneezing constantly, unless it's a cold that won't quit.

b. The van was in bad shape. One door panel had been deeply dented, and since the dent had never been repaired, rust filled the dented places. The rear tires were so worn out that they shone smoothly where tread should have been. Tires like that are really dangerous, especially on slick roads. One of the van windows was missing, and a piece of cardboard covered the opening. The whole van was covered in dust. It doesn't cost that much to run a van through a car wash, so they could have taken care of it. An odor of burnt oil drifted up from under the vehicle.

▶ **E X E R C I S E   2 :** **Revising a Paragraph for More Specific Details**

In the following paragraphs, the details that are underlined are not specific. Change the underlined sentences to a more specific description. Write the changes in the lines below each paragraph, and share your revisions with a writing partner or with a group.

a. It was the most beautiful beach I had ever seen. The beach itself was very wide; it was almost a quarter mile from the sand to the water. The sand was a pale beige, almost white in color, and it was as fine as cake flour. Shining up from the sand were small pink and ivory shells. <u>The water was nice, too.</u>

revisions: _____

_____

b. The house seemed to say, "We don't want you here." There was a heavy iron fence around the yard, and the iron gate had two locks on it. <u>A plant clung to the iron fence, and a dog patrolled the yard.</u> Black bars crossed the windows of the first story of the house, and the second story windows were tinted black.

revisions: _____

_____

Transitions

As you revise your descriptive paragraph, you may notice places that seem choppy or abrupt. That is, one sentence may end, and another may start, but the two sentences don't seem to be connected. Reading your paragraph aloud, you might sense that it is not very smooth.

You can make the writing smoother and make the content clearer by using *transitions*. Transitions are words or phrases that link one idea to another. They tell the reader what he or she has just read and what is coming next. Every kind of writing has its own transitions. Here are some transitions you may want to use in writing a description:

Transitions for a Descriptive Paragraph

To show ideas brought together: and, also, in addition, as well as

To show a contrast: but, although, on the other hand, however, in contrast, unlike, yet, on the contrary

To show a similarity: both, like, similarly, all, each

To show a time sequence: after, always, before, first, second, third, (and so forth), often, meanwhile, next, soon, then, when, while

To show a position in space: above, ahead of, alongside, among, around, away, below, beside, between, beneath, beyond, by, close, down, far, here, in front of, inside, near, nearby, next to, on, on top of, outside, over, there, toward, under, up, underneath

---

There are many other transitions you can use, depending on what you need to link your ideas. Take a look at a revised draft of the descriptive paragraph on an apartment. Pay particular attention to the transitions.

A Roughlines Revised Draft of a Descriptive Paragraph
(Transitions are underlined.)

My first apartment showed what I could do with a little cash and plenty of ideas. To furnish my small apartment, I started with an old bed I got at a thrift shop. I took off the headboard and covered the bed with a blue tablecloth. <u>Then</u>, to make the bed look like a couch, I covered the wall side of the bed with lots of blue and red pillows. I <u>also</u>

---

got an armchair from the thrift shop. It had yellow plastic cushions, <u>but</u> I camouflaged those cushions with lots of blue pillows. I made a bookcase out of bricks and lumber. The bookcase was five feet high, <u>and</u> I used it as a wall unit. <u>On it</u>, I put my cassette player and speakers, some books, some framed photos, and a candle in a wine bottle dripped with wax. <u>For the windows</u>, I made curtains out of red and blue striped sheets <u>and</u> hung them on brass rods. I was proud of those curtains. <u>On the wall</u>, I had movie posters of *2001: A Space Odyssey* and *Close Encounters of the Third Kind*. They had lots of blue in them.

▶ **E XERCISE 1:** **Recognizing Transitions**

Underline the transitions in the following paragraph. When you have finished the exercise, share your answers with a partner or a group.

My sister designed a children's fantasy for her little boy's birthday party. She decorated the walls with streamers in neon yellow and green. From the ceiling she hung clusters of yellow and blue balloons. Then, on the food table, she spread a tablecloth printed with hundreds of small Barney dinosaurs. Meanwhile, my brother finished decorating an enormous cake slathered in white and yellow icing. On top of the cake he placed a small purple dinosaur. After he put the cake in the middle of the table, my sister added baskets filled with cookies and candy. Beneath the table she hid a huge box of prizes for all the party games. When she added a bag of treats for each child at the party, my sister finished her work. Now came the enjoyment of seeing her son celebrate his third birthday.

FINAL LINES: DESCRIPTION

In the *final lines* stage of writing a description, you add the finishing touches to your paragraph, such as changing words, combining sentences, changing or adding transitions, and sharpening details. If you look over the roughlines draft of the description of an apartment, you'll notice that the phrase "lots of" is used often, as in

lots of blue and red pillows
lots of blue pillows
lots of blue in them

When you are drafting, it is easy to get into the habit of using vague words like "lots of" or "a lot" and of being repetitive. In the final version of the descriptive paragraph, the "lots of" phrases are replaced.

Rereading the draft paragraph, you may notice that the ending of the paragraph is a little sudden. The paragraph needs a sentence that pulls all the detail together and reminds the reader of the topic sentence. The final lines version has an added sentence that ties the paragraph together.

Compare the following final lines paragraph to the roughlines version. To track the way the paragraph evolved, the outlines stage is also included for you.

Before you prepare the final lines copy of your descriptive paragraph, check your latest draft for errors in spelling and punctuation, and for any errors made in typing or recopying.

An Outlines Version of a Descriptive Paragraph

topic sentence: My first apartment showed what I could do with little cash and plenty of ideas.

details: It was a small apartment.
I got an old bed from a thrift shop.
I took off the headboard.
I covered the bed with a blue tablecloth to look like a couch.
I covered the wall side with red and blue pillows.
I got an armchair from the thrift shop.
It had plastic cushions.
I camouflaged the yellow plastic cushions with lots of blue pillows.
I made a bookcase out of bricks and lumber.
It was five feet high, like a wall unit.
I put my cassette player and speakers on the bookcase.
I also put some books, framed photos, a candle in a wine bottle dripped with wax.
I made curtains out of blue and red striped sheets.
I hung them on brass rods.
I was proud of them.
On the wall I had movie posters of *2001: A Space Odyssey* and *Close Encounters of the Third Kind*.
They had lots of blue in them.

A Roughlines Version
of a Descriptive Paragraph

My first apartment showed what I could do with a little cash and plenty of ideas. To furnish my small apartment, I started with an old bed I got at a thrift shop. I took off the headboard and covered the bed with a blue tablecloth. Then, to make the bed look like a couch, I covered the wall side of the bed with lots of blue and red pillows. I also got an armchair from the thrift shop. It had yellow plastic cushions, but I camouflaged those cushions with lots of blue pillows. I made a bookcase out of bricks and lumber. The bookcase was five feet high, and I used it as a wall unit. On it, I put my cassette player and speakers, some books, some framed photos, and a candle in a wine bottle dripped with wax. For the windows, I made curtains out of red and blue striped sheets and hung them on brass rods. I was proud of those curtains. On the wall I had movie posters of *2001: A Space Odyssey* and *Close Encounters of the Third Kind*. They had lots of blue in them.

A Final Lines Version
of a Descriptive Paragraph
(Changes from the roughlines
version are underlined.)

My first apartment showed what I could do with a little cash and plenty of ideas. To furnish my apartment, I started with an old bed I got at a thrift shop. I took off the headboard and covered the bed with a blue tablecloth. Then, to make the bed look like a couch, I covered the wall side of the bed with piles of blue and red pillows. I also got an armchair from the thrift shop. It had yellow plastic cushions, but I camouflaged those cushions with more blue pillows. I made a bookcase out of bricks and lumber. The bookcase was five feet high, and I used it as a wall unit. On it, I put my cassette player and speakers, some books, some framed photos, and a candle in a wine bottle dripped with wax. For the windows, I made curtains out of red and blue striped sheets and hung them on brass rods. I was proud of those curtains. On the wall I had movie posters of *2001: A Space Odyssey* and *Close Encounters of the Third Kind*. They were filled with shades of blue, and I thought they added the perfect final touch to my stylish but inexpensive apartment.

▶ **E XERCISE 1 : Correcting Errors in Final Lines**

Following is a descriptive paragraph with the kinds of errors that are easy to overlook when you write the final version of an assignment. Correct the errors, writing above the lines.

I have an old dilapidated sweatshirt that I'll allways cherish for the memmories it holds. It is a ratty-looking, gray shirt that belongs in the rag pile but I wore that shirt on many happy occassions. The greasy stain on one sleeve is a memory of how I got covered in oil when i was working on my first motorcycle the tear at the neck reminds me of a crazy game of football. At the game where I tore the shirt, I also met my current girlfreind. The pale white blotches acrost the front of the shirt are from bleech. But to me they are a memory of the time my girlfriend and I was fooling around at the laundry room and put to much bleach in the washer. Every mark or stain on my shirt has a meaning to me and I'll never through that old shirt away.

Lines of Detail: A Walk-Through Assignment

Your assignment is to write a paragraph describing a popular place for socializing. Follow these steps:

Step 1: To begin the thoughtlines, freewrite about a place where people socialize. For example, you could write about a place where people go to eat, or dance, or swim, or just "hang out."

Step 2: Read your freewriting. Underline all the words, phrases, and sentences of description.

Step 3: List everything you underlined, grouping the ideas in some order. Maybe the details can be listed from inside to outside, or can be put into categories, like walls, floor, and furniture, or scenery and people.

Step 4: After you've surveyed the list, write a sentence about the dominant impression of the details.

Step 5: Using the dominant impression as your topic sentence, write an outline. Add specific details where you need them. Concentrate on details that appeal to the senses.

Step 6: Write a roughlines version of your paragraph. Be sure to check the order of your details. Combine short sentences and add transitions.

Step 7: Revise your first roughlines version, paying particular attention to order, specific details, and transitions.

Step 8: After a final check for punctuation, spelling, and word choice, prepare the final lines version of the paragraph.

Writing Your Own Descriptive Paragraph

When you write on any of these topics, follow the stages of thoughtlines, outlines, roughlines, and final lines in preparing your descriptive paragraph. Be sure that your paragraph is based on a dominant impression, and put the dominant impression into your topic sentence.

1. Write a paragraph that describes one of the following items:

   the contents of your purse or wallet
   items in the glove compartment of your car
   what is in your top bureau drawer, or what is in your top kitchen drawer
   a piece of clothing
   a hospital waiting room
   what you wear on your day off
   a perfect meal
   a family member
   a favorite relative
   an enemy
   a very young baby
   an irritating customer
   your first impression of a school
   a person who was a positive influence in your life

2. Describe a place that creates one of these impressions:

peace	tension	depression
excitement	cheerfulness	hurry
friendliness	danger	

3. Describe a person that conveys one of these impressions:

confidence	warmth	pride
hostility	fear	style
shyness	rebellion	intelligence
conformity	strength	beauty

4. Select a photograph of a person or place. You can use a photograph from a magazine or newspaper, or one of your own photographs. Write a paragraph describing that photograph. Attach the photograph to the completed paragraph.

5. Interview a partner so that you and your partner can gather details and then write a descriptive paragraph with the title, "My Perfect Room."

   First, prepare a list of at least six questions to ask your partner. Write down the answers your partner gives and use these answers to form more questions. For example, if your partner says her dream room would be a game room, ask her what games she'd like to have in it. If your partner says his perfect room would be a workshop, ask him what kind of workshop.

   When you've finished the interview, switch roles. Let your partner interview you. Feel free to add more questions or to follow up on previous ones.

   Finally, give your partner his or her interview responses, then take your own responses and use them as the basis for gathering as many details as you can on your perfect room in order to create the thoughtlines part of your paragraph. Then go on to the outlines, roughlines, and final lines stages. Be prepared to read your completed paragraph to your partner.

6. Describe photograph A. Be sure that your description includes details about the children and the setting.

7. Describe the people and the location in photograph B. Look carefully at the details of the scene and include them in your description.

ALONG THESE LINES/Prentice-Hall, Inc.

Photograph A

Photograph B

PEER REVIEW

Name: _____   **Section:** _____

Peer Review Form for a Descriptive Paragraph

After you've written a roughlines version of your descriptive paragraph, let a writing partner read it. When your partner has completed the following form, discuss his or her comments. Then repeat the same process for your partner's paragraph.

The dominant impression of the paragraph is this sentence:

_____

_____

The details of the description are in a specific order (for example, top to bottom, time order, and so forth). That order is

_____

_____

The part of the description I like best begins with the words

_____

_____.

The part that can use more details or more specific details begins with the words

_____

_____.

I have questions about

_____

_____.

I noticed these transitions:

_____

_____

A place where transitions could be added or improved is right before the words

_____

_____

Other comments on the paragraph:

_____

_____

_____

Reviewer's name: _____

Writing from Reading: Description

A PRESENT FOR POPO
Elizabeth Wong

The child of Chinese immigrants, Elizabeth Wong was born in Los Angeles, California. She has a Master's degree in Fine Arts and has worked as a writer for newspapers and television. She has also written several plays. In "A Present for Popo," Wong describes a beloved grandmother.

Before you read this essay, consider these questions:

Are you afraid of growing old?
Do you think most old people in our country are treated well?
Are they respected? Ignored?
Are you close to anyone over sixty-five?
Did you grow up in close contact with a grandparent?
Is there one person who holds your family together?

Words You May Need to Know

nimbly: quickly, gracefully
vain: excessively proud of your appearance
co-opted: taken over
niggling: unimportant

dim sum: a light meal
terrarium: a small container where plants and small creatures are kept alive under conditions imitating their natural environment

A PRESENT FOR POPO
Elizabeth Wong

When my Popo opened a Christmas gift, she would shake it, smell it, listen to it. She would size it up. She would open it nimbly, with all enthusiasm and delight, and even though the mittens were ugly or the blouse too small or the card obviously homemade, she would coo over it as if it were the baby Jesus.

Despite that, buying a gift for my grandmother was always problematic. Being in her late 80s, Popo didn't seem to need any more sweaters or handbags. No books certainly, as she only knew six words of English. Cosmetics might be a good idea, for she was just a wee bit vain.

But ultimately, nothing worked. "No place to put anything anyway," she used to tell me in Chinese. For in the last few years of her life, Popo had a bed in a room in a house in San Gabriel owned by one of her sons. All her belongings, her money, her very life was now co-opted and controlled by her sons and their wives. Popo's daughters had little power in this matter. This was a traditional Chinese family.

For you see, Popo had begun to forget things. Ask her about something that happened 20 years ago, and she could recount the details in the heartbeat of a New York minute. But it was those niggling little everyday matters that became so troubling. She would forget to take her heart medicine. She would forget where she put her handbag. She would forget she talked to you just moments before. She would count the few dollars in her billfold, over and over again. She would ask me for the millionth time, "So when are you going to get married?" For her own good, the family decided she should give up her beloved one-room Chinatown flat.

Popo herself recognized she might be a danger to herself, "I think your grandmother is going crazy," she would say.

That little flat was a bothersome place, but Popo loved it. Her window had a view of several import-export shops below, not to mention the grotesque plastic hanging lanterns and that nasty loudspeaker serenading tourists with 18 hours of top-40 popular hits.

My brother Will and I used to stand under her balcony on Mei Ling Way, shouting up, "Grandmother on the Third Floor! Grandmother on the Third Floor!" Simultaneously, the wrinkled faces of a half-dozen grannies would peek cautiously out their windows. Popo would come to the balcony and proudly claim us: "These are my grandchildren coming to take me to *dim sum*." Her neighbors would cluck and sigh, "You have such good grandchildren. Not like mine."

In that cramped room of Popo's, I could see past Christmas presents. A full-wall collage of family photos that my mother and I made together and presented one year with lots of fanfare. Popo had attached additional snapshots by way of paper clips and Scotch tape. And there, on the window sill, a little terrarium to which Popo had tied a small red ribbon. "For good luck," as she gleefully pointed out the sprouting buds. "See, it's having babies."

Also, there were the utility shelves on the wall, groaning from a wide assortment of junk, stuff and whatnot. Popo was fond of salvaging discarded things. After my brother had installed the shelving, she did a little jig, then took a whisk broom and lightly swept away any naughty spirits that might be lurking on the walls. "Shoo, shoo, shoo, away with you, Mischievous Ones!" That apartment was her independence, and her pioneer spirit was everywhere in it.

Popo was my mother's mother, but she was also a second mother to me. Her death was a great blow. The last time I saw her was Christmas, 1990, when she looked hale and hearty. I thought she would live forever. Last October, at 91, she had her final heart attack. The next time I saw her, it was at her funeral.

An open casket, and there she was, with a shiny new penny poised between her lips, a silenced warrior woman. Her sons and daughters placed colorful pieces of cloth in her casket. They burned incense and paper money. A small marching band led a New Orleans-like procession through the streets of Chinatown. Popo's picture, larger than life, in a flatbed truck to survey the world of her adopted country.

This little 4-foot, 9-inch woman had been the glue of our family. She wasn't perfect, she wasn't always even nice, but she learned from her mistakes, and, ultimately, she forgave herself for being human. It is a lesson of forgiveness that seems to have eluded her own sons and daughters.

And now she is gone. And with her—the tenuous, cohesive ties of blood and duty that bound us to family. My mother predicted that once the distribution of what was left of Popo's estate took place, no further words would be exchanged between Popo's children. She was right.

But this year, six of the 27 grandchildren and two of the 18 great-grandchildren came together for a holiday feast of honey-baked ham and mashed potatoes. Not a gigantic family reunion. But I think, for now, it's the one yuletide present my grandmother might have truly enjoyed.

Merry Christmas, Popo!

Writing from Reading "A Present for Popo"

1. Elizabeth Wong uses many details about her grandmother's apartment to describe the woman. Write a paragraph in which you use many details about a person's environment (for example, her office, his apartment) to describe that person.

2. Wong's essay includes a description of a funeral in a Chinese-American family. Write a description of some custom or ritual in your family. You could write, for instance, about a wedding, a funeral, the celebration of a holiday, or a religious occasion.

3. "A Present for Popo" is a tribute to a beloved person. Write a description of someone who holds a special place in your life.

4. The grandmother in Wong's essay is an immigrant, a Chinese woman who moved to America. Describe an immigrant that you know. Focus on how the person is a combination of two countries or cultures.

5. Describe an older person you know well. In your description, you can use details of appearance and behavior. Focus on how these details reveal personality.

6. Describe yourself at age ninety. Use your imagination to give details of appearance, behavior, and family relationships.

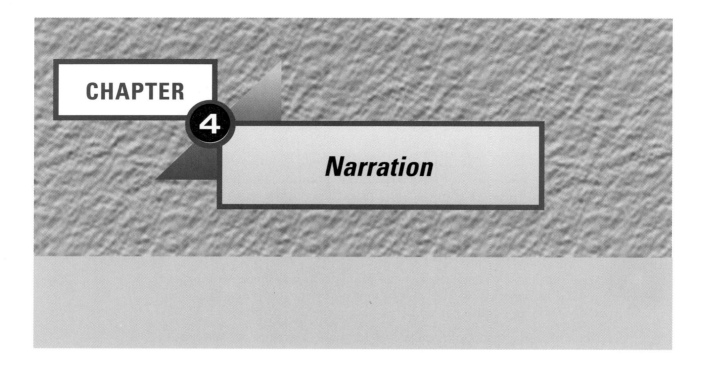

Narration

WHAT IS NARRATION?

Narration means telling a story. Everybody tells stories; some people are better storytellers than others. When you write a narrative paragraph, you can tell a story about something that happened to you or to someone else, or about something that you saw or read.

Because it relies on specific details, a narrative is like a description. But it is also different from a description because it covers events in a time sequence. That is, a description can be about a person, a place, or an object, but a narrative is always about happenings: events, actions, incidents.

Interesting narratives do more than tell what happened. They help the reader become involved in the story by providing vivid detail. You can get that detail from your memory or observation or reading. *Don't just tell the story; show it.*

Giving the Narrative a Point

We all know people who tell long stories that seem to lead nowhere. These people talk on and on; they recite an endless list of activities and soon become boring. Their narratives have no point.

The difficult part of writing a narrative is making sure that it has a *point.* That point will be included in the *topic sentence. The point of a narrative is the meaning of the incident or incidents you are writing about.* To get to the point of your narrative, ask yourself questions like these:

What did I learn?
What's the meaning of this story?
What's my attitude towards what happened?
Did it change me?
What emotion did it make me feel?
Was the experience a good example of something (like unfairness, or kindness, or generosity)?

The answers to such questions can lead you to the topic sentence.

ALONG THESE LINES/Prentice-Hall, Inc.

An effective topic sentence for a narrative is

not this: I'm going to tell you about the time I flunked my driving test.
(This is an announcement; it does not make a point.)
but this: When I failed my driving test, I learned not to be
overconfident.

not this: Yesterday my car stalled in rush-hour traffic. (This identifies the
incident but does not make a point. It is also too narrow to be a good
topic sentence.)
but this: When my car stalled in rush-hour traffic, I was annoyed and
embarrassed.

*The topic sentence, stating the point of your narrative paragraph, can be
placed in the beginning or middle or end of the paragraph.* You may want to start
your story with the point, so that the reader knows exactly where your story is
headed, or you may want to conclude your story by leaving the point until last.
Sometimes the point can even fit smoothly into the middle of your paragraph.

Consider the following narrative paragraphs. The topic sentences are in various places.

Topic Sentence at the Beginning

<u>When I was five, I learned how serious it is to tell
a lie.</u> One afternoon, my seven-year-old friend Tina
asked me if I wanted to walk down the block to play ball
in an empty lot. When I asked my mother, she said
I couldn't go because it was too near dinner time.
I don't know why I lied, but when Tina asked me if
my mother had said yes, I nodded my head in a lie. I
wanted to go play, and I did. Yet as I played in the
dusty lot, a dull buzz of guilt or fear distracted me.
As soon as I got home, my mother confronted me. She
asked me whether I had gone to the sandlot and whether
I had lied to Tina about getting permission. This time,
I told the truth. Something about my mother's tone of
voice made me feel very dirty and ashamed. I had let
her down.

ALONG THESE LINES/Prentice-Hall, Inc.

Topic Sentence in the Middle

When I was little, I was afraid of diving into water. I thought I would go down and never come back up. Then one day, my father took me to a pool where we swam and fooled around, but he never forced me to try a dive. After about an hour of playing, I walked round and round the edge of the pool, trying to get the courage to dive in. Finally, I did it. <u>When I made that first dive, I felt blissful because I did something I had been afraid to do.</u> As I came to the surface, I wiped the water from my eyes and looked around. The sun seemed more dazzling, and the water sparkled. Best of all, I saw my father looking at me with a smile. "You did it," he said. "Good for you! I'm proud of you."

Topic Sentence at the End

It seemed like I'd been in love with Reeza for years. Unfortunately, Reeza was always in love with someone else. Finally, she broke up with her boyfriend Nelson. I saw my chance. I asked Reeza out. After dinner, we talked and talked. Reeza told me all about her hopes and dreams. She told me about her family and her job, and I felt very close to her. We talked late into the night. When she left, Reeza kissed me. "Thanks for listening," she said. "You're like a brother to me." <u>Reeza meant to be kind, but she shattered my hopes and dreams.</u>

▶ **EXERCISE 1:** Finding the Topic Sentence in a Narrative Paragraph

Underline the topic sentence in each of the following narrative paragraphs.

Paragraph a

I was eager to get a place of my own. I figured that having my own apartment meant I was free at last because there would be no rules, no curfew, no living by someone else's schedule. My first day in the apartment started well. I arranged the furniture, put up all my pictures, and called all my friends. Then I called out for pizza. When it came, I tried to start a conversation with the delivery man, but he was in a hurry. I ate my pizza alone while I watched the late movie. It was too late to call any of my friends, and I definitely wasn't going to call my mother and let her know I wanted some company. In truth, my first day in my apartment showed me the lonely side of living on my own.

Paragraph b

Last Saturday I took a bus downtown to have lunch with a friend. After lunch, my friend and I split the bill, and I reached for my wallet to pay my share. I was horrified to discover I had lost my wallet. My friend drove me home, and the first thing I saw was the blinking message light on my answering machine. The message said someone had found my wallet and wanted to return it. I couldn't believe anyone in the city would be so kind and honest, but losing something changed my mind. When I met the man in a nearby coffee shop, he gave me the wallet with all my money and credit cards still in it. He said he had found it on a seat in the bus and had been calling my apartment for hours. He was such a good person he wouldn't even take a small reward. He even paid the check at the coffee shop because he said I'd had a bad day and deserved a break!

Paragraph c

Yesterday, one person showed me what it means to be a good parent. I was walking in the mall, and just ahead of me a toddler was holding his father's hand and struggling to keep up. Pretty soon, the child got tired and started to cry. Within minutes, his crying had become a full-fledged tantrum. The little boy squatted on the ground, refusing to go any farther, his face purple. Some parents would have shouted at the child, threatened him, or scooped him up and carried him away. This father, however, just sat down on the ground by his son and talked to him, very calmly and quietly. I couldn't hear his words, but I got the feeling he was sympathizing with the tired little boy. Pretty soon, the child's screams became little sniffles, and father and son walked quietly away.

▶ **EXERCISE 2:** **Writing the Missing Topic Sentences in Narrative Paragraphs**

Following are three paragraphs. If the paragraph already has a topic sentence, write it in the lines provided. If it doesn't have a topic sentence, create one. (Two of the paragraphs have no topic sentence.)

Paragraph a

When I got up, I realized I must have turned off my alarm clock and gone back to sleep because I was already an hour behind schedule. I raced into the shower, only to find I had used up the last of the shampoo the day before. I barely had time to make a cup of coffee to take with me in the car. I grabbed the cup of coffee, rushed to the car, and turned the ignition. The car wouldn't start. Two hours later, the emergency service finally came to jump-start the car. I arrived at work three hours late, and the supervisor was not happy with me.

If the paragraph already has a topic sentence, write it here. If it doesn't have a topic sentence, create one. _____

_____

_____

Paragraph b

Since I gave my first speech in my Public Speaking class, I'm not as shy as I used to be. On the day I was supposed to give my speech, I seriously considered cutting class, taking an F on the speech, or even dropping the course. All I could think of was what could go wrong. I could freeze up and go blank, or I could say something really stupid. In spite of my terror, I managed to walk up to the front of the class. When I started talking, I could hear my voice shaking. I wondered if everyone in the room could see the cold sweat on my forehead. By the middle of the speech, I was concentrating so intensely on what to say that I forgot about my nerves. When I finished, I couldn't believe people were clapping! I never believed I could stand up and speak to the entire class. Once I did that, it seemed so easy to talk in a class discussion. Best of all, the idea of making another speech doesn't seem as frightening anymore.

ALONG THESE LINES/Prentice-Hall, Inc.

If the paragraph already has a topic sentence, write it here. If it doesn't have a topic sentence, create one._____

_____

_____

Paragraph c

Last weekend I was driving home alone, at about ten p.m., when a carload of young men pulled their car up beside mine. They began shouting and making strange motions with their hands. At first I ignored them, hoping they'd go away. But then I got scared because they wouldn't pass me. They kept driving right alongside of my car. I rolled up my car windows and locked the doors. I couldn't hear their shouts, but I was still afraid. I was more afraid when I stopped at a red light and they pulled up next to me. Suddenly, one of the men screamed at me, at the top of his lungs, "Hey! You have a broken tail light!"

If the paragraph already has a topic sentence, write it here. If it doesn't have a topic sentence, create one._____

_____

_____

Hints for Writing a Narrative Paragraph

Everyone tells stories, but some people tell stories better than others. When you write a story, be sure to

- be clear,
- be interesting,
- stay in order,
- pick a topic that is not too big.

1. *Be clear.* Put in all the information the reader needs in order to follow your story. Sometimes you need to explain the time, or place, or the relationships of the people in your story in order to make the story clear. Sometimes you need to explain how much time has elapsed between one action and another. This paragraph is not clear:

```
     I've never felt so stupid as I did on my first day of
work. I was stocking the shelves when Mr. Cimino came up
to me and said, "You're doing it wrong." Then he showed
me how to do it. An hour later, he told me to call the
produce supplier and check on the order for grapefruit.
Well, I didn't know how to tell Mr. Cimino that I didn't
know what phone to use or how to get an outside line. I
also didn't know how to get the phone number of the pro-
duce supplier, or what the order for the grapefruit was
supposed to be and when it was supposed to arrive. I felt
really stupid asking these questions.
```

What's wrong with the paragraph? It lacks all kinds of information. Who is Mr. Cimino? Is he the boss? Is he a produce supervisor? And, more importantly, what kind of place is the writer's workplace? The reader knows the place has something to do with food, but is it a supermarket, or a fruit market, or a warehouse?

2. *Be interesting.* A boring narrative can make the greatest adventure sound dull. Here is a dull narrative:

```
I had a wonderful time on prom night. First, we went
out to dinner. The meal was excellent. Then we went to
the dance and saw all our friends. Everyone was dressed
up great. We stayed until late. Then we went out to
breakfast. After breakfast we watched the sun come up.
```

Good specific detail is the difference between an interesting story and a dull one.

3. *Stay in order.* Put the details in a clear order, so that the reader can follow your story. Usually, time order is the order you follow in narration. This narrative has a confusing order:

```
My impatience cost me twenty dollars last week. There
was a pair of shoes I really wanted. I had wanted them
for weeks. So, when payday came around, I went to the
mall and checked the price on the shoes. I had been
checking the price for weeks before. The shoes were
expensive, but I really wanted them. On payday, my
friend, who works at the shoe store, told me the shoes
were about to go on sale. But I was impatient. I bought
them at full price, and three days later, the shoes were
marked down twenty dollars.
```

There's something wrong with the order of events here. Tell the story in the order it happened: first, I saw the shoes and wanted them; second, the shoes were expensive; third, I checked the price for several weeks; fourth, I got paid; fifth, I checked the price again; sixth, my friend told me the shoes were about to go on sale; seventh, I paid full price right away; eighth, the shoes went on sale. A clear time sequence helps the reader follow your narrative.

4. *Pick a topic that is not too big.* If you try to write about too many events in one paragraph, you run the risk of being superficial. You can't describe anything well if you cover too much. This paragraph covers too much:

```
Starting my sophomore year at a new high school was
a difficult experience. Because my family had just moved
to town, I didn't know anybody at school. On the first
day of school, I sat by myself at lunch. Finally, two
students at another table started a conversation with
me. I thought they were just feeling sorry for me. At
the end of the first week, it seemed like the whole
school was talking about exciting plans for the week-
end. I spent Friday and Saturday night at home, doing
all kinds of things to keep my mind off my loneliness.
On Monday, people casually asked, "Have a good weekend?"
I lied and said, "Of course."
```

This paragraph would be better if it discussed one shorter time period in greater depth and detail. It could cover the first day at school, or the first lunch at school, or the first Saturday night at home alone, when the writer was doing "all kinds of things" to keep from feeling lonely.

Using a Speaker's Exact Words in Narrative

Some of the examples of narrative that you have already seen have included the *exact words* someone said. You may want to include part of a conversation in your narrative. To do so, you need to know how to punctuate speech.

A person's *exact words need quotation marks around them.* If you change the words, you do not use quotation marks.

exact words: "You're being silly," he told me.
not exact words: He told me that I was being silly.

exact words: My sister said, "I'd love to go to the party."
not exact words: My sister said she would love to go to the party.

There are a few other points to remember about punctuating a person's exact words. *Once you've started quoting a person's exact words, periods and commas generally go inside the quotation marks.* Here are two examples:

Richard said, "Nothing can be done."
"Be careful," my mother warned us.

When you introduce a person's exact words with phrases like "She said," or "The teacher told us," put a comma before the quotation marks. Here are two examples:

She said, "You'd better watch out."
The teacher told us, "This will be a challenging class."

If you are using a person's exact words and have other questions about punctuation, check the section on punctuation at the back of this book.

WRITING THE NARRATIVE PARAGRAPH IN STEPS

THOUGHTLINES: NARRATION

Finding something to write about can be the hardest part of writing a narrative paragraph because it is usually difficult to think of anything interesting or significant that you've experienced. By answering the following questions, you can gather topics for your paragraph.

▶ **EXERCISE 1:** Collaborative Questionnaire for Gathering Narrative Topics

Answer the following questions as best you can. Then read your answers to a group. The members of the group should then ask you follow-up questions. Write your answers on the lines provided; the answers will add detail to your list.

Finally, tear out the page, and ask each member of your group to circle one topic or detail that could be developed into a narrative paragraph. Discuss the suggestions. Repeat this process for each member of the group.

Narrative Questionnaire

1. Did you ever have a close call? When? _____ Write four details you remember about it:

   a. _____

   b. _____

   c. _____

   d. _____

   Additional details to add after working with the group:

   _____

   _____

2. Have you ever tried out for a team? Write four details about what happened before, during, and after:

   a. _____

   b. _____

   c. _____

   d. _____

   Additional details to add after working with the group:

   _____

   _____

3. Have you ever had a day when everything went wrong? Write four details about that day:

   a. _____

   b. _____

   c. _____

   d. _____

   Additional details to add after working with the group:

   _____

   _____

4. Have you ever applied for a job? Write four details about what happened when you applied for a job:

   a. _____

   b. _____

   c. _____

   d. _____

   Additional details to add after working with the group:

   _____

   _____

ALONG THESE LINES/Prentice-Hall, Inc.

Freewriting for a Narrative Topic

One good way to discover something to write about is to freewrite. For example, if your instructor asks you to write a narrative paragraph about something that changed you, you might begin by **freewriting**.

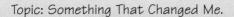

Freewriting for a Narrative Paragraph

Topic: Something That Changed Me.

Something that changed me. I don't know. What changed me? Lots of things happened to me, but I can't find one that changed me. Graduating from high school? Everybody will write about that, how boring, and anyway, what was the big deal? I haven't gotten married. No big change there. Divorce. My parents' divorce really changed the whole family. A big shock to me. I couldn't believe it was happening. I was really scared. Who would I live with? They were real calm when they told me. I've never been so scared. I was too young to understand. Kept thinking they'd just get back together. They didn't. Then I got a step-mother. The year of the divorce a hard time for me. Kids suffer in divorce.

Narrowing and Selecting a Suitable Narrative Topic

After you freewrite, you can assess your writing, looking for words, phrases, or sentences that you could expand into a paragraph. The sample writing has several ideas for a narrative:

> high school graduation
> learning about my parents' divorce
> adjusting to a stepmother
> the year of my parents' divorce

Looking for a topic that is not too big, you could use

> high school graduation
> learning about my parents' divorce

Since the freewriting has already labeled graduation as a boring topic, the divorce seems to be a more attractive subject. In the freewriting, you already have some details related to the divorce; add to these by **brainstorming**. Follow-up questions and answers might include the following:

Q A

Question: How old were you when your parents got divorced?
Answer: I was seven years old when my mom and dad divorced.

Question: Are you an only child?
Answer: My sister was ten.

Question: Where did you parents tell you? Did they both tell you at the same time?
Answer: They told us at breakfast, in the kitchen. Both my folks were there. I was eating toast. I remember I couldn't eat it when they both started talking. I remember a piece of toast with one bite out of it.

Question: What reasons did they give?
Answer: They said they loved us, but they couldn't get along. They said they would always love us kids.

Question: If you didn't understand, what did you *think* was happening?
Answer: At first I just thought they were having another fight.

Question: Did you cry? Did they cry?
Answer: I didn't cry. My sister cried. Then I knew it was serious. I kept thinking I would have to choose which parent to live with. Then I knew I'd really hurt the one I didn't choose. I felt so much guilt about hurting one of them. A part of me kept saying they'd get back together.

Question: How did the scene end? Did your father leave the house?
Answer: My dad got up. I saw him leave the apartment carrying a bunch of his things.

Question: What made you scared?
Answer: I didn't know if I'd ever see him again.

Question: What else did you feel?
Answer: I was confused.

Question: What were you thinking?
Answer: I felt ripped apart.

Questions can help you form the point of your narrative. After brainstorming, you can go back and survey all the details. Do they lead you to a point? Try asking yourself the questions listed earlier in this chapter: What did I learn? What's the meaning of this story? What's my attitude towards what happened? Did it change me? What emotion did it make me feel? Was the experience a good example of something (like unfairness, or kindness, or generosity)?

For the topic of the divorce, the details refer to a number of emotions:

I was confused.
I felt ripped apart.
It was a big shock to me.
I couldn't believe it was happening.
I've never been so scared.
I was too young to understand.
I felt so much guilt.

The *point* of the paragraph can't list all these emotions, but it could say

When my parents announced they were divorcing, I felt confused by all my emotions.

Now that you have a point and a good-sized list of details, you can move to the outlines stage of writing a narrative paragraph.

▶ **EXERCISE 1:** Distinguishing Good Topic Sentences from Bad Ones in Narration

Following are sentences. Some would make good topic sentences for a narrative paragraph. Others would not; they are too big to develop in a single paragraph, or they are so narrow they can't be developed, or they make no point about an incident or incidents. Put an *X* by the sentences that would not make good topic sentences.

    a. _____ Sarah went to her first job interview last week.

    b. _____ I learned a lot when I was in the Army.

    c. _____ The motorist who stopped to help me on the highway taught me a valuable lesson about trust.

    d. _____ My two-year battle for child custody was a nightmare.

    e. _____ This is the story of the birth of my son.

    f. _____ I saw true compassion when I visited the home for babies with AIDS.

    g. _____ Our team's victory over the Rangers demonstrated the power of endurance.

    h. _____ I've seen guns ruin the lives of four of my friends in four years.

    i. _____ The robbery took place at the deli near my house.

    j. _____ I never knew what it was like to be afraid until our house was burglarized.

    k. _____ Our team won the semifinals last week.

▶ **E x e r c i s e 2 :** **Developing a Topic Sentence from a List of Details**

Following are two lists of details. Each has an incomplete topic sentence. Read the details carefully; then complete each topic sentence.

    a. **topic sentence:** When he _____, my brother

                 made me feel _____.

    details: My brother always borrows my clothes.
               Sometimes I wish he wouldn't.
               Last week he took my new leather jacket.
               I went to my closet, and the jacket wasn't there.
               I wanted to wear it that night.
               Later, he came home wearing it.
               I could have punched him.
               He gave it back.
               He swore he didn't know it had a big slash in the back.
               He acted innocent.
               I told him he'd have to pay to fix the jacket.
               He still hasn't paid me.

    b. **topic sentence:** An incident at a traffic light showed me_____

               _____.

    details: I was stopped at a traffic light one afternoon.
               Cars were stopped on all sides of me.
               Suddenly, a driver from the car beside me leaped out of his car.
               He ran to the car in front of me.

E X E R C I S E

He started screaming at the driver of the car.
The driver inside that car wouldn't open his window.
The man who was screaming began to pound on the window.
Then he started kicking the car, hard.
I watched, in terror.
I couldn't drive out of this situation.
I was stuck and afraid of being the next victim.
The crazy, shouting driver stopped.
He got back in his car.
When the light changed, he raced into the intersection.
I felt safer, but still shaken.

⊙UTLINES: NARRATION

The topic of how an experience changed you has led you to a point and a list of details. You can now write a rough outline, with the *point* as the *topic sentence*. Once you have the rough outline, check it for these qualities:

Relevance: Does all the detail connect to the topic sentence?
Order: Is the detail in a clear order?
Development: Does the outline need more detail? Is the detail specific enough?

Your revised outline might look like the following:

A Revised Outline for a Narrative Paragraph

topic sentence: When my parents announced that they were divorcing, I felt confused by all my emotions.

details:

background of the narrative
- I was seven when my mom and dad divorced.
- My sister was ten.
- Both my folks were there.
- They told us at breakfast, in the kitchen.
- I was eating toast.
- I remember I couldn't eat anything when they started talking.
- I remember a piece of toast with one bite out of it.

story of the divorce announcement
- My parents were very calm when they told us.
- They said they loved us but couldn't get along.
- They said they would always love us kids.

my reactions
at each
stage

It was a big shock to me.
I couldn't believe it was happening.
At first I just thought they were
having another fight.
I was too young to understand.
I kept thinking my parents would get
back together.
I didn't cry.
My sister cried.
Then I knew it was serious.
I kept thinking I would have to
choose which parent to live with.
I knew I'd really hurt the one I
didn't choose.
I felt so much guilt about hurting
one of them.
Meanwhile, a part of me kept saying
they'd get back together.
Then my dad got up.
I saw him leave the apartment
carrying a bunch of his clothes.
I didn't know if I'd ever see him
again.
I was ripped apart.

Once you have a revised outline, you're ready to move on to the roughlines stage of the narrative paragraph.

▶ **EXERCISE 1:** **Finding Details That Are Out of Order in a Narrative Outline**

The following outlines have details that are out of time sequence. Put them in the correct time order by numbering the first event with a 1, and so on.

a. **topic sentence:** Renewing my driver's license was a frustrating experience.

details: _____ I got on the shortest line.

_____ The office was packed with people.

_____ When I got through the crowd, I went straight to the information desk.

_____ The clerk at the information desk just gave me a form and said, "Get in line."

_____ After an hour, I got to the head of the line.

_____ I gave my form to the man behind the counter.

_____ I waited in line for an hour.

_____ The man behind the counter said, "You're in the wrong line."

E X E R C I S E

b. topic sentence: Yesterday I saw something that showed me the good side of people.

details: _____ My traffic lane was at a standstill, so I had time to look around.

_____ I was driving down the highway.

_____ As I waited for the traffic to move, I saw a ragged man by the side of the road, holding a sign.

_____ The sign said, "Will Work for Food."

_____ I saw a car pull off the road, right next to the man.

_____ The ragged man shrank back, as if he were afraid the car would hit him.

_____ The driver motioned to the homeless man through the open window.

_____ The driver of the car rolled down his window on the passenger side.

_____ The homeless man crept over.

_____ The driver handed him a big bag of food from Burger King.

c. topic sentence: A good friend let me down yesterday.

details: _____ Last week Jerome and I had planned a trip to Island Park for swimming, sun, and fun.

_____ Yesterday morning I got up early because Jerome had said he wanted to leave early and beat the traffic.

_____ I was really angry when he called at noon and said he'd been out late the night before and overslept.

_____ At nine-thirty, I figured something had come up and he'd call.

_____ He hadn't come by nine o'clock.

_____ At ten, he still hadn't come or called.

_____ I started calling him at ten-fifteen, but I kept getting his answering machine.

▶ **EXERCISE 2:** **Recognizing Irrelevant Details in a Narrative Outline**

Following are three outlines. Two of them have details that aren't relevant to the topic sentence. Cross out the details that don't fit.

a. topic sentence: I saw another side of my sister when her husband was in a car accident.

details: My sister Julia is usually very helpless.
She lets her husband Leo make all the decisions.
She doesn't like to go anywhere without him.
Then one day she got a call from the hospital.

Leo had been in a car accident.
He was in critical condition.
Julia suddenly became very strong.
She calmly told us she was going to the hospital to wait.
She went right up to the desk at the emergency room and requested to see Leo.
When the nurses tried to make her wait, she demanded to see him.
She stayed by Leo's side for twenty-four hours.
The only time she left was to talk to his doctors.
She was very firm and businesslike with the doctors.
She questioned them about the right treatment for Leo.
She got the name of a famous surgeon.
She called the surgeon and got him to come to the hospital.
Today, Leo says she saved his life.

b. topic sentence: The most embarrassing thing I've ever experienced happened to me in the supermarket checkout line.

details: I always shop with a list of what I need to buy.
The cashier was running the items through the scanner.
Our store uses scanners now instead of cash registers.
When he was finished, he said, "That'll be $23.50."
I reached into my wallet for the money.
All I found was a ten-dollar bill.
I searched frantically through all the folds of my wallet.
There was nothing but the ten-dollar bill.
I was *sure* I had put a twenty in my wallet when I left for the store.
Then I remembered—I had spent the twenty at the gas station.
I whispered to the cashier, "Oops! I didn't bring enough money."
He just looked at me.
The groceries were already bagged.
I had to take them out of the bags and get rid of items that added up to $13.50.
Meanwhile, the people in line behind me wanted to kill me.
At that moment, I wished they had.

c. topic sentence: I felt like a real outsider when I went to a friend's party recently.

details: A friend at work, Tim, asked me to come to his house for a big party.
I went to elementary school with Tim's brother.
Tim is older than I am.
Tim said the party would be pretty extravagant; he was going to have live music and catered food.
It sounded good, so I went.
I did not know one person there, except for Tim.
When I came in, he took me around and introduced me to people.
They were nice and talked to me, but they all knew each other.
They talked about people and things I didn't know.
I wound up holding a drink and trying to look like I was studying Tim's CD collection.

Then I sort of lingered at the buffet table.
The food was outstanding.
I kept moving from place to place, so no one would see me standing in a corner and feel sorry for me.
Finally, I slipped out without saying good-bye to Tim.

ⓇOUGHLINES: NARRATION

After you have a revised outline for your narration paragraph, you can begin working on a rough draft of the paragraph. As you write your first draft, you can combine some of the short sentences of the outline. Once you have a draft, you can check it for places you'd like to improve. The list below may help you check your draft.

A Checklist for Revising the Draft of a Narrative Paragraph

✔ Is my narrative vivid?

✔ Are the details clear and specific?

✔ Does the topic sentence fit all the details?

✔ Are the details written in a clear order?

✔ Do the transitions make the narrative easy to follow?

✔ Have I made my point?

Revising for Sharper Details

A good idea for a narrative can be made better if you revise for sharper detail. In the following paragraph, the underlined words and phrases could be revised to create better details. In the following example, see how the second draft has more vivid details than the first draft.

First Draft: Details Are Dull

A woman at the movies showed me just how rude and selfish people can be. It all started when I was in line with a lot of other people. We had been waiting a long time to buy our tickets. We were outside, and it wasn't pleasant. We were impatient because time was running out and the movie was about to start. Some people were making remarks, and others were pushing. Then a woman

ALONG THESE LINES/Prentice-Hall, Inc.

<u>cut to</u> the front of the line. The cashier at the ticket window <u>told</u> the woman there was a line and she would have to go to the end of it. The woman <u>said she didn't want to wait because her son didn't want to miss the beginning of the movie.</u>

Second Draft: Better Details

A woman at the movies showed me just how rude and selfish people can be. It all started when I was in line with <u>forty or fifty other people</u>. We had been waiting to buy our tickets for <u>twenty minutes</u>. We were outside, <u>where the temperature was about 90 degrees, and it looked like rain</u>. We were all getting impatient because time was running out and the movie was about to start. <u>I heard two people mutter about how ridiculous the wait was, and someone else kept saying, "Let's go!" The man directly behind me kept pushing me, and each new person at the end of the line pushed the whole line forward, against the ticket window. Then a woman with a loud voice and a large purse thrust her purse and her body in front of the ticket window.</u> The cashier <u>politely</u> told the woman there was a line and she had to to the end of it. But the woman answered <u>indignantly</u>. <u>"Oh no,"</u> <u>she said. "I'm with my son Mickey. And Mickey really wants to see *The Cable Guy*. And he hates to miss the first part of any movie. So I can't wait. I have got to have those tickets now."</u>

Checking the Topic Sentence

Sometimes you think you have a good idea and a good topic sentence and details, but when you write the draft of the paragraph, you realize the topic sentence doesn't quite fit all the details. When that happens, you can either revise the details or rewrite the topic sentence.

In the following paragraph, the topic sentence (underlined) doesn't quite fit all the details, so it needs to be rewritten.

<u>I didn't know what to do when a crime occurred in front of my house.</u> At nine p.m. I was sitting in my living room, watching television, when I heard what sounded like a crash outside. At first I thought it was a garbage can that had fallen over. Then I heard another crash and a shout. I ran to the window, and I looked out into the dark. I couldn't see anything because the street light in front of my house was broken. But I heard at least two voices, and they sounded angry and threatening. I heard another voice, and it sounded like someone moaning. I was afraid. I ran to the telephone. I was going to call 911, but then I froze in fear. What if the police came and people got arrested? Would the suspects find out I was the one who had called the police? Would they come after *me*? Would I be a witness at a trial? I didn't want to get involved. So I just stood behind the curtain, peeking out and listening. Pretty soon the shouting stopped, but I still heard sounds like hitting. I couldn't stand it any more. I called the police. When they came, they found a young teenager, badly beaten, in the street. They said my call may have saved his life.

The preceding paragraph has good details, but the story has more of a point than "I didn't know what to do." The person telling the story did, finally, do something. A better topic sentence would cover the whole story.

topic sentence rewritten: <u>I finally found the courage to do the right thing when a crime occurred in front of my house.</u>

▶ **EXERCISE 1:** **Adding Better Details to the Draft of a Narrative**

Do this exercise alone, with a partner, or with a group. The following paragraph has some details that could be more vivid. Rewrite the paragraph in the lines below, replacing the underlined details with more vivid words, phrases, or sentences.

    Roberto showed he is a great athlete when he lost the wrestling match. The match had been very close, but someone had to lose, and that someone turned out to be Roberto. After the match, the winner, Tom, was <u>getting all the attention.</u> He was acting very <u>full of himself.</u> Roberto was just <u>keeping to himself.</u> Roberto <u>looked hurt.</u> His eyes <u>were sad.</u> Nevertheless, he went to Tom and shook hands. Tom looked <u>mean</u> and <u>didn't say much.</u> Roberto, on the other hand, <u>said the right thing.</u> Then Roberto walked away, his head held high.

Rewrite:_____

_____

_____

_____

_____

_____

_____

_____

_____

_____

▶ **EXERCISE 2:** **Collaborative Exercise: Writing a Better Topic Sentence for a Narrative**

Do this exercise with a partner or with a group. The following paragraphs could use better topic sentences. (In each paragraph, the current topic sentence is underlined.) Read each paragraph carefully, then write a new topic sentence for it in the lines provided.

  a. <u>My visit to my old school was interesting.</u> I hadn't been back to Miller Road Elementary since fifth grade, so I expected it to be changed. I just didn't expect it to be so drastically changed. When I entered the schoolyard, I saw that the playground that had once been full of trees and bright green grass was now a muddy, empty lot. All the trees were gone.

The school, once a new, golden brick building, was sooty and decrepit. Several of the windows were broken. I walked into the entrance hall and saw graffiti all over the walls. The school was silent. Wandering the halls, I peeped into the classrooms. I saw rickety desks and blackboards so faded you could hardly see the words chalked on them. Then I found Room 110, my old first grade classroom. I went in and sat down at one of the desks, and the room that had once seemed so big and so exciting suddenly seemed small and sad.

new topic sentence: _____

_____

b. <u>I had dinner with my family last week.</u> My two younger brothers, Simon and David, started it by fighting over who was going to sit in the seat next to my father. When we all sat down to eat, my sister provoked my mother by complaining, "Chicken again? All we eat is chicken." Of course, my mother jumped right in and said if my sister wanted to take the responsibility for planning menus and cooking meals, she could go right ahead. Meanwhile, my father was telling David not to kick Simon under the table, and Simon was spitting mashed potatoes at David. I got irritated and said I wished that once, just once, we could eat dinner like a normal family. So then my father and I had an argument about what I meant by a normal family. By that time, Simon had spilled his milk on the floor, and my mother had caught my sister feeding chicken to the dog. We all left the dinner table in a bad mood.

new topic sentence: _____

_____

Using Transitions Effectively in Narration

When you tell a story, you have to be sure that your reader can follow you as you move through the steps of your story. One way to make your story easier to follow is to use *transitions*, words that connect one event to another. Most of the transitions in narration have to do with time. Following is a list of transitions that writers often use in writing narration.

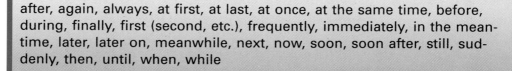

Transitions for a Narrative Paragraph

after, again, always, at first, at last, at once, at the same time, before, during, finally, first (second, etc.), frequently, immediately, in the meantime, later, later on, meanwhile, next, now, soon, soon after, still, suddenly, then, until, when, while

The Revised Draft

Following is a revised draft of the paragraph on divorce. It has been revised several ways, using the checklist. Some ideas from the outline have been combined. The details have been put in order and transitions have been added. Exact words of dialogue have been used to add vivid details.

ALONG THESE LINES/Prentice-Hall, Inc.

A Roughlines Revised Draft of a Narrative Paragraph
(Transitions are underlined.)

<u>When</u> my parents announced that they were divorcing, I felt confused by all my emotions. <u>At the time</u> of their announcement, I was seven and my sister was ten. Both my folks were there to tell us. They told us at breakfast, in the kitchen. I was eating toast, but I remember I couldn't eat anything when they started talking. I remember a piece of toast with one bite taken out of it. My parents were very calm when they told us. "We love both you kids very much," my father said, "but your mother and I aren't getting along." They said they would always love us. The announcement was such a shock to me that I couldn't believe it was happening. <u>At first</u>, I just thought they were having another fight. I was too young to understand, and I kept thinking my folks would get back together. I didn't cry. <u>Suddenly</u>, my sister started to cry, <u>and then</u> I knew it was serious. I kept thinking I would have to choose which parent to live with. I knew I'd really hurt the one I didn't choose, <u>so</u> I felt so much guilt about hurting one of them. <u>Yet</u> a part of me still kept thinking that they'd get back together. <u>Then</u> my dad got up. I saw him leaving the apartment carrying a bunch of clothes. I didn't know if I'd ever see him again. I felt torn apart.

▶ **EXERCISE 1: Recognizing Transitions in a Narrative Paragraph**

Underline the transitions in the following paragraph.

The salesman who called last night was a master of manipulation. He first asked for me by name. He didn't ask for the head of the house, which is always a sure sign that the call is a sales pitch. After confirming I was Mr. Johnson, he told me he was checking on my newspaper delivery. Then he asked if I had been getting my paper regularly and on time. When I said yes, he quickly added that I could get a better deal by extending my subscription, right away, at a discounted rate for long-term customers. By that time, I was getting tired of what I now knew was a sales call. Just before I tried to end the conversation, the salesman offered me a chance to win a trip to the Bahamas. Suddenly, he had my interest again. While I listened to him explain the contest, I seriously thought about extending my newspaper subscription.

ALONG THESE LINES/Prentice-Hall, Inc.

Finally, I even thanked him for the information about the vacation contest. Maybe the next time a salesman calls, I'll first ask him about any contests and my real chances of winning.

FINAL LINES: NARRATION

When you prepare the final copy of the narrative paragraph, make any minor changes in word choice or transitions that will refine your writing. Following are the revised outline, second draft, and the final copy of the narrative paragraph on divorce. Look at them carefully to see how the paragraph evolved from outlines to roughlines to final lines. Notice these changes in the final lines version:

- The roughlines version used both formal and informal words such as "folks", "parents", "dad", and "father."
- The final lines uses only "parents" and "father."
- A word or two of detail has been added.
- A word or two of detail has been changed.
- A transition has been added.

Before you prepare the final lines copy of your narrative paragraph, check your latest draft for errors in spelling and punctuation, and for any errors made in typing or recopying.

An Outlines Version of a Narrative Paragraph

topic sentence:	When my parents announced that they were divorcing, I felt confused by all my emotions.
details:	I was seven when my mom and dad divorced. My sister was ten. Both my folks were there. They told us at breakfast, in the kitchen. I was eating toast. I remember I couldn't eat anything when they started talking. I remember a piece of toast with one bite out of it. My parents were very calm when they told us. They said they loved us but couldn't get along. They said they would always love us kids. It was a big shock to me.

ALONG THESE LINES/Prentice-Hall, Inc.

I couldn't believe it was happening.
At first I just thought they were having another fight.
I was too young to understand.
I kept thinking my parents would get back together.
I didn't cry.
My sister cried.
Then I knew it was serious.
I kept thinking I would have to choose which parent to live with.
I knew I'd really hurt the one I didn't choose.
I felt so much guilt about hurting one of them.
A part of me kept saying they'd get back together.
Then my dad got up.
I saw him leaving the apartment carrying a bunch of his clothes.
I didn't know if I'd ever see him again.
I was ripped apart.

A Roughlines Version of a Narrative Paragraph

When my parents announced that they were divorcing, I felt confused by all my emotions. At the time of their announcement, I was seven and my sister was ten. Both my folks were there to tell us. They told us at breakfast, in the kitchen. I was eating toast, but I remember I couldn't eat anything when they started talking. I remember a piece of toast with one bite taken out of it. My parents were very calm when they told us. "We both love you very much," my father said. "But your mother and I aren't getting along." They said they would always love us. The announcement was such a shock to me that I couldn't believe it was happening. At first, I just thought they were having another fight. I was too young to understand, and I kept thinking my folks would get back together. I didn't cry. Suddenly, my sister started to cry, and then I knew it was serious. I kept thinking I would have to choose which parent to live with. I knew I'd really hurt the one I didn't choose, so I felt so much guilt about hurting one of them. Yet a part of me still kept thinking that they'd get back together. Then my

> dad got up. I saw him leaving the apartment carrying
> a bunch of clothes. I didn't know if I'd ever see
> him again. I felt torn apart.

**A Final Lines Version
of Narrative Paragraph**
(Changes from the roughlines
version are underlined.)

When my parents announced that they were
divorcing, I felt confused by all my emotions. At
the time of the announcement, I was seven, and my
sister was ten. Both <u>my parents</u> were there to tell
us. They told us at breakfast, in the kitchen. I was
eating toast, but I remember I couldn't eat anything
when they started talking. <u>In fact,</u> I remember
<u>staring at</u> a piece of toast with one bite taken out
of it. My parents were very calm when they told us.
"We both love you very much," my father said. "But
your mother and I aren't getting along." They said
they would always love us. The announcement was such
a shock to me that I couldn't believe it was
happening. At first, I just thought they were having
another fight. I was too young to understand, and I
kept thinking <u>my parents</u> would get back together. I
didn't cry. Suddenly, my sister started to cry, and
then I knew it was serious. I kept thinking I would
have to choose which parent to live with. I knew I'd
really hurt the one I didn't choose, so I felt
<u>terrible</u> guilt about hurting one of them. Yet a part
of me kept thinking that they'd get back together.
Then my <u>father</u> got up. I saw him leaving the
apartment carrying a bunch of clothes. I didn't know
if I'd ever see him again. I felt torn apart.

▶ **EXERCISE 1:** **Proofreading the Final Lines of a Narrative
Paragraph**

Proofread the following paragraph. Correct any errors in spelling, punctuation,
or recopying. Write your corrections in the line above each error.

When my girl friend tossed my ring out the window, I knew she was not
ready to forgive me one more time. It all started on Saturday, at MacDon-
ald's, when I ran into my girlfriend Lakisha. I could see she was'nt in a good
mood. As soon as we sat down, she asked me about Yvonne. A girl I've been
seeing behind Lakisha's back. Well, of course I lied and said "Yvonne was
nothing to me." However, Lakisha said she seen me and Yvonne at the mall

the night before, and we looked like was rommanticly involved. I asked, "How could you tell?" Well, naturally that was the wrong thing to say since I was admitting Yvonne and I had been together. After I asked that stupid question, Lakisha took my ring off her finger and tossed that ring right threw the window at McDonalds.

Lines of Detail: A Walk-Through Assignment

Write a paragraph about an incident in your life that embarrassed, or amused, or frightened, or saddened, or angered you. In writing the paragraph, follow these steps:

Step 1: Begin by freewriting. Then read your freewriting, looking for both the details and the focus of your paragraph.

Step 2: Brainstorm for more details. Then write all the freewriting and the brainstorming as a list.

Step 3: Survey your list. Write a topic sentence that makes a point about the details.

Step 4: Write an outline. As you write the outline, check that your details fit the topic sentence and are in a clear order. As you revise your outline, add details where they are needed.

Step 5: In the roughlines stage, write and revise a draft of your paragraph. Revise until your details are specific and in a clear order, and your transitions are smooth. Combine any sentences that are short and choppy. Add a speaker's exact words if they will make the details more specific.

Step 6: In preparing the final lines copy, check for punctuation, spelling, and word choice.

Writing Your Own Narrative Paragraph

When you write a narrative paragraph on any of the following topics, be sure to work through the steps of thoughtlines, outlines, roughlines, and final lines.

1. Write about some event you saw that you'll never forget. Begin by freewriting. Then read your freewriting, looking for both the details and the focus of your paragraph.

    If your instructor agrees, ask a writing partner or a group to (a) listen to you read your freewriting, (b) help you focus it, (c) help you add details by asking questions.

2. Write a narrative paragraph about how you met your boyfriend or girlfriend, husband or wife. Start by listing as many details as you can, and, if your instructor agrees, ask a writing partner or a group to (a) survey your list of details, (b) ask questions that will lead you to more details.

3. Write about a time when you got what you wanted. Start by listing as many details as you can, and, if your instructor agrees, ask a writing partner or a group to (a) survey your list of details, and (b) ask questions that will lead you to more details.

4. Interview an older family member or friend. Ask him or her to tell you an interesting story about the past. Ask questions as the person speaks. Take notes. If you have a tape recorder, you can tape the interview, but take notes as well.

   When you've finished the interview, review the information with the person you've interviewed. Would he or she like to add anything? If you wish, ask follow-up questions.

   Next, on your own, find a point to the story. Work through the stages of outlines, roughlines, and final lines to turn the interview into a narrative paragraph.

5. Write a narrative paragraph about the men in photograph A. Explain what they are saying, and include what happened before and after this scene. You may want to include some dialogue in your paragraph.

6. Write a narrative paragraph about the man waiting in photograph B. You can write about an incident that led to his situation or an incident that happened right after the scene in the photo. Pay attention to the expensive car and its possible role in the narrative.

Photograph A

Photograph B

Name: _____   **Section:** _____

Peer Review Form for a Narrative Paragraph

After you've written a roughlines version of your narrative paragraph, let a writing partner read it. When your partner has completed the following form, discuss the responses. Repeat the same process for your partner's paragraph.

I think the topic sentence of this paragraph is

_____

_____. (Write the sentence.)

I think the topic sentence (a) states the point well, or (b) could be revised.

The part of the narrative I liked best begins with the words

_____

_____

The part that could use more or better details begins with the words

_____

_____

An effective transition is

_____ (write the words of a good transition).

I have questions about

_____

_____

I would like to see something added about

_____

_____

I would like to take out the part about

_____

_____

I think the narrative is (a) easy to follow, or (b) a little confusing.

Other comments on the paragraph:

_____

_____

_____

Reviewer's name: _____

Writing from Reading: Narration

ROCKY ROWF

Edna Buchanan

Edna Buchanan is famous as a former crime reporter for the Miami Herald *and as the author of nonfiction books and novels about murder and mayhem. In this essay, she writes about a lighter subject: how she met and got to know Rocky Rowf, her dog.*

Before you read this selection, consider these questions:

Are pets smarter than most people think?
Do pets have ways of communicating with their owners?
Do individual pets have distinct personalities?
Have you ever brought home a stray dog or cat?
Have you ever panicked during an emergency with a pet?

Words You May Need to Know

dehydrated: lacking water
clambered: climbed
nonchalantly: coolly, casually
dotes: shows great love for
deferential: respectful
obsequious: slavelike, submissive

abject: humiliating
fawning: submissive behavior
disdainfully: scornfully, arrogantly
pretext: excuse
repertoire: collection of tricks

ROCKY ROWF

Edna Buchanan

I was a pushover.

I met Rocky on a sizzling Fourth of July weekend. I never intended to take him home with me. He was sprawled under a park bench on South Beach trying to stay cool. I was there to exercise, to bend and stretch in the shade of the sea grape trees, and to look at the blue-green summer sea. Two elderly men, friendly regulars in the park, were sitting on the bench.

"Is that your dog?" I asked.

They said no. He was so quiet they had barely noticed him. He was panting in the heat, and I grew alarmed as I patted him. His tongue was purple—eggplant purple. I was certain that it meant the animal was dangerously dehydrated. I filled a paper cup several times from a faucet used by bathers to rinse sand off their feet and he drank politely. But his tongue stayed purple.

That is its normal color, something I did not learn until later. It may mean he is part chow chow, though he does not look it. He looks like the kind of mutt that everybody has owned at some time in their life: black with buff-colored paws, medium sized, and affable. His ears are floppy, his grin silly. He wore a battered, old leather collar with no tag. After he drank, he watched me exercise, then followed as I walked along the seawall. This little romance will end now, I thought, as I returned to my car.

When I opened the door, he pushed right past me, scrambling into the front seat. Obviously accustomed to traveling by car, he was determined to have his way. When ordered out, he slunk into the backseat and set-

ALONG THESE LINES/Prentice-Hall, Inc.

tled stubbornly on the floor, on the far side, out of arm's reach. What the heck, I thought, I'll keep him until I find his owner. As we pulled away from the curb, however, I reconsidered: I can't take this dog home, what about all those cats?

I stopped at the main lifeguard station, and the dog clambered out after me, trotting right alongside. The guard said he had seen the dog roaming the beach alone for the past three days. He would call Animal Control, he said, and held the dog, so I could get away. "Bye, puppy," I said, and headed for the car. My mistake was in looking back. The dog was whimpering and struggling to follow, his eyes fixed on me, pleading.

"You sure this isn't your dog?" The lifeguard looked suspicious.

I insisted I had never seen that animal before in my life. The lifeguard let go, and the dog bounded to me, wagging his tail.

On the way home we stopped at the supermarket for dog food. It was too hot to leave him in the car, so I left him just outside the store and told him to wait. He'll probably be gone, finding a new friend, by the time I get the dog food through the checkout counter, I thought. But as I turned the next aisle, there he was, trotting past the produce, wriggling with delight when he spotted me. Somebody had opened the door.

"Is that your dog?" the store manager wanted to know. I denied it.

"Are you sure?" he said, staring pointedly at the dog food and the Milk-Bone box in my cart.

He ejected the dog, who was waiting when I came out. I looked around the parking lot vaguely, wondering where I had left my car. He knew. All I had to do was follow as he trotted briskly ahead, found the car, and sat down next to it waiting for me. When we got home, he scampered up the front steps without hesitation and waited as I unlocked the door. It was as though he had lived there all his life. Misty and Flossie were snoozing on the highly polished hardwood floor in the living room when this strange dog walked nonchalantly into their home. Both shot straight up in the air, then fled so fast that for several seconds they ran in place on the slick surface. They skidded into my bedroom and dove out the window. Luckily it was open. The screen landed in the middle of the lawn.

After the initial shock, they sized him up at once. He must have lived with other animals, because he dotes on them, especially smaller ones, and is particularly deferential to cats. He was so obsequious in fact, rolling on his back in abject surrender whenever they entered the room, that they quickly became disgusted at his fawning. Within two days the cats were stealing his food and stepping disdainfully over him as he napped.

For two weeks we walked up and down that stretch of South Beach seawall looking for his owner. Lots of people had seen the friendly dog, but always alone. A middle-aged Puerto Rican busboy with no teeth grinned and greeted him as Blackie. I thought we had found the owner, but he said he had fed the dog a hamburger and some water at about one o'clock the same morning I found him performing his hungry-and-thirsty act.

After two weeks I gave up, took him to the vet, got him a license, and he joined the household.

He chose his own name. I ran through dozens of appropriate possibilities. None appealed to him. He would not even open his eyes at most. But when I said Rocky, he looked up, wagged his tail, and grinned. So Rocky it is—Rocky Rowf.

His past remains a mystery. Housebroken and well-behaved, he did

ALONG THESE LINES/Prentice-Hall, Inc.

not seem to understand even the most simple commands. Perhaps, I decided, his owner spoke a language other than English. We went to an obedience school, taught by a cop in charge of the Coral Gables police K-9 unit. The only mutt, Rocky was the smartest in the class. However, he did refuse to be a watchdog. In an attempt to agitate him, they thrust him between a Doberman pinscher and a German shepherd. The big dogs were ferocious, leaping in frenzies, snarling, and barking. Rocky Rowf sat between them, grinning and drooling. A very laid-back dog, he hates trouble, rolling his eyes and whining when the cats quarrel among themselves. If the chips were down and we were attacked by strangers, he would do the sensible thing—run for his life.

The day after his first visit to the vet, I got home from the *Herald* after nine o'clock at night. When I opened the back door and called, he did not come bounding in from the yard as usual. I stepped out into the dark and could barely make him out, curled up next to the banana tree. I called to him again and again. He did not move. My heart sank. Frightened, I approached the still form, reached out, and touched the fur ruffled by a summer breeze. It felt cool.

He was dead.

Poor stray dog, doing fine until I took him home; now he was dead. How did it happen? My mind raced. The vet had said he was in good health thirty-six hours earlier. It had to be poison, or maybe he had been shot. It was too dark to see anything in the yard. I dialed the vet's emergency number. He's dead, I cried accusingly, probably an allergic reaction to the shots you gave him.

"What makes you think he's dead," asked Dr. Hal Nass.

"I know a dead dog when I see one!" I screamed.

He told me to bring the body to his office. He would get dressed and meet me there; together we would find out what happened.

The dog weighed forty-seven pounds. The backyard was dark, and I didn't even own a flashlight. The only neighbor I knew was across the street, in a big house on the bay. When I had moved in months earlier he introduced himself and invited me to call on him if I ever needed help.

His wife answered. They had gone to bed early. I said I needed her husband's assistance. I whimpered to him that somebody or something had killed my dog and asked if he had seen any strangers prowling the neighborhood. I told him I had to get the dead dog out of my shadowy and unlit backyard and into my car. Poor Rocky Rowf's last ride would be to the vet for an autopsy.

A sympathetic man and a good neighbor, Larry Helfer climbed out of bed, got dressed and brought a flashlight. "I think it was poison," I said, greeting him in tears. "The doctor said he was fine yesterday."

I offered him a blanket to wrap the body in. "Where is it?" he said grimly. Out there, I said, pointing. He pushed open the back door, stared into the darkness, then slowly turned and looked at me, his face strange. I stepped past him to look. Sitting at the back door, gazing up at us was Rocky. He was grinning.

Never taking his eyes off me, Larry Helfer began to back slowly toward the front door. He obviously believed that, using the pretext of a dead dog, I had lured him out of his bed and across the street, for some unknown purpose.

ALONG THESE LINES/Prentice-Hall, Inc.

"I could have sworn he was dead. He didn't answer when I called him," I babbled. "He was just lying there."

It was his turn to babble. "My, eh, wife, is worried. I better go tell her everything's all right," he said and made a run for it.

I caught the vet, just as he was leaving his home. "Never mind," I said.

Larry Helfer and his wife avoided me for several years after that. When we did meet by chance, they always asked politely after the health of my dog.

Nowadays, I point an index finger at Rocky Rowf and say, "Bang, you're dead!" He falls on the floor, then rolls over on his back. It's one of the best tricks in his repertoire.

It wasn't difficult to teach him at all. He already knew how.

Writing from Reading "Rocky Rowf"

When you write on any of the following topics, be sure to work through the stages of thoughtlines, outlines, roughlines, and final lines.

1. Write a narrative paragraph about an animal you know that has a distinct personality. As part of the thoughtlines stage of writing, you may want to freewrite about all your memories of this animal.

2. Write a narrative paragraph about how you got a pet. In the thoughtlines stage of writing, you may want to list all the steps included in getting your pet.

3. Write the story of an emergency with a pet. If your instructor agrees, you may want to begin the thoughtlines part of this assignment by asking a writing partner to interview you, asking questions such as the following:

   How did you feel during this emergency?
   What was the worst part of the incident?
   Did your feelings change during the emergency?

   After the interview, you can then interview your partner to collect ideas for his or her paragraph.

4. Write the story of how your pet got its name.

5. Write a narrative paragraph that shows that dogs (or cats) are smarter than people.

6. Edna Buchanan writes about a time she helped an animal, a lost dog. Write a narrative paragraph about a time you helped a person who was in trouble.

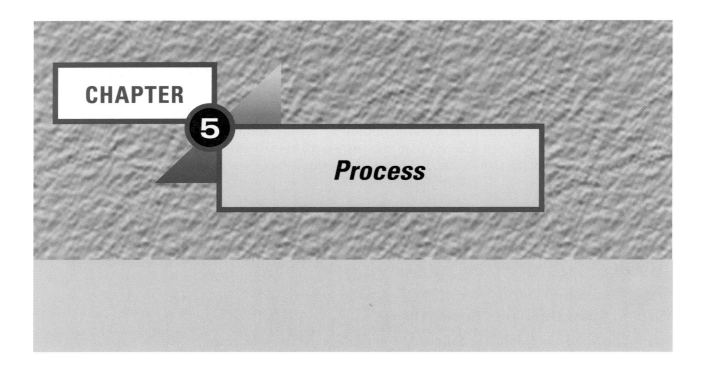

5

Process

WHAT IS PROCESS?

A process paragraph explains *how to do something* or describes *how something happens* or is done. When you tell the reader how to do something (a *directional process*), you speak directly to the reader and give him or her clear, specific instructions about performing some activity. Your purpose is to *explain an activity so that a reader can do it.* For example, you may have to leave instructions telling a new employee how to close the cash register or use the copy machine.

When you describe how something happens (an *informational process*), your purpose is to *explain an activity, but not to tell a reader how to do it.* For example, you may have to explain how a boxer trains for a fight or how the special effects for a film were created. Instead of speaking directly to the reader, an informational process speaks about "I," "he," "she," "we," "they," or about a person by his or her name. A directional process uses "you" or, in the way it gives directions, the word "you" is understood.

A Process Involves Steps in Time Order

Whether a process is directional or informational, it *describes something that is done in steps,* and these steps are in a specific order: a *time order.* The process can involve steps that are followed in minutes, hours, days, weeks, months, or even years. For example, the steps in changing a tire may take minutes, whereas the steps taken to lose ten pounds may take months.

The important thing to remember is that a process involves steps that *must* follow a certain order, not just a range of activities that can be placed in any order.

This sentence signals a process:

Learning to use a word processor is easy if you follow a few simple directions. (Using a word processor involves following steps in order; that is, you can't set the margins before you turn the machine on.)

The following sentence does *not* signal a process:

ALONG THESE LINES/Prentice-Hall, Inc.

There are several ways to get a person to like you. (Each way is separate; there is no time sequence here.)

Telling a person, in a conversation, how to do something or how something is done gives you the opportunity to add important points that you may have forgotten or to throw in details that you may have left out. Your listener can ask questions if he or she doesn't understand you. Writing a process is more difficult. Your reader isn't there to stop you, to ask you to explain further, to question you. In writing a process, you must be *organized* and *clear*.

Hints for Writing a Process Paragraph

1. In choosing a topic, find an activity you know well. If you write about something familiar to you, you'll have a clearer paragraph.

2. Choose a topic that includes steps that must be done in a specific time sequence.

not this: I find lots of things to do on a rainy day.
but this: I have a specific plan for cleaning out my closet.

3. Choose a topic that is fairly small. A complicated process cannot be covered well in one paragraph. If your topic is too big, the paragraph can become superficial, incomplete, or boring.

too big: There are many stages in the process of a bill before Congress becoming a law.
smaller and manageable: Will power and support were the most important elements in my struggle to quit smoking.

4. Write a topic sentence that makes a point. Your *topic sentence should do more than announce.* Like the topic sentence for any paragraph, it should have a point. As you plan the steps of your process and gather details, ask yourself some questions: What point do I want to make about this process? Is the process hard? Is it easy? Does the process require certain tools? Does the process require certain skills, like organization, patience, endurance?

an announcement: This paragraph is about how to change the oil in your car.
a topic sentence: You don't have to be a mechanic to change the oil in your car, but you do have to take a few simple precautions.

5. Put in all the steps. If you are explaining a process, you are writing for someone who does not know the process as well as you do. So keep in mind that what seems clear or simple to you may not be clear or simple to the reader. Be sure to tell what is needed before the process starts, too. For instance, what ingredients are needed to cook the dish? Or what tools are needed to assemble the toy?

6. Put the steps in the right order. Nothing is more irritating to a reader than trying to follow directions that skip back and forth. Careful planning and revision can help you get the time sequence right.

7. Be specific in the details and steps. To be sure you have sufficient detail and clear steps, keep your reader in mind. Put yourself in the reader's place. Could you follow your own directions or understand your steps?

Take a close look at the following process paragraph. Check it to see if it (1) explains something the writer knows well, (2) uses a topic that includes steps, (3) uses a fairly small topic, (4) includes a topic sentence that makes a point, (5) includes all the steps, (6) puts the steps in the right order, and (7) is specific in details and steps.

> Good scrambled eggs are easy to make if you don't rush the process. To start, you will need a bowl, a frying pan, some butter, eggs, milk, and salt and pepper. Mix the eggs and milk in a bowl. When they are mixed, put the mixture into a frying pan, already heated to medium heat and coated with melted butter. Stir the eggs so that they remain creamy and don't stick. Take your time. Add salt and pepper to taste. Then you have delicious scrambled eggs.

You probably noticed that this paragraph needs some revision so that the steps are explained in more detail. Anyone who didn't know how to cook would have real problems following these directions. For instance, the reader might ask, "How many eggs and how much milk should I mix together if I want to make scrambled eggs for two people? And what do I mix the eggs and milk with? A fork? A spoon? A whisk? How do I know when they're mixed sufficiently? How much butter should I melt in the frying pan? What do I use to stir the eggs? What happens if the eggs start to stick? Should I lower the heat? How do I know when the eggs are done?"

If you remember that a process explains, you will focus on being clear. Now that you know the purpose and strategies of writing a process, you can begin the thoughtlines step of writing one.

▶ **EXERCISE 1:** **Recognizing Good Topic Sentences for Process Paragraphs**

If a sentence is a good topic sentence for a process paragraph, put *OK* on the line provided. If a sentence has a problem, label that sentence with one of these letters:

   A   This is an announcement; it makes no point.
   B   This sentence covers a topic that is too big for one paragraph.
   S   This sentence describes a topic that does not require steps.

   a. _____   I've developed a plan for doing my laundry that saves time and keeps my clothes in good shape.

   b. _____   How I learned to wash and wax my car is the subject of this paragraph.

   c. _____   There are several reasons for buying a home computer.

   d. _____   The steps involved in brain surgery are complicated.

   e. _____   Trying out for the cheerleading squad meant I had to overcome a series of obstacles.

   f. _____   This paper shows the method of refinishing an antique chair.

   g. _____   Civil rights in America evolved in several stages.

   h. _____   There are many things to remember when you enter college.

   i. _____   If you learn just a few trade secrets, you can give yourself a professional manicure at home.

j. ____ Fred learned the right way to apply for a car loan.

k. ____ I've learned that patience is the most important part of house-breaking a puppy.

l. ____ My sister, who sells dresses at an elegant store, follows a specific plan when she closes a sale.

m. ____ I am going to discuss things you need to do to change the oil in your car.

n. ____ Steps to a healthier body are the topic to be explained.

o. ____ David gave me a few good suggestions for making job contacts.

▶ **E X E R C I S E 2 :** **Collaborative Exercise in Including Necessary Materials in a Process**

Following are three possible topics for a process paragraph. For each topic, work with a partner or a group and list the items (materials, ingredients, tools, utensils, supplies) that the reader would have to gather before he or she begins the process. When you've finished the exercise, check your lists with another group to see if you've missed any items.

topic: washing a car

needed items: _____

_____

_____

topic: cooking a hamburger on a grill

needed items: _____

_____

_____

topic: preparing a package for mailing (the package contains a breakable item)

needed items: _____

_____

_____

WRITING THE PROCESS PARAGRAPH IN STEPS

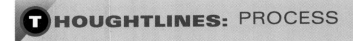

THOUGHTLINES: PROCESS

The easiest way to start writing a process paragraph is to pick a small topic, one that you can cover well in one paragraph. Then you can gather ideas by listing or freewriting or both.

If you decided to write about how you entertained your nephew for an afternoon, you might begin by freewriting. Then you might check your freewriting, looking for details that have to do with the process of that afternoon. You can *underline* those details, as in the example that follows.

Freewriting for a Process Paragraph

Topic: Entertaining a nephew.

I had to find something to do with Albert for a whole afternoon. I don't know Albert that well. I only see him two or three times a year when my sister visits my mom. I like Albert. What do I know about <u>five-year-olds</u>? Sports? But I can't play sports well. I can't get him on a team of kids his own age. So I <u>decided, the zoo.</u> Everybody likes zoos. I like the zoo. Probably why I decided the zoo. Albert was awfully quiet in the car <u>on the way there</u>. <u>A little scared of me.</u> Then, <u>at the zoo,</u> wouldn't go near the animals <u>at first.</u> And <u>he raced</u> from exhibit to exhibit. I thought he'd want to spend some time looking at each animal. But he was always <u>racing ahead</u> to see what was next. He warmed up to me a lot <u>later</u>. Even <u>at the zoo, when he got excited,</u> he really talked up a storm. I had to drag him out of the souvenir shop at the zoo exit, or I'd have been broke! One souvenir is enough! What a racket. But I let him go at his own pace <u>through the zoo.</u> Let him eat what he wanted later, too.

Next, you can *put what you've underlined into a list, in correct time sequence:*

before the trip

decided on the zoo
Albert was quiet on the way there
a little scared of me

at the zoo

first, wouldn't go near the animals
raced from exhibit to exhibit to see what was ahead
then, after he got excited, talked up a storm

after the zoo

he warmed up to me

Check the list. Are some details missing? Yes. A reader might ask, "Did you tell Albert how to behave before he got to the zoo? How did you keep control of a five-year-old? What else happened at the zoo? What animals did you see first, second, etc? How did the afternoon end? Was it a success?" Answers to questions like these can give you the details needed to write a clear and interesting informational process paragraph.

Writing a Topic Sentence for a Process Paragraph

Freewriting and a list can now help you focus your paragraph by *identifying the point* of your process. You already know what the subject of your paragraph is:

ALONG THESE LINES/Prentice-Hall, Inc.

entertaining a five-year-old for a whole afternoon. But what's the point? Is it easy to entertain a five-year-old? Is it difficult? What does it take to have a successful afternoon with a five-year-old?

Maybe a topic sentence could be

I've learned that the way to have an enjoyable afternoon with a five year-old is to plan for both our interests, but to let him set the pace and make some choices.

Once you have a topic sentence, you can think about adding details that explain your topic sentence and can begin the outlines stage of writing.

▶ **E X E R C I S E 1 : Finding the Steps of a Process in Freewriting**

Read the following freewriting, then reread it, looking for all the words, phrases, or sentences that have to do with steps. Underline all those items. Once you've underlined the freewriting, put what you've underlined into a list, in a correct time sequence.

How I Found My First Apartment: Freewriting

My first apartment. Could I afford the rent was my first question. So I designed a budget and came up with a figure for the highest rent I could pay. Rents are high in this area. I didn't know what places went for until I looked around. Looked in the classified ads in the paper to see what typical one-bedroom apartments cost in different neighborhoods. Had decided I needed a one-bedroom, not an efficiency. Found the names of two or three places that matched my budget. Didn't call right away. Why call if the place is a dump? So took a ride in my car first. Checked out those two or three places. Then called the phone numbers of the two nicest-looking places. Set up a time to visit. Asked to see a copy of the leases at the visits. Brought my older brother with me on the visits. He's experienced. Took leases home. Drove back to apartments at several times of day to see how noisy the neighborhoods are, how safe, to check out things I forgot to look for. Read leases carefully. Considered which apartment was cheaper. Which was newer and cleaner and nicer. The cheaper one was not so new but was larger. Called apartment manager and set up a time to sign lease.

Your List of Steps, in Time Sequence

_____

_____

_____

_____

_____

_____

_____

_____

_____

_____

_____

⊙ OUTLINES: PROCESS

Using the freewriting and topic sentence on entertaining a nephew, you could make an outline. Then you could revise it, checking the topic sentence and list of details, improving them where you think they could be better. A revised outline of an afternoon with Albert follows.

An Outline for a Process Paragraph

topic sentence: I've learned that the way to have an enjoyable afternoon with a five-year-old is to plan for both our interests, but to let him set the pace and make some choices.

details:

Before the zoo

Albert, my five-year-old nephew, was visiting.
I had to find a way to entertain him one Saturday afternoon.
Before Saturday, I decided on the zoo.
When I picked Albert up, I brought lots of cash to pay for tickets, snacks, and souvenirs.
I brought an umbrella and Albert's sweater.
It could rain or get cold.
Albert was quiet in the car.
He was a little scared of me.
I left him alone.
I just told him what to expect at the zoo.
I told him to stay close to me.

| At the zoo | At the zoo, the first animals we saw were gorillas. Albert was scared. He wouldn't go near the gorilla compound. I didn't push him. Then he raced from exhibit to exhibit to see what was ahead. The second group of animals was lions. Albert loved them. But he raced on to the next animals. I let him set his own pace. The last animals were in the Snake House. Albert started talking up a storm. |
| After the zoo | At the end of the afternoon, he wanted to do it again—the next day! |

The following checklist may help you to revise an outline for your own process paragraph.

A Checklist for Revising a Process Outline

✔ Is my topic sentence focused on some point about the process?

✔ Does it cover the whole process?

✔ Do I have all the steps?

✔ Are they in the right order?

✔ Have I explained clearly?

✔ Do I need better details?

▶ **E X E R C I S E   1**: Collaborative Exercise: Revising the Topic Sentence in a Process Outline

The following topic sentence doesn't cover all the steps of the process. Read the outline several times; then write a topic sentence that covers all the steps of the process and has a point. When you've written a topic sentence, exchange this exercise with a partner. Add a topic sentence to the first one on the sheet you just received. Exchange these exercises once more, with another person, and repeat the process. After each of you has three different topic sentences, discuss which sentences work best.

topic sentence: If you want to save money at the supermarket, write a list at home.

details: First, leave a pencil and a piece of paper near your refrigerator.

Each time you use the last of some item, like milk, write that item on the paper.

Before you go to the store, read what's written on the paper and add to the list.

Then rewrite the list, organizing it according to the layout of your store.

Put all the dairy products together on the list, for instance.

Put all the fresh fruits and vegetables together.

At the store, begin with the first items on your list.

Move purposefully through the aisles.

Keep your eyes on your list so you don't see all kinds of goodies that you don't need.

Pass by the gourmet items.

Keep going through each aisle, buying only what is on your list.

At the end of the last aisle, check what's in your cart against your list.

Get any item you forgot.

When you stand in the checkout line, avoid looking at the overpriced and tempting snacks that fill the area.

revised topic sentences:

1. _____

_____

_____

2. _____

_____

_____

3. _____

_____

_____

▶ **E X E R C I S E   2 :   Revising the Order of Steps in a Process Outline**

The steps in each of these outlines are out of order. Put numbers in the spaces provided, indicating what step should be first, second, and so forth.

a. topic sentence: Danielle knows all the steps in spreading a rumor.

details: _____   Danielle figures it's OK to tell *one* person, her best friend Vicky.

_____   Vicky figures it's OK to tell *one* person, her dear friend Jack.

_____   Danielle always swears she can keep a secret.

_____   Somebody tells Danielle some great gossip, making her promise to keep it a secret.

_____   Jack figures his whole group of friends, except him, has already heard the gossip, so he thinks it's OK to tell anybody.

ALONG THESE LINES/Prentice-Hall, Inc.

_____ Jack tells several people.

_____ The whole town is talking about the big secret.

b. topic sentence: My neighbor has a Saturday routine that never changes.

details: _____ Every Saturday at 8 a.m. he starts cutting his lawn.

_____ The roar of his lawn mower wakes me up.

_____ He barbecues steaks on Saturday nights.

_____ In the afternoon, he sits on a lawn chair in his yard.

_____ After he's been in the lawn chair for a while, he falls asleep.

_____ He reads the paper as he grills the steaks.

_____ I see him in the deli at noon, buying pumpernickel bagels for lunch.

c. topic sentence: Getting my cat to take a pill is a real chore.

details: _____ I have to hide the pill inside a clump of mashed tuna.

_____ My cat Princess hates pills.

_____ She runs when she hears the rattle of the pill container.

_____ I have to take out one pill, very quietly.

_____ I coax Princess by allowing her to sniff at the tuna.

_____ I lure her further, until I have her out in the open.

_____ I pop the tuna into her mouth.

_____ Princess swallows the tuna and the hidden pill.

▶ **EXERCISE 3: Collaborative Exercise in Listing All the Steps in an Outline**

Following are three topic sentences for process paragraphs. Working with a partner or group, write all the steps needed to complete an outline for each sentence. After you've listed all the steps, number them in the correct time order.

a. topic sentence: There are a few simple steps to giving a dog a bath.

steps: _____

_____

_____

_____

_____

_____

_____

_____

_____

b. topic sentence: Anyone can make a delicious salad.

steps: _____

_____

_____

_____

_____

_____

_____

_____

_____

_____

c. topic sentence: You can devise a plan for getting to work on time.

steps: _____

_____

_____

_____

_____

_____

_____

_____

_____

_____

d. topic sentence: Sewing on a button is not as easy as it looks.

steps: _____

_____

_____

_____

_____

_____

_____

_____

_____

_____

ⓇOUGHLINES: PROCESS

You can take the outline and write it in paragraph form, and you'll have a first draft of the process paragraph. As you write the first draft, you can combine some of the short sentences from the outline. Then you can review your draft and revise it for organization, detail, clarity, grammar, style, and word choice.

Using the Same Grammatical Person

Remember that the *directional* process speaks directly to the reader, calling him or her "you." Sentences in a directional process use the word "you," or they imply "you."

> directional: <u>You</u> need a good paint brush to get started.
> Begin by making a plan. ("You" is implied.)

Remember that the *informational* process involves somebody doing the process. Sentences in an informational process use words like "I" or "we" or "he" or "she" or "they" or a person's name.

> informational: <u>Chip</u> needs a good paint brush to get started.
> First, <u>I</u> can make a list.

One problem in writing a process is shifting from describing how somebody *did* something to telling the reader how *to do* an activity. When that shift happens, the two kinds of processes get mixed. That shift is called a *shift in persons*. In grammar, the words "I" and "we" are considered to be in the first person, "you" is the second person," and "he," "she," "it," and "they" are in the third person.

If these words refer to one, they are called "singular"; if they refer to more than one, they are called "plural." The following list may help.

A List of Persons

1st person singular: I

2nd person singular: you

3rd person singular: he, she, it, or a person's name

1st person plural: we

2nd person plural: you

3rd person plural: they, or the names of more than one person

In writing your process paragraph, *decide whether your process will be directional or informational, and stay with one kind.* Following are two examples of a shift in persons. Look at them carefully and study how the shift is corrected.

Part of a Process with a Shift in Persons

> After I preheat the oven to 350 degrees, I mix the egg whites and sugar with an electric mixer set at high speed. Mix until stiff peaks form. Then I put the mixture in small mounds on an ungreased cookie sheet. (This

process went from "I preheat" and "I mix" to giving directions: "Mix until stiff peaks form." Giving directions implies "you." Then the process went back to "I," in "I put.")

Correcting the Shift in Persons

After I preheat the oven to 350 degrees, I mix the egg whites and sugar with an electric mixer set at high speed. I mix until stiff peaks form. Then I put the mixture in small mounds on an ungreased cookie sheet.

Part of a Process with a Shift in Persons

A salesman has to be very tactful when customers try on clothes. The salesman can't hint that a suit may be a size too small. You can insult a customer with a hint like that. (The sentences shifted from "salesman" to "you.")

Correcting the Shift in Persons

A salesman has to be very careful when customers try on clothes. The salesman can't hint that a suit may be a size too small. He can insult a customer with a hint like that.

Using Transitions Effectively

As you revise your draft, you can add transitions. Transitions are particularly important in a process paragraph because you are trying to show the steps in a *specific sequence*, and you are trying to show the *connections* between steps. Good transitions will also keep your paragraph from sounding like a choppy, boring list.

Below is a list of some of the transitions you can use in writing a process paragraph.

Transitions for a Process Paragraph

after, afterward, as, as he is . . ., as soon as . . ., as you are . . ., at last, at the same time, before, begin by, during, eventually, finally, first, second, third, etc., first of all, gradually, in the beginning, immediately, initially, last, later, meanwhile, next, now, quickly, sometimes, soon, suddenly, the first step, the second step, etc., then, to begin, to start, until, when, whenever, while, while I am . . .

When you write a process paragraph, you must pay particular attention to clarity. As you revise, keep thinking about your audience: are your steps easy to follow? The following checklist can help you revise your draft.

A Checklist for Revising a Process Paragraph

✔ Does the topic sentence cover the whole paragraph?

✔ Does the topic sentence make a point about the process?

✔ Is any important step left out?

✔ Should any step be explained further?

✔ Are the steps in the right order?

✔ Should any sentences be combined?

✔ Have I used the same person to describe the process throughout the paragraph?

✔ Have I used transitions effectively?

▶ **E X E R C I S E 1:** **Correcting Shifts in Person in a Process Paragraph**

Following is a paragraph that shifts in several places from being an informational to a directional process. Those places are underlined. Rewrite the underlined parts, directly above the underlining, so that the whole paragraph is an informational process.

Jesse has perfected a whole routine for getting out of chores. He starts as soon as his mother says, "Jesse?" with that certain tone in her voice. Before she can go any further, he says, "What?" in a hurt, tired, exasperated way. He also looks very tired as he says this. <u>You have to look tired,</u> or the trick won't work. When she asks him to do something like take out the garbage, he goes into phase two of the routine. He tells her that he always takes out the garbage and now it's Lynette's turn. Of course, Lynette instantly chimes in and says she's sick of doing all the chores for a lazy bum like Jesse. The fight between Lynette and Jesse usually distracts their mother. Sometimes she forgets what she originally <u>wanted you to do.</u> If she can remember, Jesse has one last tactic. <u>You can always agree to do the chore</u> and then procrastinate until somebody else does it. <u>Live by the rule,</u> "Always put off till tomorrow what you can do today."

▶ **E X E R C I S E 2:** **Revising Transitions in a Process Paragraph**

The transitions in this paragraph could be better. Rewrite the underlined transitions, directly above each one, so that the transitions are smoother.

You can set an attractive dinner table with just a few steps and a little creativity. First, clear the table and make sure the surface is clean. <u>Second,</u> place some placemats around the table. You can use your imagination with placemats. You can use different colored ones, or different shaped ones, from different sets; you can also use brightly colored dish towels. <u>Third,</u> place your prettiest dinner plates on each mat. <u>Fourth,</u> put a knife and fork on either side of each plate. <u>Fifth,</u> find pretty, bright-colored napkins and find an interesting way to place them. You can twist each napkin into a roll or fold it so it stands in the middle of the plate. <u>Sixth,</u> choose a matching glass for each place setting. <u>Seventh,</u> find a centerpiece for the table. The centerpiece can be anything from a a bowl of fruit or fresh vegetables to a single flower in a vase. <u>Eighth,</u> sit back and enjoy your creativity.

The Revised Draft

Below is the revised draft of the process paragraph on entertaining a five-year-old. The draft has more details than the outline, and one detail from the outline, about Albert racing around, has been moved. Some short sentences have been combined, and transitions have been added.

A Roughlines Revised Draft of a Process Paragraph

I've learned that the way to have an enjoyable afternoon with a five-year-old is to plan for both our interests, but to let him set the pace and make some choices. I learned all this when Albert, my five-year-old nephew, was visiting, and I had to find a way to entertain him one Saturday afternoon. Before Saturday rolled around, I wanted to pick something we both liked, so I decided on the zoo. When I picked Albert up on Saturday, I brought lots of cash to pay for tickets, snacks, and souvenirs. I also brought an umbrella and Albert's sweater, in case the weather got wet or cold. In the car, Albert was quiet, as if he was scared of me. But I didn't pump him with questions. I left him alone, just telling him what to expect at the zoo and warning him to stay close to me once we got there. At the zoo, Albert was scared of the gorillas, the first animals we saw. He wouldn't go near the gorilla compound. I didn't push him. The second group of animals was the lions, and Albert loved them. Still, he raced on to the next group of animals. Throughout our visit, Albert raced from exhibit to exhibit to see what was ahead. I thought he would spend some time looking at each exhibit, but I let him set his own pace and just stayed close to him. The last animals were in the Snake House, and Albert was so fascinated he started talking up a storm. By the end

ALONG THESE LINES/Prentice-Hall, Inc.

```
of our afternoon, Albert had warmed up to me so much
that he said he wanted to do it all over again, the
next day!
```

⒡INAL LINES: PROCESS

Before you prepare the final copy of your process paragraph, you can check your latest draft for any places where grammar, word choice, and style need revision.

Below are the revised outline, revised draft, and final lines version of the process paragraph on entertaining a five-year-old. When you compare the rough-lines and final lines versions, you'll notice that the final lines version has some changes:

- The topic sentence has been rewritten; the meaning has not been changed, but it is more clearly stated.
- The point of the topic sentence is reinforced in a new sentence, placed just before the last sentence.
- A transition, "again," has been added to stress the point of the topic sentence.
- The word "raced" has been changed to "ran" to avoid repetition.

Before you prepare the final lines copy of your process paragraph, check your latest draft for errors in spelling and punctuation, and for any errors made in typing or recopying.

```
              An Outlines Version
           of a Process Paragraph
```

```
topic sentence: I've learned that the way to have
                an enjoyable afternoon with a five-
                year-old is to plan for both our
                interests but to let him set the
                pace and make some choices.

       details: Albert, my five-year-old nephew, was
                visiting.
                I had to find a way to entertain
                him one Saturday afternoon.
                Before Saturday, I decided on the
                zoo.
                When I picked Albert up, I brought
                lots of cash to pay for tickets,
                snacks, and souvenirs.
                I brought an umbrella and Albert's
                sweater.
                It could rain or get cold.
```

Albert was quiet in the car.
He was a little scared of me.
I left him alone.
I just told him what to expect at
the zoo.
I told him to stay close to me.
At the zoo, the first animals we saw
were gorillas.
Albert was scared.
He wouldn't go near the gorilla
compound.
I didn't push him.
Then he raced from exhibit to
exhibit to see what was ahead.
The second group of animals was
lions.
Albert loved them.
But he raced on to the next animals.
I let him set his own pace.
The last animals were in the snake
house.
Albert started talking up a storm.
At the end of the afternoon, he
wanted to do it again, the next day!

A Roughlines Version of a Process Paragraph

I've learned that the way to have an enjoyable
afternoon with a five-year-old is to plan for both
our interests but to let him set the pace and make
some choices. I learned all this when Albert, my
five-year-old nephew, was visiting, and I had to
find a way to entertain him one Saturday afternoon.
Before Saturday rolled around, I wanted to pick
something we both liked, so I decided on the zoo.
When I picked Albert up on Saturday, I brought lots
of cash to pay for tickets, snacks, and souvenirs.
I alos brought an umbrella and Albert's sweater, in
case the weather got wet or cold. In the car,
Albert was quiet, as if he was scared of me. But I
didn't pump him with questions. I left him alone,
just telling him what to expect at the zoo and
warning him to stay close to me once we got there.
At the zoo, Albert was scared of the gorillas, the
first animals we saw. He wouldn't go near the
gorilla compound. I didn't push him. The second
group of animals was lions, and Albert loved them.

Still, he raced on to the next group of animals. Throughout our visit, Albert raced from exhibit to exhibit to see what was ahead. I thought he would spend some time looking at each exhibit, but I let him set his own pace and just stayed close to him. The last animals were in the Snake House, and Albert was so fascinated he started talking up a storm. By the end of our afternoon, Albert had warmed up to me so much that he said he wanted to do it all over again, the next day!

A Final Lines Version of a Process Paragraph
(Changes from the roughlines version are underlined.)

I've learned that the way to have an enjoyable afternoon with a five-year-old is to plan something that interests us both but to let him set the pace and make some choices. I learned all this when Albert, my five-year-old nephew, was visiting, and I had to find a way to entertain him one Saturday afternoon. Before Saturday rolled around, I wanted to pick something we both liked to do, so I decided on the zoo. When I picked Albert up on Saturday, I brought lots of cash to pay for tickets, snacks, and souvenirs. I also brought an umbrella and Albert's sweater, in case the weather got wet or cold. In the car, Albert was quiet, as if he was scared of me. But I didn't pump him with questions. I left him alone, just telling him what to expect at the zoo and warning him to stay close to me once we got there. At the zoo, Albert was scared of the gorillas, the first animals we saw. He wouldn't go near the gorilla compound. Again, I didn't push him. The second group of animals was lions, and Albert loved them. Still, he ran on to the next group of animals. Throughout our visit, Albert raced from exhibit to exhibit to see what was ahead. I thought he would spend some time looking at each exhibit, but I let him set his own pace and just stayed close to him. The last animals were in the snake house, and Albert was so fascinated he started talking up a storm. By letting Albert move and talk according to his own timetable, I had given him a good time. By the end of our afternoon, Albert had warmed up to me so much that he said he wanted to do it all again, the next day!

► **E X E R C I S E   1 :   Correcting Errors in a Final Lines Process Paragraph**

The following process paragraph has the kind of errors you might make on a final copy. You can catch and correct such errors by proofreading. Correct the errors you find by writing the corrections directly above each error.

I have a foolproof system for making my bed neatly. First, I dump all the pillow's on the flore. I then pull the bedspread back to the bottom of the bed. Once you've pulled the bedspread back, I can pull back the blanket and the top sheet. Next, i smooth the bottom sheet and pull it tight, tucking the extra material into the corners of the mattress. When the bottom sheet is tucked in tightly, I pull up the top sheet and blanket, smoothing them as I go and making sure they are tucked into the bottom and lower corners of the bed. At the top end of the bed, fold the edge of the top sheet over the blanket, and I smooth the folded sheet and blanket across the bed. Finly, I put the pillows back and arrange the bedspread over the bed, making sure the bedspread dosen't drag on one side. In a few move, I have a well-made bed.

Lines of Detail: A Walk-Through Assignment

Your assignment is to write a paragraph on how you planned a special day. Follow these steps:

Step 1:   Focus on one special day. If you can't think of a day you planned, ask yourself questions such as, Have you ever planned a birthday party? Baby or wedding shower? Surprise party? Picnic? Reunion? Celebration of a religious holiday?

Step 2:   Once you have picked the day, freewrite. Write anything you can remember about the day and how you planned it.

Step 3:   When you've completed the freewriting, read it. Underline all the details that refer to steps in planning that event. List the underlined details, in time order.

Step 4:   Add to the list by brainstorming. Ask yourself questions that can lead to more details. For example, if an item on your list is, "I decorated the room," ask questions like, "What did I use for decorations? What colors did I use?"

Step 5:   Survey your expanded list. Write a topic sentence that makes some point about your planning for this special day. To reach a point, think of questions like, "Was the planning successful?" or "What did I learn from the planning?"

Step 6:   Use the topic sentence to prepare an outline. Be sure that the steps in the outline are in the correct time order.

Step 7:   Write a roughlines version of the paragraph. In this first draft, add more details and combine short sentences.

ALONG THESE LINES/Prentice-Hall, Inc.

Step 8: Revise your draft. Be careful to use smooth transitions, and check that you have included all the necessary steps.

Step 9: Prepare and proofread the final lines copy of your paragraph.

Writing Your Own Process Paragraph

When you write on one of these topics, be sure to work through the stages of thoughtlines, outlines, roughlines, and final lines.

1. Write a directional or informational process about one of these topics:

   packing a suitcase   falling out of love
   preparing for a garage sale   getting up in the morning
   painting a room   getting ready to go out for a
   taking a test   special occasion
   losing weight   sizing up a new acquaintance
   training a roommate   fixing a clogged drain
   doing holiday shopping early   changing the oil in a car
   breaking up with a boyfriend or   washing and waxing a car
   girlfriend   breaking a specific habit
   getting good tips while working as   gaining weight
   a waiter or waitress   giving a pet a bath
   finding the right mate

2. Write about the wrong way to do something, or the wrong way you (or someone else) did it. You can use any of the topics in the list in question 1, or you can choose your own topic.

3. Imagine that a relative who has never been to your state is coming to visit. This relative will arrive at the nearest airport, rent a car, and drive to your house. Write a paragraph giving your relative clear directions for getting from the airport to your house. Be sure to have an appropriate topic sentence.

4. Interview one of the counselors at your college. Ask the counselor to tell you the steps for applying for financial aid. Take notes or tape the interview. Get copies of any forms that are included in the application process. Ask questions about these forms.

   After the interview, write a paragraph explaining the process of applying for financial aid. Your explanation is directed at a high school senior who has never applied for aid.

5. Interview someone whose cooking you admire. Ask that person to tell you the steps involved in making a certain dish. Take notes or tape the interview.

   After the interview, write a paragraph, *not* a recipe, explaining how to prepare the dish. Your paragraph will explain the process to someone who is a beginner at cooking.

PEER REVIEW

Name: _____ **Section:** _____

Peer Review Form for a Process Paragraph

After you've written a roughlines version of your process paragraph, let a writing partner read it. When your partner has completed the following form, discuss it. Repeat the same process for your partner's paragraph.

The steps that are most clearly described are

_____

_____

I'd like more explanation about this step:

_____

_____

Some detail could be added to the part that begins with the words

_____

_____

A transition could be added to the part that begins with the words

_____

_____

I have questions about

_____

_____

The best thing about this paragraph is

_____

_____

Other comments on the paragraph:

_____

_____

_____

_____

_____

Reviewer's name: _____

Writing from Reading: Process

HOW TO LAND THE JOB YOU WANT
Davidyne Mayleas

Davidyne Mayleas studied banking and finance before becoming a writer. She has published books and articles about the job market. In this essay, she gives a step-by-step explanation of how you can become your own job counselor and teach yourself to get the job you want. Her explanation is made clear and interesting through her use of examples.

Before you read this selection, consider these questions:

Do you think a job search is a humiliating experience?
Have you ever been turned down for a job that you thought you deserved?
Have you ever been interviewed for a job? If so, how did you feel during the interview, and what did you learn from it?
Have you ever interviewed anyone who was applying for a job? If so, how did you feel during the interview, and what did you learn from it?
Do you know people who are in the job or career you'd like to have?

Words You May Need to Know

résumé: a brief account of personal, educational, and professional qualifications and experience, used in applying for a job
asset: useful thing or quality
classified ads: small advertisements in the newspaper, often called the "Want Ads"
actuarial department: the department that calculates the insurance rates, risks, etc., according to probabilities based on statistical records
prospective: potential
route: send, direct
geriatric: having to do with elderly people
perseverance: persistence
traits: personal characteristics
leads: guides to other jobs, suggestions to follow

HOW TO LAND THE JOB YOU WANT
Davidyne Mayleas

Louis Albert, 39, lost his job as an electrical engineer when his firm made extensive cutbacks. He spent two months answering classified ads and visiting employment agencies—with zero results. Albert might still be hunting if a friend, a specialist in the employment field, had not shown him how to be his own job counselor. Albert learned how to research unlisted openings, write a forceful résumé, perform smoothly in an interview, even transform a turndown into a job.

Although there seemed to be a shortage of engineering jobs, Albert realized that he still persuaded potential employers to see him. This taught him something—that his naturally outgoing personality might be as great an asset as his engineering degree. When the production head of a small electronics company told him that they did not have an immediate opening, Albert told his interviewer, "You people make a fine product. I think you could use additional sales representation—someone like me who understands and talks electrical engineer's language, and who enjoys selling." The interviewer decided to send Albert to a senior vice president. Albert got a job in sales.

You too can be your own counselor if you put the same vigorous effort into *getting* a job as you would into *keeping one*. Follow these three basic rules, developed by placement experts:

1. *Find the hidden job market.* Classified ads and agency listings reveal only a small percentage of available jobs. Some of the openings that occur through promotions, retirements and reorganization never reach the personnel department. There are three ways to get in touch with this hidden market:

Write a strong résumé with a well-directed cover letter and mail it to the appropriate department manager in the company where you'd like to work. Don't worry whether there's a current opening. Many managers fill vacancies by reviewing the résumés already in their files. Dennis Mollura, press-relations manager in the public-relations department of American Telephone and Telegraph, says, "In my own case, the company called me months after I sent in my résumé."

Get in touch with people who work in or know the companies that interest you. Jobs are so often filled through personal referral that Charles R. Lops, executive employment manager of the J. C. Penney Co., says, "Probably our best source for outside people comes from recommendations made by Penney associates themselves."

"Drop in" on the company. Lillian Reveille, employment manager of Equitable Life Assurance Society of the United States, reports: "A large percentage of the applicants we see are 'walk-ins'—and we do employ many of these people."

2. *Locate hidden openings.* This step requires energy and determination to make telephone calls, see people, do research, and to keep moving despite turndowns.

Contact anyone who may know of openings, including relatives, friends, teachers, bank officers, insurance agents—anyone you know in your own or an adjacent field. When the teachers' union and employment agencies produced no teaching openings, Eric Olson, an unemployed high-school math instructor, reviewed his talent and decided that where an analytical math mind was useful, there he'd find a job. He called his insurance agent, who set up an interview with the actuarial department of one of the companies he represented. They hired Olson.

It's a good idea to contact not only professional or trade associations in your field, but also your local chamber of commerce and people involved in community activities. After Laura Bailey lost her job as retirement counselor in a bank's personnel department, she found a position in customer relations in another bank. Her contact: a member of the senior-citizens club that Mrs. Bailey ran on a volunteer basis.

Use local or business-school libraries. Almost every field has its own directory of companies, which provides names, addresses, products and/or services, and lists officers and other executives. Write to the company president or to the executive to whom you'd report. The vice president of personnel at Warner-Lambert Co. says, "When a résumé of someone we could use—now or in the near future—shows up 'cold' in my in-basket, that's luck for both of us."

Consult telephone directories. Sometimes the telephone company will send you free the telephone directories of various cities. Also, good-sized public libraries often have many city directories. Fred Lewis, a cabinet maker, checked the telephone directories of nine different cities where he knew furniture was manufactured. At the end of five weeks he had a sizable telephone bill, some travel expenses—and ten interviews which resulted in three job offers.

3. *After you find the opening, get the job.* The applicants who actually get hired are those who polish these six job-getting skills to perfection:

Compose a better résumé. A résumé is a self-advertisement, designed to get you an interview. Start by putting yourself in an employer's place. Take stock of your job history and personal achievements. Make an inventory of your skills and accomplishments that might be useful from the employer's standpoint. Choose the most important and describe them in words that stress accomplishments. Avoid such phrases as "my duties included . . ." Use action words like planned, sold, trained, managed.

Ask a knowledgeable business friend to review your résumé. Does it stress accomplishment rather than duties? Does it tell an employer what you can do for him? Can it be shortened? (One or two pages should suffice.) Generally, it's not wise to mention salary requirements.

Write a convincing cover letter. While the résumé may be a copy, the cover letter must be personal. Sy Mann, director of research for Aceto Chemical Co., says: "When I see a mimeographed letter that states, 'Dear Sir, I'm sincerely interested in working for your company,' I wonder, 'How many other companies got this valentine?' " Use the name and title of the person who can give you the interview, and be absolutely certain of accuracy here. Using a wrong title or misspelling a prospective employer's name may route your correspondence directly to an automatic turndown.

Prepare specifically for each interview. Research the company thoroughly; know its history and competition. Try to grasp the problems of the job you're applying for. For example, a line in an industry journal that a food company was "developing a new geriatric food" convinced one man that he should emphasize his marketing experience with vitamins rather than with frozen foods.

You'll increase your edge by anticipating questions the interviewer might raise. Why do you want to work for us? What can you offer us that someone else cannot? Why did you leave your last position? What are your salary requirements?

An employer holds an interview to get a clearer picture of your work history and accomplishments, and to look for characteristics he considers valuable. These vary with jobs. Does the position require emphasis on attention to detail or on creativity? Perseverance or aggressiveness? Prior to the interview decide what traits are most in demand. And always send a thank-you note immediately after the interview.

Follow up. They said you would hear in a week; now it's two. Call them. Don't wait and hope. Hope and act.

Supply additional information. That's the way Karen Halloway got her job as fashion director with a department store. "After my interview I sensed that the merchandise manager felt I was short on retail experi-

ALONG THESE LINES/Prentice-Hall, Inc.

ence. So I wrote to him describing the 25 fashion shows I'd staged yearly for the pattern company I'd worked for."

Don't take no for an answer. Hank Newell called to find out why he had been turned down. The credit manager felt he had insufficient collection experience. Hank thanked him for his time and frankness. The next day, Hank called back saying, "My collection experience is limited, but I don't think I fully emphasized my training in credit checking." They explored this area and found Hank still not qualified. But the credit manager was so impressed with how well Hank took criticism that when Hank asked him if he could suggest other employers, he did, even going so far as to call one. Probing for leads when an interview or follow-up turns negative is a prime technique for getting personal referrals.

The challenge of finding a job, approached in an active, organized, realistic way, can be a valuable personal adventure. You can meet new people, develop new ideas about yourself and your career goals, and improve your skills in dealing with individuals. These in turn can contribute to your long-term job security.

Writing from Reading "How to Land the Job You Want"

When you write on any of these topics, be sure to work through the stages of thoughtlines, outlines, roughlines, and final lines.

1. Interview someone who has a job you'd like to have. Ask him or her how you can prepare yourself, with the proper education and job experience, to be ready for a similar job. Use the information from the interview to write a process paragraph.

2. Write a paragraph on how to fire an employee as painlessly as possible. As part of the thoughtlines stage, you might want to freewrite on how it feels to be fired or to fire someone. Then you can consider how to minimize those bad feelings.

3. Write a process paragraph on how you—or someone else—got over losing a job.

4. Interview a business professor or job placement counselor at your college. Ask him or her to explain how to put together a good résumé. Take notes.

    After the interview, do further research on writing a résumé. Ask the person you interviewed and/or your college librarian for books on the subject. Use the information from the interview and from books to write a paragraph on how to prepare an effective résumé.

5. Write a summary of "How to Land the Job You Want." Include Mayleas' three basic rules and give some details about each rule.

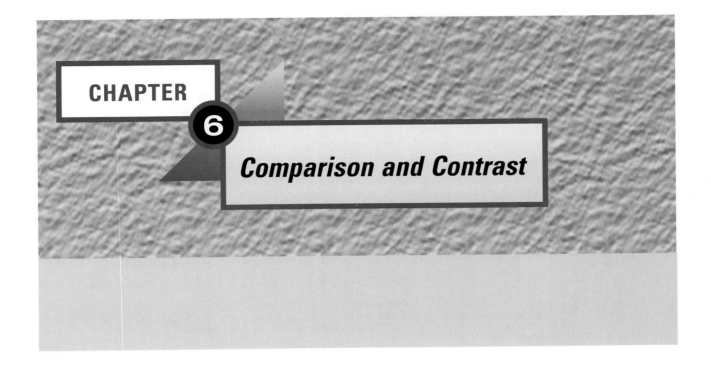

CHAPTER 6

Comparison and Contrast

WHAT IS COMPARISON? WHAT IS CONTRAST?

To *compare* means to point out similarities. To *contrast* means to point out differences. *When you compare or contrast, you need to come to some conclusion.* It's not enough to say, "These two things are similar," or "They are different." Your reader will be asking, "So what? What's your point?" You may be showing the differences between two restaurants to explain which is the better buy:

> If you like Mexican food, you can go to either
> Cafe Mexicana or Juanita's, but Juanita's has lower
> prices.

Or you may be explaining the similarities between two family members to show how people with similar personalities can clash.

> My cousin Bill and my brother Karram are both so
> stubborn they can't get along.

Hints for Writing a Comparison or Contrast Paragraph

1. *Limit your topic.* When you write a comparison or contrast paragraph, you might think that the easiest topics to write about are broad ones with many similarities or differences. However, if you make your topic too large, you will not be able to cover it well, and your paragraph will be full of very large, boring statements.

Here are some topics that are too large for a comparison or contrast paragraph: two countries, two periods in history, two kinds of addiction, two wars, two economic or political systems, two presidents.

2. *Avoid the obvious topic.* Some students may think it is easier to write about two things if the similarities or differences between them are obvious, but with

an obvious topic you'll have nothing new to say, and you'll risk writing a boring paragraph.

Here are some obvious topics: the differences between high school and college, the similarities between *Terminator I* and *Terminator II*. If you are drawn to an obvious topic, *try a new angle* on the topic. Write about the unexpected, using the same topic. Write about the similarities between high school and college, or the differences between *Terminator I* and *Terminator II*. You may have to do more thinking before you come up with ideas, but your ideas may be more interesting to write about and to read.

Writing the Topic Sentence for a Comparison or Contrast Paragraph

The topic sentence makes the point of your comparison or contrast paragraph. It should also indicate whether the paragraph is about similarities or differences, like this:

> Because he is so reliable and loyal, Michael is a much better friend to me than Stefan. (The phrase "much better" indicates differences.)

> My two botany teachers share a love of the environment and a passion for protecting it. (The word "share" indicates similarities.)

The topic sentence should *not* announce. The sentences below are announcements, not topic sentences:

> This paper will explain the similarities between my two botany teachers.

> Let me tell you about why Michael is a different kind of friend than Stefan.

The topic sentence should do more than indicate similarities or differences; it should *focus on the specific kind of comparison or contrast you will make.*

> not focused: My old house is different from my new house.
> focused: My new home is bigger, brighter, and more comfortable than my old one.

The topic sentence should cover both subjects to be compared or contrasted.

> covers only one subject: The beach at Santa Lucia was dirty and crowded.
> covers both subjects: The beach at Santa Lucia was dirty and crowded, but the beach at Fisher Bay was clean and private.

Be careful. It's easy to get so carried away by the details of your paragraph that you forget to put both subjects into one sentence.

Organizing Your Comparison or Contrast Paragraph

Whether you decide to write about similarities (to compare) or differences (to contrast), you will have to decide how to organize your paragraph. You can choose between two patterns of organization: *subject-by-subject* or *point-by-point.*

Subject-by-Subject In the subject-by-subject pattern, you support and explain your topic sentence by first writing all your details on *one subject* and then writing all your details on *the other subject.* If you choose a subject-by-subject pattern, be sure to discuss the points for your second subject *in the same order* as you did for the first subject. For example, if your first subject is an amusement park, you might cover (1) the price of admission, (2) the long lines at rides, and (3) the quality of the rides. When you discuss the second subject, another amusement park, you should write about its prices, lines, and quality of rides *in the same order*.

Look carefully at the outline and following comparison paragraph for a subject-by-subject pattern.

A Comparison Outline: Subject-by Subject Pattern

topic sentence: Once I realized that my brother and my mother are very much alike in temperament, I realized why they don't get along.

details:

first subject, James—temper
My brother James is a hot-tempered person.
It is easy for him to lose control of his temper.

unkind words
When he does, he often says things he later regrets.

stubbornness
James is also very stubborn.
In an argument, he will never admit he is wrong.
Once we were arguing about baseball scores.
Even when I showed him the right score, printed in the paper, he wouldn't admit he was wrong.
He said that the newspaper had made a mistake.
James' stubbornness overtakes his common sense.

second subject, mother—temper
James has inherited many of his character traits from our mother.
She has a quick temper, and anything can provoke it.
Once, she got angry because she had to wait too long at a traffic light.

unkind words
She also has a tendency to use unkind words when she's angry.

stubbornness
She never backs down from a disagreement or concedes that she was wrong.
My mother even quit a job because she refused to admit she'd made a mistake in taking inventory.
Her pride can lead her into foolish acts.
After I realized how similar my brother and mother are, I understood how such inflexible people are likely to clash.

A Comparison Paragraph: Subject-by-Subject Pattern

first subject, James

Once I realized that my brother and my mother are very much alike in temperament, I realized why they don't get along. My brother James is a hot-tempered person. It's easy for him to lose control of his temper, and when he does, he often says things he regrets. James is also very stubborn. In an argument, he will never admit he is wrong. I remember one time when we were arguing about baseball scores. Even when I showed him the right score, printed in the newspaper, he wouldn't admit he was wrong. James insisted that the newspaper must have made a mistake in printing the score. As this example overtakes shows, sometimes James' stubbornness James' common sense. It took me a while to realize that my stubborn

second subject, mother

brother James has inherited many of his traits from our mother. Like James, she has a quick temper, and almost anything can provoke it. She once got angry because she had to wait too long at a traffic light. She also shares James' habit of saying unkind things when she's angry. And just as James refuses to back down when he's wrong, my mother will never back down from a disagreement or concede she's wrong. In fact, my mother once quit a job because she refused to admit she'd made a mistake in taking inventory. Her pride is as powerful as James' pride, and it can be just as foolish. After I realized how similar my mother and brother are, I understood how such inflexible people are likely to clash.

Look carefully at the paragraph in the *subject-by-subject* pattern, and you'll note that it

- begins with a topic sentence about both subjects—James and his mother,
- gives all the details about one subject—James,
- then gives all the details about the second subject—his mother, in the same order.

Point-by-Point   In the point-by-point pattern, you support and explain your topic sentence by discussing each point of comparison or contrast, switching back and

ALONG THESE LINES/Prentice-Hall, Inc.

forth between your subjects. You explain one point for each subject, then explain another point for each subject, and so on.

Look carefully at the outline and the following comparison paragraph below for the point-by-point pattern.

A Point-by-Point Outline for a Comparison Paragraph

topic sentence: Once I realized that my brother and my mother are very much alike in temperament, I realized why they don't get along.

details:

1st point, temper
> My brother James is a hot-tempered person.
> It is easy for him to lose control of his temper.
> My mother has a quick temper, and anything can provoke it.
> Once she got angry because she had to wait too long at a traffic light.

2nd point, unkind words
> When my brother gets angry, he often says things he regrets.
> My mother has a tendency to use unkind words when she's angry.

3rd point, stubbornness
> James is very stubborn.
> In an argument, he will never admit he is wrong.
> Once we were arguing about baseball scores.
> Even when I showed him the right score, printed in the paper, he wouldn't admit he was wrong.
> He said the newspaper had made a mistake.
> James' stubbornness overtakes his common sense.
> My mother will never back down from a disagreement or admit that she is wrong.
> She even quit a job because she refused to admit she'd made a mistake in taking inventory.
> She was foolish in her stubbornness.

> After I realized how similar my mother and brother are, I understood how such inflexible people are likely to clash.

Comparison Paragraph: Point-by-Point Pattern

1st point

Once I realized that my brother and my mother are very much alike in temperament, I realized why they don't get along. My brother is a hot-tempered person, and it is easy for him to lose control of his temper. My mother shares James' quick temper, and anything can provoke her anger. Once, she got angry because she had to wait too long at a traffic light. When my brother gets

2nd point

angry, he often says things he regrets. Similarly, my mother is known for the unkind things she's said in anger. James is a very stubborn person. In an

3rd point

argument, he will never admit he's wrong. I can remember one argument we were having over baseball scores. Even when I showed him the right score, printed in the newspaper, he wouldn't admit he had been wrong. He simply insisted the paper had made a mistake. At times like this, James' stubbornness overtakes his common sense. Like her son, my mother will never back down from an argument or admit she was wrong. She even quit a job because she refused to admit she'd made a mistake in taking inventory. In that case, her stubbornness was as foolish as James'. It took me a while to see the similarities between my brother and mother. Yet after I realized how similar these two people are, I understood how two inflexible people are likely to clash.

Look carefully at the paragraph in the *point-by-point pattern*, and you'll note that it

- begins with a topic sentence about both subjects—James and his mother,
- discusses how both James and his mother are alike in these points: their quick tempers, the unkind things they say in a temper, their often foolish stubbornness,
- switches back and forth between the two subjects.

Subject-by-subject and point-by-point patterns can be used for either a comparison or a contrast paragraph. But whatever pattern you choose, remember these hints:

1. *Be sure to use the same points to compare or contrast two subjects.* If you are contrasting two cars, you can't discuss the price and safety features of one,

ALONG THESE LINES/Prentice-Hall, Inc.

and the styling and speed of the other. You must discuss the price of both, or the safety features, or styling, or speed of both.

You don't have to list the points in your topic sentence, but you can include them, like this: "My old Celica turned out to be a cheaper, a safer, and a faster car than my boyfriend's new Taurus."

2. *Be sure to give roughly equal space to both subjects.* This rule doesn't mean you must write the same number of words—or even sentences—on both subjects. It does mean you should be giving fairly equal attention to the details of both subjects.

Because you will be writing about two subjects, this type of paragraph can involve more details than other paragraph formats. Thus, a comparison or contrast paragraph may be longer than twelve sentences.

▶ **E X E R C I S E   1 :   Collaborative Exercise: Identifying Suitable Topic Sentences for a Comparison or a Contrast Paragraph**

Do this exercise with a partner or with a group. Following is a list of possible topic sentences for a comparison or contrast paragraph. Some would make good topic sentences; others wouldn't. The ones that wouldn't make good topic sentences have one or more of these problems:

A They are announcements.
B They don't indicate whether the paragraph will be about similarities or differences.
C They don't focus on the specific kind of comparison or contrast to be made.
D They cover subjects that are too big to write about in one paragraph.
E They don't cover both subjects.

Mark the following problem sentences by using one or more of the letters above. If a sentence would make a good topic sentence for a comparison or a contrast paragraph, mark it *OK*.

1. _____ I have two friends, Rick and Luke.

2. _____ My two close friends, Rick and Luke, are very similar.

3. _____ My two close friends, Rick and Luke, are alike in their athletic ability and obsession with sports.

4. _____ The United States and Canada are similar in their economic system, history, and culture.

5. _____ The Palm Club has better music and a friendlier atmosphere.

6. _____ I'd like to discuss the similarities between my cat and my beagle.

7. _____ Men and women are different in their physical, intellectual, and emotional make-up.

8. _____ On the one hand, there is Jack's Pizza Parlour, and then there is the Italian Palace.

9. _____ Mr. Sheridan is a more energetic and enthusiastic teacher than Mr. Smith.

10. _____ My second date with Carla was a big improvement over my first one.

11. _____ Here are some significant differences between roller skating and in-line skating.

12. _____ Communism and democracy are contrasting systems of government.

Using Transitions Effectively for Comparison or Contrast

The transitions you use in a comparison or a contrast paragraph, how to use them, and when to use them all depend on the answers to two questions:

1. Are you writing a comparison or a contrast paragraph?

   • When you choose to write a *comparison* paragraph, you use transition words, phrases, or sentences that point out *similarities*.
   • When you choose to write a *contrast* paragraph, you use transition words, phrases, or sentences that point out *differences*.

2. Are you organizing your paragraph in the point-by-point or subject-by-subject pattern?

   • When you choose to organize your paragraph in the *point-by-point pattern*, you need transitions *within each point*, and *between points*.
   • If you choose to organize in the *subject-by-subject pattern*, you need *most of your transitions* in the *second half* of the paragraph, to remind the reader of the points you made in the first half.

Here are some transitions you can use in writing comparison or contrast. (There are many others that may be appropriate for your ideas.)

Transitions for a Comparison or a Contrast Paragraph

To show similarities: additionally, again, also, and, as well as, both, each of, equally, furthermore, in addition, in the same way, just like, like, likewise, similarly, similar to, too, so

To show differences: although, but, conversely, different from, despite, even though, except, however, in contrast to, instead of, in spite of, nevertheless, on the other hand, otherwise, still, though, unlike, whereas, while, yet

---

Some examples may help you to understand how to use transitions in a point-by-point or subject-by-subject pattern.

Using Transitions in a Contrast Paragraph, Point-by-Point Pattern

When you organize in a point-by-point pattern, some of your transitions will come within each point. For example, you might want to write about the different styles of houses as one point. You might want to say:

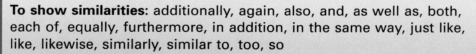

```
Our first house was a farm house out in the country.
Our second house was a row house in the city.
```

ALONG THESE LINES/Prentice-Hall, Inc.

You can combine the sentences when you add a transition:

> <u>While</u> our first house was a farm house out in the country, our second house was a row house in the city.

When you organize around a point-by-point pattern, some of your transitions will come between your points. For example, you may have just finished writing about the differences in prices at two local supermarkets. Now you want to discuss the differences in products. To avoid a choppy style, you can add words, phrases, or even a sentence of transition.

Following is part of a paragraph that shows you a *transition between points*. The transition sentence is underlined.

first point: differences in price	Prices at Food Circus tend to be high. Last week, for instance, I paid 99 cents for a head of iceberg lettuce. Two cans of tomato soup cost me a dollar. At Superfood Mart, prices are generally lower. Iceberg lettuce sold for 49 cents a head last week, and two cans of tomato soup were on sale for 67 cents.
transition sentence	<u>Just as the two stores vary in price, they offer different products.</u> Food Circus has a wide range of gourmet
second point: differences in products	items, expensive ice creams, and a fancy baking section. Superfood Mart offers very little gourmet food or high-priced ice cream, and it doesn't have a bakery. But it offers more choice in fresh produce than Food Circus does.

Using Transitions in a Contrast Paragraph, Subject-by-Subject Pattern

When you organize in a subject-by-subject pattern, a *transition, usually a sentence, will come between the end of the first subject and the beginning of the second subject.* This transition is important in linking the two parts of your paragraph.

And when you use a subject-by-subject pattern, *more transitions* will be used in the *second half* of your paragraph than in the first half. The transitions in the second half remind your reader that you are comparing or contrasting two things.

Following is a contrast paragraph written in a subject-by-subject pattern. Notice the transition sentence in the middle of the paragraph, the number of transitions in the second half of the paragraph, and the way transitions are used to remind the reader of the points in the first half of the paragraph.

Transitions in a Contrast Paragraph, Subject-by-Subject Pattern (Transitions are underlined.)

Food Circus and Superfood Mart differ in price, products, and appearance. Prices at Food Circus tend to be high. Last week, for instance, I paid 99 cents for a head of iceberg lettuce. Two cans of tomato soup cost me a dollar. <u>Just like the prices</u>, the products at Food Circus tend to be fancy. Food Circus has a wide range of gourmet items, expensive ice creams, and a fancy bakery full of elaborate cakes and cookies. The appearance of this store is elegant, with gleaming chrome counters, bright lights, neon signs over the deli and bakery, and wide aisles. <u>Superfood Mart is a big contrast to Food Circus, in several ways. While iceberg lettuce costs 99 cents at Food Circus</u>, it costs 69 cents at Superfood Mart. <u>Instead of Food Circus' tomato soup at a dollar a can</u>, Superfood Mart sells it at 67 cents for two cans. <u>Although Superfood Mart doesn't sell the gourmet food, expensive ice cream, and bakery goods available at Food Mart</u>, it does have a greater selection of fresh produce like tomatoes and corn. <u>Another important contrast</u> between the stores is their appearance. <u>Unlike Food Circus</u>, Superfood Mart is small and dark, with narrow aisles. It looks like an old-fashioned grocery store <u>instead of a modern food market like Food Circus.</u> Each store appeals to different shoppers; Food Circus offers luxuries and a pleasant setting to those who can afford them, <u>while</u> Superfood Mart offers bargains and fresh produce to the budget-conscious.

Writing a comparison or contrast paragraph challenges you to make decisions: Will I compare or contrast? Will I use a point-by-point or a subject-by-subject pattern? These decisions will determine what kind of transitions you will use and where you will use them.

► **EXERCISE 1: Writing Appropriate Transitions for a Comparison or Contrast Paragraph**

Following are pairs of sentences. First, decide whether each pair shows a comparison or a contrast. Then combine the two sentences into one, using an appropriate transition (a word or phrase).

You may have to rewrite parts of the original sentences to create one smooth sentence. When you've finished the exercise, compare your new sentences with your classmates.

The first pair is done for you.

a. Dr. Cheung is a professor of art.

   Dr. Mbala is a professor of history.

combined: <u>Dr. Cheung is a professor of art while Dr. Mbala is a professor of</u>

<u>history</u>.

b. *The Brady Bunch* was a show about a happy, well-adjusted family that was too good to be true.

   The Fresh Prince of Bel Air was a show about a family that lived a fantasy lifestyle.

combined: _____

   _____

c. Small children are often afraid to leave their parents.

   Teenagers can't wait to get away from their parents.

   combined: _____

   _____

d. Phillippe was an intelligent dog who learned all sorts of tricks.

   Elvis, our basset hound, refused to do the simplest tricks.

   combined: _____

   _____

e. Exercise can help you lower cholesterol levels, fight heart disease, and relieve stress.

   A doctor can give you medicine for heart disease, high cholesterol, or stress.

   combined: _____

   _____

f. Edward is dedicated to helping the homeless at the food bank where he works.

   His sister Irene has devoted her life to protecting the rights of Central American refugees.

   combined: _____

   _____

g. My father spends many hours volunteering at a local food bank.

   Every Saturday, my boyfriend donates his time to the food bank, where he collects free food from donors.

   combined: _____

   _____

WRITING THE COMPARISON OR CONTRAST PARAGRAPH IN STEPS

THOUGHTLINES: COMPARISON OR CONTRAST

One way to get started on a comparison or a contrast paragraph is to list as many differences or similarities on one topic as you can. Then you can see whether you have more similarities (comparisons) or more differences (contrasts), and decide which approach to use. For example, if you are asked to compare or contrast two restaurants, you could begin with a list like this:

> ### Thoughtlines List for Two Restaurants: Victor's or The Garden
>
> similarities
>
> both offer lunch and dinner
> very popular
> nearby
>
> differences
>
> | Victor's | The Garden |
> |---|---|
> | formal dress | informal dress |
> | tablecloths | placemats |
> | food is bland | spicy food |
> | expensive | moderate |
> | statues, fountains, fresh flowers | dark wood, hanging plants |

Getting Points of Comparison or Contrast

Whether you compare or contrast, you are looking for *specific points of comparison or contrast,* items you can discuss about both subjects.

If you surveyed the list on the two restaurants and decided you wanted to contrast the two restaurants, you'd see that you already have these points of contrast:

dress
decor
food
prices

To write your paragraph, start with several points of comparison or contrast. As you work through the stages of writing, you may decide you don't need all the points you've jotted down, but it is better to start with too many points than with too few.

▶ **E X E R C I S E 1: Collaborative Exercise in Developing Points of Comparison or Contrast**

Following are some topics that could be used for a comparison or a contrast paragraph. Underneath each topic, write three points of comparison or contrast. Then, working with a partner or with a group, add to the list of points so that you have five points for each topic. Be prepared to read your list to the class. The first topic is done for you.

a. topic: Compare or contrast two television talk shows.

Points of comparison or contrast:

1. the host
2. the kinds of topics discussed on the show
3. the length of the program

4. the time of day it is broadcast _____

5. what the studio audience is like _____

b. **topic:** Compare or contrast a movie and its sequel.

Points of comparison or contrast:

1. _____

2. _____

3. _____

4. _____

5. _____

c. **topic:** Compare or contrast two friends.

Points of comparison or contrast:

1. _____

2. _____

3. _____

4. _____

5. _____

d. **topic:** Compare or contrast two college courses.

Points of comparison or contrast:

1. _____

2. _____

3. _____

4. _____

5. _____

e. **topic:** Compare or contrast two professional basketball players.

Points of comparison or contrast:

1. _____

2. _____

3. _____

4. _____

5. _____

▶ **E X E R C I S E   2:   Finding Differences in Subjects That Look Similar**

Following are pairs of subjects that are similar but have some differences. Working alone, with a partner, or with a group, list three differences for each pair.

a. Burger King and McDonald's

differences: 1. _____

2. _____

3. _____

b. Pepsi and Coke

differences: 1. _____

2. _____

3. _____

c. swimming in the ocean and swimming in a pool

differences: 1. _____

2. _____

3. _____

d. preschool and kindergarten

differences: 1. _____

2. _____

3. _____

Adding Details to Your Points

Once you have some points, you can begin adding details, which will lead you to more points. Even if they don't, the process will help you to develop the ideas of your paragraph.

If you were to write about the differences in restaurants, for example, your new list with added details might look like this:

Thoughtlines List for a Contrast of Restaurants

Victor's	The Garden
dress—formal	informal dress
men in jackets, women in dresses	all in jeans
decor—pretty, elegant statues, fountains	place mats, on table is a card listing specials
fresh flowers on tables, tablecloths	lots of dark wood, brass, green hanging plants
food—bland tasting, traditional, broiled fish or chicken, traditional steaks, appetizers like shrimp cocktail, onion soup	spicy and adventurous, pasta in tomato sauces, garlic in everything, curry, appetizers like tiny tortillas, ribs in honey-mustard sauce
price—expensive	moderate
everything costs extra, like appetizer, salad	price of dinner includes appetizer and salad

ALONG THESE LINES/Prentice-Hall, Inc.

Once you have a list of points and some details, you can review your list and ask yourself, "What's my main idea? Where is the list taking me?"

Reading the list about restaurants, you might conclude that you prefer The Garden to Victor's. Why? There are several hints within your list: The Garden has cheaper food, better food, and a more casual atmosphere.

Now that you have a point, you can put it into a topic sentence. A topic sentence contrasting the restaurants could be written this way:

I'd rather eat at The Garden than at Victor's because The Garden gives me better, cheaper food in a more casual environment.

Once you have a possible topic sentence, you can begin working on the outlines stage of your paragraph.

▶ **E X E R C I S E   1 :   Writing Topic Sentences for Comparison or Contrast**

Following are lists of details. Some are for comparison paragraphs; some are for contrast paragraphs. Read each list carefully; then write a topic sentence for each list.

a. topic sentence:_____

_____

List of Details

frozen yogurt	ice cream
taste—light, milky, a little sour	sweet, heavy, creamy
nutritional value—low fat or fat free, low calorie, a healthy dessert or snack	more fat, higher calories, acceptable as an occasional treat
popularity—younger generation, parents with small children who want a healthy snack, dieters	lovers of gourmet food, people who want to splurge on calories

b. topic sentence:_____

_____

List of Details

frozen yogurt	ice cream
availability—frozen yogurt stores, supermarkets, fast food places, college cafeterias	ice cream stores, supermarkets, college cafeterias, snack bars
ways to buy it—in cones, cups, quarts, pints, in cakes, soft serve	cones, cups, pints, quarts, half gallon, gallon, cakes, a little soft serve
flavors—mostly fruit, some chocolate, some with mixed-in ingredients like Heath bars	chocolate, fruit, mixed-in ingredients like cherries or cookies

E X E R C I S E

c. topic sentence:_____

_____

List of Details

pick-up truck	sport utility vehicle (like Bronco, Explorer)
seating—for two	seats four or five
room to carry things—large truck bed, can be open space, covered by a canvas cover, or permanently closed	large covered space behind seats, but not as big as pick-up's space
uses—good for rough terrain, hunting and fishing, hauling and moving, construction work	good for country driving but also for suburban families with space for toys, baby strollers, car seats

d. topic sentence:_____

_____

List of Details

pick-up truck	sport utility vehicle
buyers—popular with young people, sportsmen, farmers	people in their twenties, people who camp or fish
image—a rugged, solid, practical vehicle	fashionable, rugged, useful
accessories available—CD players, fancy speakers, air conditioning	luxurious interiors, CD players and speakers, air conditioning

OUTLINES: COMPARISON OR CONTRAST

When you have a topic sentence, you can begin to draft an outline. Before you can write an outline, however, you have to make a decision: What pattern do you want to use in organizing your paragraph? Do you want to use the subject-by-subject or the point-by-point pattern?

The following is an outline of a contrast paragraph in point-by-point form.

> ### An Outline of a Contrast Paragraph: Point-by-Point
>
> **topic sentence:** I'd rather eat at The Garden than at Victor's because The Garden gives me better, cheaper food in a more casual environment.

details:

1st point:
food

> Food at Victor's is bland-tasting and traditional.
> The menu has broiled fish, chicken, traditional steaks.
> The spices used are mostly parsley and salt.
> The food is the usual American food, with a little French food on the list.
> Appetizers are the usual things like shrimp cocktail or onion soup.
> Food at The Garden is more spicy and adventurous.
> There are many pasta dishes in tomato sauce.
> There is garlic in just about everything.
> The Garden serves four different curry dishes.
> It has all kinds of ethnic food.
> Appetizers include items like tiny tortillas and hot, honey-mustard ribs.

2nd point:
prices

> The prices of the two restaurants differ.
> Victor's is expensive.
> Everything you order costs extra.
> An appetizer and a salad costs extra.
> Food at The Garden is more moderately priced.
> The price of a dinner includes an appetizer and a salad.

3rd point:
environment

> I feel uncomfortable in Victor's, which has a formal environment.
> Everyone is dressed up, the men in jackets and ties and the women in dresses.
> I'd rather eat in a more casual place.
> People don't dress up to go to The Garden; they wear jeans.

conclusion

> I guess I prefer a place where I can relax, with reasonable prices and unusual food, to a place that's a little stuffy, with a traditional and expensive menu.

Once you've drafted an outline, check it. Use the checklist below to help you review and revise your outline.

A Checklist for an Outline of a Comparison or a Contrast Paragraph

✔ Do I have enough details?

✔ Are all my details relevant?

✔ Have I covered all the points on both sides?

✔ If I'm using a subject-by-subject pattern, have I covered the points in the same order on both sides?

✔ Have I tried to cover too many points?

✔ Have I made my main idea clear?

Using this checklist as your guide, compare the outline with the thoughtlines list. You may notice several changes:

- Some details on decor in the thoughtlines have been omitted because there were too many points.
- A concluding sentence has been added to reinforce the main idea.

▶ **EXERCISE 1: Adding a Point and Details to a Comparison or a Contrast Outline**

The following draft outline is too short. Develop it by adding a point of contrast and details to both subjects, to develop the contrast.

topic sentence: Carson College is a friendlier place than Wellington College.

details: When a person enters Carson College, he or she sees groups of students who seem happy.
They are sprawled on the steps and on the lawns, looking like they are having a good time.
They are laughing and talking to each other.
At Wellington College, everyone seems to be a stranger.
Students are isolated.
They lean against the wall or sit alone, reading intently or staring into space.
The buildings at Carson seem open and inviting.
There are many large glass windows in each classroom.
There are wide, large corridors.
Many signs help newcomers find their way around.
Wellington College seems closed and forbidding.
It has dark, windowless classrooms.
The halls are narrow and dirty.
There are no signs or directions posted on the buildings.

ALONG THESE LINES/Prentice-Hall, Inc.

Add a new point of contrast, and details, about each college: _____

_____

_____

_____

_____

_____

_____

▶ E X E R C I S E   2 :   **Finding Irrelevant Detail in a Comparison**
or Contrast Outline

The following draft outline contains some irrelevant details. Cross out the details
that don't fit.

topic sentence: Bill, a student in my chemistry class, behaves like my two-
year-old son Toby.

details: Toby has a hard time sitting still for very long.
When we go to a restaurant, Toby gets impatient waiting for his
food.
He will sit still only until he's finished eating.
Then he begins to fidget.
Sometimes he starts dropping things, like French fries or spoons,
on the floor.
Bill finds it hard to sit through class.
Sometimes he gets impatient when the professor is telling a long
story.
Bill does not have good grades in this class.
If Bill is taking a quiz, he will sit quietly only until he's finished
taking the quiz.
Dr. Berthoff's quizzes are hard.
Then Bill begins to squirm at his desk.
He shifts his seat around.
Sometimes he drops pencils on the floor.
Toby likes a great deal of attention.
I'm divorced, and Toby doesn't see his father often.
To get my attention, Toby misbehaves.
He interrupts when I have company.
He teases our dog.
He throws something.
Bill likes attention, too.
He misbehaves in class to get attention from the professor.
Sometimes he makes smart remarks while the professor is
lecturing.
Sometimes he teases the girl who sits next to him.
Once, he threw a crumpled ball of paper across the room, into the
wastebasket.
Bill and Tony both behave like children, but in Bill's case, it's time
to grow up.

▶ **E X E R C I S E   3 :** **Revising the Order in a Comparison or a Contrast Outline**

Following is an outline written in the subject-by-subject pattern. Rewrite the part of the outline that is in italics so that the points in the second half follow the order of the first half. You do not have to change any sentences; just rearrange them.

topic sentence: Young people and old people are both victims of society's prejudices.

details: Some people think young people are not capable of mature thinking.
They think the young are on drugs.
They think the young are alcoholics.
The young are considered parasites because they do not earn a great deal of money.
Many young people are in college and not working full time.
Many young people rely on help from their parents.
The young are outcast because their appearance is different.
The young wear trendy fashions.
They have strange haircuts.
People may think the young are punks.
The way young people look makes other people afraid.
Old people are also judged by their appearance.
They are wrinkled or scarred or frail-looking.
People are afraid of growing old and looking like that.
So they are afraid of the old.
Some people think elderly people are not capable of mature thinking.
They think the old are on too much medication to think straight.
They think the old are senile.
Some people consider the old to be parasites because elderly people do not earn a great deal of money.
Some of the elderly have small pensions.
Some have only Social Security.
The young and the old are often stereotyped.

Rewritten order: _____

_____

_____

_____

_____

_____

_____

_____

_____

_____

_____

_____

ROUGHLINES: COMPARISON OR CONTRAST

When you've revised your outline, you can write the first draft of the restaurant paragraph. After making a first draft, you may want to combine more sentences, rearrange your points, fix your topic sentence, or add vivid detail. You may also need to add transitions.

Revising the Draft

Here is a revised version of the paragraph on contrasting two restaurants. As you read it, notice the changes from the outline: the order of some detail in the outline has been changed, sentences have been combined, and transitions have been added.

> **Roughlines Revised Draft
> of a Contrast Paragraph:
> Point-By-Point**
> (Transitions are underlined.)
>
> I'd rather eat at The Garden than at Victor's because The Garden gives me better and cheaper food in a more casual environment. The food at Victor's is bland-tasting and traditional. The menu has broiled fish, chicken, and traditional steaks. The food is the usual American food with a little French food on the list. Appetizers are the usual things like shrimp cocktail and onion soup. The spices used are mainly parsley and salt. Food at The Garden, <u>however,</u> is more spicy and adventurous. The restaurant has all kinds of ethnic food. There are many pasta dishes with tomato sauce. The menu has four kinds of curry on it. The appetizers include items like tiny tortillas and hot, honey-mustard ribs. <u>And if parsley is the spice of choice at Victor's,</u> garlic is the favorite spice at The Garden. The prices at the restaurants differ, <u>too.</u> Victor's is expensive because everything you order costs extra. An appetizer or a salad costs extra. Food at The Garden, <u>in contrast,</u> is more moderately priced because the price of a dinner includes an appetizer and a salad. <u>Price and menu are important, but the most important difference between the restaurants has to do with environment</u>. I feel uncomfortable at Victor's, which has a formal kind of atmosphere. Everyone is dressed up, the men in jackets and ties and the women in dresses. I'd rather eat in a more casual place like The Garden,

> where everyone wears jeans. I guess I prefer a place
> where I can relax, with reasonable prices and
> unusual food, to a place that's a little stuffy,
> with a traditional and expensive menu.

The following checklist may help you revise your own draft:

A Checklist for Revising the Roughlines of a Comparison or a Contrast Paragraph

✔ Did I include a topic sentence that covers both subjects?

✔ Is the paragraph in a clear order?

✔ Does it stick to one pattern, either subject-by-subject or point-by-point?

✔ Are both subjects given roughly the same amount of space?

✔ Do all the details fit?

✔ Are the details specific and vivid?

✔ Do I need to combine any sentences?

✔ Are transitions used effectively?

✔ Have I made my point?

▶ **EXERCISE 1:** Revising the Roughlines of a Comparison or a Contrast Paragraph by Adding Vivid Details

You can do this exercise alone, with a writing partner or with a group. The following contrast paragraph lacks the vivid details that could make it interesting. Read it; then rewrite the underlined parts in the space above the underlining. Replace the original words with more vivid detail.

   Nelson and Byron are so different in appearance that most people wouldn't believe the men are brothers. Nelson is tall and lanky. At six feet, he seems even taller because he has a bony, long-limbed body. His hair is <u>cut short</u>, and it is a <u>dark color</u>. Nelson's face is notable for its bone structure. He has high, prominent cheekbones, a sharp, prominent nose, and a long, jutting chin. His face has a lean, sculptured look. Byron looks nothing like his brother. First of all, he is short and stocky. He is <u>short in height</u> and seems even shorter because his body is <u>kind of fat</u>. His hair, unlike Nelson's, is long and straight and is usually pulled into a ponytail. Byron's hair is <u>lighter</u>

ALONG THESE LINES/Prentice-Hall, Inc.

<u>than Nelson's</u>. His face is rounded, with a snub nose, round cheeks like apples, and a round chin. Byron's face has a soft, chubby look. Byron looks like an overweight wrestler; Nelson looks like a basketball player.

FINAL LINES: COMPARISON OR CONTRAST

Contrast Paragraph: Point-by-Point Pattern

Following are the revised outline, revised draft, and final lines versions of the paragraph contrasting restaurants, using a point-by-point pattern. When you read the roughlines and final lines versions, you'll notice several changes:

- "usual" or "usually" was used too often, so synonyms were substituted,
- "onion soup" became "*French* onion soup," to emphasize the detail,
- "everything *you* order" was changed to "everything *a person* orders," to avoid sounding as if the reader is ordering food at Victor's, and
- "a formal *kind of atmosphere*" became "a formal environment" to eliminate extra words.

Before you prepare the final lines copy of your comparison or contrast paragraph, check your latest draft for errors in spelling and punctuation, and for any errors made in typing or recopying.

An Outlines Version of a Contrast Paragraph: Point-by-Point

topic sentence: I'd rather eat at The Garden than at Victor's because The Garden gives me better, cheaper food in a more casual environment.

details: Food at Victor's is bland-tasting and traditional.
The menu has broiled fish, chicken, traditional steaks.
The spices used are mainly parsley and salt.
The food is the usual American food, with a little French food on the list.
Appetizers are the usual things like shrimp cocktail or onion soup.
Food at the Garden is more spicy and adventurous.
There are many pasta dishes in tomato sauce.

There is garlic in just about
everything.
The Garden serves four different
curry dishes.
It has all kinds of ethnic food.
Appetizers include items like tiny
tortillas and hot, honey-mustard
ribs.
The prices of the two restaurants
differ.
Victor's is expensive.
Everything you order costs extra.
An appetizer or a salad costs extra.
Food at The Garden is more
moderately priced.
The price of a dinner includes an
appetizer and a salad.
I feel uncomfortable in Victor's,
which has a formal environment.
Everyone is dressed up, the men in
jackets and ties and the women in
dresses.
I'd rather eat in a more casual
place.
People don't dress up to go to The
Garden; they wear jeans.
I guess I prefer a place where I can
relax, with reasonable prices and
unusual food, to a place that's a
little stuffy, with a traditional
and expensive menu.

A Roughlines Version of a Contrast Paragraph: Point-by-Point

I'd rather eat at The Garden than at Victor's
because The Garden gives me better and cheaper food
in a more casual environment. The food at Victor's
is bland-tasting and traditional. The menu has
broiled fish, chicken, and traditional steaks. The
food is the usual American food with a little
French food on the list. Appetizers are the usual
things like shrimp cocktail and onion soup. The
spices used are mainly parsley and salt. Food at
The Garden, however, is more spicy and adventurous.
The restaurant has all kinds of ethnic food. There
are many pasta dishes with tomato sauce. The menu

ALONG THESE LINES/Prentice-Hall, Inc.

has four kinds of curry on it. The appetizers
include items like tiny tortillas and hot, honey-
mustard ribs. And if parsley is the spice of choice
at Victor's, garlic is the favorite spice of The
Garden. The prices at the restaurants differ, too.
Victor's is expensive because everything you order
costs extra. An appetizer or a salad costs extra.
Food at The Garden, in contrast, is more moderately
priced because the price of a dinner includes an
appetizer and a salad. Price and menu are important,
but the most important difference between the
restaurants has to do with environment. I feel
uncomfortable at Victor's, which has a formal kind
of atmosphere. Everyone is dressed up, the men in
jackets and ties and the women in dresses. I'd
rather eat in a more casual place like The Garden,
where everyone wears jeans. I guess I prefer a place
where I can relax, with reasonable prices and
unusual food, to a place that's a little stuffy,
with a traditional and expensive menu.

**A Final Lines Version
of a Contrast Paragraph:
Point-by-Point
(Changes from the roughlines
version are underlined.)**

   I'd rather eat at The Garden than at Victor's
because The Garden gives me better and cheaper food
in a more casual environment. The food at Victor's
is bland-tasting and traditional. The menu has
broiled fish, chicken, and traditional steaks. The
food is <u>typical</u> American food with a little French
food on the list. Appetizers are <u>standard items</u>
like shrimp cocktail and <u>French</u> onion soup. The
spices are mostly parsley and salt. Food at The
Garden, however, is more spicy and adventurous. The
restaurant has all kinds of ethnic food. There are
many pasta dishes with tomato sauce. The menu has
four kinds of curry on it. The appetizers include
items like tiny tortillas and hot, honey-mustard
ribs. And if parsley is the spice of choice at
Victor's, garlic is the favorite spice at The
Garden. The prices at the restaurants differ, too.
Victor's is expensive because everything <u>a person</u>
orders costs extra. An appetizer or a salad costs
extra. Food at The Garden, in contrast, is more
moderately priced because the price of a dinner

includes an appetizer and a salad. Price and menu are important, but the most important difference between the two restaurants has to do with environment. I feel uncomfortable at Victor's, which has a formal <u>environment</u>. Everyone is dressed up, the men in jackets and ties and the women in dresses. I'd rather eat in a more casual place like The Garden, where everyone wears jeans. I guess I prefer a place where I can relax, with reasonable prices and unusual food, to a place that's a little stuffy, with a traditional and expensive menu.

The Same Contrast Paragraph: Subject-by-Subject

To show you what the same paragraph contrasting restaurants would look like in a subject-by-subject pattern, the outlines, roughlines, and final lines versions follow.

An Outlines Version: Subject-by-Subject

topic sentence: I'd rather eat at The Garden than at Victor's because The Garden gives me better, cheaper food in a more casual environment.

details:

1st subject: Victor's
Food at Victor's is bland-tasting and traditional.
The menu has broiled fish, chicken, and traditional steaks.
The spices used are mostly parsley and salt.
The food is the usual American food, with a little French food on the list.
Appetizers are the usual things like shrimp cocktail and onion soup.
Victor's is expensive.
Everything you order costs extra.
An appetizer or salad costs extra.
I feel uncomfortable at Victor's, which has a formal environment.
Everyone is dressed up, the men in jackets and ties and the women in dresses.

2nd subject: The Garden
Food at The Garden is more spicy and adventurous.

There are many pasta dishes in
tomato sauce.
There is garlic in just about
everything.
The Garden serves four different
curry dishes.
It has all kinds of ethnic food.
Appetizers include items like tiny
tortillas and hot, honey-mustard
ribs.
Food at The Garden is moderately
priced.
The price of a dinner includes an
appetizer and a salad.
The Garden is casual.
People don't dress up to go there;
they wear jeans.
I guess I prefer a place where I can
relax, with reasonable prices and
unusual food, to a place that's a
little stuffy, with a traditional
and expensive menu.

A Roughlines Version: Subject-by-Subject
(Transitions are underlined.)

   I'd rather eat at The Garden than at Victor's
because The Garden gives me better, cheaper food in
a more casual environment. The food at Victor's is
bland-tasting and traditional. The menu has broiled
fish, chicken, and traditional steaks on it. The
food is the usual American food, with a little
French food on the list. Appetizers are the usual
things like shrimp cocktail and onion soup. At
Victor's, the spices are mostly parsley and salt.
Eating traditional food at Victor's is expensive
because everything you order costs extra. An
appetizer or a salad, for instance, costs extra.
Victor's prices make me nervous, and the
restaurant's formal environment makes me
uncomfortable. At Victor's, everyone is dressed up,
the men in jackets and ties and the women in
dresses. <u>I guess the formal atmosphere, the food,
and the prices attract some people, but I'd rather
go to The Garden for a meal.</u> The food at The Garden
is more spicy and adventurous <u>than the offerings at</u>

<u>Victor's.</u> The place has all kinds of ethnic food. There are many pasta dishes in tomato sauce, and The Garden serves four different curry dishes. Appetizers include items like tiny tortillas and hot, honey-mustard ribs. <u>If Victor's relies on parsley and salt to flavor its food</u>, The Garden sticks to garlic, which is in just about everything. Prices are lower at The Garden <u>than they are at Victor's</u>. The Garden's meals are more moderately priced because, <u>unlike Victor's</u>, The Garden includes an appetizer and a salad in the price of a dinner. <u>And in contrast to Victor's</u>, The Garden is a casual restaurant. People don't dress up to go to The Garden; everyone wears jeans. I guess I prefer a place where I can relax, with unusual food at reasonable prices, to a place that's a little stuffy, with a traditional and expensive menu.

A Final Lines Version: Subject-by-Subject
(Changes from the roughlines version are underlined.)

I'd rather eat at The Garden than at Victor's because The Garden gives me better, cheaper food in a more casual environment. The food at Victor's is bland-tasting and traditional. The menu has broiled fish, chicken, and traditional steaks on it. The food is typical American food, with a little French food on the list. Appetizers are the <u>standard</u> things like shrimp cocktail and <u>French</u> onion soup. At Victor's, the spices are mostly parsley and salt. Eating traditional food at Victor's is expensive because everything <u>a person</u> orders costs extra. An appetizer or a salad, for instance, costs extra. Victor's prices make me nervous, and the restaurant's formal environment makes me uncomfortable. At Victor's, everyone is dressed up, the men in jackets and ties and the women in dresses. I guess the formal <u>atmosphere</u> and the prices attract some people, but I'd rather go to The Garden for a meal. The food at The Garden is more spicy and adventurous than the offerings at Victor's. The place has all kinds of ethnic food. There are many pasta dishes in tomato sauce, and The Garden serves four different curry dishes. Appetizers include items like tiny tortillas and hot, honey-mustard ribs. If Victor's relies on

parsley and salt to flavor its food, The Garden
sticks to garlic, which is in just about everything.
Prices are lower at The Garden than they are at
Victor's. The Garden's meals are moderately priced
because, unlike Victor's, The Garden includes an
appetizer and a salad in the price of a dinner. And
in contrast to Victor's, The Garden is a casual
restaurant. People don't dress up to go to The
Garden; everyone wears jeans. I guess I prefer The
Garden because I prefer a place where I can relax,
with unusual food at reasonable prices, to a place
that's a little stuffy, with a traditional and
expensive menu.

▶ **E X E R C I S E   1 :   Correcting the Errors in a Final Lines
Comparison or Contrast Paragraph**

Following is a comparison paragraph with the kinds of errors that are easy to
overlook in a final copy of an assignment. Correct the errors, writing your corrections above the lines.

My nephew's stuffed dog and my portable tape player meet the same
needs in both of us. Brendan, who is four, won't go anywhere without the
ragged stufed dog he loves. To him, that dog represents security I have seen
him cry so long and so hard that his parents had to turn the car around and
drive fifty miles to pick up the dog they forgot. My tape player is my security, and I take it everywere. I even take it to the library when I study; I just
plug in the earphones. When Brendan feels tense, he runs to grab his dog. One
day Brendans mother was yelling at him, an his face got puckered up and red.
Brendan ran out of the room and hid in the corner of the hallway. He was
clutching his dog. While I dont clutch my tape player, I do turn to my mussic
to relax whenever I felt anxious. Brendan uses his toy to excape the world. I
seen him sit silent for half an hour, holding his dog and starring into space.
He is involved in some fantasy with his puppy. Whenever I feel tense, I turn
on my music. It soothes me and puts me in a world of my own. I guess adults
and children have there own ways of coping with conflict, and they have
their own toys, too!

Lines of Detail: A Walk-Through Assignment

Write a paragraph that compares or contrasts any experience you've heard about
with the same experience as you lived it. For example, you could compare or contrast what you heard about starting college with your actual experience of start-

ing college. You could compare or contrast what you heard about falling in love with your experience of falling in love, or what you heard about playing a sport with your own experience playing that sport. To write your paragraph, follow these steps:

Step 1: Choose the experience you will write about; then list all the similarities and differences between the experience as you heard about it and the experience as you lived it.

Step 2: To decide whether to write a comparison or a contrast paragraph, survey your list to see which has more details, similarities or differences.

Step 3: Add details to your comparison or contrast list. Survey your list again, and group the details into points of comparison or contrast.

Step 4: Write a topic sentence that includes both subjects, focuses on comparison or contrast, and makes a point.

Step 5: Decide whether your paragraph will be in the subject-by-subject or point-by-point pattern. Write your outline in the pattern you choose.

Step 6: Write a roughlines draft of your paragraph. Revise your draft, checking the transitions, the order of the points and the space given to each point for each subject, the relevance and vividness of the details. Combine any short, choppy sentences.

Step 7: Before you prepare the final copy of your paragraph, edit for word choice, spelling, punctuation, and transitions.

Writing Your Own Comparison or Contrast Paragraph

When you write on one of these topics, be sure to follow the stages of thought-lines, outlines, roughlines, and final lines.

1. Contrast what your appearance (or your behavior) makes others think of you and what you are like below the surface of your appearance (or behavior). If your instructor agrees, you can ask a writing partner or a group to give you ideas on what your appearance or behavior says about you.

2. Contrast something you did in the past with the way you do the same thing today. For example, you could contrast the two ways (past and present) of studying, shopping, treating your friends, spending your free time, driving a car, or getting along with a parent or child.

3. Compare or contrast any of the following:

two pets	two performers	two movies
two cars	two bosses	two TV shows
two stores	two family members	two jobs
two athletic teams	two birthdays	two classes

If your instructor agrees, you may want to brainstorm points of comparison or contrast with a writing partner or with a group.

4. Imagine that you are a reporter who specializes in helping consumers get the best for their money. Imagine that you are asked to rate two brands

of the same supermarket item. Write a paragraph advising your readers which is the better buy. You can rate two brands of cola, or yogurt, or potato chips, or toothpaste, or ice cream, or chocolate chip cookies, or paper towels—any item you can get in a supermarket.

Be sure to come up with *enough* points of contrast. You can't, for example, do a well-developed paragraph on just the taste of two cookies. But you can also discuss texture, color, smell, price, fat content, calories, number of chocolate chips, etc. If you instructor agrees, you may want to brainstorm topics or points of contrast with a group, as a way of beginning the thoughtlines stage. Then work on your own on the outlines, roughlines, and final lines stages.

5. Contrast your taste in music, or dress, or ways of spending leisure time with that of another generation.

6. Interview a person of your age group who comes from a different part of the country. (Note: There may be quite a few people from different parts of the country in your class.) Ask him or her about similarities or differences between his or her former home and this part of the country. You could ask about similarities or differences in dress, music, dating, nightlife, ways to spend leisure time, favorite entertainers, or anything else that you like.

After the interview, write a paragraph that either shows how people of the same age group, from different parts of the country, have different tastes in music, dress, etc., or share the same tastes in music, dress, etc. Whichever approach you use, use details you collected in the interview.

Name: _____   **Section:** _____

Peer Review Form for a Comparison or Contrast Paragraph

After you've written the roughlines version of your paragraph, let a writing partner read it. When your partner has completed the following form, discuss the comments. Then repeat the same process for your partner's paragraph.

I think the topic sentence of this paragraph is

_____

_____

The pattern of this paragraph is (a) subject-by-subject or (b) point-by- point.

The points used to compare or contrast are

_____

_____

The part of the paragraph I liked best was about

_____

The comparison or contrast is (a) easy to follow, (b) a little confusing.

I have questions about

_____

I would like to see something added about

_____

I would like to take out the part about

_____

I would like to add or change a transition in front of the words

_____

Other comments on the paragraph:

_____

_____

_____

_____

_____

_____

Reviewer's name: _____

ALONG THESE LINES/Prentice-Hall, Inc.

Writing from Reading: Comparison or Contrast

AGAINST ALL ODDS, I'M JUST FINE
Brad Wackerlin

When Brad Wackerlin wrote this essay in 1990, he had just graduated from high school. He writes about the differences between society's view of teenagers and the real teens who "do fine" in the real world.

Before you read this selection, consider these questions:

Do you consider yourself typical of people in your age group? Why or why not?
Do you think newspapers, magazines, and television influence the way we perceive different age groups? For example, do the media influence the way we perceive old people? Or teens?
Do you ever find yourself saying or thinking something like, "That's typical high school behavior," or "That's just like an old person"?
Do you think there is a generation gap?
Is it hard to be yourself in the teen years?

Words You May Need to Know

warping: twisting out of shape
baby boomers: People born between 1946 and 1964, when the record number of births was called a Baby Boom

preconceived: formed in advance
generation gap: the distance (in attitudes, values, goals, etc.) between two generations

AGAINST ALL ODDS, I'M JUST FINE
Brad Wackerlin

What troubled times the American teenager lives in! Ads for Nike shoes urge us to "Just do it!" while the White House tells us to "Just say no." The baby boomers have watched their babies grow into teens and history has repeated itself: the punk teens of the '80s have taken the place of the hippie teens of the '60s. Once again, the generation gap has widened and the adults have finally remembered to remember that teenagers are just no good. They have even coined a name for their persecution of adolescents: "teen-bashing."

If what is being printed in the newspapers, viewed on television and repeated by adults is correct, it is against all odds that I am able to write this article. Adults say the average teenager can't write complete sentences and has trouble spelling big words. Their surveys report that I can't find Canada on a map. According to their statistics, my favorite hobbies are sexual intercourse and recreational drug use. It's amazing that I've found time to write this; from what they say, my time is spent committing violent crimes or just hanging out with a gang. In fact, it is even more amazing that I'm here at all, when you consider that the music I listen to is supposedly "warping" my mind and influencing me to commit suicide.

Nonetheless, here I am. I write this article to show that a teenager can survive in today's society. Actually, I'm doing quite well. I haven't fathered any children, I'm not addicted to any drugs, I've never worshiped Satan and I don't have a police record. I can even find Canada on a map along with its capital, Ottawa. I guess my family and friends have been supportive of me, for I've never been tempted to become one of those teenage runaways I'm always reading about. Call me a rebel, but I've stayed in school and (can it be true?!) I enjoy it. This month, I graduate from high school and join other graduates as the newest generation of adults. I'm looking forward to four years of college and becoming a productive member of society. I may not be America's stereotypical teen, but that only proves there is something wrong with our society's preconceived image of today's teenager.

My only goal in writing this article is to point out the "bum rap" today's teenager faces. I feel the stereotypical teen is, in fact, a minority. The true majority are the teenagers who, day in and day out, prepare themselves for the future and work at becoming responsible adults. Our time is coming. Soon we will be the adults passing judgment on the teenagers of tomorrow. Hopefully, by then, we will have realized that support and encouragement have a far more positive effect on teenagers than does "bashing" them.

Writing from Reading "Against All Odds, I'm Just Fine"

When you write on any of the following topics, be sure to work through the stages of thoughtlines, outlines, roughlines, and final lines in preparing your paragraph.

1. Write a paragraph that contrasts society's image of any age group (teens, twenties, thirties, etc.) with the reality. As part of the thoughtlines stage of writing, interview one or more members of that age group. Before the interview, prepare a list of questions. They might be questions such as the following:

   How does television depict your age group?
   What do most people think is wrong with people in your age group?
   Are there stereotypes about how your age group dresses, talks, etc.?

   Try to have at least eight questions before you begin the interview. At the interview, jot down answers, ask follow-up questions, and ask the person(s) being interviewed to review and add to your notes.

2. Contrast your first impression of someone with the way you feel about the person after knowing him or her longer.

3. Show the similarities between teens of today and teens of thirty years ago. If your instructor agrees, brainstorm for similarities, with a partner or group.

4. Compare or contrast yourself with the kind of person you think is "typical" of your age group.

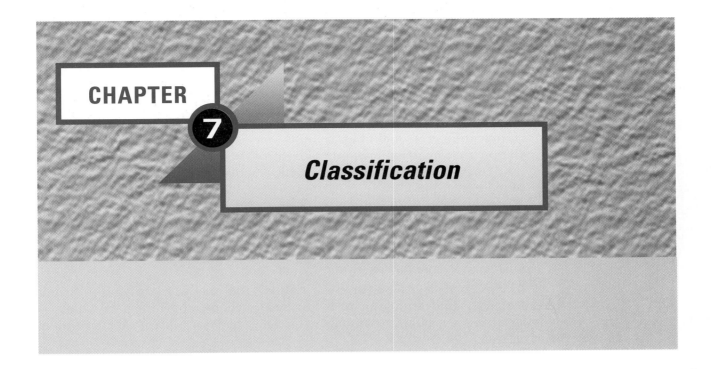

Classification

WHAT IS CLASSIFICATION?

When you *classify*, you divide something into different categories, and you do it according to some basis. For example, you may classify the people in your neighborhood into three categories: those you know well, those you know slightly, and those you don't know at all. Although you may not be aware of it, you have chosen a *basis* for this classification; that is, you are classifying the people in your neighborhood according to how well you know them.

Hints for Writing a Classification Paragraph

1. Divide your subject into three or more categories. If you are thinking about classifying VCRs, for instance, you might think about dividing them into cheap VCRs and expensive VCRs. Your basis for classification would be the price of VCRs. But you would need at least one more price category—moderately-priced VCRs. *Using at least three categories helps you to be reasonably complete in your classification.*

2. Pick *one* basis for classification and stick with it. If you're classifying VCRs on the basis of price, you can't divide them into cheap, expensive, and Japanese. Two of the categories relate to price, but "Japanese" does not.

In the following examples, notice how one item doesn't fit its classification and has been crossed out:

fishermen

fishermen who fish every day
weekend fishermen
~~fishermen who own their own boat~~
(If you are classifying fishermen on the basis of how often they fish, "fishermen who own their own boat" doesn't fit.)

tests

essay tests
objective tests
math tests
combination essay and objective tests
(If you are classifying tests on the basis of the type of questions they ask, "math tests" doesn't fit because it describes the subject being tested.)

3. Be creative in your classification. While it is easy to classify drivers according to their age, your paragraph will be more interesting if you choose another basis of comparison, such as how drivers react to a very slow driver in front of them.

4. Have a reason for your classification. You may be classifying to help a reader understand a topic or to help a reader choose something. You may be trying to prove a point, to criticize something, or to attack someone's position on an issue.

A classification paragraph must have a unifying reason behind it, and the details for each category should be as descriptive and specific as possible. Determining your audience and deciding why you are classifying can help you stay focused and make your paragraph more interesting.

▶ **EXERCISE 1:** **Collaborative Exercise on Finding a Basis for Classifying**

Do this exercise with a partner. First, write one basis for classifying each of the following topics. Then change papers with your partner; add a basis for each topic and trade papers again. Keep going until you and your partner have four different bases for classifying each topic. Be prepared to read your answers to the class.

The first topic is done for you.

a. topic to classify: dogs

You can classify dogs on the basis of

1. how easy they are to train
2. their size
3. how frisky they are
4. the way they behave in cars

b. topic to classify: cars

You can classify cars on the basis of

1. _____
2. _____
3. _____
4. _____

c. topic to classify: football players

You can classify football players on the basis of

1. _____

2. _____

3. _____

4. _____

d. topic to classify: music videos

You can classify music videos on the basis of

1. _____

2. _____

3. _____

4. _____

▶ **E X E R C I S E   2 :   Identifying What Doesn't Fit
                        the Classification**

In each of the following lists, one item doesn't fit because it is not classified on the same basis as the others in the list. First, determine the basis for the classification. Then cross out the one item on each list that doesn't fit.

a. topic: parties

basis for classification: _____

list: anniversary parties
     birthday parties
     small parties
     retirement parties

b. topic: hair

basis for classification: _____

list: black
     gray
     brown
     straight

c. topic: jewelry

basis for classification: _____

list: earring
     diamond
     necklace
     bracelet

d. **topic:** sleepers

basis for classification: _____

list: late sleepers
     people who snore
     people who toss and turn
     sleepers who talk in their sleep

e. **topic:** police

basis for classification: _____

list: Captain
     Detective
     Officer of the Year
     Sergeant

f. **topic:** teenagers

basis for classification: _____

list: have full-time job
     work part time
     have no job
     pay for their own clothes

g. **topic:** teenagers

basis for classification: _____

list: like heavy metal
     prefer rap
     listen to country
     attend concerts

h. **topic:** teenagers

basis for classification: _____

list: live with both parents
     live at home while attending college
     live with mother
     live with father

i. **topic:** teenagers

basis for classification: _____

list: in Midwest
     in cities
     in South
     in Northeast

▶ **E X E R C I S E 3 : Finding Categories That Fit One Basis
for Classification**

In the lines under each topic, write three categories that fit the basis of classification that is given. The first one is done for you.

a. topic: cartoons on television

basis for classification: when they are shown

categories:

1. *Saturday morning cartoons*

2. *weekly cartoon series shown in the evening*

3. *cartoons that are holiday specials*

b. topic: desserts

basis for classification: how fattening they are

categories:

1. _____

2. _____

3. _____

c. topic: teenagers

basis for classification: popularity with peers

categories:

1. _____

2. _____

3. _____

d. topic: toys

basis for classification: price

categories:

1. _____

2. _____

3. _____

e. topic: chicken

basis for classification: how it is cooked

categories:

1. _____

2. _____

3. _____

f. topic: mail

basis for classification: the purpose for sending it

categories:

1. _____

E X E R C I S E

2. _____

3. _____

WRITING THE CLASSIFICATION PARAGRAPH IN STEPS

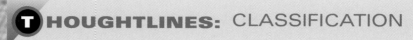

THOUGHTLINES: CLASSIFICATION

First, pick a topic for your classification. The next step is to choose some basis for your classification.

Brainstorming a Basis for Classification

Sometimes the easiest way to choose one basis is to brainstorm about different categories related to your topic and to see where your brainstorming leads you. For example, if you were to write a paragraph classifying phone calls, you could begin by listing anything about phone calls that occurs to you:

Phone Calls

sales calls at dinner time	people talk too long
short calls	calls I hate getting
calls in middle of night	wrong number
long distance calls	waiting for a call

The next step is to survey your list. See where it is leading you. The list of phone calls includes a few *unpleasant* phone calls:

sales calls at dinner time
wrong number
calls in middle of night

Maybe you can label these calls, Calls I Don't Want, and that will lead you toward a basis for classification. You might think about Calls I Don't Want, and Calls I Want. Remember, however, that you need at least three categories. If you stick with this basis for classification, you can come up with three categories:

Calls I Want to Receive
Calls I Don't Want to Receive
Calls I Really Don't Want to Receive

You can then gather details about your three categories by brainstorming:

Calls I Want to Receive

from boyfriend
good friends
catch-up calls—someone I haven't talked to for a while
make me feel close

Calls I Don't Want to Receive

sales calls at dinner time
wrong numbers

calls that irritate or interrupt
invade privacy

Calls I Really Don't Want to Receive
emergency call in middle of night
"let's break up" call from boyfriend
change my life, indicate some bad change

Matching the Points within the Types

As you begin thinking about details for each of your categories, try to write about the same points in each category. For instance, in the list of phone calls, each category includes some details about who made the call.

Calls I want—from good friends, my boyfriend
Calls I don't want—from salespeople, unknown callers
Calls I really don't want—from the emergency room, my boyfriend

If you decide to classify dogs on the basis of their breeds, you could talk about what each breed is used for, its size, and intelligence. As another illustration, if you are classifying babysitters on the basis of age, you might choose to talk about these points for each age group: how much the sitter charges, when the sitter arrives (early, on time, late), how strict the sitter is, why the child likes or dislikes the sitter. The idea is to achieve unity by covering the same points for each age group of babysitters.

Writing a Topic Sentence for a Classification Paragraph

The topic sentence for a classification paragraph should do two things:

1. It should mention what you are classifying,
2. It should indicate the basis for your classification by stating the basis or listing your categories, or both.

Consider the details on phone calls. To write a topic sentence about the details, you

1. mention what you are classifying: phone calls, and
2. indicate the basis for classifying by (a) stating the basis (whether I want to get the calls), or (b) listing the categories (calls I want to get, calls I don't want to get, and calls I really don't want to get). You may also state both the basis and the categories in the topic sentence.

Following these guidelines, you can write a topic sentence like this:

I can classify phone calls according to whether I want to get them.

or

Phone calls can be grouped into the ones I want to get, the ones I don't want to get, and the ones I really don't want to get.

Both of these topic sentences state what you're classifying and give some indication of the basis for the classification. Once you have a topic sentence, you are ready to begin the outlines phase of writing the classification paragraph.

▶ **EXERCISE 1:**   **Collaborative Exercise in Creating**
                     Questions to Get Details
                     for a Classification Paragraph

Do this exercise with a partner or with a group. Each of the following lists includes a topic, the basis for classifying that topic, and three categories. For each list, think of three questions that you could ask to get more details about the categories. The first list is done for you.

a. topic: moviegoers

basis for classification: what they eat and drink during the movie

categories: the traditional munchers, the healthy munchers, the really hungry
            munchers

questions you can ask:

1. *What does each type eat and drink?*

2. *What does each type look like?*

3. *Does each group stock up on more supplies during the movie?*

b. topic: sports fans at a game

basis for classification: how much they like the sport

categories: fanatics, ordinary fans, and bored observers

questions you can ask:

1. _____

2. _____

3. _____

c. topic: people at the dentist's office

basis for classification: how nervous they are

categories: the mildly anxious, the anxious, and the terrified

questions you can ask:

1. _____

2. _____

3. _____

d. topic: children at a preschool

basis for classification: how they interact with others

categories: shy, friendly, aggressive

questions you can ask:

1. _____

2. _____

3. _____

e. **topic:** older female relatives

basis for classification: how they greet you

categories: those who shake hands, those who peck you on the cheek, those
    who hug you to death

questions you can ask:

1. _____

2. _____

3. _____

▶ **E X E R C I S E   2 :** **Writing Topic Sentences for a Classification
                             Paragraph**

Review the topics, bases for classification, and categories in Exercise 1. Then,
using that material, write a good topic sentence for each topic.

Topic Sentences

for topic a: _____

_____

_____

for topic b:_____

_____

_____

for topic c:_____

_____

_____

for topic d:_____

_____

_____

for topic e:_____

_____

_____

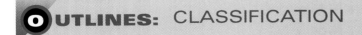

OUTLINES: CLASSIFICATION

Effective Order in Classifying

After you have a topic sentence and a list of details, you can create an outline.
Think about which category you want to write about first, second, and so forth.
The order of your categories will depend on what you're writing about. If you're

classifying ways to meet people, you can save the best for last. If you're classifying three habits that are bad for your health, you can save the worst one for last.

If you list your categories in the topic sentence, list them in the same order that you will explain them in the paragraph.

Following is an outline for a paragraph classifying phone calls. The thought-lines have been put into categories. The underlined sentences have been added to clearly define each category before the detail is given.

	An Outline for a Classification Paragraph
topic sentence:	Phone calls can be grouped into the ones I want to get, the ones I don't want to get, and the ones I really don't want to get.
category 1	<u>There are some calls I really want to receive.</u>
details	They make me feel close to someone. I like calls from my boyfriend, especially when he calls just to say he is thinking of me. I like to hear from good friends. I like catch-up calls. These are calls from people I haven't talked to in a while.
category 2	<u>There are some calls I don't want.</u>
details	These calls invade my privacy. Sales calls always come at dinner time. They offer me newspaper subscriptions or "free" vacations. I get at least four wrong number calls each week. All these calls irritate me, and I have to interrupt what I'm doing to answer them.
category 3	<u>There are some calls I really don't want to receive.</u>
details	They are the calls that tell me about some bad change in my life. I once got a call in the middle of the night. It was from a hospital emergency room. The nurse said my brother had been in an accident. I once got a call from a boyfriend. He said he wanted to break up.

When you make your own classification outline, you can use the guidelines that follow as a check.

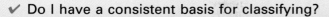

> ## A Checklist for Revising the Classification Outline
>
> ✔ Do I have a consistent basis for classifying?
> ✔ Does my topic sentence mention what I'm classifying and indicate the basis for classification?
> ✔ Do I have enough to say about each category in my classification?
> ✔ Are the categories presented in the most effective order?
> ✔ Am I using clear and specific detail?

With a revised outline, you can begin the roughlines stage of your writing.

▶ **E X E R C I S E 1: Recognizing the Basis for Classification within the Topic Sentence**

The topic sentences below do not state a basis for classification, but you can recognize the basis nevertheless. After you've read each topic sentence, write the basis for classification on the lines provided. The first one is done for you.

a. topic sentence: Neighbors can be classified into complete strangers, acquaintances, and buddies.

basis for classification: *how well you know them*

b. topic sentence: Men who wear earrings can be grouped in The One-Earring Type, The Two-Earring Type, and The Three-or-More-Earring Type.

basis for classification: _____

c. topic sentence: Dates can be categorized as those who pay the check, those who split the check, and those who "forget" their money.

basis for classification: _____

d. topic sentence: In the dog world, there are yipper-yappers, authoritative barkers, and boom-box barkers.

basis for classification: _____

e. topic sentence: At the Thai restaurant, you can order three kinds of hot sauce: hot sauce for beginners, hot sauce for the adventurous, and hot sauce for fire eaters.

basis for classification: _____

f. topic sentence: When it comes to photographs of yourself, there are three types: the ones that make you look good, the ones that make you look fat, and the ones that make you look ridiculous.

basis for classification: _____

g. topic sentence: Beer commercials on television can be grouped into the ones with pretty women, the ones with celebrities, and the ones with good buddies having good times.

basis for classification: _____

► EXERCISE 2: Collaborative Exercise in Adding Detail to an Outline

Do this exercise with a partner or group. In this rough outline, add detail where the blank lines indicate. Match the points covered in the other categories.

topic sentence: My friends can be categorized as best friends, good friends, and casual friends.

details: I know my best friends so well they are like family.
I have two best friends.
We talk about everything, from our problems to our secret ambitions.
I have known my best friends for years.
I can spend time with my best friends any time, good or bad.
I am close to my good friends, but not that close.

I have about six good friends.

_____

I have known all my good friends for at least a year.
I like to be around good friends when I'm in a good mood and want to share it.
Casual friends are people I like but am not close to.
I have about a dozen casual friends.

_____

_____

I like to be around casual friends when I am in a large crowd, so I feel less alone.

ⓡOUGHLINES: CLASSIFICATION

You can transform your outline into a first draft of a paragraph by writing the topic sentence and the detail in paragraph form. As you write, you can begin combining some of the short sentences and adding detail. You can add transitions to make the connections smoother. Various transitions can be used in a classification paragraph. The transitions you select will depend on what you are classifying and the basis you choose for classifying. For example, if you are classifying roses according to how pretty they are, you can use transitions like, "One lovely kind of rose," and "Another, more beautiful kind," and "The most beautiful kind." In other classifications you can use transitions like "the first type," "another type," or "the final type." In revising your classification paragraph, use the transitions that most clearly connect your ideas.

As you write your own paragraph, you may want to refer to a "kind" or a "type." For variety, try other words like "class," "category," "group," "species," "form," or "version," but only use them if they are appropriate.

After you have a draft of your paragraph, you can revise and review it. The checklist below may help you with your revisions.

A Checklist for Revising the Draft of a Classification Paragraph

✔ Does my topic sentence include what I'm classifying?

✔ Does it indicate the basis of my classification?

✔ Should any of my sentences be combined?

✔ Do my transitions clearly connect my ideas?

✔ Should I add more details to any of the categories?

✔ Are the categories presented in the most effective order?

Following is a revised draft of the classification paragraph on phone calls with these changes from the outline:

- an introduction has been added, in front of the topic sentence, to make the paragraph smoother,
- some sentences have been combined,
- some detail has been added,
- transitions have been added, and
- a final sentence has been added, so that the paragraph makes a stronger point.

A Roughlines Revised Draft of a Classification Paragraph

    I get many phone calls, but they fit into three
types. Phone calls can be grouped into the ones I
want to get, the ones I don't want to get, and the
ones I really don't want to get. There are some
calls I really want to receive because they make me
feel close to someone. I like calls from my
boyfriend, especially when he calls just to say he
is thinking of me. I like to hear from my good
friends. I like catch-up calls, the calls from
people I haven't talked to in a while that fill me
in on what friends have been doing. There are also
calls I don't want because they invade my privacy.
Sales calls, offering me newspaper subscriptions and
"free" vacations, always come at dinner time. In
addition, I get at least four wrong number calls
each week. All these calls irritate me, and I have

> ```
> to interrupt what I'm doing to answer them. The more
> serious calls are the ones I really don't want to
> receive. They are the calls that tell me about some
> bad change in my life. Once, in the middle of the
> night, a call from a hospital emergency room told me
> my brother had been in an accident. Another time, a
> boyfriend called to tell me he wanted to break up.
> When I get bad news by phone, I realize that the
> telephone can bring frightening calls as well as
> friendly or irritating ones.
> ```

▶ **E X E R C I S E 1 : Combining Sentences for a Better Classification Paragraph**

The following paragraph has some short sentences that would be more effective if they were combined. Combine each pair of underlined sentences into one sentence. Write the new sentence in the space above the old ones. Be prepared to share your revisions with a group.

I categorize my junk mail according to how sneaky it is. <u>The first kind of junk mail isn't very sneaky at all. It looks like junk mail.</u> This kind of mail is obviously out to sell me something. It is a catalog or an envelope that has the name of the product right there, so I can see what's for sale. A second type of junk mail is more deceptive. <u>This type comes in an envelope. The envelope tells me I am a big winner in a sweepstakes.</u> I'm not sure what this letter is selling until I open the envelope. Last, and most sneaky, is the mail disguised to look like something important. <u>Some junk mail now comes in an envelope. The envelope says, "Important Tax Information."</u> It looks like an envelope from the Internal Revenue Service, but it's just another piece of junk mail. <u>Other junk mail is made to look like it contains a telegram. And some other sneaky junk mail is made to look like it contains a check.</u> All these tricks have made me more suspicious than ever about what comes in the mail.

▶ **E X E R C I S E 2 : Identifying Transitions in a Classification Paragraph**

Underline all the transitions in the following paragraph. The transitions may be words or groups of words.

I classify my jeans according to when and where I wear them. At the bottom of the list are the ragged, worn out old jeans I wear around the house—and *only* around the house. I wouldn't want to be seen in public in such disgraceful clothes. These jeans have holes in them, are faded, ripped, and out of style. But they are also comfortable and perfect for relaxing and for doing chores. My mid-level jeans are the ones I wear to school. These jeans are presentable looking, and they are a classic style. I've worn and washed them enough to soften them up, and they're perfect for long days of sitting at a desk or studying in the library. Finally, the highest class of jeans I have is my good jeans. I wear my good jeans to parties and clubs. They are stylish and new and carry the label of a trendy company. Yet I must admit they're a little stiff and tight. When it comes to jeans, I guess I have to give up comfort to get style.

FINAL LINES: CLASSIFICATION

Following are the revised outline, the revised draft, and the final lines version of the classification paragraph on phone calls. If you compare the roughlines version to the final lines version, you'll notice these changes:

- The first sentence has been rewritten so that it is less choppy.
- The topic sentence has been rewritten so that it is smoother and less repetitive.
- Some words have been eliminated and sentences rewritten so that they are not too wordy.
- The word choice has been refined: "bad change" has been replaced by "crisis," "someone" has been changed to "a person I care about," to make the details more precise.

Now review all three versions of the paragraph and trace its development.

Before you prepare the final lines of your own classification paragraph, check your latest draft for errors in spelling and punctuation, and for any errors made in typing or recopying.

An Outlines Version of a Classification Paragraph

topic sentence: Phone calls can be grouped into the ones I want to get, the ones I don't want to get, and the ones I really don't want to get.

details: There are some calls I really want to receive.
They make me feel close to someone.
I like calls from my boyfriend, especially when he calls just to say he is thinking of me.
I like to hear from good friends.
I like catch-up calls.

These are calls from people I haven't talked to in a while.
There are some calls I don't want.
These calls invade my privacy.
Sales calls always come at dinner time.
They offer me newspaper subscriptions or "free" vacations.
I get at least four wrong number calls each week.
All these calls irritate me, and I have to interrupt what I'm doing to answer them.
There are some calls I really don't want to receive.
They are the calls that tell me about some bad change in my life.
I once got a call in the middle of the night.
It was from a hospital emergency room.
The nurse said my brother had been in an accident.
I once got a call from a boyfriend.
He said he wanted to break up.

A Roughlines Version of a Classification Paragraph

I get many phone calls, but they fit into three types. Phone calls can be grouped into the ones I want to get, the ones I don't want to get, and the ones I really don't want to get. There are some calls I want to receive because they make me feel close to someone. I like calls from my boyfriend, especially when he calls just to say he is thinking of me. I like to hear from my good friends. I like catch-up calls, the calls from people I haven't talked to in a while that fill me in on what friends have been doing. There are also calls I don't want because they invade my privacy. Sales calls, offering me newspaper subscriptions or "free" vacations, always come at dinner time. In addition, I get at least four wrong number calls each week. All these calls irritate me, and I have to interrupt what I'm doing to answer them. The more serious calls are the ones I really don't want to receive. They are the calls that tell me about some

ALONG THESE LINES/Prentice-Hall, Inc.

bad change in my life. Once, in the middle of the
night, a call from a hospital emergency room told
me my brother had been in an accident. Another time,
a boyfriend called to tell me he wanted to break
up. When I get bad news by phone, I realize the
telephone can bring frightening calls as well as
friendly or irritating ones.

**A Final Lines Version of a
Classification Paragraph**
(Changes from the roughlines
version are underlined.)

    I get many phone calls, but most of them fall
into one of three types. My phone calls can be
grouped into the ones I want to get, the ones I'd
rather avoid, and the ones I dread. There are some
calls I want to receive because they make me feel
close to a person I care about. I like calls from my
boyfriend, especially when he calls just to say he
is thinking of me. I like to hear from my good
friends. I like catch-up calls from friends I
haven't talked to in a while. There are also calls I
don't want because they invade my privacy. Sales
calls, offering me newspaper subscriptions and "free"
vacations, always come at dinner time. In addition,
I get at least four wrong number calls each week.
All these calls irritate me, and I have to interrupt
what I'm doing to answer them. The more serious
calls are the ones I really don't want to receive.
They are the calls that tell me about some crisis in
my life. I once got a midnight call from a hospital
emergency room, informing me my brother had been in
an accident. Another time, a boyfriend called to
tell me he wanted to break up. When I get bad news
by phone, I realize that the telephone can bring
frightening calls as well as friendly or irritating
ones.

► **EXERCISE 1:** **Correcting Errors in a Final Lines Version
of a Classification Paragraph**

After you've read the following paragraph, reread it and correct any errors by
writing above the lines.

    My experince in school has shown me their are three kinds of pencils, and
they are the pencils that work great, the pencils that barely work, and the pencils that dont work at all. The pencil's that work are the ones that are per-

fectly sharpened to a razor-fine point and have huge, clean erasers at the end. These pencils produce a dark, clear line when I write with them unfortunatly, I never do write with them. Great pencils are the ones I always come accross, all over the house, when i'm looking for something else. The pencils I usually rite with are the damaged pencils. They work, but not well. They need sharpening, or their erasers are worn so far down that using them leaves rips across the page. Sometimes these pencils leave a faded, weak line on the paper. Sometimes the line is so thick it look like a crayon. The third kind of pencl is the worst of all. Pencils in this group just don't work. They have no point. Or if they have a point, it brakes off as soon as I write. They have no eraser. The pencils are so chewed and mutilated they might have been previously owned by woodpeckers. Non-working pencils are the ones I bring to class on test days. I just do'nt seem to have much luck with pencils.

Lines of Detail: A Walk-Through Assignment

Write a paragraph that classifies bosses on the basis of how they treat their employees. To write the paragraph, follow these steps.

Step 1: List all the detail you can remember about bosses you have worked for or known.

Step 2: Survey your list. Then list three categories of bosses, based on how they treat their employees.

Step 3: Now that you have three categories, study your list again, looking for matching points for all three categories. For example, all three categories could be described by this matching point: where the boss works.

Step 4: Write a topic sentence that (a) names what you are classifying, and (b) states the basis for classification or names all three categories.

Step 5: Write an outline. Check that your outline defines each category, uses matching points for each category, and puts the categories in an effective order.

Step 6: In the roughlines stage, write a draft of the classification paragraph. Check the draft, revising it until it has specific detail, smooth transitions, and effective word choice.

Step 7: Before you prepare the final lines copy of your paragraph, check your last draft for any errors in punctuation, spelling, word choice, or mechanics.

Writing Your Own Classification Paragraph

When you write on any of these topics, be sure to work through the stages of thoughtlines, outlines, roughlines, and final lines.

ALONG THESE LINES/Prentice-Hall, Inc.

1. Write a classification paragraph on any of the following topics. If your instructor agrees, brainstorm with a partner or with a group to come up with (1) a basis for your classification, (2) categories related to the basis, and (3) points you can make to give details about each of the categories.

horror movies	cars
romantic movies	football players
children	fans at a concert
parents	fans at a sports event
students	neighbors
teachers	restaurants
drivers	dates
salespeople	cats
insects	dogs
excuses	fears
birthdays	weddings

2. Adapt one of the topics in question 1 by making your topic smaller. You can classify Chinese restaurants, for example, instead of restaurants, or sports cars, instead of cars. Then write a classification paragraph that helps your reader make a choice about your topic.

3. Following are some topics. Each one already has a basis for classification. Write a classification paragraph on one of these choices. If your instructor agrees, work with a partner or with a group to brainstorm categories, matching points and details for the categories.

Classify

a. exams on the basis of how difficult they are.

b. weekends on the basis of how busy they are.

c. valentines on the basis of how romantic they are.

d. breakfasts on the basis of how healthy they are.

e. skindivers (or some other sportspersons) on the basis of how experienced they are.

f. singers on the basis of the kind of audience they appeal to.

g. parties on the basis of how much fun they are.

h. television commercials on the basis of what time of day or night they are broadcast.

i. radio stations on the basis of what kind of music they play.

PEER REVIEW

Name: _____ **Section:** _____

Peer Review Form for a Classification Paragraph

After you've written a draft of your classification paragraph, let a writing partner read it. When your partner has completed the following form, discuss his or her comments. Then repeat the same process for your partner's paragraph.

This paragraph classifies

_____ (write the topic).

The basis for classification is according to

_____

_____

The matching points are

_____

_____

The part that could use more or better details is

_____

_____

I have questions about

_____

I would like to see something added about

_____

_____

I would like to take out the part about

_____

_____

The part of this paragraph I like best is

_____

_____

Other comments on the paragraph:

_____

_____

_____

Reviewer's name: _____

Writing from Reading: Classification

THREE DISCIPLINES FOR CHILDREN

John Holt

John Holt is an educator and activist who believes our system of education needs a major overhaul. In this essay, he classifies the ways children learn from their disciplines, and he warns against overusing one kind of discipline.

Before you read this essay, consider these questions:

Do you believe that children today need more parental control?
Do you believe that better discipline is needed in our schools?
Do you remember what your elementary school classes were like?
How do you learn best—by doing, seeing, or hearing?
Do you believe children learn by imitating adults?

Words You May Need to Know

discipline: the training effect of experience
impersonal: without personal or human connection
impartial: fair
indifferent: not biased, not prejudiced

wheedled: persuaded by flattery or coaxing
ritual: an established procedure, a ceremony
yield: give in to, submit
impotent: powerless

THREE DISCIPLINES FOR CHILDREN

John Holt

A child, in growing up, may meet and learn from three different kinds of disciplines. The first and the most important is what we might call the Discipline of Nature or of Reality. When he is trying to do something real, if he does the wrong thing or doesn't do the right one, he doesn't get the result he wants. If he doesn't pile one block right on top of another, or tries to build on a slanting surface, his tower falls down. If he hits the wrong key, he hears the wrong note. If he doesn't hit the nail squarely on the head, it bends, and he has to pull it out and start with another. If he doesn't measure properly what he is trying to build, it won't open, close, fit, stand up, fly, float, whistle, or do whatever he wants it to do. If he closes his eyes when he swings, he doesn't hit the ball. A child meets this kind of discipline every time he tries to *do* something, which is why it is so important in school to give children more chances to do things, instead of just reading or listening to someone talk (or pretending to). This discipline is a great teacher. The learner never has to wait long for his answer; it usually comes quickly, often instantly. Also it is clear, and very often points toward the needed correction; from what happened he cannot only see what he did was wrong, but also why, and what he needs to do instead. Finally, and most important, the giver of the answer, call it Nature, is impersonal, impartial, and indifferent. She does not give opinions, or make judgments; she cannot be wheedled, bullied, or fooled; she does not get angry or disappointed; she does not praise or blame; she does not remember past failures or hold grudges; with her one always gets a fresh start, this time is the one that counts.

The next discipline we might call the Discipline of Culture, of Society, of What People Really Do. Man is a social, a cultural animal. Children sense around them this culture, this network of agreements, customs, habits, and rules binding the adults together. They want to understand it and be a part of it. They watch very carefully what people around them are doing and want to do the same. They want to do right, unless they become convinced they can't do right. Thus children rarely misbehave seriously in church, but sit as quietly as they can. The example of all those grownups is contagious. Some mysterious ritual is going on, and children, who like rituals, want to be part of it. In the same way, the little children that I see at concerts or operas, though they may fidget a little, or perhaps take a nap now and then, rarely make any disturbance. With all those grownups sitting there, neither moving nor talking, it is the most natural thing in the world to imitate them. Children who live among adults who are habitually courteous to each other, and to them, will soon learn to be courteous. Children who live surrounded by people who speak a certain way will speak that way, however much we may try to tell them that speaking that way is bad or wrong.

The third discipline is the one most people mean when they speak of discipline—the Discipline of Superior Force, of sergeant to private, of "you do what I tell you or I'll make you wish you had." There is bound to be some of this in a child's life. Living as we do surrounded by things that can hurt children, or that children can hurt, we cannot avoid it. We can't afford to let a small child find out from experience the danger of playing in a busy street, or of fooling with the pots on the top of a stove, or of eating up the pills in the medicine cabinet. So, along with other precautions, we say to him, "Don't play in the street, or touch things on the stove, or go into the medicine cabinet, or I'll punish you." Between him and the danger too great for him to imagine we put a lesser danger, but one he can imagine and maybe therefore want to avoid. He can have no idea of what it would be like to be hit by a car, but he can imagine being shouted at, or spanked, or sent to his room. He avoids these substitutes for the greater danger until he can understand it and avoid it for its own sake. But we ought to use this discipline only when it is necessary to protect the life, health, safety, or well-being of people or other living creatures, or to prevent destruction of things that people care about. We ought not to assume too long, as we usually do, that a child cannot understand the real nature of the danger from which we want to protect him. The sooner he avoids the danger, not to escape our punishment, but as a matter of good sense, the better. He can learn that faster than we think. In Mexico, for example, where people drive their cars with a good deal of spirit, I saw many children no older than five or four walking unattended on the streets. They understood about cars, they knew what to do. A child whose life is full of the threat and fear of punishment is locked into babyhood. There is no way for him to grow up, to learn to take responsibility for his life and acts. Most important of all, we should not assume that having to yield to the threat of our superior force is good for the child's character. It is never good for anyone's character. To bow to superior force makes us feel impotent and cowardly for not having had the strength or courage to resist. Worse, it makes us resentful and vengeful. We can hardly wait to make someone pay for our humiliation, yield to us as we were once made to yield. No, if we cannot always avoid using the Discipline of Superior Force, we should at least use it as seldom as we can.

ALONG THESE LINES/Prentice-Hall, Inc.

Writing from Reading "Three Disciplines for Children"

When you write on any of the following topics, be sure to work through the stages of thoughtlines, outlines, roughlines, and final lines.

1. John Holt writes a very clear classification with a clear purpose: he is trying to explain how children should learn. Write a one-paragraph summary of the article. In your summary, include his definitions of all three categories of discipline and when they should be used.

2. Holt says that it is very important "in school to give children more chances to do things, instead of just reading or listening to someone talk."

   Write a paragraph classifying your elementary or high school classes according to how much they allowed you to do. Include your opinion of each category in the paragraph.

   If your instructor agrees, begin the thoughtlines part of this assignment with an interview. Ask a writing partner to interview you about your learning experiences, as a way of gathering ideas for this topic. Then do the same for your partner. Before any interviewing begins, write at least seven questions to ask your partner.

3. Holt says children want to understand society and to be a part of it: "They watch very carefully what people around them are doing and want to do the same."

   Write a paragraph classifying children according to the behavior they have learned from their parents. If your instructor agrees, freewrite on this topic, and then share your freewriting with a writing partner or with a group for reaction and further ideas.

4. Instead of classifying disciplines for children, write a paragraph classifying parents according to their attitudes toward their children.

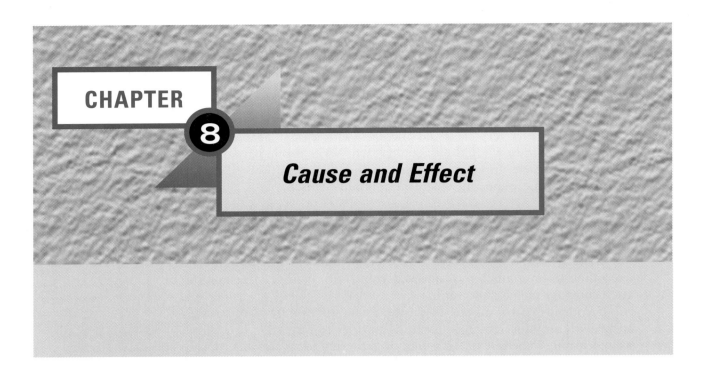

Cause and Effect

WHAT IS CAUSE AND EFFECT?

Almost every day, you consider the causes or effects of events so that you can make choices and take action. In writing a paragraph, when you explain the *reasons* for something, you are writing about *causes*. When you write about the *results* of something, you are writing about *effects*. Often in writing, you consider both the causes and effects of a decision, an event, a change in your life, or change in society, but in this chapter, you will be asked to concentrate on either causes (reasons) or effects (results).

Hints for Writing a Cause or Effect Paragraph

1. Pick a topic you can handle in one paragraph. A topic you can handle in one paragraph is one that (a) is *not too big*, and (b) *doesn't require research*.

Some topics are so large that you probably can't cover them in one paragraph. *Topics that are too big* include ones like

Why People Get Angry
Effects of Unemployment on My Family

Other topics require you to research the facts and to include the opinions of experts. They would be good topics for a research paper, but not for a one-paragraph assignment. *Topics that require research* include ones like

The Causes of Divorce
The Effects of Television Viewing on Children

When you write a cause or effect paragraph, choose a topic you can write about by using what you already know. That is, make your topic smaller and more personal. *Topics that use what you already know* are ones like

Why Children Love Video Games
The Causes of My Divorce
What Enlistment in the Navy Did for My Brother
How Alcoholics Anonymous Changed My Life

ALONG THESE LINES/Prentice-Hall, Inc.

2. Try to have at least three causes or effects in your paragraph. Be sure you consider immediate and remote causes or immediate and remote effects. Think about your topic and gather as many causes or effects as you can *before* you start drafting your paragraph.

An event usually has more than one cause. Think beyond the obvious, the *immediate cause*, to more *remote causes*. For example, the immediate cause of your car accident might be the other driver who hit the rear end of your car. But more remote causes might include the weather conditions or the condition of the road.

Situations can have more than one result, too. If you take Algebra I for the second time and you pass the course with a "C," an *immediate result* is that you fulfill the requirements for graduation. But there may be other, *more remote results*. Your success in Algebra may help to change your attitude towards mathematics courses. Or your success may build your confidence in your ability to handle college work. Or your success may lead you to sign up for another course taught by the same teacher.

3. Make your causes and effects clear and specific. If you are writing about why short haircuts are popular, don't write, "Short haircuts are popular because everybody is getting one," or "Short haircuts are popular because they're a trend." If you write either of these statements, you're really saying, "Short haircuts are popular because they're popular."

Think further. Have any celebrities been seen with this haircut? Write the names of actors, athletes, or musicians who have the haircut, or the name of the movie and the actor who started the trend. By giving specific details that explain, illustrate, or describe a cause or effect, you help the reader understand your point.

4. Write a topic sentence that indicates whether your paragraph is about causes or effects. You shouldn't announce, but you can *indicate*.

not this: The effects of my winning the scholarship are going to be
discussed. (an announcement)
but this: Winning the scholarship changed my plans for college. (indicates
effects will be discussed)

You can *list* a short version of all your causes or effects in your topic sentence, like this:

Frozen yogurt's popularity has forced ice cream makers to change their products, driven ice cream parlors out of business, and created a whole new line of dessert products.

You can *hint* at your points by summarizing them, like this:

Frozen yogurt's popularity has challenged and even threatened its competition, but it has also created new business opportunities.

Or you can use words that *signal* causes or effects.

words that signal causes: reasons, why, because, motives, intentions
words that signal effects: results, impact, consequences, changed, threatened, improved

▶ **E X E R C I S E　1:**　**Selecting a Suitable Topic for a Cause or Effect Paragraph**

Following is a list of topics. Some topics are suitable for a cause or effect paragraph. Some are too large to handle in one paragraph, some would require research, and some are both too large and would require research. Put an *X* next to any topic that is not suitable, and be prepared to discuss why the topic is not suitable for writing one paragraph.

Topics—Suitable and Not Suitable

a. _____ Why Children Fail in School

b. _____ Effects of Smoking Cigarettes

c. _____ Reasons I Attend College Part Time

d. _____ Why Kids Love Baseball

e. _____ The Impact of Computers on Education

f. _____ The Causes of Drug Abuse

g. _____ The Effects of AIDS on Our Society

h. _____ How Magic Johnson Changed My Perceptions of AIDS

i. _____ Why Marriages Fail

j. _____ The Causes of Anorexia

k. _____ The Effects of Nike Ads on Teens

l. _____ The Impact of Television on American Family Life.

▶ **EXERCISE 2:** **Recognizing Cause and Effect in Topic Sentences**

In the following list, if the topic sentence is for a cause paragraph, put a *C* next to it. If the sentence is for an effect paragraph, put an *E* next to it.

Topic Sentences for Cause or Effect Paragraphs

a. _____ Adopting a stray dog had startling consequences for my family.

b. _____ I decided to pierce my ears out of a desire to look different, to do something exciting, and to shock my parents.

c. _____ Jack has several motives for proposing marriage.

d. _____ Until I actually owned one, I never knew how a computer could change a person's work habits.

e. _____ The television's remote control device has created conflicts in my marriage.

f. _____ Children enjoy horror movies because the movies allow them to deal with their fears in a non-threatening way.

g. _____ People buy clothes with designer labels to impress others, to feel successful, and to feel accepted into a high social class.

h. _____ The birth of my little sister had an unexpected impact on my life.

i. _____ I am beginning to understand why my mother was a strict disciplinarian.

j. _____ Video cassette recorders have changed the movie industry.

WRITING THE CAUSE OR EFFECT PARAGRAPH IN STEPS

T HOUGHTLINES: CAUSE OR EFFECT

Once you've picked a topic, the next—and very important—step is getting ideas. Remember that you must have a sufficient number of causes or effects, along with specific details, to write a developed paragraph.

Freewriting on a Topic

One way to get ideas is to *freewrite* on your topic. Because causes and effects are clearly connected, you can begin by freewriting about both and then choose either causes or effects to write about, later.

If you were thinking about writing a cause or effect paragraph on owning a car, you could begin by freewriting something like this:

Freewriting on Owning a Car

A car of my own. Why? I needed it. Couldn't get a part-time job without one. Because I couldn't get to work. Needed it to get to school. Of course I could have taken the bus to school. But I didn't want to. Feel like a grown-up when you have a car of your own. Freedom to come and go. I was the last of my friends to have a car. Couldn't wait. An old Camaro. But I fixed it up nicely. Costs a lot to maintain. Car payments, car loan. Car insurance.

Now you can review the freewriting and make separate lists of causes and effects you wrote down:

Causes (Reasons)

needed to get a part-time job
needed to get to school
my friends had cars

Effects (Results)

feel like a grown-up
freedom to come and go
costs a lot to maintain
car payments
car loan
car insurance

Because you have more details on the effects of owning a car, you decide to write an effects paragraph.

Brainstorming and Interviewing for Ideas

Another way to get ideas is to brainstorm. Ask yourself questions about your topic. Start with a small number of questions (perhaps five), but try to use each question and answer to lead you to more questions and answers.

If you like, you can use the brainstorming technique with a partner or with a group. Ask another person or several people to interview you. Tape or jot down your answers. Start with five questions, but try to use each question and answer to lead you to more questions and answers. Soon, you will have a list of ideas.

Working with a List

Your list can be used several ways. You can add to it if you think of ideas as you are reviewing your list. You can begin to group ideas in your list and then add to it. On the list below, the ideas that fit together have * next to them:

Effects of Getting My Own Car

felt like a grown-up
* costs a lot to maintain
freedom to come and go
* car payments
* car loan

The ideas that fit together are all about the *costs* of owning a car. They are connected because one effect of owning a car is having to pay for it.

Look at the list again to see if you have at least three effects, with details, to write about.

> one effect: I had to pay for the car and related expenses.
> details: costs a lot to maintain
> car payments
> car loan
> car insurance
>
> second effect: I had the freedom to come and go.
> details: none
>
> third effect: I felt like a grown-up.
> details: none

Will these effects work in a paragraph? One way to decide is to try to add details to the effects that have no details. Now ask questions to get the details.

second effect: I had the freedom to come and go.
Question: What do you mean?
Answer: Well, I didn't have to beg my father for his truck anymore. I didn't have to get rides from friends. I could go to the city when I wanted. I could ride around just for fun.

third effect: I felt like a grown-up.
Question: What do you mean, "like a grown-up"?
Answer: Adults can go where they want, when they want. They drive themselves.

If you look carefully at the answers to the preceding questions, you'll find that the two effects are really *the same*. By adding details to both effects, you'll find that both are saying that owning a car gives you the adult freedom to come and go.

So the list needs *another effect* of owning a car. What else happened, how else did things change when you got your car? You might answer:

> I worried about someone hitting my car.
> I worried about bad drivers.
> I wanted to avoid the scratches you get in parking lots.

With answers like these, your *third effect* could be

> I became a more careful driver.

Now that you have three effects and some details, you can rewrite your list. You can add details as you rewrite.

> **List of Effects of Getting My Own Car**
>
> one effect: I had to pay for the car and related expenses.
> 　　details: costs a lot to maintain
> 　　　　　　car payments
> 　　　　　　car loans
> 　　　　　　car insurance
>
> second effect: I had the adult freedom to come and go.
> 　　　details: didn't have to beg my father for his truck
> 　　　　　　didn't have to get rides from friends
> 　　　　　　could go to the city when I wanted
> 　　　　　　could ride around for fun
>
> third effect: I became a more careful driver.
> 　　details: worried about someone hitting the car
> 　　　　　　worried about bad drivers
> 　　　　　　wanted to avoid the scratches cars get in parking
> 　　　　　　lots

Designing a Topic Sentence

With at least three effects and some details for each effect, you can create a topic sentence. The topic sentence for this paragraph should indicate that the subject is the *effects* of getting a car. You can summarize all three effects in your topic sentence, or you can just hint at them. A possible topic sentence for the paragraph can be

> Owning my own car cost me money, gave me freedom, and made me more careful about how I drive.

or

> Once I got a car of my own, I realized the good and bad sides of ownership.

With a topic sentence and a fairly extensive list of details, you are ready to begin the outlines step in preparing your paragraph.

E X E R C I S E

▶ **EXERCISE 1:** **Collaborating to Design Questions and Gather Details for a Cause or Effect Paragraph**

Following are three topics for cause or effect paragraphs. For each of the following topics, write five questions that could lead you to ideas on the topic. (The first one is a sample and is completed for you.) After you've written five questions for each topic, give your list to a member of your writing group. Ask him or her to add one question to each topic and then to pass the exercise on to the next member of the group. Repeat the process so that each group member adds to the lists of all the other members.

At the end of the process, take your copy of the exercise back. Each group member can read his or her own copy aloud. As the questions are read, add to your own list if you hear a question you'd like to remember.

Later, if your instructor agrees, you can answer the questions (and add more questions and answers) as a way to begin writing a cause or effect paragraph.

Topics for Cause or Effect Paragraphs

a. topic: the effects of expensive proms on high school students
questions that can lead to ideas and details:

1. Can all students afford to go to the prom?

2. What are the costs of a prom?

3. How much do male students pay for a prom?

4. How much do female students pay for a prom?

5. Do some students feel left out because they can't afford to go?

additional questions: Will proms get more expensive?

Will proms be eliminated?

Will proms become simpler and less expensive?

Are expensive proms worth it?

Do they give a special memory?

b. topic: why teenagers watch soap operas
questions that can lead to ideas and details:

1. _____

2. _____

3. _____

4. _____

5. _____

additional questions: _____

_____

_____

_____

c. **topic:** the effects of festival seating* at concerts
* festival seating is the policy of selling tickets that are *not* for assigned seats. That is, concertgoers usually stand, not sit, as close to the stage as possible.
questions that can lead to ideas and details:

1. _____

2. _____

3. _____

4. _____

5. _____

additional questions: _____

_____

_____

_____

d. **topic:** why Americans are eating more meals away from home
questions that could lead to ideas and details:

1. _____

2. _____

3. _____

4. _____

5. _____

additional questions: _____

_____

_____

_____

▶ **E X E R C I S E   2 :** **Creating Causes or Effects for Topic Sentences**

For each of the following topic sentences, create three causes or effects, depending on what the topic sentence requires. The first one is completed for you, as a sample. After you've completed the exercise, read your answers to a writing partner or to a group.

a. **topic sentence:** The telephone answering machine has both improved and complicated my life.

1. I don't miss important calls any more.

2. Now I have to deal with all the messages left on my answering machine.

3. I also have to decide whether to answer my phone or to "screen" calls when I am at home and the phone rings.

b. topic sentence: Small children may fear the dark for a number of reasons.

1. _____

_____

2. _____

_____

3. _____

_____

c. topic sentence: There are many reasons why teens join gangs.

1. _____

_____

2. _____

_____

3. _____

_____

d. topic sentence: Credit cards can have negative effects on those who use them.

1. _____

_____

2. _____

_____

3. _____

_____

e. topic sentence: Taking too many college courses at one time can have serious consequences.

1. _____

_____

2. _____

_____

3. _____

_____

OUTLINES: CAUSE OR EFFECT

With a topic sentence and a list of causes or effects, and details, you can draft a rough outline of your paragraph. Once you have a rough outline, you can work

ALONG THESE LINES/Prentice-Hall, Inc.

on revising it. You may want to add to it, take out certain ideas, rewrite the topic sentence, or change the order of the ideas. The checklist below may help you revise your outline.

> ## A Checklist for Revising the Outline of a Cause or Effect Paragraph
>
> ✔ Does my topic sentence make my point?
>
> ✔ Does it indicate whether my paragraph is about causes or effects?
>
> ✔ Does the topic sentence fit the rest of the outline?
>
> ✔ Have I included enough causes or effects to make my point?
>
> ✔ Have I included enough details?
>
> ✔ Should I eliminate any ideas?
>
> ✔ Is the order of my causes or effects clear and logical?

The Order of Causes or Effects

Looking at a draft outline can help you decide on the best order for your reasons or results. There is no single rule for organizing reasons or results. Instead, you should think about the ideas you are presenting and decide on the most logical and effective order. For example, if you are writing about some immediate and some long-range effects, you might want to discuss the effects in a *time order*. You might begin with the immediate effect, then discuss what happens later, and end with what happens last of all. If you are discussing three or four effects that are not in any particular time order, you might save the most important effect for last, for an *emphatic order*. If one cause leads to another, then use the *logical order* of discussing the causes.

In the outline below, notice that the carefree side of owning a car comes first, and the cares of owning a car, the expense and the worry, come later. The topic sentence follows the same order.

> ## An Outline for an Effects Paragraph
>
> | revised topic sentence | topic sentence: Owning my own car gave me freedom, cost me money, and made me careful about how I drive. |
> |---|---|
> | effect 1 | I had the adult freedom to come and go. I didn't have to beg my father for his truck. I didn't have to get rides from my friends. I could go to the city when I wanted. I could ride around for fun. |

effect 2 {
I had to pay for the car and related expenses.
A car costs a lot to maintain.
I had car payments.
I had a car loan to pay.
I had car insurance.

effect 3 {
I became a more careful driver.
I worried about someone hitting the car.
I worried about bad drivers.
I wanted to avoid the scratches cars can get in a parking lot.

Once you have a revised outline of your cause or effect paragraph, you are ready to begin the roughlines stage of writing.

▶ **E X E R C I S E   1 :** **Writing Topic Sentences for Cause or Effect Outlines**

Following are two outlines. They have no topic sentences. Read the outlines carefully, several times. Then write a topic sentence for each. If your instructor agrees, you can design the topic sentences by working with a partner or with a group.

a. topic sentence: _____

_____

_____

When I don't get enough sleep, I get irritable.
Little things, like my friend's wise remarks, make me angry.
At work, I am not as patient as I usually am when a customer complains.
Lack of sleep also slows me down.
When I'm tired, I can't think as fast.
For instance, it takes me ten minutes to find a number in the phone book when I can usually find one in a minute.
When I'm tired, I am slower in restocking the shelves at the store where I work.
Worst of all, I make more mistakes when I'm tired.
Last Monday, I was so tired I locked myself out of my car.
And a sleepless night can cause me to ring up a sale the wrong way.
Then I have to spend hours trying to fix my mistake before my boss catches it.

b. topic sentence:_____

_____

_____

Denise wasn't really interested in the things I like to do.
She hated sports.
She always complained when we went to football games together.
Denise was not much fun to be with.
Whenever we were together, we wound up fighting over some trivial thing.

For example, we once spent a whole evening fighting about what movie we should see.
My main reason for breaking up was Denise's lack of trust in me.
Denise couldn't believe I cared about her unless I showed her, every minute.
She made me call her at least three times a day.
She needed to know where I was at all times.
She was jealous of the time I spent away from her.

▶ **EXERCISE 2: Revising the Order of Causes or Effects**

Following are topic sentences and lists of causes or effects. Reorder each list according to the directions given at the end of the list. Put 1 by the item that would come first, and so forth.

a. topic sentence: My brother went on a diet for several reasons.

_____ He couldn't exercise for as long as he was used to.

_____ His clothes were too tight.

_____ A doctor told him his weight was raising his cholesterol to a dangerous level.

Use this order: From least important to most important.

b. topic sentence: Rappers started something when they began wearing baseball caps backward.

_____ Fans imitated the look.

_____ When rap became popular, fans noticed the caps.

_____ The caps started showing up on people who never listen to rap.

Use this order: Time order.

c. topic sentence: Losing my job had negative and positive effects on me.

_____ I was in a state of shock because I had no idea I'd be laid off.

_____ I eventually realized the job had been a dead-end job and I could do better.

_____ I went from shock to a feeling of failure.

Use this order: The order indicated by the topic sentence, from bad to good.

▶ **EXERCISE 3: Developing an Outline**

The following outlines need one more cause or effect and related details. Fill in the missing parts. When you've completed the exercise, share your answers with a writing partner or with a group.

a. topic sentence: Stress at work can lead to many emotional and physical problems.

effect: Stressed-out people get caught in a cycle of worry and stress.

details: When I am under stress at the office, for instance, I worry about getting everything done on deadline.

EXERCISE

The pressure to meet deadlines creates more stress and more worry for me.

effect: Stress can cause high blood pressure.

details: I know an executive who pushed herself to work twelve-hour days.
She never stopped working and never felt she was good enough.
She wound up in the hospital, where she was treated for dangerously high blood pressure.

third effect: _____

_____

details (at least two sentences): _____

_____

_____

_____

b. topic sentence: People look for mates in the personals columns for many reasons.

cause: It's hard to meet the right person in a bar or club.

details: Everyone in a bar or club is trying hard to look trendy or rich.
Conversation is often insincere or superficial.

cause: The personals columns allow people to screen their dates.

details: Those who write the ads can describe who they are and what they want in a mate.
For instance, the person who places the ad can say he or she is looking for someone who likes sports, or who doesn't smoke.
Those who answer personals have to send a letter describing themselves and often send a photo.

cause: _____

_____

details (at least two sentences): _____

_____

_____

_____

ⓇOUGHLINES: CAUSE OR EFFECT

Once you have an outline in good order, with a sufficient number of causes or effects and a fair number of details, you can write a first draft of the paragraph. When the first draft is complete, you can read and reread it, deciding how you'd like to improve it. The checklist that follows may help you revise.

ALONG THESE LINES/Prentice-Hall, Inc.

A Checklist for Revising the Roughlines Draft of a Cause or Effect Paragraph

✔ Does my topic sentence indicate cause or effect?

✔ Does it fit the rest of the paragraph?

✔ Do I have enough causes or effects to make my point?

✔ Do I have enough details for each cause or effect?

✔ Are my causes or effects explained clearly?

✔ Is there a clear connection between my points?

✔ Have I shown the links between my ideas?

✔ Do I need to combine sentences?

✔ Do I need an opening or closing sentence?

Linking Ideas in Cause or Effect

When you write about how one event or situation causes another, or about how one result leads to another, you have to be clear in showing the connections between events, situations, or effects. One way to be clear is to rely on transitions. Some transitions are particularly helpful in writing cause and effect paragraphs.

Transitions for a Cause or Effect Paragraph

For cause paragraphs: because, due to, for, for this reason, since

For effect paragraphs: as a result, consequently, hence, in consequence, then, therefore, thus, so

Making the Links Clear

Using the right transition word is not always enough to make your point. Sometimes you have to *write the missing link* in your line of thinking so that the reader can understand your point. To write the missing link means writing phrases, clauses, or sentences that help the reader follow your point.

> not this: Many mothers are working outside the home.
> Consequently, microwave ovens are popular.
> but this: Many mothers are working outside the home and have less time
> to cook. Consequently, microwave ovens, which can cook food in minutes,
> are popular.

The hard part of making clear links between ideas is that you have to put yourself in your reader's place. Remember that your reader cannot read your mind, only your paper. Connections between ideas may be clear in your mind, but you must spell them out on paper.

Revising the Draft

Following is the revised draft of the paragraph on owning a car. When you read it, you'll notice many changes from the outlines stage:

- The details on "car payments" and "a car loan" said the same thing, so the repetition has been cut out.
- Some details about the costs of maintaining a car and about parking have been added.
- The order of the details about the costs of a car has been changed. Now, paying for a car comes first, maintaining it comes after.
- Sentences have been combined.
- Transitions have been added.

**A Roughlines Revised Draft
of an Effects Paragraph**
(Transitions are underlined.)

Owning my own car gave me freedom, cost me money, and made me more careful about how I drive. <u>First of all</u>, my car gave me the adult freedom to come and go. I didn't have to beg my father for his truck or get rides from my friends anymore. I could go to the city or even ride around for fun when I wanted. <u>On the negative side,</u> I had to pay for the car and related expenses. I had to pay for the car loan. I also paid for car insurance. <u>A car costs a lot to maintain, too</u>. I paid for oil changes, tune ups, tires, belts, and filters. <u>With so much of my money put into my car,</u> I became a more careful driver. I worried about someone hitting the car and watched out for bad drivers. <u>In addition,</u> I wanted to avoid the scratches a car can get in a parking lot, so I always parked far away from other cars.

▶ **E X E R C I S E 1: Making the Connections Clear**

Following are ideas that are connected, but the connection is not clearly explained. Rewrite each pair of ideas, making the connection clear.

If your instructor agrees, share your answers with a partner or with a group to get reactions.

a. I had a bad attitude towards homework in high school. Therefore, I did poorly in my freshman college courses.

rewrite: _____

_____

_____

_____

(*hint:* Did the bad attitude follow you to college?)

b. People want stylish clothes. They don't have much money to spend. So they go to discount stores.

rewrite: _____

_____

_____

_____

(*hint:* Do discount stores offer style? Or cheaper clothes? Or both?)

c. I drank three cups of coffee last night. Consequently, I couldn't sleep.

rewrite: _____

_____

_____

_____

(*hint:* Do you usually or rarely drink coffee at night? What substance in the coffee kept you awake?)

d. Pine Tree College was nearer home than Lake College. As a result, I went to Pine Tree College.

rewrite: _____

_____

_____

_____

(*hint:* Did you want a college close to home? Did you want to save money by attending college and living at home? Did you want a shorter trip to school?)

▶ **E X E R C I S E 2: Revising a Paragraph by Adding Details**

Each of the following paragraphs is missing details. Add details—at least two sentences—to each paragraph.

If your instructor agrees, read your revisions to a partner or to a group.

a. I had good reasons for getting a German Shepherd. First of all, I have always had a dog, and I needed a dog when my collie, Buff, died. After I lost Buff, I just couldn't stand walking into an empty house. There was no excited buddy, wagging his tail, thrilled to see me. I missed the companionship of walking my dog, talking to my dog, playing with my dog. Second, German Shepherds are a breed I've always admired. They are fiercely loyal dogs, and they are extremely intelligent. My grandmother had a German Shepherd who was smarter than some people I know. My third reason for getting my shepherd was for security. _____

_____

_____

_____

_____

All in all, a shepherd was the breed that gave me the companionship, loyalty, intelligence, and security I wanted.

b. My first day of college had three significant effects on me. One effect was to reassure me. I had expected my teachers to be cold, formal, and distant. I was sure they would never stoop to being friendly to a mere freshman like me. But my teachers turned out to be friendly and warm, and they stressed their desire to meet with students during office hours. My reassurance was mixed with a second reaction, excitement. It was exciting to start a new part of my life and to see all the people and places I would be getting to know. Maybe the guy sitting next to me in English class would become a friend. Or maybe the girl in my art class would go out with me. My third reaction was less positive; it was fear._____

_____

_____

_____

So I was afraid on the first day, but I was also reassured and excited. Only time would tell how correct my first reactions had been.

▶ **EXERCISE 3:** **Revising a Draft by Combining Sentences**

Combine the underlined sentences in the following paragraph. Write your combinations in the space above the original sentences.

The latest television commercial is designed to make viewers think that freedom, excitement, and nature come with the car. First of all, the ad starts with a tired executive. The executive rips off his tie and leaps into his convertible. As he speeds out of the city, the viewers get a sense of freedom. The freedom is connected to a sense of excitement. The car zips past slower cars. Loud rock-'n-roll plays on the soundtrack. The car, a Nighthawk, races around curves and conquers dangerous corners. Soon, viewers see the ultimate effect of owning a Nighthawk. The car brings the executive to the middle of a green area. There is a gorgeous lake. Everything is unspoiled. The rock-'n-roll music fades away, and the only sounds heard are bird calls and gentle

EXERCISE

breezes. Truly, this commercial says, a new car can change viewers' lives. This ad is not really for a car; instead, it sells a dream of excitement and escape.

F INAL LINES: CAUSE OR EFFECT

Following are the revised outline, the revised draft, and the final version of the paragraph on owning a car. When you contrast the roughlines and final lines versions, you'll notice several changes:

- an introductory sentence has been added,
- some sentences have been combined,
- transitions have been revised, and
- some words have been changed so that the language is more precise.

Changes in style, word choice, sentence variety, and transitions can all be made before you decide on the final version of your paragraph. You may also want to add an opening or closing to your paragraph. Then, before you prepare the final lines copy of your paragraph, check your latest draft for errors in spelling and punctuation, and for any errors made in typing or recopying.

Look carefully at the outlines, roughlines, and final lines versions of the following effects paragraph so that you can see how it evolved.

An Outlines Version of an Effects Paragraph	
topic sentence:	Owning my own car gave me freedom, cost me money, and made me careful about how I drive.
details:	I had the adult freedom to come and go. I didn't have to beg my father for his truck. I didn't have to get rides from my friends. I could go to the city when I wanted. I could ride around for fun. I had to pay for the car and related expenses. A car costs a lot to maintain. I had car payments. I had a car loan to pay. I had car insurance. I became a more careful driver. I worried about someone hitting the car. I worried about bad drivers. I wanted to avoid the scratches cars can get in a parking lot.

A Roughlines Version of an Effects Paragraph

Owning my own car gave me freedom, cost me money, and made me careful about how I drive. First of all, my car gave me the adult freedom to come and go. I didn't have to beg my father for his truck or get rides from my friends anymore. I could go to the city or even ride around for fun when I wanted. On the negative side, I had to pay for the car and related expenses. I had to pay for the car loan. I also paid for car insurance. A car costs a lot to maintain, too. I paid for oil changes, tune ups, tires, belts, and filters. With so much of my money put into my car, I became a more careful driver. I worried about someone hitting the car and watched out for bad drivers. In addition, I wanted to avoid the scratches cars can get in a parking lot, so I always parked away from other cars.

A Final Lines Version of an Effects Paragraph
(Changes from the roughlines version are underlined.)

<u>When I bought my first car, I wasn't prepared for all the changes it made in my life.</u> Owning my own car gave me freedom, cost me money, and made me careful about how I drive. First of all, my car gave me the adult freedom to come and go. I didn't have to beg my father for his truck or get rides from my friends anymore. I could go to the city or even ride around for fun when I wanted. On the negative side, I had to pay for the car and related expenses. <u>I had to pay for both the car loan and car insurance</u>. A car costs <u>money</u> to maintain, too. I paid for oil changes, tune ups, tires, belts, and filters. With so much of my money put into my car, I became a more careful driver. I worried about someone hitting the car and watched out for bad drivers. <u>To avoid dangers in the parking lot as well as on the road</u>, I always parked <u>my car far</u> away from other cars, <u>keeping my car safe from scratches</u>.

▶ **EXERCISE 1:** Correcting a Final Copy of a Cause or Effect Paragraph

Following is a cause paragraph. It contains the kinds of errors that are easy to make in preparing the final lines copy of a paragraph. Correct all the errors in the lines above.

I signed up for an Introduction to Computers class this semster so that I could get some useful skills. One reason I took the Course is that I am thinking of bying a home computer to use for my college assinments. But if I don't know how to use a computer, what good would it do to own one. If I can learn to use a computer, I can learn word processing on it and do my college papers. Secondly, my ability to use a computer will help me at home. I have a freind who does her household accounts and stores financial information on her home computer another friend has a program that helps her plan her investments. The most important reason I am studing computers is that I think I get a better job if I know the basics of computers. Even though I am majoring in social work, not math, science, or buisness, a computer will be essential in my field. I'll use it to look up clients' records and to store data. I'll use it in research and writing. I think that, in the future, every job will require a knowlege of computer.

Lines of Detail: A Walk-Through Assignment

Write a paragraph on this topic: Why Americans are eating more meals away from home. To write your paragraph, follow these steps:

Step 1: Go back to Exercise 1 on page 219. Topic d is the same topic as this assignment. If you have already done that exercise, you have 5 or more questions that can lead you to ideas and details. If you haven't done the exercise, do part d now.

Step 2: Use the answers to your questions to prepare a list of ideas and details. Put the items on your list into groups of reasons and related details. Add to the groups until you have at least three reasons (and related details) why Americans are eating more meals away from home.

Step 3: Write a topic sentence that fits your reasons.

Step 4: Write an outline. Check that your outline has sufficient details and that you have put the reasons in the best order.

Step 5: Write a roughlines draft of your paragraph. Revise it until you have enough specific details to explain each reason, and the links between your ideas are smooth and clear. Check whether any sentences should be combined and whether your paragraph could use an opening sentence or a concluding one.

Step 6: Before you prepare the final lines copy of your paragraph, check your latest draft for word choice, punctuation, transitions, and spelling.

Writing Your Own Cause or Effect Paragraph

When you write on any of the topics below, be sure to work through the stages of thoughtlines, outlines, roughlines, and final lines.

1. Write a cause paragraph on one of the following topics. Create the topic by filling in the blanks.

   Why I Chose _____

   Why I Stopped _____

   Why I Enjoy _____

   Why I Started _____

   Why I Hate _____

   Why I Bought _____

   Why I Decided _____

2. Write a one-paragraph letter of complaint to the manufacturers of a product you bought or to the company that owns a hotel, restaurant, airline, or some other service you used. In your letter, write at least three reasons why you (1) want your money refunded or (2) want the product replaced. Be clear and specific about your reasons. Be sure your letter has a topic sentence.

   If your instructor agrees, read a draft of your letter to a writing partner, and ask your partner to pretend to be the manufacturer or the head of the company. Ask your partner to point out where your ideas are not clear or convincing and where you make your point effectively.

3. Think of a current fad or trend. The fad can be a popular style of clothing, a kind of movie, a kind of music, a sport, a pastime, an actor, an athlete, a gadget, an invention, or an appliance. Write a paragraph on the causes of this fad or trend or the effects of it.

   If your instructor agrees, begin by brainstorming with a group. Create a list of three or four fads or trends. Then create a list of questions to ask (and answer) about each fad or trend. If you are going to write about causes, for example, you might ask questions like

   What changes in society have encouraged this trend?
   Have changes in the economy helped to make it popular?
   Does it appeal to a specific age group? Why?
   Does it meet any hidden emotional needs? For instance, is it a way to gain status, or to feel safe, or powerful?

   If you are going to write about effects, you might ask questions like

   Will this trend last?
   Has it affected competitors?
   Is it spreading?
   Is the fad changing business, or education, or the family?
   Has it improved daily life?

ALONG THESE LINES/Prentice-Hall, Inc.

Name: _____   **Section:** _____

Peer Review Form for a Cause or Effect Paragraph

After you've written a roughlines version of your cause or effect paragraph, let a writing part-ner read it. When your partner has completed the following form, discuss the comments. Then repeat the same process for your partner's paragraph.

This is a cause paragraph/an effect paragraph. (Circle one.)

In this paragraph, the causes or effects are

_____

_____

_____

(Briefly list all of them.)

The topic sentence uses these words to indicate cause or effect:

_____

_____ (Write the exact words.)

The cause or effect that is most clearly explained is

_____

_____

I would like to see more detail added to

_____

_____

I have questions about

_____

_____

I would like to take out the part about

_____

_____

Other comments on the paragraph:

_____

_____

_____

_____

Reviewer's name: _____

Writing from Reading: Cause and Effect

STUDENTS IN SHOCK
John Kellmayer

John Kellmayer, an educator, explores the reasons why college students are stressed beyond their limits. He also discusses how colleges are reacting to student problems.

Before you read this selection, consider these questions:

Is college more stressful than you thought it would be?
Do you think many college students suffer from anxiety or depression?
Have you chosen a college major?
When you feel stressed out, who provides emotional support or advice?
Do you think college students today face more pressures than college students fifty years ago did?

Words You May Need to Know

warrant: demand, call for, require
magnitude: great importance
biofeedback: A method of monitor-
ing your blood pressure, heart rate, and so forth as a way of assessing and controlling stress

STUDENTS IN SHOCK
John Kellmayer

If you feel overwhelmed by your college experiences, you are not alone—many of today's college students are suffering from a form of shock. Going to college has always had its ups and downs, but today the "downs" of the college experience are more numerous and difficult, a fact that the schools are responding to with increased support services.

Lisa is a good example of a student in shock. She is an attractive, intelligent twenty-year-old college junior at a state university. Having been a straight-A student in high school and a member of the basketball and softball teams there, she remembers her high school days with fondness. Lisa was popular then and had a steady boyfriend for the last two years of school.

Now, only three years later, Lisa is miserable. She has changed her major four times already and is forced to hold down two part-time jobs in order to pay her tuition. She suffers from sleeping and eating disorders and believes she has no close friends. Sometimes she bursts out crying for no apparent reason. On more than one occasion, she has considered taking her own life.

Dan, too, suffers from student shock. He is nineteen and a freshman at a local community college. He began college as an accounting major but hated that field. So he switched to computer programming because he heard the job prospects were excellent in that area. Unfortunately, he discovered that he had little aptitude for programming and changed majors again, this time to psychology. He likes psychology but has heard horror stories about the difficulty of finding a job in that field without a graduate degree. Now he's considering switching majors again. To help pay for school, Dan works nights and weekends as a sales clerk at K-Mart. He doesn't get along with his boss, but since he needs the money, Dan feels he has no choice except to stay on the job. A few months ago, his girlfriend of a year and a half broke up with him.

Not surprisingly, Dan has started to suffer from depression and migraine headaches. He believes that in spite of all his hard work, he just isn't getting anywhere. He can't remember ever being this unhappy. A few times he considered talking to somebody in the college psychological counseling center. He rejected that idea, though, because he doesn't want people to think there's something wrong with him.

What is happening to Lisa and Dan happens to millions of college students each year. As a result, roughly one-quarter of the student population at any time will suffer from symptoms of depression. Of that group, almost half will experience depression intense enough to warrant professional help. At schools across the country, psychological counselors are booked up months in advance. Stress-related problems such as anxiety, migraine headaches, insomnia, anorexia, and bulimia are epidemic on college campuses. Suicide rates and self-inflicted injuries among college students are higher now than at any other time in history. The suicide rate among college youth is fifty percent higher than among nonstudents of the same age. It is estimated that each year more than five hundred college students take their own lives. College health officials believe that these reported problems represent only the tip of the iceberg. They fear that most students, like Lisa and Dan, suffer in silence.

There are three reasons today's college students are suffering more than in earlier generations. First is a weakening family support structure. The transition from high school to college has always been difficult, but in the past there was more family support to help get through it. Today, with divorce rates at a historical high and many parents experiencing their own psychological difficulties, the traditional family is not always available for guidance and support. And when students who do not find stability at home are bombarded with numerous new and stressful experiences, the results can be devastating.

Another problem college students face is financial pressure. In the last decade tuition costs have skyrocketed—up about sixty-six percent at public colleges and ninety percent at private schools. For students living away from home, costs range from five thousand dollars to as much as twelve thousand a year and more. And at the same time that tuition costs have been rising dramatically, there has been a cutback in federal aid to students. College loans are now much harder to obtain and are available only at near-market interest rates. Consequently, most college students must work at least part-time. And for some students, the pressure to do well in school while holding down a job is too much to handle.

A final cause of student shock is the large selection of majors available. Because of the magnitude and difficulty of choosing a major, college can prove a time of great indecision. Many students switch majors, some a number of times. As a result, it is becoming commonplace to take five or six years to get a degree. It can be depressing to students not only to have taken courses that don't count towards a degree but also to be faced with the added tuition costs. In some cases these costs become so high that they force students to drop out of college.

While there is no magic cure-all for student shock, colleges have begun to recognize the problem and are trying in a number of ways to help students cope with the pressures they face. First of all, many colleges are upgrading their psychological counseling centers to handle the greater demand for services. Additional staff is being hired, and experts are doing research to learn more about the psychological problems of college students. Some schools even advertise these services in student newspapers

ALONG THESE LINES/Prentice-Hall, Inc.

and on campus radio stations. Also, upperclassmen are being trained as peer counselors. These peer counselors may be able to act as a first line of defense in the battle for students' well-being by spotting and helping to solve problems before they become too big for students to handle. In addition, stress-management workshops have become common on college campuses. At these workshops, instructors teach students various techniques for dealing with stress, including biofeedback, meditation, and exercise.

Finally, many schools are improving their vocational counseling services. By giving students more relevant information about possible majors and career choices, colleges can lessen the anxiety and indecision often associated with choosing a major.

If you ever feel that you're "in shock," remember that your experience is not unique. Try to put things in perspective. Certainly, the end of a romance or failing an exam is not an event to look forward to. But realize that rejection and failure happen to everyone sooner or later. And don't be reluctant to talk to somebody about your problems. The useful services available on campus won't help you if you don't take advantage of them.

Writing from Reading "Students in Shock"

When you write on any of the following topics, be sure to work through the stages of thoughtlines, outlines, roughlines, and final lines.

1. Write a one-paragraph summary of "Students in Shock." Include the three significant reasons college students are in distress, and discuss how colleges are reacting to student stress. Remember to use logical and effective transitions throughout your summary.

2. Write a paragraph about the main causes of stress in your life. To begin, list everything that caused you stress in the past twenty-four hours. Don't think about whether the cause was minor or major; just list all the causes you can remember. If you felt stress waiting for a traffic light to change, for example, write it down.

   When you've completed your list, read it to a writing partner or to a group. Ask your listener(s) to help you identify three or more causes of stress in your life. Then work alone to prepare your paragraph.

3. Write a paragraph on the positive effects of your attending college. Be sure you have at least three effects.

4. Write a paragraph on the negative effects of your attending college. Be sure you include at least three effects.

5. Write a letter to your college instructors. Your letter will be a paragraph giving at least three reasons why students seem tired in class.

6. Stress has different effects on different people. Freewrite about the effects of college stress on you and people you know. Use your freewriting to plan and write a paragraph on the effects of college stress. Use your and your friends' experiences as examples of the different effects of college stress.

WHAT IS ARGUMENT?

A written argument is an attempt to *persuade* a reader to think or act in a certain way. When you write an argument paragraph, your goal is to get people to see your point, to agree with it, and perhaps to act on it.

In an argument paragraph, you take a stand. Then you support your stand with reasons. In addition, you give details for each reason. Your goal is to persuade your reader by making a point that has convincing reasons and details.

Hints for Writing an Argument Paragraph

1. Pick a topic you can handle. Your topic should be small enough to be covered in one paragraph. For instance, you can't argue effectively for world peace in just one paragraph. However, you may be able to argue effectively in favor of a cultural diversity celebration at your school.

2. Pick a topic you can handle based on your own experience and observation. Such topics as drug legalization, gun control, capital punishment, or acid rain require extensive research into facts, figures, and expert opinions to make a complete argument. They are topics you can write about convincingly in a longer research paper, but for a one-paragraph argument, pick a topic based on what you've experienced yourself.

not this topic: Organized Crime
but this topic: Starting a Crime Watch Program in My Neighborhood

3. Do two things in your topic sentence: Name the subject of your argument, and take a stand. The following topic sentences do both.

subject   takes a stand
The <u>college cafeteria should serve more healthy snacks.</u>

subject   takes a stand
<u>High school athletes who fail a course should not be allowed to play on a school team.</u>

You should take a stand, but *don't announce it*:

not this: This paragraph will explain why Springfield needs a teen center.
but this: Springfield should open a teen center. (A topic sentence with a subject and a stand.)

4. Consider your audience. Consider why these people should support your points. How will they be likely to object? How will you get around these objections? For instance, you might want to argue, to the residents of your community, that the intersection of Hawthorne Road and Sheridan Street needs a traffic light. Would anyone object?

At first, you might think, "No. Why would anyone object? The intersection is dangerous. There's too much traffic there. People risk major accidents getting across the intersection." But if you think further about your audience, which is the people in your community, you might identify these objections: Some town residents may not want to pay for a traffic signal. Some drivers may not want to spend extra time waiting for a light to change.

There are several ways to handle objections:

1. First, you can *refute* an objection. To refute it means to prove it isn't valid; it isn't true. For instance, if someone says that a light wouldn't do any good, you might say that a new light has already worked in a nearby neighborhood.

2. Sometimes it's best to admit that the other side has a point. You have to *concede* that point. For instance, traffic lights do cost money. And waiting for a light to change does take time.

3. Sometimes you can *turn an objection into an advantage*. When you acknowledge the objection and yet use it to make your own point, you show that you've intelligently considered both sides of the argument. For instance, you might say that the cost of a traffic signal at the intersection is well worth it because that light will buy safety for all the drivers who try to cross Hawthorne Road and Sheridan Street. Or you might say that waiting a few moments for the light to change is better than waiting many minutes for an opening in the heavy traffic of the intersection.

4. Be specific, clear, and logical in your reasons. As always, think before you write. Think about your point and your audience. Try to come up with at least three reasons for your position.

Be careful that your reasons do not overlap. For instance, you might write the following:

```
topic sentence: College students should get discounts
                on movie tickets.
      audience: Owners of movie theaters
       reasons: 1. Many college students can't afford
                current ticket prices.
                2. The cost of tickets is high for
                most students.
                3. More people in the theater means
                more popcorn and candy sold at the
                concession stand.
```

Notice that Reasons 1 and 2 overlap; they are really part of the same reason.

Be careful *not to argue in a circle*. For instance, if you say, "One reason for having an afterschool program at Riverside Elementary School is that we need one there," you've just said, "We need an afterschool program because we need an afterschool program."

Finally, *be specific in stating your reasons.*

not this: One reason to start a bus service to and from the college is to help people.

but this: A bus service to and from the college would encourage students to leave their cars at home and use travel time to study.

▶ **EXERCISE 1: Recognizing Good Topic Sentences in an Argument Paragraph**

Some of the following topic sentences are appropriate for an argument paragraph. Some are not appropriate. They are for topics that are too large for one paragraph, require research, are announcements, or do not take a stand. Put OK next to the sentences that would work well in an argument paragraph.

If your instructor agrees, discuss your answers with a writing group, identifying the specific problem in each sentence that is not marked OK.

a. _____ People should try to cure their own addictions.

b. _____ The empty lot by the post office is a serious problem.

c. _____ We must ban offshore oil drilling in American waters.

d. _____ Bicycle safety should be taught at Deerfield Elementary School.

e. _____ We need stricter penalties for criminals.

f. _____ Something should be done about victims' rights.

g. _____ The City Parks and Recreation Department should put more picnic tables at Veterans' Park.

h. _____ The Savings and Loan scandal shows the need for stricter banking laws.

i. _____ National Federal Savings Bank should be open on Saturday so that working people can do their banking.

j. _____ The reasons to ban skateboarding at Miller Mall will be the subject of this essay.

▶ **EXERCISE 2: Collaborative Exercise in Recognizing and Handling Objections**

Following are topic sentences of arguments. Working with a group, list two possible objections to each argument that might come from the specific audience identified. Then think of ways to handle each objection, either by refuting it, or conceding it, or trying to turn it to your advantage. On the lines provided, write the actual sentence(s) you would use in a paragraph.

a. topic sentence: The college library, which is currently open until 10 p.m., should be open until midnight every night.

audience: the deans, the vice president and the president of the college

possible objections from this audience:

1. _____

2. _____

answering objections:

1. _____

   _____

2. _____

   _____

b. topic sentence: The local mall [you pick a specific mall] needs more security officers to patrol inside and outside the mall.

audience: the owners of the mall

possible objections from this audience:

1. _____
2. _____

answering objections:

1. _____

   _____

2. _____

   _____

c. topic sentence: Atlantic Township should ban parking at the beach parking lot after midnight.

audience: teen residents of Atlantic Township

possible objections from this audience:

1. _____
2. _____

answering objections:

1. _____

   _____

2. _____

   _____

d. topic sentence: The Crispy Donut Shop should stop serving coffee in styrofoam cups.

audience: the owners of the Crispy Donut Shop

possible objections from this audience:

1. _____
2. _____

answering objections:

1. _____

   _____

ALONG THESE LINES/Prentice-Hall, Inc.

2. _____

_____

e. topic sentence: Local day-care centers should be required, by law, to provide one adult supervisor for every two children under the age of one year.

audience: The owners of the Happy Child Day-care Center, which currently has one adult supervisor for every three children under the age of one year.

possible objections from this audience:

1. _____

2. _____

answering objections:

1. _____

_____

2. _____

_____

WRITING THE ARGUMENT PARAGRAPH IN STEPS

❚T❚HOUGHTLINES: ARGUMENT

Imagine that your instructor has given you this assignment:

> Write a one-paragraph letter to the editor of your local newspaper. Argue for something in your town that needs to be changed.

One way to begin is to *brainstorm* for some specific point that you can write about.

> Is there a part of town that needs to be cleaned up?
> Should something be changed at a school?
> What do I notice on my way to work, or school, that needs improvement?
> What could be improved in my neighborhood?

By answering these questions, you may come up with one topic, and then you can list ideas on it.

> topic: Cleaning up Roberts Park
> ideas: dirty and overgrown
>   benches are all cracked and broken
>   full of trash
>   could be fixed up
>   I work nearby
>   I'd use it

You can consider your audience and possible objections:

audience: Local people of all ages who read the local paper.
possible objections from this audience:
    Would cost money
    More important things to spend money on
answering objections:
    Money would be well spent to beautify the downtown.
    City children could play there in the fresh air and in nature; workers could eat lunch there.

Grouping Your Ideas

Once you have a list, you can start grouping the ideas in your list. Some of the objections you wrote down may actually lead you to reasons that support your argument. That is, by answering objections, you may come up with reasons that support your point. Following is a possible list for an argument, some supporting reasons, and some details about cleaning up Roberts Park.

A Rough List for an Argument Paragraph

point: We should clean up Roberts Park.
reason: Would make the downtown area more attractive.
details: ?
reason: City children could play there.
details: get fresh air
       not have to play in traffic
       play in natural setting
reason: Workers could eat lunch outdoors.
details: I work nearby.
       I'd eat there.

One part of this list needs attention. The reason, "Would make the downtown area more attractive," has no details and isn't specific. That is, the reason seems to overlap the point of the argument. If a downtown park is cleaned up, which is the point of the argument, obviously the downtown will be more attractive.

Brainstorming for Clarity and Details

To come up with a more specific reason and better details, you might brainstorm with a series of questions:

Who will be attracted to the downtown area?
Why is it important to make the downtown area attractive?
What will happen if the downtown area looks better?

By answering these questions, you can improve your list of reasons and details.

A Revised List for an Argument Paragraph

point: We should clean up Roberts Park.
reason: Improving the park would make the downtown area more attractive to shoppers.
details: Shoppers could stroll in the park or rest from their shopping.
       Friends could meet in the park for a day of shopping and lunch.
reason: City children could play in the park.

details: They could get fresh air.
          They could play in a natural setting.
reason: Workers could eat lunch outdoors.
details: I work nearby.
          I'd eat outside.

With three reasons and some details for each, you can draft a topic sentence. Remember that your topic sentence for an argument should (1) *name your subject*, and (2) *take a stand*. Following is a topic sentence about Roberts Park that does both.

    subject   takes a stand
<u>Roberts Park should be cleaned up and improved.</u>

With a topic sentence, you are ready to move on to the outlines stage of preparing an argument paragraph.

▶ **E X E R C I S E   1 :   Distinguishing between Reasons and Details**

Each of the following lists has three reasons supporting the topic sentence. There are also details for each reason. First, find the reasons and label them Reason 1, Reason 2, and Reason 3. Then find the details and label them either Detail 1, Detail 2, or Detail 3 to match each reason.

    a. topic sentence: The city needs to pick up garbage at my apartment complex three times, not twice, a week.

_____ Garbage spills out past the dumpster.

_____ People throw their garbage on top of already loaded dumpsters; the bags fall and split open.

_____ Garbage that piles up, uncovered, is a health hazard.

_____ Too much garbage accumulates when the schedule allows for only two pickups.

_____ Flies buzz over the garbage, a sign of dangerous contamination that can spread.

_____ The roaches from the garbage area move into the apartments, carrying disease.

_____ Trash piles make people lose pride in their neighborhood.

_____ Apartment residents are starting to litter the parking lot because they've lost respect for their homes.

_____ One long-time resident is thinking of moving to a better neighborhood.

    b. topic sentence: Children under ten years of age should not be permitted in the Mountain Mall unless they are accompanied by an adult.

_____ It is not safe for children to be alone in the mall.

_____ Unsupervised children cause trouble for mall
                          merchants.

_____ Children left alone in the mall are not always
                          happy with their freedom.

_____ I saw one nine-year-old boy roam the mall for
                          hours, looking forlorn.

_____ Sometimes pairs of sad, young girls wait by the
                          food court for an hour, until Mom, who is
                          "late," remembers to pick them up.

_____ Once I saw two seven-year-old boys walk back
                          and forth in front of my store for half an hour,
                          with nothing to do.

_____ Children have been kidnapped in malls.

_____ If a child gets sick at the mall, will he or she
                          know what to do?

_____ Bored children run through stores, chasing each
                          other.

_____ I saw one child shoplifting.

▶ **E X E R C I S E 2 : Collaborative Exercise in Finding Reasons
                          to Support an Argument**

Working with a partner or with a group, give three reasons that support each
point. In each case, the readers of your local newspaper will be the audience for
an argument paragraph.

    a. point: The state should ban all telephone sales calls between the hours
               of 5 p.m. and 8 p.m.

    reasons: 1. _____

              2. _____

              3. _____

    b. point: Our state must ban the ultra-dark window tinting of cars and
               trucks.

    reasons: 1. _____

              2. _____

              3. _____

    c. point: Parenting should be a required course for all high school
               students.

    reasons: 1. _____

              2. _____

              3. _____

E X E R C I S E

d. point: Dogs should not be permitted on the public beach.

reasons: 1. _____

2. _____

3. _____

OUTLINES: ARGUMENT

With a topic sentence and a list of reasons and details, you can draft an outline. Then you can review it, making whatever changes you think it needs. The following checklist may help you to review and revise your outline.

A Checklist for Revising an Argument Outline

✔ Does my topic sentence make my point? Does it state a subject and take a stand?

✔ Have I considered the objections to my argument so that I am arguing intelligently?

✔ Do I have all the reasons I need to make my point?

✔ Do any reasons overlap?

✔ Are my reasons specific?

✔ Do I have enough details for each reason?

✔ Are my reasons in the best order?

The Order of Reasons in an Argument

When you are giving several reasons, it is a good idea to keep the most convincing or most important reason for last. Saving the best for last is called using *emphatic* order. For example, you might have these three reasons to tear down an abandoned building in your neighborhood: (1) The building is ugly, (2) Drug dealers are using the building, and (3) The building is infested with rats. The most important reason, the drug dealing, should be used last, for an emphatic order.

Following is a revised version of the outline on improving Roberts Park. When you look at the revised outline, you'll notice *several changes* from the thoughtlines list:

- Since the safety of children at play is important, it is put as the last detail.
- Some details have been added.
- A sentence has been added to the end of the outline. It explains why improving the park is a good idea even to people who will never use the park themselves. It is a way of answering their objections.

ALONG THESE LINES/Prentice-Hall, Inc.

E X E R C I S E

An Outline for an Argument Paragraph

topic sentence:	Roberts Park should be cleaned up and improved.
reason:	Improving the park would make the downtown area more attractive to shoppers.
details:	Shoppers could stroll through the park or rest there after shopping. Friends could meet at the park for a day of shopping and lunch.
reason:	Workers from nearby offices and stores could eat lunch outdoors.
details:	I work in a bank nearby. I'd eat outside. An hour outdoors is a pleasant break from work.
reason:	City children could play there.
details:	They would get fresh air. They would play on grass, not on asphalt. They would not have to play near traffic.
final idea:	An attractive park improves the city, and all residents benefit when the community is beautified.

▶ **E X E R C I S E 1 :** **Working with the Order of Reasons in an Argument Outline**

Following are topic sentences and lists of reasons. For each list, put an *X* by the reason that is the most significant, the reason you would save for last in an argument paragraph.

   a. topic sentence: Manufacturers of vitamins should stop the double packaging of their products.

reason 1. _____ Putting a small jar into a big box is deceptive, making the buyer think he or she is getting more for their money.

reason 2. _____ Buyers get irritated trying to open both a box and a jar.

reason 3. _____ Double packaging wastes valuable natural resources.

   b. topic sentence: Our city should permit a snack bar to open at Greenwood Lake.

reason 1. _____ Visitors to the lake would appreciate the chance to buy hot dogs, potato chips, and soda.

reason 2. _____ There are no restaurants or stores near the lake.

reason 3. _____ The profits from the snack bar could be used to maintain the natural beauty of the lake area, which looks seedy.

c. topic sentence: Parents should not let their children play in the sun for hours.

reason 1. _____ Too much sun in childhood can lead to skin cancer later in life.

reason 2. _____ Too much sun, even in childhood, can cause premature wrinkling in adults.

reason 3. _____ The sun can cause headaches and irritability in all age groups.

d. topic sentence: Seven-year-olds should be given a small allowance, to spend as they wish.

reason 1. _____ Seven-year-olds see other children their age with spending money.

reason 2. _____ Children need to learn to handle money responsibly.

reason 3. _____ Learning to make change develops math skills.

▶ **E X E R C I S E 2 : Recognizing Reasons That Overlap**

Following are topic sentences and lists of reasons. In each list, two reasons overlap. Put an X by the two reasons that overlap.

a. topic sentence: The college cafeteria should lower its prices.

1. _____ Prices are too high for most students.

2. _____ Lower prices would actually mean a profit for the cafeteria because more students would use it.

3. _____ Many students can't afford to eat in the cafeteria.

4. _____ The cafeteria has to compete with nearby, cheaper restaurants.

b. topic sentence: Advertising should be banned from all children's Saturday morning TV programs.

1. _____ Young children are too innocent to know the way advertising works.

2. _____ Much advertising is for unhealthy food, like sugary cereals and junk food.

3. _____ Advertising manipulates unsuspecting children.

4. _____ Toy commercials push expensive toys that many parents cannot afford.

c. topic sentence: Our college needs a larger, lighted sign at the entrance.

1. _____ Some residents of our town have never heard of our college, so a large sign would be good publicity.

2. _____ Visitors to the college have a hard time finding it.

3. _____ Students who are preoccupied sometimes drive right past the entrance to their college at night.

4. _____ A better sign would make people more aware of the college.

▶ **EXERCISE 3:** **Identifying a Reason That is Not Specific**

In each of the following lists put an *X* by the reason that is not specific.

a. **topic sentence:** The senior class should hold a Senior Citizens' Day, and bring elderly people to school for a day of fun and entertainment.

1. _____ Teenagers would enjoy talking to older people, especially since many teens do not have much contact with their own grand-parents.

2. _____ Planning a day's entertainment would teach teens how to organize a major event.

3. _____ The older people would benefit from the day.

4. _____ Each generation would learn not to stereotype the other.

b. **topic sentence:** American college students should learn a foreign language.

1. _____ Countries that compete with us economically, like Japan and Germany, have a competitive edge because their children routinely learn English.

2. _____ It is often easier for a person to get a good job when he or she speaks two languages.

3. _____ Learning a new language broadens a person's horizons.

4. _____ Most Americans, at home or at work, have to interact with immigrants or visitors who do not speak English.

c. **topic sentence:** Our college should open a fitness center in the gym.

1. _____ Health clubs are too expensive for many students.

2. _____ A fitness center would be good for students.

3. _____ Students who have an hour or two between classes could work out in the gym.

4. _____ Students who were new to the college could make friends by using the fitness center.

▶ **EXERCISE 4:** **Adding Details to an Outline**

Following is part of an outline. It includes a topic sentence and three reasons. Add at least two sentences of detail to each reason. Your details may be examples or descriptions.

topic sentence: The staff at Bargain Supermarket should enforce the "9 Items or Less" rule at the Express Checkout lane.

reason: Customers who follow the rule must suffer because of people who don't obey the rule.

detail:_____

_____

detail:_____

_____

reason: Not enforcing the rule can create unpleasant confrontations among customers.

detail:_____

_____

detail:_____

_____

reason: If it doesn't enforce the rule, Bargain Supermarket may lose customers.

detail:_____

_____

detail:_____

_____

ROUGHLINES: ARGUMENT

Once you are satisfied with your outline, you can write the first draft of your paragraph. When you have completed it, you can begin revising the draft so that your argument is clear, smooth, and convincing. The checklist below may help you with your revisions.

A Checklist for Revising the Roughlines Draft of an Argument Paragraph

- ✔ Do any of my sentences need combining?
- ✔ Have I left out a serious or obvious reason?
- ✔ Should I change the order of my reasons?
- ✔ Do I have enough details?
- ✔ Are my details specific?
- ✔ Do I need to explain the problem or issue I am writing about?
- ✔ Do I need to link my ideas more clearly?
- ✔ Do I need a final sentence to stress my point?

Checking Your Reasons

Be sure that your argument has covered all the serious or obvious reasons. Sometimes writers get so caught up in drafting their ideas that they forget to mention something very basic to the argument. For instance, if you were arguing for a leash law for your community, you might give the reason that dogs who run free can hurt people and damage property. But don't forget to mention another serious reason to keep dogs on leashes: Dogs that are not restrained can get hurt or killed.

One way to see if you have left out a serious or obvious reason is to ask a friend or classmate to read your draft and to react to your argument. Another technique is to put your draft aside for an hour or two and then read it as if you were a reader, not the writer.

Explaining the Problem or the Issue

Sometimes your argument discusses a problem so obvious to your audience that you don't need to explain it. On the other hand, sometimes you need to explain a problem or issue so your audience can understand your point. If you tell readers of your local paper about teenage vandalism at Central High School, you probably need to explain what kind of vandalism has occurred there and how often. Sometimes it's smart to convince readers of the seriousness of a situation by giving them background information, so they'll be more persuaded by your argument.

Transitions That Emphasize

In writing an argument paragraph, you can use any transition, depending on how you present your point. But no matter how you present your reasons, you will probably want to *emphasize* one of them. Following are some transitions that can be used for emphasis.

Transitions to Use for Emphasis: above all, especially, finally, mainly, most important, most of all, most significant, primarily

---

For example, by saying, "*Most important,* broken windows at Central High School are a safety problem," you put the emphasis for your audience on this one idea.

A Revised Draft

Following is a revised draft of the argument paragraph on Roberts Park. When you read it, you'll notice these changes from the outline:

- A description of the problem has been added.
- Details have been added.
- Short sentences have been combined.
- Transitions, including two sentences of transition, have been added. "Most important" and "Best of all"—transitions that show emphasis—have been included.

A Roughlines Revised Draft of an Argument Paragraph
(Transitions are underlined.)

Roberts Park was once a pretty little park, but today it is overgrown with weeds, cluttered with trash and rusty benches. Roberts Park should be cleaned up and improved. Improving the park would make the downtown area more attractive to shoppers. Shoppers could stroll through a renovated park or rest there after shopping. Friends could <u>also</u> meet there for a day of shopping and lunch. <u>Shoppers are not the only ones who could enjoy the park.</u> Workers from nearby offices and stores could eat lunch outdoors. I work in a bank near the park, and I would bring my lunch to work and eat outside in good weather. I think many people would agree that an hour spent outdoors is a pleasant break from work. <u>Most important</u>, city children could play in an improved Roberts Park. They would get fresh air while they played on grass, not asphalt. <u>Best of all</u>, they would not have to play near traffic. <u>Children, shoppers, and workers would benefit from a clean-up of Roberts Park, but so would others.</u> An attractive park improves the city, and all residents benefit when a community is beautified.

▶ **EXERCISE 1:** **Adding an Explanation of the Problem to an Argument Paragraph**

This paragraph could use an explanation of the problem. Write a short explanation of the problem in the lines provided. When you have completed it, be ready to share it with a group or with the class.

Crystal Springs Apartments should get rid of its speed bumps. The majority of the residents at Crystal Springs did not want the bumps. They were installed without a vote of the residents. If the management at the apartments had asked the residents to vote, most residents would have voted against the bumps. Residents dislike the bumps because the structures can damage cars. Even when a driver drives at the speed limit, he or she can wreck the alignment of a car because the bumps are very high. More serious damage can occur if a driver drives just five miles over the speed limit. Worst of all, the bumps, which were installed for safety reasons, are creating safety hazards. Drivers are avoiding the bumps by swerving onto the grass. Residents who walk through the apartment complex are in danger of being hit by drivers who swerve onto the lawn. Clearly, the bumps have not improved life at Crystal Springs Apartments; they have made it worse.

Explanation:_____

_____

_____

▶ E X E R C I S E 2 : **Recognizing Transitions in an Argument Paragraph**

Underline all the transitions—words, phrases, or sentences—in the following paragraph. Put a double line under any transitions that emphasize.

Every time I go into my favorite restaurant, I am greeted by a server who hands me a menu and then puts a glass of ice water on the table. I need one of those items, the menu, but I <u>may not</u> need the water. Restaurants should not give customers a glass of water unless the customers request it. For one thing, giving everyone a glass of water wastes water. Most people order some kind of drink, like iced tea or Pepsi, and they don't touch the water. At the end of the meal, the water is thrown down the drain. Our whole country is trying to conserve our natural resources, and yet we waste all this water. Water is not the only thing we'd save if restaurants stopped giving it routinely. We'd save energy. The glasses holding all that water need to be washed. Running the dishwasher takes electricity. More glasses mean more use of the dishwasher. More important than conserving water or energy is the message the new policy would send. If customers had to ask for their water, they'd think about the restaurant's reason for not providing it: conservation. People who think about saving water or energy may think about how they can save water or electricity at home. And so a simple restaurant policy can do a little towards saving our earth.

▶ E X E R C I S E 3 : **Adding a Final Sentence to an Argument Paragraph**

The following paragraph can use a final sentence to sum up the reasons or to reinforce the topic sentence. Add that final sentence. Be prepared to share your sentence with a group or with the class.

My boyfriend is away at basic training for the Marines. He calls me often, and I love his calls. But I wish he would write me letters. People who are away from their loved ones should write letters if they want to show they care. It's easy to pick up the phone, but writing a letter takes more effort. A letter shows me the writer spent some time thinking about me and about what to tell me. Taking that time is a way of telling me I'm special. A letter can also say things a speaker can't. Sometimes it's hard to say "I'm sorry" or "I miss you" on the phone. But words of intimacy can be easier to write than to say. Most important, a letter can be read over and over. The words last. I can carry a letter with me, or hide it in a special place, and every time I read it, I can feel close to the writer.

_____

_____

_____

ALONG THESE LINES/Prentice-Hall, Inc.

Ⓕ**INAL LINES:** ARGUMENT

Following are the revised outline, the revised draft, and the final lines version of the argument paragraph on Roberts Park. When you read the final lines version, you'll notice several changes from the draft version:

- Some words have been changed to improve the detail.
- The first sentence has been changed so that it is more descriptive and uses a parallel pattern for emphasis.

Look carefully at all three stages of the paragraph to see how it evolved.

Before you prepare the final lines copy of your argument paragraph, check your latest draft for errors in spelling and punctuation, and look for any errors made in typing or recopying.

An Outlines Version of an Argument Paragraph

topic sentence: Roberts Park should be cleaned up and improved.

details: Improving the park would make the downtown area more attractive to shoppers.
Shoppers could stroll through the park and rest there after shopping.
Friends could meet at the park for a day of shopping and lunch.
Workers from nearby offices and stores could eat lunch outdoors.
I work in a bank nearby.
I'd eat outside.
An hour outdoors is a pleasant break from work.
City children could play there.
They would play on grass, not on asphalt.
They would not have to play near traffic.
An attractive park improves the city, and all residents benefit when the community is beautified.

A Roughlines Version of an Argument Paragraph

Roberts Park was once a pretty little park, but today it is overgrown with weeds, cluttered with trash and rusty benches. Roberts Park should be cleaned up and improved. Improving the park would make the downtown area more attractive to shoppers. Shoppers could stroll through a renovated park or rest there after shopping. Friends could also meet at the park for a day of shopping and lunch. Shoppers are not the only ones who could enjoy the park. Workers from nearby offices and stores could eat lunch outdoors. I work in a bank near the park, and I would bring my lunch to work and eat outside in good weather. I think many people would agree that an hour spent outdoors is a pleasant break from work. Most important, city children could play in an improved Roberts Park. They would get fresh air while they played on grass, not asphalt. Best of all, they would not have to play near traffic. Children, shoppers, and workers would benefit from a clean-up of Roberts Park, but so would others. An attractive park improves the city, and all residents benefit when a community is beautified.

A Final Lines Version of an Argument Paragraph
(Changes from the roughlines version are underlined.)

Roberts Park was once a pretty little park, but today it is overgrown with weeds, <u>littered with trash, and cluttered with rusty benches.</u> Roberts Park should be cleaned up and improved. Improving the park would make the downtown area more attractive to shoppers. Shoppers could stroll through a <u>restored</u> park or rest there after shopping. Friends could also meet at the park for a day of shopping and lunch. Shoppers are not the only ones who could enjoy the park. Workers from nearby offices and stores could eat lunch outdoors. I work in a bank near the park, and I would bring <u>a bag</u> lunch to work and eat outside in good weather. I think many people would agree that an hour spent outdoors is a pleasant break from work. Most important, city children could play in an improved Roberts Park. They would get fresh air while they played on grass, not asphalt. Best of all, they would not have to play near traffic. Children, shoppers, and workers would benefit from a clean-up of Roberts Park, but so would others. An attractive park improves the city, and all residents benefit when a community is beautified.

ALONG THESE LINES/Prentice-Hall, Inc.

▶ **E X E R C I S E 1 : Proofreading an Argument Paragraph**

Following is a final lines copy of a paragraph. It contains the kinds of errors that are easy to overlook in a final copy. Correct the errors in the lines above each error.

Our college should put a pencil sharpener in every classroom. First of all putting a sharpener in each class would help many students. Most student take notes and tests in pencil. Often, a pencil point breaks or gets worn down while a student is writing. A pencil sharpener in the room takes care of the problem. Secondly, a pencil sharpner would eliminate distractions in class. For instance, I was in my math class yesterday when my pencil point broke. I did'nt have another pencil, and there was no sharpener in the room. I had to interrupt the lesson to ask to borow a pencil. last of all, a pencil sharpner in each room would solve the problem of wandering students. At least once a day, a student comes into one of my classes, politely asking, "Does this room have a pencil sharpener? Its embarrassing to have to do this. And its worse to wander desperately threw the halls, trying to find one of the few rooms with a sharpener. Pencil sharpeners wouldn't cost the college much, but they would sure make a diference.

Lines of Detail: A Walk-Through Assignment

Write a one-paragraph letter to the editor of your local newspaper. Argue for some change you want for your community. You could argue for a traffic light, turn signal, or stop sign at a specific intersection. Or you could argue for bike paths in certain places, a recycling program, more bus service, or for any other specific change you feel is needed. To write your paragraph, follow these steps:

Step 1: Begin by listing all the reasons and details you can think of, on your topic. Survey your list and consider any possible objections. Answer the objections as well as you can, and see if the objections can lead you to more reasons.

Step 2: Group your reasons, listing the details that fit under each reason. Add details where they are needed and check to see if any reasons overlap.

Step 3: Survey the reasons and details and draft a topic sentence. Be sure that your topic sentence states the subject and takes a stand.

Step 4: Write an outline. Then revise it, checking that you have enough reasons to make your point. Also check that your reasons are specific and in an effective order. Be sure that you have sufficient details for each reason. Check that your outline includes answers to any significant objections.

Step 5: Write a draft of your argument. Revise the draft until it includes any necessary explanations of the problem being argued, all serious or obvious reasons, and sufficient specific details. Also check that the most important reason is stated last. Add all the transitions that are needed to link your reasons and details.

Step 6: Before you prepare the final lines copy of your paragraph, decide whether you need a final sentence to stress you point and whether your transitions are smooth and logical. Refine your word choice. Then check for errors in spelling, punctuation, and grammar.

Writing Your Own Argument Paragraph

When you write on any of the following topics, be sure to work through the stages of thoughtlines, outlines, roughlines, and final lines.

1. Write a paragraph for readers of your local newspaper, arguing for one of the following:

   a. a ban on all advertising of alcohol
   b. mandatory jail terms for those convicted of drunk driving
   c. a ban on smoking in all public, enclosed places

2. In a paragraph, argue one of the following topics to the audience specified. If your instructor agrees, brainstorm your topic with a group before you start writing. Ask the group to "play audience," reacting to your reasons, raising objections, asking questions.

   Topic a.   Early morning classes should be abolished at your college.
   Audience: The Dean of Academic Affairs

   Topic b.   Attendance in college classes should be optional.
   Audience: The instructors at your college

   Topic c.   College students should get discounts at movie theaters.
   Audience: The owner of your local movie theater

   Topic d.   Your college should provide a day-care facility for students with children.
   Audience: The president of your college

   Topic e.   Businesses should hire more student interns.
   Audience: The president of a company (name it) you'd like to work for

3. Write a paragraph for or against any of the following topics. Your audience for the argument is your classmates and your instructor.

For or Against

   a. seat belt laws
   b. ratings for music CDs and tapes
   c. dress codes in high school
   d. uniforms in elementary schools
   e. mandatory student activities fees for commuter students

Name: _____   **Section:** _____

Peer Review Form for an Argument Paragraph

After you've written a roughlines version of your argument paragraph, let a writing partner read it. When your partner has completed the following form, discuss his or her comments. Then repeat the same process for your partner's paragraph.

The topic sentence has this subject:

_____

It takes this stand:

_____

The most convincing part of the paragraph started with the words _____

and ended with the words _____.

After reading this paragraph, I can think of an objection to this argument. The objection is

_____

_____

The paragraph has/has not handled this objection. (Pick one.)

The part of the argument with the best details is the part about

_____

The part that could use more or better details is

_____

_____

The order of reasons (a) is effective (b) could be better. (Pick one.)

I have questions about

_____

_____

Other comments on the paragraph:

_____

_____

_____

_____

_____

_____

Reviewer's name: _____

Writing from Reading: Argument

THE MYTH OF COMPUTER LITERACY
Douglas Noble

Douglas Noble, a former teacher and computer programmer, argues that a knowledge of computers is not as important as many people think.

Before you read this selection, consider these questions:

Have computers made your work or studies easier? More difficult?
Or have they had little effect?
Do computers create new jobs? Do they eliminate jobs?
Do you expect to use a computer in your career?
Can computers invade your privacy?

Words You May Need to Know

infrastructure: underlying framework
insinuates: introduces, injects
clamor: cry, demand
dubious: doubtful
acquiescence: submission

dissent: disagreement, opposition
propaganda: information spread to promote a cause
nostalgia: a longing for the experiences and things of the past

THE MYTH OF COMPUTER LITERACY
Douglas Noble

We are witnessing the creation of an enormous computer education infrastructure in this country. As the computer insinuates itself further and further into our jobs and our lives, the need for everyone to acquire some form of computer literacy (CL) is coming to be accepted as reasonable. Failure to learn to use computers, we are told again and again, will leave one functionally illiterate, devoid of the skills needed to survive in the "information society."

The great justification of the CL movement is that high-tech jobs require high-tech skills. Early in this century, the introduction of machinery made many unskilled jobs semiskilled; just so, we are told, the introduction of computers will transform many jobs into "knowledge work" requiring computer proficiency. True, computers are being introduced into millions of jobs, but it hardly follows that those jobs will become intellectually more demanding. In fact, the contrary is more often the case: the jobs become deskilled and less creative.

It is also important to realize that many jobs are simply eliminated by computers and that a large part of the service sector will remain unaffected by them. The majority of jobs that will be affected call for a level of computer expertise that can be acquired in a week or two of practical instruction. In the computer field itself, the number and quality of jobs has been greatly overstated, and anyway, a computer literacy course is hardly preparation for a career in programming.

If, as I have suggested, the practical claims for computer literacy are nonsense, how has the movement gotten so far? Whose interests does it serve? Certainly those of the hardware and software manufacturers—the cry for computer literacy is nothing if not a good way to sell computers. And the educational establishment stands to benefit from the clamor for computer courses. But the real weavers of CL's dubious cloth are the prime movers behind the computerized society itself—the corporate leaders and their ideological allies who mean to transform the workplace, the home, and the school into an efficient, highly controlled, and easily monitored technological marketplace. The makers of the "information society" have perpetrated the CL movement in order to ensure public acquiescence in their grand design.

How does the computer literacy movement ensure this acquiescence? First, it introduces people to computers, gives them some hands-on experience, and deludes them into thinking that all computers are as friendly as their little micro. In this way, computer literacy mystifies in the name of demystification.

Second, as manufacturers and designers produce computers that are ever more user-friendly, so CL helps "produce" people who are ever more computer-friendly. A person who is familiar with a school computer or, even better, who has a personal computer at home is less likely to be apprehensive about a computerized society than a person who is uninitiated.

Third, computer literacy helps ensure public acquiescence in the information society by psychologizing dissent. Anyone who is reluctant to get involved with computers is labeled "computerphobic."

The unequivocal message of CL propaganda is this: Computers are important, very important, and learning about them is equally important. This propaganda portrays the computer society as inevitable and, in the process, suggests that any misgivings about it amount to nothing more than nostalgia. Add to this a fervent appeal to national prestige, along with a challenge to overcome our foreign competition, and it becomes hard to find anyone who will even admit the possibility that all this computer talk may be exaggerated. But the relative unimportance of computer knowledge must be stated plainly and often so people will see that the picture of the future woven into the CL tapestry remains essentially a fiction.

Writing from Reading "The Myth of Computer Literacy"

When you write on any of the following topics, be sure to work through the stages of thoughtlines, outlines, roughlines, and final lines in preparing your paragraph.

1. Using your personal experience for reasons and details, argue one of the following topics:

   a. Writing with a computer can make a person a better writer.
   b. Writing with a computer can make it easier to write.
   c. Writing with a computer has little effect on the quality of a person's writing.

   Your audience is your classmates and your instructor.

2. Douglas Noble argues that not all computers are friendly. Write a paragraph that argues one of the following topic sentences. Your audience is your classmates and your instructor.

   a. Computerization of records can violate your privacy.
   b. The Internet can be a source of family problems.
   c. Computers are taking jobs from people.
   d. E-mail can be a dangerous tool.

If your instructor agrees, begin by brainstorming one of the sentences. Share your knowledge and experiences, ask questions, write reasons and details. Use brainstorming to begin the thoughtlines stage of writing.

3. Technology is changing the way people work. Fax machines and computers, for example, have made it possible for many people to work at home rather than at an office. However, working at home has drawbacks as well as benefits. Write a paragraph arguing one of the following to an audience of your classmates and your instructor:

   a. Working at home makes workers' jobs harder and more stressful than ever.
   b. Working at home gives workers greater freedom and flexibility.

4. Investigate how, when, and where computers are available to students on your campus. Then argue for a specific improvement in the availability of computers. You may want to argue for more computers, or for extended hours in a computer lab. Your audience is the academic dean of your campus.

5. Noble says that many jobs are unaffected by computers. If you work or have worked at a job that requires computer literacy, argue that a knowledge of computers is an essential skill in today's workplace. Use your experiences to develop reasons and details. Your audience is your classmates and your instructor.

6. Write a paragraph arguing one of the following to an audience of your classmates and your instructor:

   a. Computers can enhance your creativity.
   b. Home computers are expensive toys.
   c. Most people don't need computers.

7. Write a paragraph arguing that every college student should take a computer literacy course in his or her first semester. Your audience is the readers of the college newspaper, which includes students, teachers, and administrators.

   Begin your assignment by listing all the ways that computers are linked to college learning, such as computerized library resources, writing labs, and so forth. Then list careers that may require a knowledge of computers. Survey the list of ideas for those that can become reasons.

AFROCENTRIC EDUCATION POINTLESS IF GIRLS ARE EXCLUDED
Julianne Malveaux

Julianne Malveaux is a professor of African-American Studies at the University of California at Berkeley. In this editorial, she explores a recent move to create schools exclusively for black males. She identifies several problems with such schools, particularly their impact on black females.

Before you read this selection, consider these questions:

Do you think black males should have their own schools? Why or why not? Do you think schools should be allowed to limit their enrollment to one race?

ALONG THESE LINES/Prentice-Hall, Inc.

Do you believe in all-male or all-female schools?

Do you think female teachers can teach males effectively?

Do you think male teachers can teach females effectively?

If you are male, would you consider attending an all-male college, military, or technical institute?

If you are female, would you consider attending an all-female college, military, or technical institute?

Do you think boys who are raised by single mothers grow up with a disadvantage?

Words You May Need to Know

Afrocentric: centered on African-American history, culture, and concerns

ACLU: The American Civil Liberties Union, a national organization that fights to maintain constitutional rights

NOW: The National Organization for Women, a group that supports women's rights

role models: people that others may try to imitate, heroes

gnaws: eats away, wears away, wastes

curriculum: a course of study, a plan of study in school

denigrate: put down, speak damagingly of

implicitly: in a hidden manner, without saying so openly

proponents: supporters

stigmatizing: branding, giving a mark of disgrace

parochial school: an elementary, middle, or high school operated by a religious organization

addressed: dealt with, paid attention to

AFROCENTRIC EDUCATION POINTLESS IF GIRLS ARE EXCLUDED
Julianne Malveaux

They have been proposed in New York and Milwaukee, and public schools just for black boys were supposed to open in Detroit this fall but were stopped by a successful lawsuit filed by the ACLU and the NOW Legal Defense Fund. A federal judge ruled that the Detroit plan for three all-male academies was unconstitutional.

Why should black boys have their own schools? Those who support them say black men are "endangered" and cite statistics on dropout status and arrest rates to back themselves up. They say that too many black boys, raised by their mothers, lack positive male role models and are all too vulnerable to negative influences, like gangs.

They say that the public school curriculum ignores black achievement and gnaws away at self-esteem, and that an Afrocentric curriculum taught by black men is necessary to rebuild this esteem for black boys. And they say these schools address some of these problems.

But every problem that black boys face is also faced by black girls. Girls rarely are arrested, but they, too, drop out and get caught up in all of the urban negatives—teen pregnancy, dead-end careers and sometimes worse. Like black boys, many black girls would benefit from male attention and positive male role models. Like boys, they are vulnerable to gangs and others in the absence of those models. And girls, like boys, read books that denigrate African Americans, those histories that mention only Booker T. Washington, Dr. Martin Luther King, or blacks in the context of slavery.

Black girls, like black boys, would greatly benefit from an improvement in the quality of urban education. These girls are sent a stunning negative message when they observe a shift in resources from all students to male students. They are being told, implicitly, that their educations are less important than black male educations.

Proponents of all-black boy schools, like Chicago author Juwanza Kunjufu, would not only segregate students. Kunjufu, alleging that "black women cannot teach black men," would also make teaching environments almost entirely male. Yet if Kunjufu is right, if black women can't teach black men, then the illiteracy rate among African Americans would be even higher than it is now, as black women teachers have historically been the backbone of urban school systems.

Those who say black boys need their own schools are crying "crisis." Their argument does not stand up unless we believe that the black man is "endangered." To protect against "endangered species" status, these boys bond under the leadership of African-American male teachers.

But these separate schools seem simply to reinforce the notion of "endangerment," stigmatizing black male youngsters and separating them from the general school population. And it sends these boys the message that something is so wrong with girls and women that they are incapable or learning in their presence!

The existence of all-black boy schools suggests that black boys are special, but black girls are not. And this is a message girls may carry through womanhood. If black boys/men are so special, must black women support them financially when they cannot find work? Should they put up with violent or abusive behavior because the black man is so special? Should she cling to traditional roles to please this "special" man? Should she make her needs secondary to his?

Because of students' different capabilities, there is no one model of education that serves every child. Some learn best in a highly disciplined parochial or military school, others in loosely structured programs for the gifted and talented.

Under the umbrella of education, there may well be room for Afrocentric academies targeted toward black male youth. But these academies may cause more problems than they solve unless the educational needs of black girls are also addressed.

Writing from Reading "Afrocentric Education Pointless if Girls Are Excluded"

1. Write a one-paragraph summary of Malveaux's article. Focus on the point of her argument and the details she uses to support her point.

2. Write an argument for or against any one of the following. Your audience is your classmates and instructor.

   all-male schools   all-female schools
   all-male colleges   all-female colleges
   all-male military colleges all-male clubs
   all-female clubs

ALONG THESE LINES/Prentice-Hall, Inc.

3. Write an argument that agrees or disagrees with any of the statements below. You can support your argument with reasons or specific examples. Your audience is your classmates and instructor.

The public school curriculum ignores black achievement.
Black women cannot teach black males.
Black boys need their own schools.

WHAT IS AN ESSAY?

You write an *essay* when you have more to say than can be covered in one paragraph. An essay can be one paragraph, but in this book, we take it to mean a writing of more than one paragraph. An essay has a main point, called a *thesis*, which is supported by subpoints. The subpoints are the *topic sentences*. Each paragraph in the *body*, or main part, of the essay has a topic sentence. In fact, every paragraph in the body of an essay is like the paragraphs you've already written because each one makes a point and then supports it.

COMPARING THE SINGLE PARAGRAPH AND THE ESSAY

Read the paragraph and the essay that follow, both about Bob, the writer's brother. You'll notice many similarities.

A Sample Single Paragraph

```
     I think I'm lucky to have a brother who is two years
older than I am. For one thing, my brother Bob fought
all the typical child-parent battles, and I was the
real winner. Bob was the one who made my parents under-
stand that seventeen-year-olds shouldn't have an 11 p.m.
curfew on weekends. He fought for his rights. By the
time I turned seventeen, my parents had accepted the
later curfew, and I didn't have to fight for it. Bob
also paved the way for me at school. He was such a great
athlete that I benefited from his reputation. When I
tried out for the basketball team, I had an advantage
before I hit the court. I was Bob Cruz's younger
```

ALONG THESE LINES/Prentice-Hall, Inc.

brother, so the coach thought I had to be pretty good. At home and at school, my big brother was a big help to me.

A Sample Essay

Some people complain about being the youngest child or the middle child in the family. These people believe older children get all the attention and grab all the power. I'm the younger brother in my family, and I disagree with the complainers. I think I'm lucky to have a brother who is two years older than I am.

For one thing, my brother Bob fought all the typical child-parent battles, and I was the real winner. Bob was the one who made my parents understand that seventeen-year-olds shouldn't have an 11 p.m. curfew on weekends. He fought for his rights, and the fighting wasn't easy. I remember months of arguments between Bob and my parents as Bob tried to explain that not all teens on the street at 11:30 are punks or criminals. Bob was the one who suffered from being grounded or who lost the use of my father's car. By the time I turned seventeen, my parents had accepted the later curfew, and I didn't have to fight for it.

Bob also paved the way for me at school. Because he was so popular with the other students and the teachers, he created a positive image of what the boys in our family were like. When I started school, I walked into a place where people were ready to like me, just as they liked Bob. I remember the first day of class when the teachers read the new class rolls. When they got to my name, they asked, "Are you Bob Cruz's brother?" When I said yes, they smiled. Bob's success opened doors for me in school sports, too. He was such a great athlete that I benefited from his reputation. When I tried out for the basketball team, I had an advantage before I hit the court. I was Bob Cruz's younger brother, so the coach thought I had to be pretty good.

I had many battles to fight as I grew up. Like all children, I had to struggle to gain independence and respect. In my struggles at home and at school, my big brother was a big help to me.

If you read the two sample selections carefully, you noticed that they make the same main point, and they support that point with two subpoints.

main point: I think I'm lucky to have a brother who is two years older than I am.

subpoints: 1. My brother Bob fought all the typical child-parent battles, and I was the real winner.
2. Bob also paved the way at school.

ALONG THESE LINES/Prentice-Hall, Inc.

You'll notice that the essay is longer because it has more details and examples to support the points.

ORGANIZING AN ESSAY

When you write an essay of more than one paragraph, the *thesis* is the focus of your entire essay; it is the major point of your essay. The other important points that are part of the thesis are in topic sentences.

Thesis: Working as a salesperson has changed my character.

Topic sentence: I have had to learn patience.
Topic sentence: I have developed the ability to listen.
Topic sentence: I have become more tactful.

Notice that the thesis expresses a bigger idea than the topic sentences following it, and that it is supported by the topic sentences. The essay has an introduction, a body, and a conclusion.

1. *Introduction:* The first paragraph is usually the introduction. The thesis goes here.
2. *Body:* This central part of the essay is the part where you support your main point (the thesis). Each paragraph in the body of the essay has its own topic sentence.
3. *Conclusion:* Usually one paragraph long, the conclusion reminds the reader of the thesis by reemphasizing it.

WRITING THE THESIS

There are several characteristics of a thesis:

1. It is expressed in a *sentence*. A thesis is *not* the same as the topic of the essay, or as the title of the essay:

topic: quitting smoking
title: Why I Quit Smoking
thesis: I quit smoking because I was concerned for my health, and I wanted to prove to myself that I could break the habit.

2. A thesis *does not announce*; it makes a point about the subject:

announcement: This essay will explain the reasons why young adults should watch what they eat.
thesis: Young adults should watch what they eat so they can live healthy lives today and prevent future health problems.

3. A thesis *is not too broad*. Some ideas are just too big to cover well in an essay. A thesis that tries to cover too much can lead to a superficial or boring essay.

thesis too broad: People all over the world should work on solving their interpersonal communications problems.
an acceptable thesis: As a Southerner, I had a hard time understanding that some New Yorkers think slow speech is ignorant speech.

4. A thesis *is not too narrow*. Sometimes, students start with a thesis that looks good because it seems specific and precise. Later, when they try to support such a thesis, they can't find anything to say.

thesis too narrow: My sister pays forty dollars a week for a special formula for her baby.
an acceptable thesis: My sister had no idea what it would cost to care for a baby.

Hints for Writing a Thesis

1. Your thesis can *mention the specific subpoints* of your essay. For example, your thesis might be

I hated *The Silence of the Lambs* because the film was extremely violent and it glorified criminals.

With this thesis, you have indicated the two subpoints of your essay: *The Silence of the Lambs* was extremely violent; *The Silence of the Lambs* glorified criminals.

2. Or your thesis can *make a point* without listing your subpoints. For example, you can write a thesis like the following:

I hated *The Silence of the Lambs* because of the way it made the unspeakable into entertainment.

With this thesis, you can still use the subpoints stating that the movie was extremely violent and glorified criminals. You just don't have to mention all your subpoints in the thesis.

▶ **E X E R C I S E   1 :**   **Recognizing Good Thesis Sentences**

Following is a list of thesis statements. Some are acceptable, but others are too broad, too narrow, or have some other problem. Some are announcements; others are topics, not sentences. Put a *G* next to the good thesis sentences. Be prepared to discuss the flaws in the other topic sentences.

a. _____ Why oat bran is an important part of a healthy diet will be discussed in the following essay.

b. _____ My family was a small family unit.

c. _____ The environment is a major concern of people in today's society.

d. _____ How to install speakers in a car.

e. _____ Computers are changing the world.

f. _____ Being an only child has its advantages.

g. _____ The government should stop making pennies because they have outlived their usefulness.

h. _____ A crisis in the banking industry.

i. _____ St. Augustine, Florida, is the oldest city in the United States.

j. _____ The advantages of buying an American car.

    k. _____ Learning to play a musical instrument can bring a person much pleasure.

    l. _____ The effects of a limited job market on graduating college students is the subject to be explored.

▶ E X E R C I S E　2:　**Writing a Thesis That Relates to the Subpoints**

Following are lists of subpoints that could be explained in an essay. Write a thesis for each list. Remember that there are two ways to write a thesis: you can write a thesis that includes the subpoints, or you can write one that makes a point without listing the subpoints. As an example, the first one is done for you, using both kinds of topic sentences.

    a. **one kind of thesis:** *If you want a pet, a cat is easier to care for than a dog.*

    another kind of thesis: *Cats make better pets than dogs because cats don't need to be walked, don't mind being alone, and don't make any noise.*

    subpoints:　1. Cats don't need to be walked, but dogs need regular exercise.
               2. Cats don't mind being home alone, but dogs get lonely.
               3. Cats are quieter than dogs.

    b. **thesis:** _____

_____

    subpoints:　1. Employers look for workers who are prepared to work hard.
               2. Employers will hire people with the right training.
               3. Employers want workers who have a positive attitude.

    c. **thesis:** _____

_____

    subpoints:　1. My neighbors often give me good advice.
               2. They are willing to lend me tools when something in my house needs fixing.
               3. They also bring me delicious Indian food.

    d. **thesis:** _____

_____

    subpoints:　1. It's fun to get an unexpected card in the mail.
               2. I look forward to the free samples that sometimes come in the mail.
               3. I like looking through all the catalogs that come in the mail.

WRITING THE ESSAY IN STEPS

In an essay, you follow the same steps you learned in writing a paragraph—thoughtlines, outlines, roughlines, final lines—but you adapt them to the longer essay form.

THOUGHTLINES: ESSAY

Often the thoughtlines part begins with *narrowing a topic*. Your instructor may give you a large topic so that you can find something smaller, within the broad one, that you'd like to write about.

Some students think that, because they have several paragraphs to write, they'd better pick a big topic, one that will give them enough to say. But big topics can lead to boring, shallow, general essays. A smaller topic can challenge you to find the specific, concrete examples and details that make an essay effective.

If your instructor asked you to write about college, for instance, you might *freewrite* some ideas as you narrow the topic:

Narrowing the Topic of College

What college means to me—too big, and it could be boring
College vs. high school—everyone might choose this topic
College students—too big
College students who have jobs—better!
Problems of working and going to college—ok!

In your freewriting, you can consider your *purpose*—to write an essay about some aspect of college—and *audience*—your instructor and your classmates. Your narrowed topic will appeal to this audience because many students hold jobs and instructors are familiar with the problems of working students.

Listing Ideas

Once you have a narrow topic, you can use whatever thoughtlines process works for you. You can brainstorm by writing a series of questions and answers about your topic, you can freewrite on the topic, you can list ideas on the topic, or you can do any combination of these processes.

Below is a sample *listing of ideas* on the topic of the problems of working and going to college.

Problems of Working and Going to College: A List

early classes   weekends only time to study
too tired to pay attention   no social life
tried to study at work   apartment a mess
got caught   missed work for make-up test
got reprimanded   get behind in school
slept in class   need salary for tuition
constantly racing around   rude to customers
no sleep   girlfriend ready to kill me
little time to do homework

Marking the Ideas on Your List

After you have a list, you can survey it. Look for the ideas that fit together, *marking the related ideas* with the same number. Following is the list on working and going to college. On this list, all the items marked 1 are about problems at school; those marked 2 are about problems at work; and those marked 3 are about problems outside of school and work. You'll also notice that *some items on the list have no numbers*; these could fit into more than one place, or they might not fit anywhere.

Problems of Working and Going to College: A List Marked for Related Ideas

1	early classes	3	weekends only time to study
1	too tired to pay attention	3	no social life
2	tried to study at work	3	apartment a mess
2	got caught	2	missed work for make-up test
2	got reprimanded	1	get behind in school
1	slept in class		need salary for tuition
	constantly racing around	2	rude to customers
	no sleep	3	girlfriend ready to kill me
1	little time to do homework		

Clustering the Ideas

By *clustering* the items on the list, you'll find it easier to see the connections between ideas. The following numbered items have been clustered (grouped), and they have been listed under a subtitle.

Problems of Working and Going to College: Ideas in Clusters

Problems at School

early classes
too tired to pay attention
slept in class
little time to do homework
get behind in school

Problems at Work

tried to study at work
got caught
got reprimanded
missed work for make-up test
rude to customers

Problems Outside of Work and School

weekends only time to study
no social life
apartment a mess
girlfriend ready to kill me

When you name each cluster by giving it a subtitle, you move towards a focus for each body paragraph of your essay. By beginning to focus the body paragraphs, you also start thinking about the main point, the *thesis* of your essay. Concentrating on the thesis and on focused paragraphs helps you *unify* your essay.

Reread the clustered ideas. When you do so, you'll notice that each cluster is about problems at a different place. You can incorporate that concept into a thesis with a sentence like this:

ALONG THESE LINES/Prentice-Hall, Inc.

Students who work while they attend college face problems at school, at work, and at home.

Once you have a thesis and a list of details, you can begin working on the outlines part of your essay.

▶ **EXERCISE 1:** **Collaborative Exercise on Narrowing Topics**

Working with a partner or with a group, narrow these topics so the new topics are related, but smaller, and suitable for short essays that are between four and six paragraphs. The first topic is narrowed for you. When your group has completed the exercise, be ready to share your answers with the class.

a. **topic:** summer vacation

smaller, related topics:

1. *a car trip with children*

2. *Disney World: not a vacation paradise*

3. *my vacation job*

b. **topic:** cars

smaller, related topics:

1. _____

2. _____

3. _____

c. **topic:** sports

smaller, related topics:

1. _____

2. _____

3. _____

d. **topic:** pets

smaller, related topics:

1. _____

2. _____

3. _____

e. **topic:** money

smaller, related topics:

1. _____

2. _____

3. _____

▶ **EXERCISE 2:** Marking and Clustering Related Ideas

Following are two topics, each with a list of ideas. Mark all the related items on the list with the same number (1, 2, or 3). Some items might not get a number. When you've finished marking the list, write a title for each number that explains the cluster of ideas.

Be ready to share your marking system and titles with a group or with the entire class.

a. topic: why teenage marriages fail

_____ teens not ready to be responsible to a mate

_____ one partner is insecure

_____ jobs don't pay much without college degree

_____ rent bills

_____ in-laws interfere

_____ one mate is too critical of the other

_____ old friends create temptations

_____ friends gossip to one partner about the other

_____ novelty of being married wears off

_____ no cash for entertainment

_____ influence of media

The ideas marked 1 can be titled _____

The ideas marked 2 can be titled _____

The ideas marked 3 can be titled _____

b. topic: giving a good party

_____ circulate among all the guests

_____ invite people who'd like each other

_____ plan a menu you can cook ahead of time

_____ make sure all the guests have someone to talk to

_____ keep the guest list small

_____ the day of the party, clean up the party area

_____ an hour before the party, set up the buffet table

_____ put out glasses and ice

_____ arrange a selection of things to drink

_____ have music playing before the first guest arrives

_____ look like you're having a good time

_____ neighbors might complain

_____ invite people at least a week ahead

ALONG THESE LINES/Prentice-Hall, Inc.

The ideas marked 1 can be titled _____

The ideas marked 2 can be titled _____

The ideas marked 3 can be titled _____

OUTLINES: ESSAY

In the next stage of writing your essay, draft an outline. Use the thesis to focus your ideas. There are many kinds of outlines, but all are used to help a writer organize ideas. When you use a *formal outline*, you show the difference between a main idea and its supporting details by *indenting* the supporting details. In a formal outline, Roman numerals (numbers) and capital letters are used. Each Roman numeral represents a paragraph, and the letters beneath the numeral represent supporting details.

A sentence outline on the problems of working and going to college follows. It includes an introduction that presents the thesis and a topic sentence for each body paragraph. The topic sentences have been created from the titles of the ideas clustered earlier. The details have been drawn from ideas in the clusters. The conclusion has just one sentence that unifies the essay.

A Draft Outline for an Essay

introduction	I Thesis: Students who work while going to college face problems at school, at work, and at home.
topic sentence	II Trying to juggle job and school responsibilities creates problems at school.
	A. Early classes are difficult.
	B. I am too tired to pay attention.
details	C. Once I slept in class.
	D. I have little time to do homework.
	E. I get behind in school assignments.
topic sentence	III Work can suffer when workers attend college.
	A. I tried to study at work.
	B. I got caught by my boss.
	C. I was reprimanded.
details	D. Sometimes I am rude to customers.
	E. Another time, I had to cut work to take a make-up test.

```
topic sentence       IV  Working students face problems
                          outside of college and work.
                          A. I have no social life.
                          B. The weekends are the only time
                             to study.
details                   C. My apartment is a mess.
                          D. My girlfriend is ready to kill
                             me.
topic sentence        V   I have learned that working
                          students have to be very
                          organized to cope with their
                          responsibilities at college,
                          work, and home.
```

Revising Your Draft Outline

Before you begin a draft of your essay, survey your outline. Developing a good, clear outline now can save you hours of confused writing later. The extra time you spend to make sure your outline has sufficient details and that each paragraph stays on one point will pay off in the long run.

Some Hints in Outlining

Checking the Topic Sentences Keep in mind that the topic sentence in each body paragraph should support the thesis sentence. If a topic sentence is not carefully connected to the thesis, the structure of the essay will be confusing. Here is a thesis with a list of topic sentences. One of the topic sentences doesn't fit and is crossed out.

```
thesis:          I   A home-cooked dinner can be a
                     rewarding experience for both the cook
                     and the guests.
topic           II   Preparing a meal is a satisfying
sentences:           activity.
               III   It is a pleasure for the cook to see
                     guests enjoy the meal.
                IV   Many recipes are handed down through
                     generations.
                 V   Dinner guests are flattered when
                     someone cooks for them.
                VI   Dining at home is a treat for
                     everyone at the table or in the
                     kitchen.
```

Since the thesis of this outline is about the pleasure of dining at home, for the cook and the guests, topic sentence IV doesn't fit: it isn't about the joy of cooking *or* about being a dinner guest. It takes the essay off track. A careful check of the links between the thesis and the topic sentences will help keep your essay focused.

ALONG THESE LINES/Prentice-Hall, Inc.

Including Some Details Some students believe that they don't need many details in the outline. They feel they can fill in the details later, when they actually write the essay. Even though some writers do manage to add details later, others, who are in a hurry or who run out of ideas, run into problems.

Let's say, for example, that a writer has included very few details in an outline, like this:

```
II A burglary makes the victim feel unsafe.
   A. The person has lost property.
   B. The person's home territory has been invaded.
```

The paragraph created from this outline might be too short and lack specific details, like this:

```
   A burglary makes the victim feel unsafe. First of
all, the victim has lost property. Second, a person's
home territory has been invaded.
```

If you usually can't think of much to say when you write, try to tackle the problem in the outlines stage. The more details you put into your outline, the more detailed and effective your draft essay will be. For example, suppose the same outline on the burglary topic had more details, like this:

```
                     II A burglary makes the victim feel
                        unsafe.
                        A. The person has lost property.
                        B. The property could be worth
                           hundreds of dollars.
  more detail          C. The victim can lose a television or
  about burgulary         camera or VCR.
  itself               D. The burglars may take cash.
                        E. Worse, items with personal value,
                           like family jewelry or heirlooms,
                           can be stolen.

                        F. Even worse, a person's territory
                           has been invaded.
  more detail          G. People who thought they were
  about safety            safe know they are not
  concerns                safe.
                        H. The fear is that the invasion can
                           happen again.
```

You will probably agree that the paragraph will be more detailed, too.

Staying on One Point It's a good idea to check the outline of each body paragraph to see if each paragraph stays on one point. Compare each topic sentence, which is at the top of the list for the paragraph, against the details indented under it. Staying on one point gives each paragraph unity.

Following is the outline for a paragraph that has problems staying on one point. See if you can spot the problem areas.

Outline for a Paragraph That Doesn't Stay on One Point

```
III Sonya gives warmly of her money and of herself.
    A. I remember how freely she gave her time when
       our club had a car wash.
    B. She is always willing to share her lecture
       notes with me.
    C. Sonya gives 10 percent of her salary to her
       church.
    D. She is a member of Big Sisters and spends
       every Saturday with a disadvantaged child.
    E. She can read people's minds when they are in
       trouble.
    F. She knows what they are feeling.
```

The topic sentence of this paragraph is about generosity. But sentences E and F talk about Sonya's insight, not her generosity. When you have a problem staying on one point, you can solve the problem two ways:

1. Eliminate details that don't fit your main point.
2. Change the topic sentence so that it relates to all the ideas in the paragraph.

For example, you could cut out sentences E and F about Sonya's generosity, thus getting rid of the details that don't fit. You could even change the topic sentence in the paragraph so that it relates to all the ideas in the paragraph. A better topic sentence is *Sonya is a generous and insightful person.*

Revisiting the Thoughtlines Stage

Drafting an outline can help you identify skimpy places in your plan, places where your paragraphs need more details. You can get these details in two ways:

1. Go back to the writing you did in the thoughtlines stage. Check whether items on a list or ideas from freewriting can lead you to more details for your outline.
2. Brainstorm for more details by a question-and-answer approach. For example, if the outline includes "My apartment is a mess," you might ask, "Why? How messy?" Or if the outline includes "I have no social life," you might ask, "What do you mean? Parties? Clubs?"

The time you spend revising your outline will make it easier for you to write an essay that is well developed, unified, and coherently structured. The following checklist may help you revise.

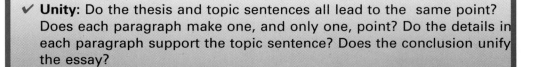

A Checklist for Revising the Outline of an Essay

✔ **Unity:** Do the thesis and topic sentences all lead to the same point? Does each paragraph make one, and only one, point? Do the details in each paragraph support the topic sentence? Does the conclusion unify the essay?

ALONG THESE LINES/Prentice-Hall, Inc.

✔ **Support:** Do the body paragraphs have enough supporting details?

✔ **Coherence:** Are the paragraphs in the most effective order? Are the details in each paragraph arranged in the most effective order?

The revised outline for the essay on working and going to college follows.

Revised Outline for an Essay

I Thesis: Students who work while going to college face problems at school, at work, and at home.

II Trying to juggle job and school responsibilities creates problems at school.
  A. Early classes are difficult.
  B. I am too tired to pay attention.
  C. Once I slept in class.
  D. I have little time to do homework.
  E. I get behind in school assignments.

III Work can suffer when workers attend college.
  A. I tried to study at work.
  B. I got caught by my boss.
  C. I was reprimanded.

added detail {
  D. Sometimes I come to work very tired.
  E. When I don't have enough sleep, I can be rude to customers.
}

revised detail {
  F. Rudeness gets me in trouble.
  G. Another time, I had to cut work to take a make-up test.
}

revised topic sentence
IV Working students suffer outside of classes and the workplace.
  A. I work nights during the week.
  B. The weekends are the only time I can study.

added detail, order of detail changed {
  C. My apartment is a mess since I have no time to clean it.
  D. Worse, my girlfriend is ready to kill me because I have no social life.
  E. We never even go to the movies anymore.
  F. When she comes over, I am busy studying.
}

> V I have learned that working
> students have to be very organized
> to cope with their responsibilities
> at college, work, and home.

▶ **EXERCISE 1:** Collaborative Exercise on Completing an Outline for an Essay

Following is part of an outline that has a thesis and topic sentences but no details. Working with a partner or with a group, add the details and write in complete sentences. Write one sentence for each capital letter. Be sure that the details are connected to the topic sentence.

I thesis: Video cameras have several beneficial uses in American society.

II Americans use their video cameras to record memorable family events.

A. _____

B. _____

C. _____

D. _____

E. _____

F. _____

III Video cameras are being used to prevent or detect crimes.

A. _____

B. _____

C. _____

D. _____

E. _____

F. _____

IV Video cameras have given ordinary people an entry into many TV programs.

A. _____

B. _____

C. _____

D. _____

E. _____

F. _____

V The video camera has changed the way Americans celebrate family rituals, has contributed to the prevention and detection of crime, and has made ordinary people into TV directors, reporters, and performers.

▶ **E X E R C I S E 2 : Focusing an Outline for an Essay**

The following outline has a thesis and details, but it has no topic sentences for the body paragraphs. Write the topic sentences.

I thesis: After my last meal at Don's Diner, I swore I'd never eat there again.

II _____

_____

    A. My friend and I were kept waiting for a table for half an hour.

    B. During that time, several tables were empty, but no one bothered to clear the dirty dishes.

    C. We just stood in the entrance, waiting.

    D. Then, when we were seated, the waitress was surly.

    E. It took fifteen minutes to get a menu.

    F. The plates of food were slammed down on the table.

    G. The orders were mixed up.

III _____

_____

    A. The hamburger was full of gristle.

    B. The French fries were as hard as cardboard.

    C. Our iced tea was instant.

    D. The iced tea powder was floating on top of the glass.

    E. The lettuce had brown edges.

    F. Ketchup was caked all over the outside of the ketchup bottle.

IV I never want to repeat the experience I had at Don's Diner.

ROUGHLINES: ESSAY

When you are satisfied with your outline, you can begin the roughlines stage of creating the essay. Start by writing a first draft of the essay which must include these parts: introduction, body paragraphs, and conclusion.

WRITING THE INTRODUCTION

Where Does the Thesis Go?

The *thesis* should appear in the introduction of the essay, in the first paragraph. But most of the time it should not be the first sentence. Write a few (three or more) sentences of introduction before the thesis. Generally, the thesis is the *last sentence* in the introductory paragraph.

Why put the thesis at the end of the first paragraph? First of all, writing several sentences in front of your main idea gives you a chance to lead into it gradually and smoothly. This method will help you build interest and gain the reader's attention. Also, by placing the thesis after a few sentences of introduction, you will not startle the reader with your main point.

Finally, if your thesis is at the end of the introduction, it states the main point of the essay just before that point is supported in the body paragraphs. Putting the thesis at the end of the introduction is like inserting an arrow that points to the supporting ideas in the essay.

Hints for Writing the Introduction

There are a number of ways to write an introduction.

1. You can *begin with some general statements* that gradually lead to your thesis:

general statements	Students face all kinds of problems when they start college. Some students struggle with a lack of basic math skills; others have never learned to write a term paper. Students who were stars in high school have to cope with being just another social security number at a large institution. Students with small children have to find a way to be good parents and good students, too. Although all these problems are common, I found an even
thesis at end	more typical conflict. <u>My biggest problem in college was learning to organize my time.</u>

2. You can *begin with a quote* that smoothly leads to your thesis. The quote can be a quote from someone famous, or it can be an old saying. It can be something your mother always told you, or it can be a slogan from an advertisement, or the words of a song.

quote	Everybody has heard the old saying, "Time flies," but I never really thought about that statement until I started college. I expected college to challenge me with demanding course work. I expected it to excite me with the range of people I would meet. I even thought it might amuse me with the fun and intrigue of dating and romance. But I never expected college to exhaust me. I was surprised to dis-
thesis at end	cover that <u>my biggest problem in college was learning to organize my time.</u>

(**Note:** You can add transitional words or phrases to your thesis, as in the sample above.)

3. You can *tell a story* as a way of leading into your thesis. You can open with the story of something that happened to you or to someone you know, a story you read about or heard on the news.

ALONG THESE LINES/Prentice-Hall, Inc.

story   My friend Phyllis is two years older than I am, and so she started college before I did. When Phyllis came home from college for the Thanksgiving weekend, I called her with a huge list of activities she and I could enjoy. I was really surprised when Phyllis told me she planned to spend most of the weekend sleeping. I didn't understand her when she told me she was worn out. When I started college myself, I understood her perfectly. Phyllis was a victim of that old college ailment: not knowing how to handle time. I developed
thesis   the same disease. <u>My biggest problem in col-</u>
at end   <u>lege was learning to organize my time.</u>

4. You can *explain why this topic is worth writing about.* Explaining could mean giving some background on the topic, or it could mean discussing why the topic is an important one.

explain   I don't remember a word of what was said during my freshman orientation, and I wish I did. I'm sure somebody somewhere warned me about the problems I'd face in college. I'm sure somebody talked about getting organized. Unfortunately, I didn't listen, and I had to learn the hard way. I hope other students will listen and learn and be spared my hard lesson
thesis   and my big problem. <u>My biggest problem in col-</u>
at end   <u>lege was learning to organize my time.</u>

5. You can *use one or more questions* to lead into your thesis. You can open with a question or questions that will be answered by your thesis. Or you can open with a question or questions that catch the reader's attention and move towards your thesis.

question   Have you ever stayed up all night to study for an exam, then fallen asleep at dawn and slept right through the time of the exam? If you have, then you were probably the same kind of college student I was. I was the student who always ran into class three minutes late, the one who begged for an extension on the term paper, the one who pleaded with the teacher to postpone the test. I just could not get things done on schedule. <u>My biggest prob-</u>
thesis   <u>lem in college was learning to organize my</u>
at end   <u>time.</u>

6. You can *open with a contradiction* of your main point as a way of attracting the reader's interest and leading to your thesis. You can begin with an idea that is the opposite of what you will say in your thesis. The contrast between your opening and your thesis creates interest.

contradiction   People who knew me in my freshman year
probably felt really sorry for me. They saw
a girl with dark circles under her blood-
shot eyes, a girl who was always racing
from one place to another. Those people
probably thought I was exhausted from over-
work. But they were wrong. My problem in
college was definitely not too much work;
it was the way I handled my work. <u>My</u>

thesis   <u>biggest problem in college was learning to</u>
at end   <u>organize my time.</u>

▶ EXERCISE 1: Writing an Introduction

Following are five thesis sentences. Pick one. Then write an introductory paragraph on the lines provided. Your last sentence should be the thesis sentence. If
your instructor agrees, read your introduction to others in the class who wrote
an introduction to the same thesis, or read your introduction to the entire class.

Pick one of these thesis sentences. Write an introduction of at least three sentences:

Thesis Sentences

    a. Americans are becoming much too fashion-conscious.
    b. A car phone can be a hazard for the user and for other drivers.
    c. Credit cards got me into trouble.
    d. A diet is only as good as the dieter.
    e. People should be more careful in protecting their homes from thieves.

Write an introduction: _____

_____

_____

_____

_____

_____

_____

_____

WRITING THE BODY OF THE ESSAY

In the body of the essay, the paragraphs *explain, support, and develop your thesis.*
In this part of the essay, each paragraph has its own topic sentence, which does
the following:

    1. It focuses the sentences in the paragraph.
    2. It makes a point connected to the thesis.

The thesis and the topic sentences are ideas that need to be supported by details, explanations, and examples. You can visualize the connections among the parts of an essay like this:

Introduction with Thesis

Body {
     Topic Sentence
     Details
     Topic Sentence
     Details
     Topic Sentence
     Details

Conclusion

When you write topic sentences, you can help to organize your essay by referring to the following checklist.

A Checklist for the Topic Sentences of an Essay

✔ Does the topic sentence give the point of the paragraph?

✔ Does the topic sentence connect to the thesis of the essay?

How Long Are the Body Paragraphs?

Remember that the body paragraphs of an essay are the place where you explain and develop your thesis. These paragraphs should be long enough to explain, not just list, your points. To do this well, try to make your body paragraphs *at least seven sentences* long. As you develop your writing skills, you may find that you can support your ideas in fewer than seven sentences.

Developing the Body Paragraphs

You can write well-developed body paragraphs by following the same steps you used in writing single paragraphs for the earlier assignments in this course. By following the steps of thoughtlines to get ideas, outlines to organize, roughlines to draft, and final lines to edit, you can create clear, effective paragraphs.

To focus and develop the body paragraphs, ask the following questions as you revise:

A Checklist for Developing Body Paragraphs for an Essay

✔ Does the topic sentence cover everything in the paragraph?

✔ Do I have enough details to explain the topic sentence?

✔ Do all the details in the paragraph support, develop, or illustrate the topic sentence?

▶ E X E R C I S E   1 :   Collaborative Exercise in Creating Topic
                                    Sentences

Do this exercise with a partner or with a group. Following are thesis sentences.
For each thesis, write topic sentences (as many as indicated by the numbered
blanks). The first one is done for you.

thesis: Cats make good pets.

topic sentence 1. *Cats are independent and don't mind being home alone.*

topic sentence 2. *Cats are easy to litter-train.*

topic sentence 3. *Cats are fun to play with.*

a. thesis: Mr. Thompson is willing to help his students both inside the
classroom and during his office hours.

topic sentence 1. _____

_____

topic sentence 2. _____

_____

b. thesis: It's easy to recognize the student who's in college to have a good
time.

topic sentence 1. _____

_____

topic sentence 2. _____

_____

topic sentence 3. _____

_____

c. thesis: When you want to get to know an attractive person at a party,
you should follow several steps.

topic sentence 1. _____

_____

topic sentence 2. _____

_____

topic sentence 3. _____

_____

d. thesis: Moving to a new town has its good and bad points.

topic sentence 1. _____

_____

topic sentence 2. _____

_____

topic sentence 3. _____

_____

topic sentence 4. _____

_____

e. thesis: The bedroom looked like something out of a movie about the rich and famous.

topic sentence 1. _____

_____

topic sentence 2. _____

_____

f. thesis: There are several reasons why men get facelifts.

topic sentence 1. _____

_____

topic sentence 2. _____

_____

topic sentence 3. _____

_____

WRITING THE CONCLUSION

The last paragraph in the essay is the *conclusion*. It does not have to be as long as a body paragraph, but it should be long enough to tie the essay together and remind the reader of the thesis. You can use any of these strategies in writing the conclusion:

1. You can *restate the thesis, in new words*. Go back to the first paragraph of your essay and reread it. For example, this could be the first paragraph of an essay:

introduction   Because I rarely watch MTV, I had little idea of what today's music videos are like. Last week, however, I happened to be running through the TV channels with my remote control, and I stopped at MTV. I was surprised and horrified by what I saw. I saw video after video that looked like a horror or a pornographic movie. I wondered how this cable channel could get away with showing such obviously controversial material. Then I realized that parents, the people who might object to the videos, rarely watch MTV. If parents started watching MTV, they would be shocked by the sex and violence.

thesis
at end

The thesis, underlined above, is the sentence that you can re-state in your conclusion. Your task is to *make the point again but to use different words*. Then work that restatement into a short paragraph, like this:

restating
the thesis

> MTV provides a daily program of entertainment for children and teens. That entertainment can include scenes of violence, particularly violence against women, and cruelty. Many parents are crusading against the words on music cassettes and disks, but they don't seem to care about the moving pictures that illustrate those words. <u>Parents who turned on MTV would be turned off by what they saw.</u>

2. You can *make a judgment, evaluation, or recommendation*. Instead of simply restating your point, you can end by making some comment on the issue you've described or the problem you've illustrated. If you were looking for another way to end the essay on MTV, for example, you could end with a recommendation.

ending with a
recommendation

> I'm no prude, but I think some of the videos on MTV are too much for my children to handle. While I don't believe I have the right to take certain videos off the air, <u>I would like MTV to restrict the showing of these videos to adult viewing time, the late evening hours.</u> If MTV made such a change to help worried parents like me, the network would have many new fans.

3. You can conclude your essay by *framing it*. With this technique, you tie your essay together neatly by *using something from your introduction* as a way of concluding. When you take an example, or a question, or even a quote from your first paragraph and refer to it in your last paragraph, you are "framing" the essay.

Take another look at the introduction to the essay on MTV: the writer talks about flipping through TV channels, seeing images of sex and violence, and being shocked. Now consider how the ideas of the introduction are used in this conclusion:

frame

frame

frame

> <u>The next time I happen to hit the MTV channel with my remote control,</u> I'll know what to expect. I won't be surprised by the <u>cruelty, sadism, and rage</u> I see on the screen. But I wonder how many parents will get the <u>same big surprise that I got</u> last week by accidentally switching to MTV. And I wonder how long it will take those shocked parents to start complaining to their cable companies.

▶ **E X E R C I S E   1:**   **Choosing a Better Way to Restate the Thesis**

Following are five clusters. Each cluster consists of a thesis sentence and two sentences that try to restate the thesis. Each restated sentence could be used as part of the conclusion to an essay. Put *B* next to the sentence in each pair that is a

ALONG THESE LINES/Prentice-Hall, Inc.

better restatement. Remember that the better choice repeats the same idea as the thesis but does not rely on too many of the same words.

a. thesis: Anyone who is thinking of buying a car should do careful research, plan a realistic budget for car payments, and negotiate intelligently.

restatement 1. _____ People in the market for a car need to check out choices and prices, set up a practical system of payment, and bargain with know-how.

restatement 2. _____ Careful research, a realistic budget for car payments, and intelligent negotiation are important for anyone who is thinking of buying a car.

b. thesis: One of the best ways to meet people is to take a college class.

restatement 1. _____ Taking a class in college is one of the best ways to meet people.

restatement 2. _____ College classes can make strangers into friends.

c. thesis: The three household chores I hate the most are cleaning closets, dusting, and folding laundry.

restatement 1. _____ Taking care of cluttered closets, dusty furniture, and wrinkled laundry makes me crazy.

restatement 2. _____ Cleaning closets, dusting, and folding laundry are the three household chores I hate the most.

d. thesis: My first job taught me the importance of being on time.

restatement 1. _____ On my first job, I learned how important it is to be on time.

restatement 2. _____ Punctuality was the key lesson of my first job.

Revising the Draft

Once you have a rough draft of your essay, you can begin revising it. The following checklist may help you to make the necessary changes in your draft.

Checklist for Revising the Draft of an Essay

✔ Does the essay have a clear, unifying thesis?

✔ Does the thesis make a point?

✔ Does each body paragraph have a topic sentence?

✔ Is each body paragraph focused on its topic sentence?

✔ Are the body paragraphs roughly the same size?

> ✔ Do any of the sentences need combining?
>
> ✔ Do any of the words need to be changed?
>
> ✔ Do the ideas seem to be smoothly linked?
>
> ✔ Does the introduction catch the reader's interest?
>
> ✔ Is there a definite conclusion?
>
> ✔ Does the conclusion remind the reader of the thesis?

Transitions within Paragraphs

In an essay, you can use two kinds of transitions: those within a paragraph and those between paragraphs.

Transitions that link ideas *within a paragraph* are the same kinds you've used earlier. Your choice of words, phrases, or even sentences depends on the type of connection you want to make. Here is a list of some common transitions and the kind of connection they express.

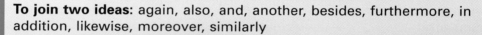

Common Transitions within a Paragraph

To join two ideas: again, also, and, another, besides, furthermore, in addition, likewise, moreover, similarly

To show a contrast or a different opinion: but, however, in contrast, instead, nevertheless, on the contrary, on the other hand, otherwise, or, still, yet

To show a cause-and-effect connection: accordingly, as a result, because, consequently, for, so, therefore, thus

To give an example: for example, for instance, in the case of, like, such as, to illustrate

To show time: after, at the same time, before, finally, first, meanwhile, next, recently, shortly, soon, subsequently, then, until

Transitions between Paragraphs

When you write something that is more than one paragraph long, you need transitions that link each paragraph to the others. There are several effective ways to link paragraphs and to remind the reader of your main idea and of how the smaller points connect to it. Here are two ways:

1. *Restate an idea* from the preceding paragraph at the start of a new paragraph. Look closely at the following two paragraphs and notice how the second paragraph repeats an idea from the first paragraph and provides a link.

> If people were more patient, driving would
> be less of an ordeal. If, for instance, the
> driver behind me didn't honk his horn as soon

as the traffic light turned green, both he and I would probably have lower blood pressure. He wouldn't be irritating himself by pushing so hard. And I wouldn't be reacting by slowing down, trying to irritate him even more, and getting angry at him. When I get impatient in heavy traffic, I just make a bad situation worse. Hurrying doesn't get me to my destination any faster; it just stresses me out.

transition
restating
an idea

<u>The impatient driver doesn't get anywhere; neither does the</u> impatient customer at a restaurant. Impatience at restaurants doesn't pay. I work as a hostess at a restaurant, and I know that the customer who moans and complains about waiting for a table won't get one any faster than the person who makes the best of the wait. In fact, if a customer is too aggressive or obnoxious, the restaurant staff may actually slow down the process of getting that customer a table.

2. *Use synonyms and repetition* as a way of reminding the reader of an important point. For example, in the following two paragraphs, notice how certain repeated words, phrases, and synonyms all remind the reader of a point about facing fear. The repeated words and synonyms are underlined.

Some people just <u>avoid</u> whatever they <u>fear.</u> I have an uncle who is <u>afraid</u> to fly. Whenever he has to go on a trip, he does anything he can to <u>avoid</u> getting on an airplane. He will drive for days, travel by train, take a bus trip. Because he is so <u>terrified</u> of flying, he lives with <u>constant anxiety</u> that some day he may have to fly. He is always thinking of the one emergency that could force him to <u>confront what he most dreads.</u> Instead of <u>dealing directly with his fear</u>, he lets it <u>haunt</u> him.

Other people are even worse than my uncle. He won't <u>attack his fear</u> of something external. But there are people who won't <u>deal with their fear</u> of themselves. My friend Sam is a good example of this kind of person. Sam has a serious drinking problem. All Sam's friends know he is an alcoholic. But Sam <u>will not admit</u> his addiction. I think he is <u>afraid to face</u> that part of himself. So he <u>denies</u> his problem, saying he can stop drinking any time he wants to. Of course, until Sam has the courage to <u>admit what he is most afraid of</u>, his alcoholism, he won't be able to change.

A Revised Draft

Following is a revised draft of the essay on working and going to college. As you read it, you'll notice many changes from the outline:

- An introduction has been added, phrased in the first person, "I," to unify the essay.

ALONG THESE LINES/Prentice-Hall, Inc.

- Transitions have been added within and between paragraphs.
- General statements have been replaced by more specific ones.
- Word choice has been improved.
- The conclusion has been rewritten. Some of the ideas added to the conclusion came from the original list of the thoughtlines phase of writing. They are ideas that didn't fit in the body paragraphs but are useful in the conclusion.

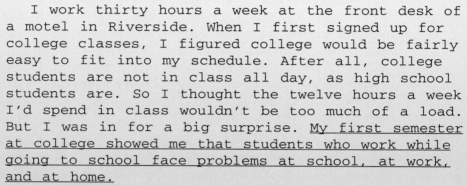

**Revised Roughlines Draft
of an Essay**
(Thesis and topic sentences are
underlined.)

I work thirty hours a week at the front desk of a motel in Riverside. When I first signed up for college classes, I figured college would be fairly easy to fit into my schedule. After all, college students are not in class all day, as high school students are. So I thought the twelve hours a week I'd spend in class wouldn't be too much of a load. But I was in for a big surprise. <u>My first semester at college showed me that students who work while going to school face problems at school, at work, and at home.</u>

<u>First of all, trying to juggle job and school responsibilities creates problems at school</u>. Early morning classes, for example, are particularly difficult for me. Because I work every weeknight from six to midnight, I don't get home until 1 a.m., and I can't fall asleep until 2 a.m. or later. I am too tired to pay attention in my 8 a.m. class. Once, I even fell asleep in that class. My work hours create other conflicts. They cut into my study time, so I have little time to do all the assigned reading and papers. I get behind in these assignments, and I never seem to have enough time to catch up. Consequently, my grades are not as good as they could be.

Because I both work and go to school, I have problems doing well at school. But <u>work can also suffer when workers attend college.</u> Students can bring school into the workplace. One night I tried to study at work, but my boss caught me reading my biology textbook at the front desk. I was reprimanded, and now my boss doesn't trust me. Sometimes I come to work very tired. When I don't get enough sleep, I can be rude to hotel guests who give me a hard time. Then the rudeness can get me into trouble. I remember one particular guest who reported me because I was sarcastic to her. She had spent half an hour complaining about her bill, and

ALONG THESE LINES/Prentice-Hall, Inc.

I had been too tired to be patient. Once again, my boss reprimanded me. Another time, school interfered with my job when I had to cut work to take a make-up test at school. I know my boss was unhappy with me then, too.

As a working student, I run into trouble on the job and at college. <u>Working students also suffer outside of college and the workplace.</u> Since I work nights during the week, the weekends are the only time I can study. Because I have to use my weekends to do schoolwork, I can't do other things. My apartment is a mess since I have no time to clean it. Worse, my girlfriend is ready to kill me because I have no social life. We never even go to the movies anymore. When she comes over, I am busy studying.

With responsibilities at home, at work, and at college, I face a cycle of stress. I am constantly racing around, and I can't break the cycle. I want a college education, and I must have a job to pay my tuition. The only way I can manage is to learn to manage my time. <u>I have learned that working students have to be very organized to cope with their responsibilities at college, at work, and at home.</u>

▶ **E X E R C I S E 1: Identifying the Main Points in the Draft of an Essay**

Following is the draft of a five-paragraph essay. Read it, then reread it and underline the thesis and the topic sentences in each body paragraph and in the conclusion.

Until this year, I had never considered spending my free time helping others in my community. Volunteer work, I thought, was something retired folks and rich people did to fill their days. Just by chance, I became a volunteer for the public library's Classic Connection, a group that arranges read-a-thons and special programs for elementary school children. Although I don't receive a salary, working with some perceptive and entertaining third graders has been very rewarding in other ways.

Currently, I meet with my small group of four girls and three boys each Saturday morning from ten to eleven o'clock, and they have actually taught me more than I ever thought possible. I usually assign the children various passages in an illustrated children's classic like *The Little Prince*, and I help them with the difficult words as they read aloud. When I occasionally read

E X E R C I S E

EXERCISE

to them, they follow right along, but when it's their turn, they happily go off track. I've learned that each child has a mind of his or her own, and I now have much more respect for day-care workers and elementary school teachers who must teach, entertain, and discipline thirty rowdy children all day long. I'm tired after just one hour with only seven children.

I have also learned the value of careful planning. I arrive at each session with a tape recorder and have them record a sound effect related to the story we'll be reading. At certain points during the session, we stop to hear the sound effects. They love to hear themselves and seem more focused on reading when I use this method. I feel more relaxed when I am well prepared and the sessions go smoothly.

I've enjoyed making several new friends and contacts through the Classic Connection. I've become friendly with the parents of the kids in my reading group, and one of the fathers has offered me a good-paying job at his printing business. He even mentioned he could be flexible about my schedule. I asked him if he could help me put a collection together of the group's most outrageous original stories, and he said he'd be glad to do it in *his* free time. I've thus learned that the spirit of volunteerism is indeed contagious.

I plan to keep volunteering for the Classic Connection's programs and look forward to a new group that should be starting soon. I don't know if I'm ready to graduate to an older group. After all, third graders still have much to teach me.

▶ **EXERCISE 2: Adding Transitions to an Essay**

The following essay needs transitions. Add the transitions where indicated, and add the type of transition—word, phrase, or sentence—that is needed. When you have completed the exercise, be ready to share your revisions with a group or with the entire class.

When I finished high school, I was determined to go to college. What I hadn't decided was *where* I would go to college. Most of my friends were planning to go away from home to attend college. They wanted to be responsible for themselves and to be free of their parents' supervision. Like my friends, I thought of going away to college. But I finally decided to go to a college near my home. I chose a college near home for several reasons.

_____ (add a phrase), I can save money by attending a community college near home. _____

ALONG THESE LINES/Prentice-Hall, Inc.

(add a word) I am still living at home, I do not have to pay for room and board at a college dorm or to pay rent for an apartment off campus. I do not have to pay for the transportation costs of visits home. My friends who are away at school tell me about all the money they are spending on the things I get at home, for free. These friends are paying for things like doing their laundry or hooking up their cable TV. _____ (add a phrase) my college expenses are basically just tuition, fees, and books. I think I have a better deal than my friends who went away to college.

_____

_____

_____ (add a sentence). By attending college near home, I have kept a secure home base. I think it would be very hard for me to handle a new school, a new town, a new set of classmates, and a new place to live all at the same time. I have narrowed my challenges to a new school and new classmates. _____ (add a word) I come home after a stressful day at college, I still have Mom's home cooking and Dad's sympathy to console me. I still sleep in my own comfortable—and comforting—room. Students who go away to school may have more freedom, _____ (add a word) I have more security.

_____

_____

_____ (add a sentence). My decision to stay home for college gave me a secure job base as well. For the past year, I've had a job I like very much. My boss is very fair, and she has come to value my work enough to let me set my own work schedule. _____ (add a word or phrase), she lets me plan my work schedule around my class schedule. If I had moved away to attend college, I would have had to find a new job. _____ (add a word or phrase) I would have had a hard time finding a boss as understanding as the one I have now.

There are many good reasons to go to a college away from home. _____ (add a word or phrase) there are probably as many good reasons to go to one near home. I know that I'm happy with my decision. It has paid off financially and has helped me maintain a secure place to live and to work.

EXERCISE

▶ **EXERCISE 3:** **Recognizing Synonyms and Repetition Used to Link Ideas in an Essay**

In the following essay, underline all the synonyms and repetition (of words or phrases) that help remind the reader of the thesis sentence. (To help you, the thesis is underlined.) When you've completed this exercise, be ready to share your answers with a group or with the class.

Whenever I turn on the TV, I hear the story of an extraordinary act of courage. A fireman, for example, rushes into a burning building to save an old man. Or a mother risks her own life to save her child from traffic. These are once-in-a-lifetime acts of courage, and they are indeed admirable. But <u>there is another, quiet kind of courage demonstrated all around us, every day.</u>

This kind of courage can be the fortitude of the person who has a terminal illness but who still carries on with living. I knew a person like that. He was the father of a family. When he found out he had a year to live, he did not waste much time in misery and despair. Instead, he used every moment to prepare his family for the time when he would no longer be there. He made financial arrangements. He spent time with his children, to show them how much he loved them. His bravery in the face of death was not unusual. Every day, there is someone who hears bad news from a doctor and quietly goes on. But because such people are so quiet in their courage, they are not given much credit.

Another example of quiet, everyday courage can be seen in people with the guts to try new and frightening things. The older person who decides to go to college, for instance, must be very scared. But he or she faces that fear and enters the classroom. And any student, of any age, who takes the course that's supposed to be hard, or the teacher who's supposed to be tough, instead of the easier one, shows a certain courage. Equally brave are the people who switch careers in middle age because they haven't found satisfaction in the workplace. It's frightening to start over at midlife, when starting over means trading job security and money for uncertainty and a lower starting salary. Yet many people make that trade, demonstrating real fortitude.

Sometimes we think that heroes are people who make the news. Granted, there are heroes splashed loudly across the papers and acclaimed on TV. Yet there are other, equally brave people who never make the news. They are the ones whose lives show a less dramatic form of courage. They are the ones who are all around us, and who deserve our admiration and respect.

Ⓕ INAL LINES: ESSAY

Creating a Title

When you are satisfied with the final draft of your essay, you can begin preparing a good copy. Your essay will need a title. Try to think of a short title that is connected to your thesis. Since the title is the reader's first contact with your essay, an imaginative title can create a good first impression. If you can't think of anything clever, try using a key phrase from your essay.

The title is placed at the top of your essay, about an inch above the first paragraph. Always capitalize the first word of the title and all other words *except* "the," "an," "a," or prepositions (like "of," "in," "with"). *Do not* underline or put quotation marks around your title.

Comparing the Stages of the Essay

Following are the revised outline, the revised draft, and the final lines version of the essay on working and going to college. When you compare the roughlines and final lines versions, you'll notice some changes in the final version:

- A title has been added.
- In the first paragraph, the words "I thought" have been added to make it clear that the statement is the writer's opinion.
- One topic sentence, in paragraph two, has been revised so that it includes the word "students" and the meaning is more precise.
- Words have been changed to sharpen the meaning.
- Transitions have been added.

Look carefully at the three stages to see how the essay evolved.

Before you prepare the final lines copy of your essay, check your latest draft for errors in spelling and punctuation, and for any errors made in typing or recopying.

An Outlines Version of an Essay	
introduction	I Thesis: Students who work while going to college face problems at school, at work, and at home.
topic sentence	II Trying to juggle job and school responsibilities creates problems at school.
	A. Early classes are difficult.
	B. I am too tired to pay attention.
	C. Once I slept in class.
	D. I have little time to do homework.
	E. I get behind in school assignments.

topic sentence   III Work can suffer when workers attend
                      college.
                      A. I tried to study at work.
                      B. I got caught by my boss.
                      C. I was reprimanded.
                      D. Sometimes I come to work very
                         tired.
                      E. When I don't have enough sleep,
                         I can be rude to customers.
                      F. Rudeness gets me in trouble.
                      G. Another time, I had to cut work
                         to take a make-up test.

topic sentence   IV Working students suffer outside of
                      classes and the workplace.
                      A. I work nights during the
                         week.
                      B. The weekends are the only time I
                         can study.
                      C. My apartment is a mess since I
                         have no time to clean it.
                      D. Worse, my girlfriend is ready to
                         kill me because I have no social
                         life.
                      E. We never even go to the movies
                         anymore.
                      F. When she comes over, I am busy
                         studying.

topic sentence   V I have learned that working
                      students have to be very organized
                      to cope with their responsibilities
                      at college, work, and home.

A Roughlines Version
of an Essay

I work thirty hours a week at the front desk of
a motel in Riverside. When I first signed up for
college classes, I figured college would be fairly
easy to fit into my schedule. After all, college
students are not in class all day, as high school
students are. So I thought the twelve hours a week
I'd spend in class wouldn't be too much of a load.
But I was in for a big surprise. My first semester
at college showed me that students who work while
going to college face problems at school, at work,
and at home.

First of all, trying to juggle job and school

ALONG THESE LINES/Prentice-Hall, Inc.

responsibilities creates problems at school. Early morning classes, for example, are particularly difficult for me. Because I work every weeknight from six to midnight, I don't get home until 1 a.m., and I can't fall asleep until 2 a.m. or later. I am too tired to pay attention in my eight o'clock class. Once, I even fell asleep in that class. My work hours create other conflicts. They cut into my study time, so I have little time to do all the assigned reading and papers. I get behind in these assignments, and I never seem to have enough time to catch up. Consequently, my grades are not as good as they could be.

Because I both work and go to school, I have problems doing well at school. But work can also suffer when workers attend college. Students can't bring school into the workplace. One night I tried to study at work, but my boss caught me reading my biology textbook at the front desk. I was reprimanded, and now my boss doesn't trust me. Sometimes I come to work very tired. When I don't get enough sleep, I can be rude to hotel guests who give me a hard time. Then the rudeness can get me into trouble. I remember one particular guest who reported me because I was sarcastic to her. She had spent half an hour complaining about her bill, and I had been too tired to be patient. Once again, my boss reprimanded me. Another time, school interfered with my job when I had to cut work to take a make-up test at school. I know my boss was unhappy with me then, too.

As a working student, I run into trouble on the job and at college. Working students also suffer outside of classes and the workplace. Since I work nights during the week, the weekends are the only time I can study. Because I have to use my weekends to do schoolwork, I can't do other things. My apartment is a mess since I have no time to clean it. Worse, my girlfriend is ready to kill me because I have no social life. We never even go to the movies anymore. When she comes over, I am busy studying.

With responsibilities at home, at work, and at college, I face a cycle of stress. I am constantly racing around, and I can't break the cycle. I want a college education, and I must have a job to pay my tuition. The only way I can manage is to learn to manage my time. I have learned that working students have to be very organized to cope with their responsibilities at college, at work, and at home.

A Final Lines Version of an Essay
(Changes from the roughlines version are underlined.)

Problems of the Working College Student

I work thirty hours a week at the front desk of a motel in Riverside. When I first <u>registered</u> for college classes, I figured college would be fairly easy to fit into my schedule. After all, <u>I thought,</u> college students are not in class all day, like high school students are. So I <u>assumed</u> the twelve hours a week I'd spend in class wouldn't be too much of a load. But I was in for a big surprise. My first semester at college showed me that students who work while going to college face problems at school, at work, and at home.

First of all, <u>students who try</u> to juggle job and school responsibilities <u>find trouble at school.</u> Early morning classes, for example, are particularly difficult for me. Because I work every week night from six to midnight, I don't get home until 1 a.m., and I can't fall asleep until 2 a.m. or later. <u>Consequently,</u> I am too tired to pay attention in my eight o'clock class. Once, I even fell asleep in that class. My work hours create other conflicts. They cut into my study time, so I have little time to do all the assigned reading and papers. I get behind in the assignments, and I never seem to have enough time to catch up. <u>As a result,</u> my grades are not as good as they could be.

Because I both work and go to school, I have problems doing well at school. But work can also suffer when workers attend college. Students can bring school into the workplace. <u>I've been guilty of this practice and have paid the price.</u> One night I tried to study at work, but my boss caught me reading my biology textbook at the front desk. I was reprimanded, and now my boss doesn't trust me. Sometimes I come to work very tired, <u>another problem.</u> When I don't get enough sleep, I can be rude to <u>motel</u> guests who give me a hard time. Then the rudeness can get me into trouble. I remember one particular guest who reported me because I was sarcastic to her. She had spent half an hour complaining about her bill, and I had been too tired to be patient. Once again, my boss reprimanded me. Another time, school interfered with my job when I had to cut work to take a make-up test at school. I know my boss was unhappy with me then, too.

ALONG THESE LINES/Prentice-Hall, Inc.

As a working student, I run into trouble on the job and at college. Working students also suffer outside of classes and the workplace. <u>My schedule illustrates the conflicts of trying to juggle too many duties.</u> Since I work nights during the week, the weekends are the only time I can study. Because I have to use my weekends to do schoolwork, I can't do other things. My apartment is a mess since I have no time to clean it. Worse, my girlfriend is ready to kill me because I have no social life. We never even go to the movies anymore. When she comes over, I am busy studying.

With responsibilities at home, at work, and at college, I face a cycle of stress. I am constantly racing around, and I can't break the cycle. I want a college education, and I must have a job to pay my tuition. The only way I can manage is to learn to manage my time. <u>In my first semester at college, I've realized</u> that working students have to be very organized to cope with the responsibilities of college, work, and home.

▶ **E X E R C I S E 1 :** **Proofreading and Correcting the Final Lines Version of an Essay**

The following essay contains the kinds of errors writers can overlook when preparing the final lines copy of their work. Correct all the errors on the lines above them.

"Three Myths About Young People"

Today, when a person says the word "teenager" or refers to "college kids," that person may be speaking with a little sneer. Young people have acquired a bad reputation. Some of the repution may be deserved, but some of it may not be. Young people are often judged according to myths, beliefs that are not true. Older people should not believe in three common myth's about the young.

We are always hearing that young people are irresponsable but their are many teens and people in their early twenties who disprove this statement. In every town, there are young people who hold full-time jobs and support a family. There are even more young people who work and go to school. All of my friends have been working since their sophmore year of High School. The fact that not one of them has ever been fired from a job implies they must be pretty good workers. Furthermore, young people today are almost forced to be responsible they must learn to work and pay for their clothes and college tuition.

Another foolish belief is that all young people take drugs. Hollywood movies encourage this myth by including a drug-crazed teenager in almost every movie. Whenever television broadcasts a public service advertisement about drugs, the drug user shown is a young person. In reality, many young people have chosen not to take drugs. For every teen with a problem of abuse, there is probally another teen who has never taken drugs or who has conquered a drug problem. In my high scool, an anonymous student poll showed that more than half of the students had never experimented with drugs.

Some older adults label young people irresponsible and addicted. Even more people are likely to say that the young are apathetic, but such critics are wrong. The young are criticized for not carring about political or social issues, for being unconscience of the problems we all face. yet high school and college students are the ones who are out there, cleaning up the litter on the highways or beaches, whenever there is a local clean-up campaign. During the holidays, every school and college collects food, clothing, and toys for the needy students organize these drives, and students distributes these items. On many weekends, young people are out on the highways, collecting for charities.

Granted, there are apathetic, addicted, and irresponsible young people. But a whole group should not be judged by the actions of a few. Each young person deserve to be treated as an individual, not as an example of a myth.

Lines of Detail: A Walk-Through Assignment

Choose two radio stations popular with your age group. They can be two stations that broadcast music, or two stations that broadcast talk shows. Write a four-paragraph essay describing who listens to each station.

To write the essay, follow these steps:

Step 1: Begin the thoughtlines with some investigation. Listen to two stations, talk or music, popular with your age group. Before you listen, prepare a list of at least six questions. The questions will help you gather details for your essay. For any radio station, you can ask:

What kinds of products or services are advertised?
Does the station offer any contests?
Does the station sponsor any events?

For two music stations, your questions might include:

What groups or individuals does the station play?
What kind of music does it play?

For two talk-radio stations, your questions might include:

What are the talk-show hosts like? Are they funny or insulting or serious?
What topics are discussed?
What kind of people call in?

Listen to the stations you chose, and as you listen, take notes. Answer your own questions, and write down anything about each station that catches your interest or that seems relevant.

Step 2: Survey your notes. Mark the related ideas with the same number. Then cluster the information you've gathered, and give each cluster a title.

Step 3: Focus all your clusters around one point. To find a focus, ask yourself whether the listeners of the two stations are people of the same social class, with the same interests, the same educational background, the same ethnic or racial background.

Try to focus your information with a thesis like one of these:

_____ (station name) and _____

(station name) appeal to the same audience.

_____ (station name) and _____

(station name) appeal to different audiences.

_____ (station name) and _____

(station name) use different strategies to appeal to the same kind

of listeners.

_____(station name) appeals to young people

who _____, but _____ (station

name) appeals to young people who _____.

While _____ (station name) is popular with

middle-aged listeners interested in _____,

_____(station name) appeals to middle-aged

listeners who like _____.

Step 4: Once you have a thesis and clustered details, draft an outline. Revise your draft outline until it is unified, expresses the ideas in a clear order, and has sufficient supporting detail.

Step 5: Write a roughlines draft of your essay. Revise the draft, checking it for balanced paragraphs, relevant and specific details, a strong conclusion, and smooth transitions.

Step 6: Before you prepare the final lines version of your essay, check for spelling, word choice, punctuation, and mechanical errors. Also, give your essay a title.

Writing Your Own Essay

When you write on any of these topics, be sure to work through the stages of thoughtlines, outlines, roughlines, and final lines in preparing your essay.

1. Take any paragraph you wrote for this class and develop it into an essay of four or five paragraphs. If your instructor agrees, read the paragraph to a partner or group, and ask your listener(s) to suggest points inside the paragraph that could be developed into paragraphs of their own.

2. Write an essay using one of the following thesis statements:

   If I won a million dollars, I know what I would do with it.

   Most families waste our natural resources every day, simply by going through their daily routines.

   TV coverage of football [or basketball, or tennis, or other sport that you choose] could be improved by a few changes.

   The one place I'll never visit again is _____ because

   _____.

   All bad romances share certain characteristics.

   If I could be someone else, I'd like to be _____ for several reasons.

3. Write an essay on earliest childhood memories. Interview three class-mates to gather details and to focus your essay. Ask each one to tell you about the earliest memory he or she has of childhood. Before you begin interviewing, make a list of questions, like, "What is your earliest memory?" "How old were you at the time of that recollection?" "What were you doing?" "Do you remember other people or events in that scene?" "If so, what were the others doing?" "Were you indoors?" "Outdoors?" "Is this a pleasant memory?" "Why do you think this memory has stayed with you?"

   Use the details collected at the interviews to write a five-paragraph essay with a thesis sentence like one of the following:

   Childhood memories vary a great deal, from person to person.
   The childhood memories of different people are surprisingly similar.
   Although some people's first memories are painful, others remember a happy time.
   Some people claim to remember events from their infancy, but others can't remember anything before their third [or fourth, or fifth, etc.] birthday.

4. Freewrite for ten minutes on the two best days of your life. After you've completed the freewriting, review it. Do the two days have much in common? Or were they very different? Write a four-paragraph essay based on their similarities or differences, with a thesis like one of these:

   The two best days of my life were both _____. (Focus on similarities.)

   While one of the best days of my life was _____, the

   other great day was _____. (Fill in with differences.)

Name: _____ **Section:** _____

Peer Review Form for an Essay

After you've written a roughlines version of your essay, let a writing partner read it. When your partner has completed the following form, discuss his or her comments. Then repeat the same process for your partner's paragraph.

The thesis of this essay is

_____

_____

The topic sentences for the body paragraphs are

_____

_____

_____

_____

The topic sentence in the conclusion is

_____

_____

The best part of the essay is the _____ (first, second, third, and so forth) paragraph.

I would like to see detail added to the part about

_____

_____.

I would take out the part about

_____.

The introduction is (a) good, (b) could be better.

The conclusion is (a) good, (b) could be better.

I have questions about

_____

Additional comments on the essay:

_____

_____

_____

Reviewer's name: _____

Writing from Reading: The Essay

ELEVEN

Sandra Cisneros

Sandra Cisneros, the child of a Mexican father and a Mexican-American mother, grew up in Chicago. She has worked as a teacher of high school dropouts and in other areas of education and the arts. A poet and writer of short stories, Cisneros incorporates her ethnic background into her writing. Her story "Eleven" is about a birthday gone wrong.

Before you read this selection, consider these questions:

Have you ever felt older than your chronological age? Younger?
Can you remember a time when someone made you feel small?
Have you ever felt like you wanted to disappear?
Is school a particularly frightening place for children? If so, why?

ELEVEN

Sandra Cisneros

What they don't understand about birthdays and what they never tell you is that when you're eleven, you're also ten, and nine, and eight, and seven, and six, and five, and four, and three, and two, and one. And when you wake up on your eleventh birthday you expect to feel eleven, but you don't. You open your eyes and everything's just like yesterday, only it's today. And you don't feel eleven at all. You feel like you're still ten. And you are—underneath the year that makes you eleven.

Like some days you might say something stupid, and that's the part of you that's still ten. Or maybe some days you might need to sit on your mama's lap because you're scared, and that's the part of you that's five. And maybe one day when you're all grown up maybe you will need to cry like if you're three, and that's okay. That's what I tell Mama when she's sad and needs to cry. Maybe she's feeling three.

Because the way you grow old is kind of like an onion or like the rings inside a tree trunk or like my little wooden dolls that fit one inside the other, each year inside the next one. That's how being eleven years old is.

You don't feel eleven. Not right away. It takes a few days, weeks even, sometimes even months before you say Eleven when they ask you. And you don't feel smart eleven, not until you're almost twelve. That's the way it is.

Only today I wish I didn't have only eleven years rattling inside me like pennies in a tin Band-Aid box. Today I wish I was one hundred and two instead of eleven because if I was one hundred and two I'd have known what to say when Mrs. Price put the red sweater on my desk. I would've known how to tell her it wasn't mine instead of just sitting there with that look on my face and nothing coming out of my mouth.

"Whose is this?" Mrs. Price says, and she holds the red sweater up in the air for all the class to see. "Whose? It's been sitting in the coatroom for a month."

"Not mine," says everybody. "Not me."

"It has to belong to somebody," Mrs. Price keeps saying, but nobody can remember. It's an ugly sweater with red plastic buttons and a collar and sleeves all stretched out like you could use it for a jump rope. It's maybe a thousand years old and even if it belonged to me I wouldn't say so.

Maybe because I'm skinny, maybe because she doesn't like me, that stupid Sylvia Saldívar says, "I think it belongs to Rachel." An ugly sweater like that, all raggedy and old, but Mrs. Price believes her. Mrs. Price takes the sweater and puts it right on my desk, but when I open my mouth nothing comes out.

"That's not, I don't, you're not. . . . Not mine," I finally say in a little voice that was maybe me when I was four.

"Of course it's yours," Mrs. Price says. "I remember you wearing it once." Because she's older and the teacher, she's right and I'm not.

Not mine, not mine, not mine, but Mrs. Price is already turning to page thirty-two, and math problem number four. I don't know why but all of a sudden I'm feeling sick inside, like the part of me that's three wants to come out of my eyes, only I squeeze them shut tight and bite down on my teeth real hard and try to remember today I am eleven, eleven. Mama is making a cake for me for tonight, and when Papa comes home everybody will sing Happy birthday, happy birthday to you.

But when the sick feeling goes away and I open my eyes, the red sweater's still sitting there like a big red mountain. I move the red sweater to the corner of my desk with my ruler. I move my pencil and books and eraser as far from it as possible. I even move my chair a little to the right. Not mine, not mine, not mine.

In my head I'm thinking how long till lunchtime, how long till I can take the red sweater and throw it over the schoolyard fence, or leave it hanging on a parking meter, or bunch it up into a little ball and toss it in the alley. Except when math period ends Mrs. Price says loud and in front of everybody, "Now, Rachel, that's enough," because she sees I've shoved the red sweater to the tippy-tip corner of my desk and it's hanging all over the edge like a waterfall, but I don't care.

"Rachel," Mrs. Price says. She says it like she's getting mad. "You put that sweater on right now and no more nonsense."

"But it's not—"

"Now!" Mrs. Price says.

This is when I wish I wasn't eleven, because all the years inside me—ten, nine, eight, seven, six, five, four, three, two, and one—are pushing at the back of my eyes when I put one arm through one sleeve of the sweater that smells like cottage cheese, and then the other arm through the other and stand there with my arms apart like if the sweater hurts me and it does, all itchy and full of germs that aren't even mine.

That's when everything I've been holding in since this morning, since when Mrs. Price put the sweater on my desk, finally lets go, and all of a sudden I'm crying in front of everybody. I wish I was invisible but I'm not. I'm eleven and it's my birthday today and I'm crying like I'm three in front of everybody. I put my head down on the desk and bury my face in my stupid clown-sweater arms. My face all hot and spit coming out of my mouth because I can't stop the little animal noises from coming out of me, until there aren't any more tears left in my eyes, and it's just my body shaking like when you have the hiccups, and my whole head hurts like when you drink milk too fast.

But the worst part is right before the bell rings for lunch. That stupid Phyllis Lopez, who is even dumber than Sylvia Saldívar, says she remembers the red sweater is hers! I take it off right away and give it to her, only Mrs. Price pretends like everything's okay.

Today I'm eleven. There's a cake Mama's making for tonight, and when Papa comes home from work we'll eat it. There'll be candles and presents and everybody will sing Happy birthday, happy birthday to you, Rachel, only it's too late.

I'm eleven today. I'm eleven, ten, nine, eight, seven, six, five, four, three, two, and one, but I wish I was one hundred and two. I wish I was anything but eleven, because I want today to be far away already, far away like a runaway balloon, like a tiny *o* in the sky, so tiny-tiny you have to close your eyes to see it.

Writing from Reading "Eleven"

1. Write about a time when you didn't feel your age. You can call the essay "Seventeen" or "Eleven," or whatever your chronological age was, but write about why you felt that you were a different age.

2. Write about a time, or several times, when an older person was wrong and you were right.

3. Write about a teacher you will always remember.

4. Write an essay on three things that children (or teens) fear.

5. You may have heard the saying, "You're only as old as you feel." Interview three people. Ask them their age; ask them how old they feel, and why. Use the information you gather to write an essay about people and age.

6. Cisneros writes that "the way you grow old is kind of like an onion or like the rings inside a tree trunk." Write an essay about three memorable "rings," or three experiences that helped you to grow in some important way.

JUST WALK ON BY: A BLACK MAN PONDERS HIS POWER
TO ALTER PUBLIC SPACE
Brent Staples

Brent Staples grew up in urban poverty but escaped his bleak background. After attending college and graduate school, he became a successful journalist. In "Just Walk on By," he writes about something he cannot escape: other people's fear of him on city streets.

Before you read this selection, consider these questions:

Have you ever been afraid in a public place? What or who frightened you?
Has anyone ever been afraid of you, in a public place?
Do you think you can recognize a mugger?
Have you ever been mistaken for someone else? How did it make you feel?

Words You May Need to Know

affluent: wealthy
unwieldy: awkward, not easily handled or managed
unnerving: disturbing, frightening
errant: unexpected, irregular
extols: praises
bandolier: a broad belt worn over the shoulder by soldiers and having a line of small loops to hold cartridges

solace: comfort
alienation: sense of being strange, isolation
entity: being
consummation: completion, perfection
labyrinthine: complicated, intricate
constitutionals: walks taken for your health

JUST WALK ON BY: A BLACK MAN PONDERS HIS POWER
TO ALTER PUBLIC SPACE
Brent Staples

My first victim was a woman—white, well dressed, probably in her early twenties. I came upon her late one evening on a deserted street in Hyde Park, a relatively affluent neighborhood in an otherwise mean, impoverished section of Chicago. As I swung onto the avenue behind her, there seemed to be a discreet, uninflammatory distance between us. Not so. She cast back a worried glance. To her, the youngish black man—a broad six feet two inches with a beard and billowing hair, both hands shoved into the pockets of a bulky military jacket—seemed menacingly close. After a few more quick glimpses, she picked up her pace and was soon running in earnest. Within seconds she disappeared into a cross street.

That was more than a decade ago. I was twenty-two years old, a graduate student newly arrived at the University of Chicago. It was in the echo of that terrified woman's footfalls that I first began to know the unwieldy inheritance I'd come into—the ability to alter public space in ugly ways. It was clear that she thought herself the quarry of a mugger, a rapist, or worse. Suffering a bout of insomnia, however, I was stalking sleep, not defenseless wayfarers. As a softy who is scarcely able to take a knife to a raw chicken—let alone hold it to a person's throat—I was surprised, embarrassed, and dismayed all at once. Her flight made me feel like an accomplice in tyranny. It also made it clear that I was indistinguishable from the muggers who occasionally seeped into the area from the surrounding ghetto. That first encounter, and those that followed, signified that a vast, unnerving gulf lay between nighttime pedestrians—particularly women—and me. And I soon gathered that being perceived as dangerous is a hazard in itself. I only needed to turn a corner into a dicey situation, or crowd some frightened, armed person in a foyer somewhere, or make an errant move after being pulled over by a policeman. Where fear and weapons meet—and they often do in urban America—there is always the possibility of death.

In that first year, my first away from my hometown, I was to become thoroughly familiar with the language of fear. At dark, shadowy intersections in Chicago, I could cross in front of a car stopped at a traffic light and elicit the *thunk, thunk, thunk, thunk* of the driver—black, white, male, or female—hammering down the door locks. On less traveled streets after dark, I grew accustomed to but never comfortable with people who crossed to the other side of the street rather than pass me. Then there were the standard unpleasantries with police, doormen, bouncers, cab drivers, and others whose business it is to screen out troublesome individuals *before* there is any nastiness.

I moved to New York nearly two years ago and I have remained an avid night walker. In central Manhattan, the near-constant crowd cover minimizes tense one-on-one street encounters. Elsewhere—visiting friends in SoHo, where sidewalks are narrow and tightly spaced buildings shut out the sky—things can get very taut indeed.

Black men have a firm place in New York mugging literature. Norman Podhoretz in his famed (or infamous) 1963 essay, "My Negro Problem— And Ours," recalls growing up in terror of black males; they "were tougher than we were, more ruthless," he writes—and as an adult on the

ALONG THESE LINES/Prentice-Hall, Inc.

Upper West Side of Manhattan, he continues, he cannot constrain his nervousness when he meets black men on certain streets. Similarly, a decade later, the essayist and novelist Edward Hoagland extols a New York where once "Negro bitterness bore down mainly on other Negroes." Where some see mere panhandlers, Hoagland sees "a mugger who is clearly screwing up his nerve to do more than just *ask* for money." But Hoagland has "the New Yorker's quick-hunch posture for broken-field maneuvering," and the bad guy swerves away.

I often witness that "hunch posture," from women after dark on the warrenlike streets of Brooklyn where I live. They seem to set their faces on neutral and, with their purse straps strung across their chests bandolier style, they forge ahead as though bracing themselves against being tackled. I understand, of course, that the danger they perceive is not a hallucination. Women are particularly vulnerable to street violence, and young black males are drastically overrepresented among the perpetrators of that violence. Yet these truths are no solace against the kind of alienation that comes of being ever the suspect, against being set apart, a fearsome entity with whom pedestrians avoid making eye contact.

It is not altogether clear to me how I reached the ripe old age of twenty-two without being conscious of the lethality nighttime pedestrians attributed to me. Perhaps it was because in Chester, Pennsylvania, the small, angry industrial town where I came of age in the 1960s, I was scarcely noticeable against a backdrop of gang warfare, street knifings, and murders. I grew up one of the good boys, had perhaps a half-dozen fist fights. In retrospect, my shyness of combat has clear sources.

Many things go into the making of a young thug. One of those things is the consummation of the male romance with the power to intimidate. An infant discovers that random flailings send the baby bottle flying out of the crib and crashing to the floor. Delighted, the joyful babe repeats those motions again and again, seeking to duplicate the feat. Just so, I recall the points at which some of my boyhood friends were finally seduced by the perception of themselves as tough guys. When a mark cowered and surrendered his money without resistance, myth and reality merged—and paid off. It is, after all, only manly to embrace the power to frighten and intimidate. We, as men, are not supposed to give an inch of our lane on the highway; we are to seize the fighter's edge in work and in play and even in love; we are to be valiant in the face of hostile forces.

Unfortunately, poor and powerless young men seem to take all this nonsense literally. As a boy, I saw countless tough guys locked away; I have since buried several, too. They were babies, really—a teenage cousin, a brother of twenty-two, a childhood friend in his mid-twenties—all gone down in episodes of bravado played out in the streets. I came to doubt the virtues of intimidation early on. I chose, perhaps even unconsciously, to remain a shadow—timid, but a survivor.

The fearsomeness mistakenly attributed to me in public places often has a perilous flavor. The most frightening of these confusions occurred in the late 1970s and early 1980s when I worked as a journalist in Chicago. One day, rushing into the office of a magazine I was writing for with a deadline story in hand, I was mistaken for a burglar. The office manager called security and, with an ad hoc posse, pursued me through the labyrinthine halls, nearly to my editor's door. I had no way of proving who I was. I could only move briskly toward the company of some-one who knew me.

Another time I was on assignment for a local paper and killing time before an interview. I entered a jewelry store on the city's affluent Near North Side. The proprietor excused herself and returned with an enormous red Doberman pinscher straining at the end of a leash. She stood, the dog extended toward me, silent to my questions, her eyes bulging nearly out of her head. I took a cursory look around, nodded, and bade her good night. Relatively speaking, however, I never fared as badly as another black male journalist. He went to nearby Waukegan, Illinois, a couple of summers ago to work on a story about a murderer who was born there. Mistaking the reporter for the killer, police hauled him from his car at gunpoint and but for his press credentials would probably have tried to book him. Such episodes are not uncommon. Black men trade tales like this all the time.

In "My Negro Problem—And Ours," Podhoretz writes that the hatred he feels for blacks makes itself known to him through a variety of avenues—one being his discomfort with that "special brand of paranoid touchiness" to which he says blacks are prone. No doubt he is speaking here of black men. In time, I learned to smother the rage I felt at so often being taken for a criminal. Not to do so would surely have led to madness—via that special "paranoid touchiness" that so annoyed Podhoretz at the time he wrote the essay.

I began to take precautions to make myself less threatening. I move about with care, particularly late in the evening. I give a wide berth to nervous people on subway platforms during the wee hours, particularly when I have exchanged business clothes for jeans. If I happen to be entering a building behind some people who appear skittish, I may walk by, letting them clear the lobby before I return, so as not to seem to be following them. I have been calm and extremely congenial on those rare occasions when I've been pulled over by the police.

And on late-evening constitutionals along streets less traveled by, I employ what has proved to be an excellent tension-reducing measure: I whistle melodies from Beethoven and Vivaldi and the more popular classical composers. Even steely New Yorkers hunching toward nighttime destinations seem to relax, and occasionally they even join in the tune. Virtually everybody seems to sense that a mugger wouldn't be warbling bright, sunny selections from Vivaldi's *Four Seasons*. It is my equivalent of the cowbell that hikers wear when they know they are in bear country.

Writing from Reading "Just Walk on By: A Black Man Ponders His Power to Alter Public Space"

1. Brent Staples says that it is dangerous to be perceived as a dangerous person. Write an essay about three instances when a person who appears dangerous can become a victim himself or herself.

2. Write a letter, several paragraphs long, to a person who misjudged or misunderstood you. Explain what the misunderstanding was, why it hurt you, and how the person can avoid making the same mistake again.

3. Write an essay about a group that many people fear. In your essay, discuss whether the fear of this group is justified. You may write about

such groups as homeless people, bikers, fraternity members, or any other group that may be feared, misunderstood, or stereotyped.

4. Write an essay on the dangers of city streets.

5. Write an essay on the dangers of the suburbs.

6. Staples refers to the "nonsense" that poor and powerless men believe: that it is manly to use one's power to frighten and intimidate others. Write an essay explaining where males learn this belief: at home, in school, from peers, from movies, or from TV.

THE BOTTOM LINE

Grammar for Writers

INTRODUCTION

Overview

In this part of the book, you'll be working with "The Bottom Line," the basics of grammar that you need to be a clear writer. If you are willing to memorize certain rules and work through various activities, you'll be able to apply grammatical rules automatically as you write.

Using the Bottom Line

Because this portion of the textbook is divided into several self-contained sections, it does not have to be read in sequence. Your instructor may suggest you review specific rules and examples, or you may be assigned various segments as either a class or a group. Several approaches are possible, and thus you can regard this section as a user-friendly grammar handbook for quick reference. Mastering the practical parts of grammar will improve your writing; you'll feel more sure of yourself because you'll know the bottom line.

CONTENTS

The Bottom Line: Grammar for Writers

Introduction	**311**
Section One: The Simple Sentence	**315**
Recognizing a Sentence	315
Recognizing Verbs	315
Recognizing Subjects	317
Word Order	322
Section Two: Beyond the Simple Sentence: Coordination	**329**
Options for Combining Simple Sentences	329
Option 1: Using a Comma with a Coordinating Conjunction	330
Option 2: Using a Semicolon Between Two Simple Sentences	333
Option 3: Using a Semicolon and a Conjunctive Adverb	334
Section Three: Beyond the Simple Sentence: Subordination	**340**
More on Combining Simple Sentences	340
Option 4: Using a Dependent Clause to Begin a Sentence	340
Option 5: Using a Dependent Clause to End a Sentence	341
Section Four: Avoiding Sentence Fragments	**348**
Recognizing Fragments	348
Correcting Fragments	352
Section Five: Using Parallelism in Sentences	**356**
Achieving Parallelism	357
Section Six: Correcting Problems with Modifiers	**363**
Correcting Modifier Problems	364
Reviewing the Steps and the Solutions	368
Section Seven: Using Verbs Correctly	**371**
Using Standard Verb Forms	371
The Past Tense	373
The Four Main Forms of a Verb	374
Irregular Verbs	375
Section Eight: More on Verbs: Consistency and Voice	**382**
Consistent Verb Tenses	382
The Present Perfect and Past Perfect Tenses	385
The Past Perfect Tense	386
Passive and Active Voice	387
Section Nine: Making Subjects and Verbs Agree	**393**
Pronouns as Subjects	394
Special Problems with Agreement	394
Compound Subjects	397
Indefinite Pronouns	398

ALONG THESE LINES/Prentice-Hall, Inc.

Collective Nouns   399
Making Subjects and Verbs Agree: The Bottom Line   400

Section Ten: Using Pronouns Correctly: Agreement and Reference   405
Agreement of a Pronoun and Its Antecedent   406
Indefinite Pronouns   406
Collective Nouns   408
Pronouns and Their Antecedents: Being Clear   410

Section Eleven: Using Pronouns Correctly: Consistency and Case   413
Choosing the Case of Pronouns   415
Common Errors with Case of Pronouns   417

Section Twelve: Punctuation   419
The Period   419
The Question Mark   419
The Semicolon   419
The Comma   421
The Apostrophe   425
The Colon   426
The Exclamation Mark   426
The Dash   427
Parentheses   427
The Hyphen   427
Quotation Marks   428
Capital Letters   429
Numbers   431
Abbreviations   431

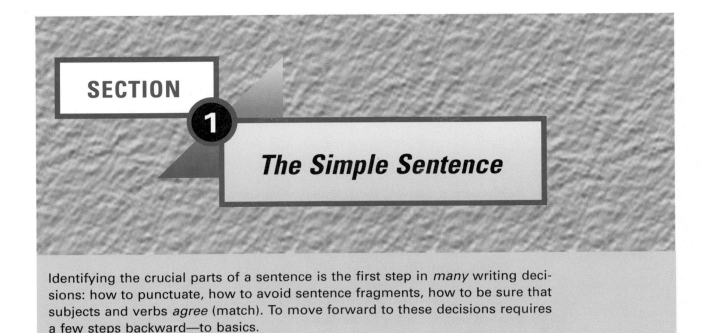

The Simple Sentence

Identifying the crucial parts of a sentence is the first step in *many* writing decisions: how to punctuate, how to avoid sentence fragments, how to be sure that subjects and verbs *agree* (match). To move forward to these decisions requires a few steps backward—to basics.

RECOGNIZING A SENTENCE

Let's start with a few basic definitions. A basic unit of language is a *word*.

> **examples:** car, dog, sun

A group of related words can be a *phrase*.

> **examples:** shiny new car; snarling, angry dog; in the bright sun

When a group of words contains a subject and a verb, it is called a *clause*. When the word group has a subject and a verb and makes sense by itself, it is called a *sentence*, or an independent clause.

If you want to check to see whether you have written a sentence, and not just a group of related words, you first have to check for a subject and a verb. It's often easier to locate the verbs first.

RECOGNIZING VERBS

Verbs are *words that express some kind of action or being*. Verbs about the five senses—sight, touch, smell, taste, and sound—are part of the group called being verbs. Look at some examples of verbs and their functions in the following sentences:

> **action verbs:**
>
> We *walk* to the store every day.
> The children *ran* to the playground.
>
> **being verbs:**
>
> My mother *is* a good cook.
> The family *seems* unhappy.
> The soup *smells* delicious.

▶ **E XERCISE 1: Recognizing Verbs**

Underline the verbs in each of the following sentences.

a. The truck stalled on the highway.

b. Early in the morning, he jogs around the park.

c. She looks worried about the driving test.

d. My cousin Bill was the best player on the team.

e. The rain floods the street on stormy days.

f. The homemade tortillas taste delicious.

g. Maria is my sister-in-law.

h. My parents called the bus station.

i. Most people love long weekends.

j. Children today are sophisticated about fashion.

k. Dalmatians are very popular pets today.

l. Single parents face many challenges at home and at work.

m. The old blanket feels rough and scratchy.

n. Her hair glistened with fragrant oil.

o. He cooked a perfect dinner of fish and rice.

More on Verbs

The verb in a sentence can be more than one word. First of all, there can be *helping verbs* in front of the main verb, the action or being verb. Here is a list of some frequently used helping verbs: *is, am, are, was, were, do, must, might, have, shall, will, can, could, may, should, would.*

I was watching the Super Bowl. (The helping verb is *was.*)
You should have called me. (The helping verbs are *should* and *have.*)
The president can select his assistants. (The helping verb is *can.*)
Leroy will graduate in May. (The helping verb is *will.*)

Helping verbs can make the verb in a sentence more than one word long. But there can also be more than one main verb:

Andrew *planned* and *practiced* his speech.
I *stumbled* over the rug, *grabbed* a chair, and *fell* on my face.

▶ **E XERCISE 2: Collaborative Exercise on Writing Sentences with Helping Verbs**

Complete this exercise with a partner or with a group. First, ask one person to add at least one helping verb to the verb given. Then work together to write two sentences using the main verb and the helping verb(s). As a final step, appoint one spokesperson for your group to read all your sentences to the class. Notice how many combinations of main verb and helping verb you hear.

The first one is done as a sample.

ALONG THESE LINES/Prentice-Hall, Inc.

a. verb: called

verb with helping verb(s): <u>has called</u>

sentence 1: <u>Sam has called me twice this week.</u>

sentence 2: <u>She has called him a hero.</u>

b. verb: moving

verb with helping verb(s): _____

sentence 1: _____

sentence 2: _____

c. verb: fly

verb with helping verb(s): _____

sentence 1: _____

sentence 2: _____

d. verb: laughed

verb with helping verb(s): _____

sentence 1: _____

sentence 2: _____

e. verb: spoken

verb with helping verb(s): _____

sentence 1: _____

sentence 2: _____

f. verb: worrying

verb with helping verb(s): _____

sentence 1: _____

sentence 2: _____

RECOGNIZING SUBJECTS

After you learn to recognize verbs, it's easy to find the subjects of sentences because subjects and verbs are linked. If the verb is an action verb, for example, the subject will be the word or words that answer the question, "Who or what is doing that action?"

The truck stalled on the highway.

Step 1: Identify the verb: *stalled*
Step 2: Ask, "Who or what stalled?"
Step 3: The answer is the subject: The *truck* stalled on the highway. The *truck* is the subject.

If your verb expresses *being*, the same steps apply to finding the subject.

Spike was my best friend.

Step 1: Identify the verb: *was*
Step 2: Ask, "Who or what was my best friend?"
Step 3: The answer is the subject: *Spike* was my best friend. *Spike* is the subject.

Just as there can be more than one word to make up a verb, *there can be more than one subject.*

examples: *David* and *Leslie* planned the surprise party.
My *father* and *I* worked in the yard yesterday.

▶ **E X E R C I S E 3 : Recognizing Subjects in Sentences**

Underline the subjects in the following sentences.

a. Maggie might have followed the directions more carefully.

b. They were stacking the records in neat piles.

c. Mike and Calvin will be coming over tomorrow.

d. Suddenly, a car appeared on the runway.

e. As a matter of fact, houses are not expensive in that neighborhood.

f. Roses are fairly easy to grow.

g. Happiness can come in many shapes and forms.

h. Colleges are facing many budget problems.

i. Complaining can sometimes make a situation worse.

j. Joy and excitement filled the locker room.

k. Sandra laughed at the man in the clown suit.

l. Nothing is wrong with my sister.

m. Books and magazines covered every table and desk.

n. The manager will be contacting you about the job interview.

o. Somebody took the last piece of cake.

More about Recognizing Subjects and Verbs

When you look for the subject of a sentence, look for the core word or words; don't include descriptive words around the subject. The idea is to look for the subject, not for the words that describe it.

The dark blue *dress* looked lovely on Anita.
Dirty *streets* and grimy *houses* destroy a neighborhood.

In these two examples, the subjects are the core words *dress*, *streets*, and *houses*, not the descriptive words *dark blue*, *dirty*, and *grimy*.

Prepositions and Prepositional Phrases

Prepositions are usually small words that often signal a kind of position or possession, as shown in the following list:

Some Common Prepositions					
about	before	beyond	inside	on	under
above	below	during	into	onto	up
across	behind	except	like	over	upon
after	beneath	for	near	through	with
among	beside	from	of	to	within
around	between	in	off	toward	without
at					

A prepositional phrase is made up of a preposition and its object. Here are some prepositional phrases. In each one, the first word is the preposition; the other words are the object of the preposition.

Prepositional Phrases

about the movie   of mice and men
around the corner   off the record
between two lanes   on the mark
during recess   up the wall
near my house   with my sister and brother

There's an old memory trick to help you remember prepositions. Think of a chair. Now, think of a series of words you can put *in front of* the chair:

around the chair   *with* the chair
by the chair   *to* the chair
behind the chair   *near* the chair
between the chairs   *under* the chair
of the chair   *on* the chair
off the chair   *from* the chair

These words are prepositions
   You need to know about prepositions because they can help you identify the subject of a sentence. Here is an important grammar rule about prepositions:

Nothing in a prepositional phrase can ever be the subject of the sentence.

Prepositional phrases describe people, places, or things. They may describe the subject of a sentence, but they never include the subject. Whenever you are looking for the subject of a sentence, begin by putting parentheses around all the prepositional phrases.

The restaurant (around the corner) makes the best fried chicken (in town.)

Notice that the prepositional phrases are in parentheses. Since *nothing* in them can be the subject, once you have eliminated the prepositional phrases you can follow the steps to find the subject of the sentence:

What's the verb? *makes*
Who or what makes the best fried chicken? The *restaurant.*
Restaurant is the subject of the sentence.

By marking off the prepositional phrases, you are left with the *core* of the sentence—less to look at.

(Behind the park), a *carousel* (with gilded horses) delighted children (from all the neighborhoods).
subject: carousel

The *dog* (with the ugliest face) was the winner (of the contest).
subject: *dog*

▶ **EXERCISE 4:** **Recognizing Prepositional Phrases, Subjects, and Verbs**

To practice identifying prepositional phrases, put parentheses around all the prepositional phrases in the following sentences. Then underline the subject and verb, putting *S* above the subject and *V* above the verb.

   a. The car in the parking lot near the bank has a huge dent in the rear.

   b. Some of the people on my street like sitting on their front steps on a hot night.

   c. Several dancers in the play stumbled on the rickety stage.

   d. During my lunch hour, I often go to the park across the street from my office.

   e. The true story beneath all his lies was a tale with some horrifying twists.

   f. She took her credit card from her wallet and handed the card to the clerk behind the counter.

   g. The doctor in the emergency room dashed down the hall toward the trauma victim.

   h. The little village above the lake gleamed in the sunlight.

   i. On sunny days, towns by the beach are usually filled with tourists.

   j. Their farm was off the main road between Springfield and Ridgewood.

▶ **EXERCISE 5:** **Collaborate on Writing Sentences with Prepositional Phrases**

Do this exercise with a partner. First, add one prepositional phrase to the core sentence given. Then ask your partner to add a second prepositional phrase to the same sentence. On the next sentence, switch places. Let your partner add the first phrase; you add the second. Keep reversing the process throughout the exercise.

ALONG THESE LINES/Prentice-Hall, Inc.

When you have completed the exercise, be ready to read to the class the sentences with two prepositional phrases. The first one has been done for you as a sample.

a. core sentence: Rain fell.

add one prepositional phrase: _Rain fell on the mountains._

add another prepositional phrase: _From a dark sky rain fell on the mountains._

b. core sentence: The school was closed.

add one prepositional phrase: _____

add another prepositional phrase: _____

_____

c. core sentence: The canoe drifted.

add one prepositional phrase: _____

add another prepositional phrase: _____

_____

d. core sentence: High school seniors are worried.

add one prepositional phrase: _____

add another prepositional phrase: _____

_____

e. core sentence: Parents must struggle.

add one prepositional phrase: _____

add another prepositional phrase: _____

_____

f. core sentence: I met her.

add one prepositional phrase: _____

add another prepositional phrase: _____

_____

g. core sentence: Jesse hid the package.

add one prepositional phrase: _____

add another prepositional phrase: _____

_____

h. core sentence: My uncle was visiting.

add one prepositional phrase: _____

add another prepositional phrase: _____

_____

WORD ORDER

When we speak, we often use a very simple word order: first, the subject; then, the verb. For example, someone would say, "I am going to the store." *I* is the subject that begins the sentence; *am going* is the verb that comes after the subject.

But not all sentences are in such a simple word order. Prepositional phrases, for example, can change the word order.

> **sentence:** Among the contestants was an older man.

> **Step 1:** Mark off the prepositional phrase(s) with parentheses: (Among the contestants) was an older man. Remember that nothing in a prepositional phrase can be the subject of a sentence.
> **Step 2:** Find the verb: *was*
> **Step 3:** Who or what was? An older man was. The subject of the sentence is *man.*

After you change the word order of this sentence, you can see the subject (*S*) and verb (*V*) more easily.

> $\overset{S}{}$ $\overset{V}{}$
> An older *man was* among the contestants.

▶ **EXERCISE 6:** **Finding Prepositional Phrases, Subjects, and Verbs in Complicated Word Order**

Start by putting parentheses around the prepositional phrases in the following sentences. Then underline the subjects and verbs, putting *S* above the subjects and *V* above the verbs.

   a. Down the street from my apartment is an all-night supermarket.

   b. Behind the counter is a cash register.

   c. Inside the student union are video games and vending machines.

   d. Around the outside of the house are tall trees with yellow blossoms on their spreading branches.

   e. Above the rooftops of the houses stands the steeple of an old church.

   f. From the back of the alley came a loud scream.

   g. Between the houses was a fence with a clinging vine of red flowers.

   h. In my closet is a raincoat with a flannel lining.

   i. Among my fondest memories is a recollection of a day at the park.

   j. With the man from Wichita came a sheriff in uniform.

More on Word Order

The expected word order of subject first, then verb will change when a sentence starts with *There is/are, There was/were, Here is/are, Here was/were.* In such cases, look for the subject after the verb.

> $\overset{V}{}$ $\overset{S}{}$ $\overset{S}{}$
> There *are* a *bakery* and a *pharmacy* down the street.

ALONG THESE LINES/Prentice-Hall, Inc.

        V   S
Here *is* the *man* with the answers.

If it helps you to understand this pattern, change the word order:

     S   S   V
A *bakery* and a *pharmacy are* there, down the street.

     S   V
The *man* with the answers *is* here.

You should also note that even when the subject comes after the verb, the verb has to *match* the subject. For instance, if the subject refers to more than one thing, the verb must also refer to more than one thing.

There are a bakery and a pharmacy down the road.
   (Two things, a bakery and a pharmacy, are down the road.)

Word Order in Questions

Questions may have a different word order. The main verb and the helping verb may not be next to each other.

question: Do you like pizza?
subject: *you*
verbs: *do, like*

If it helps you to understand this concept, think about answering the question. If someone accused you of not liking pizza, you might say, "I *do like* it." You'd use two words as verbs.

question: Will he think about it?
subject: *he*
verbs: *will, think*

question: Is Maria telling the truth?
subject: *Maria*
verbs: *is, telling*

Words That Can't Be Verbs

Sometimes there are words that look like verbs in a sentence, but they are not verbs. Such words include adverbs (words like *always, often, nearly, rarely, never, ever*) that are placed close to the verb but are not verbs. Another word that is placed between a helping verb and a main verb is *not. Not* is not a verb. When you are looking for verbs in a sentence, be careful to eliminate words like *often* and *not*.

He will not listen to me. (The verbs are *will listen*.)
Althea can often find a bargain. (The verbs are *can find*.)

Be careful with *contractions*.

They haven't raced in years. (The verbs are *have raced*. *Not* is not a part
   of the verb, even in contractions.)
Don't you come from Arizona? (The verbs are *do come*.)
Won't he ever learn? (The verbs are *will learn*. *Won't* is a contraction for
   will not.)

Recognizing Main Verbs

If you're checking to see if a word is a main verb, try the *pronoun test*. Combine your word with this simple list of pronouns:

I, you, he, she, it, we, they

A main verb is a word such as *drive* or *noticed* that can be combined with the words on this list. Now try the pronoun test.

For the word *drive:* I drive, you drive, he drives, she drives, it drives, we drive, they drive

For the word *noticed:* I noticed, you noticed, he noticed, she noticed, it noticed, we noticed, they noticed

But words like *never* can't be used, alone, with the pronouns:

~~I never, you never, he never, she never, it never, we never, they never~~
(Never did what?)

Never is not a verb. *Not* is not a verb either, as the pronoun test indicates:

~~I not, you not, he not, she not, it not, we not, you not, they not~~ (These combinations don't make sense because *not* is not a verb.)

Verb Forms That Can't Be Main Verbs

There are forms of verbs that can't be main verbs by themselves, either. An *-ing* verb, by itself, cannot be the main verb, as the pronoun test shows.

For the word *voting*: ~~I voting, you voting, he voting, she voting, we voting, they voting~~

If you see an *-ing* verb by itself, correct the sentence by adding a helping verb.

Scott ~~riding~~ his motorcycle.   (*Riding*, by itself, cannot be a main verb.)

correction: Scott was *riding* his motorcycle.

Another verb form, called an infinitive, also cannot be a main verb. An infinitive is the form of the verb that has *to* placed in front of it.

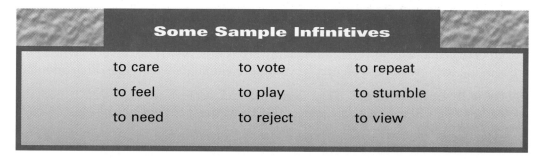

Some Sample Infinitives		
to care	to vote	to repeat
to feel	to play	to stumble
to need	to reject	to view

Try the pronoun test and you'll see that infinitives can't be main verbs:

For the infinitive *to vote:* ~~I to vote, you to vote, he to vote, she to vote, we to vote, they to vote~~

So if you see an infinitive being used as a verb, correct the sentence by adding a main verb.

We ~~to vote~~ in the election tomorrow.   (There's no verb, just an infinitive.)

correction: We *are going* to vote in the election tomorrow. (Now there's a verb.)

The infinitives and the *-ing* verbs just don't work as main verbs. You must put a verb with them to make a correct sentence.

▶ **EXERCISE 7:   Correcting Problems with *-ing* or Infinitive Verb Forms**

Most—but not all—of the following sentences are faulty; an *-ing* verb or an infinitive may be taking the place of a main verb. Rewrite the sentences with errors.

a. Everyone in the senior class to visit the amusement park for a special graduation party.

rewritten: _____

_____

b. My husband paying no attention to the feud between his sisters.

rewritten: _____

_____

c. The flashy red sportscar ahead of me speeding out of control and into the median.

rewritten: _____

_____

d. Sylvia learned to care about her health after her bout with pneumonia.

rewritten: _____

_____

e. Among his other goals, Jason to win a medal in the 200 meter race.

rewritten: _____

_____

f. After all the discussion and deliberation, the committee taking a very conservative position on the question of tenants' rights.

rewritten: _____

_____

g. One of the most famous experts in the field of forensic science to speak to my criminal justice class tomorrow.

rewritten: _____

_____

EXERCISE

h. The dog behind the fence barking uncontrollably for almost two hours.

rewritten: _____

_____

i. Ever since the accident, I have been picking tiny pieces of glass out of the carpet.

rewritten: _____

_____

j. In her lectures, the nutritionist emphasizing the importance of fiber in our diet.

rewritten: _____

_____

▶ **E X E R C I S E 8 : Finding Subjects and Verbs: A Comprehensive Exercise**

Underline the subjects and verbs in these sentences, putting *S* above the subjects and *V* above the verbs.

a. Do you ever visit your grandmother in Minneapolis?

b. They're not playing the game by the rules.

c. Behind the mall is a huge parking lot.

d. Robert needs to rehearse for the concert.

e. Won't you consider my suggestion?

f. Football players are often injured during the season.

g. My sister will never repeat that gossip.

h. There are three reasons for the price hike.

i. Jackie should have been thinking about her boyfriend's feelings.

j. There are a Mazda, a Chrysler, and a Volkswagen in the used car lot.

k. Lakeesha paid the bills and balanced her checkbook yesterday.

l. Within the fenced yard is a lovely garden of tropical plants.

m. He and my father looked tired and dirty.

n. Sweet little puppies can develop minds of their own.

o. Erin has never met her cousin from California.

▶ **E X E R C I S E 9 : Collaborate and Review: Create Your Own Text**

Complete this activity with two partners. Following is a list of rules you've just studied. Each member of the group should write one example for each rule.

When your group has completed three examples for each rule, trade your completed exercise with another group, and check their examples while they check yours.

The first rule has been done for you, as a sample.

Rule 1: The verb in a sentence can express some kind of action.

examples: a. Janelle drives to work every day.

b. Last week my cat killed a mouse in the basement.

c. My little sister dyed her hair with Kool-Aid.

Rule 2: The verb in a sentence can express some state of being or one of the five senses.

examples: a. _____

b. _____

c. _____

Rule 3: The verb in a sentence can consist of more than one word.

examples: a. _____

b. _____

c. _____

Rule 4: There can be more than one subject of a sentence.

examples: a. _____

b. _____

c. _____

Rule 5: If you take out the prepositional phrases, it's easier to identify the subject of a sentence because nothing in a prepositional phrase can be the subject of a sentence.

examples: (For examples, write sentences with at least one prepositional phrase in them; put parentheses around the prepositional phrases.)

a. _____

b. _____

c. _____

Rule 6: Not all sentences have the simple word order of subject first, then verb.

examples: (Give examples of more complicated word order.)

a. _____

b. _____

c. _____

Rule 7: Words like *not, never, often, always, ever* are not verbs.

examples: (Write sentences using those words, but underline the correct verb.)

a. _____

b. _____

c. _____

Rule 8: An *-ing* verb form by itself or an infinitive (*to* preceding the verb) cannot be a main verb.

examples: (Write sentences with *-ing* verb forms or infinitives, but underline the main verb.)

a. _____

b. _____

c. _____

SECTION 2

Beyond the Simple Sentence: Coordination

A group of words containing a subject and verb is called a clause. When that group makes sense by itself, it is called a sentence, or an independent clause.

A sentence that has *one independent clause* is called a *simple sentence*. If you rely too heavily on a sentence pattern of simple sentences, you risk writing paragraphs like

> I am a college student. I am also a salesperson in a mall. I am always busy. School is time-consuming. Studying is time-consuming. Working makes me tired. Balancing these activities is hard. I work too many hours. Work is important. It pays for school.

instead of

> I am a college student and a salesperson at a mall, so I am always busy. School and study are time-consuming, and working makes me tired. Balancing these activities is hard. I work too many hours, but that work is important. It pays for school.

OPTIONS FOR COMBINING SIMPLE SENTENCES

Good writing involves *sentence variety*. This means mixing a simple sentence with a more complicated one, and using both short and long sentences. Sentence variety is easier to achieve if you can *combine* related, short sentences into one.

Some students avoid such combining because they're not sure how to do it. They don't know how to punctuate the new combinations. It's true that punctuation involves memorizing a few rules, but once you know them, you'll be able to use them automatically and write with more confidence. Here are three options for combining simple sentences followed by the punctuation rules you need to use in each case.

ALONG THESE LINES/Prentice-Hall, Inc.

329

OPTION 1: USING A COMMA WITH A COORDINATING CONJUNCTION

You can combine two simple sentences with a comma and a coordinating conjunction. The coordinating conjunctions are *and, but, or, nor, for, yet, so.*

To *coordinate* means *to join equals.* When you join two simple sentences with a comma and a coordinating conjunction, each half of the combination remains an independent clause, with its own subject (*S*) and verb (*V*).

Here are two simple sentences:

S   V   S   V
He cooked the dinner.   *She washed* the dishes.

Here are the two simple sentences combined with a comma, and with the word *and*, a coordinating conjunction (CC):

S   V   , CC S   V
He cooked the dinner, *and she washed* the dishes.

The combined sentences keep the form they had as separate sentences; that is, they are still both independent clauses, with a subject and verb and with the ability to stand alone.

The word that joins them is the *coordinating conjunction.* It is used to join *equals.* Look at some more examples. These examples use a variety of coordinating conjunctions to join two simple sentences:

sentences combined with *but*:

S   V   , CC S V
I rushed to the bank, *but I was* too late.

sentences combined with *or*:

S   V   , CC S   V
She can write a letter to Jim, *or she can call* him.

sentences combined with *nor*:

S   V   , CC V S V
I didn't like the book, *nor did I like* the movie made from the book. (Notice what happens to the word order when you use *nor*.)

sentences combined with *for*:

S   V   , CC S V
Sam worried about the job interview, *for he saw* many qualified applicants in the waiting room.

sentences combined with *yet*:

S   V   , CC S   V
Leo tried to please his sister, *yet she never seemed* appreciative of his efforts.

sentences combined with *so*:

S V   , CC S V
I was the first in line for the concert tickets, *so I got* the best seats in the stadium.

Where Does the Comma Go?

Notice that the comma comes *before* the coordinating conjunction (*and, but, or, nor, for, yet, so*). It comes before the new idea, the second independent clause. It goes where the first independent clause ends. Try this punctuation check. After you've placed the comma, look at the combined sentences. For example:

> She joined the army, and she traveled overseas.

Now split it into two sentences at the comma:

> She joined the army. And she traveled overseas. (The split makes sense)

If you put the comma in the wrong place, after the coordinating conjunction, your split sentences become:

> She joined the army and. She traveled overseas. (The split doesn't make sense)

This test helps you see whether the comma has been placed correctly—*where the first independent clause ends.* (Notice that you can begin a sentence with *and.* You can also begin a sentence with *but, or, nor, for, yet,* or *so*—as long as you're writing a complete sentence.)

Caution: Do *not* put a comma every time you use the words *and, but, or, nor, for, yet* or *so;* put it only when the coordinating conjunction joins independent clauses. Don't put the comma when the coordinating conjunction joins words:

> blue and gold   tired but happy   hot or cold

Don't put the comma when the coordinating conjunction joins phrases:

> on the chair or under the table
> in the water and by the shore
> with a smile but without an apology

The comma is used when the coordinating conjunction joins *two independent clauses.* Another way to say the same rule is to say, the comma is used when the coordinating conjunction joins *two simple sentences.*

Placing the Comma by Using S-V Patterns

An independent clause, or simple sentence, follows this basic pattern:

> S   V
> *He ran.*

or

> S   S V
> *He* and *I ran.*

or

> S   V   V
> *He ran* and *swam.*

or

```
S         S  V       V
```
He and *I ran* and *swam.*

Study all four patterns for the simple sentence, and you'll notice that you can draw a line separating the subjects on one side and the verbs on the other:

```
S   |  V
SS  |  V
S   |  VV
SS  |  VV
```

So whether the simple sentence has one subject (or more than one), and one verb (or more than one), the pattern is subject(s) followed by verb(s).

When you combine two simple sentences, the pattern changes:

two simple sentences:

```
S     V   S  V
```
He swam. I ran.

two simple sentences combined:

```
S     V       S  V
```
He swam, but *I ran.*

In the new pattern, *SVSV,* you can't draw a line separating all the subjects on one side, and all the verbs on the other. This new pattern is called a *compound sentence:* two simple sentences, or independent clauses, joined into one.

Recognizing the *SVSV* pattern will help you place the comma for compound sentences. (If you run two independent clauses together without the necessary punctuation, you make an error called a *run-on sentence.* This error is also called a *fused sentence.*)

Here's another way to remember this rule. When you have this pattern,

```
SV      SV
```

use a comma in front of the coordinating conjunction. But with these patterns,

```
S   |  V
SS  |  V
S   |  VV
SS  |  VV
```

do not use a comma in front of the coordinating conjunctions. For example, use a comma for this pattern:

```
S     V            S   V
```
Jane followed directions, but *I rushed* ahead.

but do not use a comma for this pattern:

```
S     V                              V
```
Carol cleans her kitchen every week but never *wipes* the top of the refrigerator.

You've just studied one way to combine simple sentences. If you are going to take advantage of this method, you need to *memorize the coordinating conjunc-*

ALONG THESE LINES/Prentice-Hall, Inc.

tions—*and, but, or, nor, for, yet, so*—so that your use of them, with the correct punctuation, will become automatic.

▶ **E X E R C I S E　1 :**　**Recognizing Compound Sentences and Adding Commas**

Add commas only where they are needed in the following sentences.

  a. I came to see the play but the theater was closed.

  b. The waiter at the crowded restaurant rushed from table to table and tried to pacify the impatient customers.

  c. Before my trip I read everything in the library about Puerto Rico and I took a Spanish class in night school.

  d. The young couple are planning to save their money and are hoping to buy a small house in the suburbs.

  e. It rained all weekend so the picnic was postponed.

  f. Rosa showed signs of nervousness in her speech yet her words carried conviction and power.

  g. I looked in three stores for the perfect birthday gift for Fred but couldn't find anything at all.

  h. You have to prepare for a marathon or you can do serious damage to your body.

  i. She deserved to win first prize for she had spent years practicing her skills.

  j. The customers were not interested in my excuses nor were they sympathetic with my problems.

  k. Andrew fiddled with the TV for half an hour but he couldn't get the fuzziness out of the picture.

  l. Several of my classmates studied together in the library and shared their notes.

OPTION 2: USING A SEMICOLON BETWEEN TWO SIMPLE SENTENCES

Sometimes you want to combine two simple sentences (two independent clauses), but you don't want to use a coordinating conjunction. **If you want to join two simple sentences that are related in their ideas and you don't use a coordinating conjunction, you can combine them with a semicolon.**

two simple sentences:

S　　V　　　　S　　V
I cooked the turkey. *She made* the stuffing.

two simple sentences combined with a semicolon:

S   V   ; S V
I cooked the turkey; *she made* the stuffing.

Here's another example of this option in use:

S   V V   ; S   V
Rain can be dangerous; *it makes* the roads slippery.

Notice that when you join two simple sentences with a semicolon, the second sentence begins with a lower case letter, not a capital letter.

Caution: If you are joining two simple sentences (two independent clauses) without a coordinating conjunction, *you must use a semicolon.* A comma isn't enough. (Joining two simple sentences with a comma and no coordinating conjunction is an error called a *comma splice.*)

comma splice error:

S   V   S   V
The *crowd pushed* forward, *people began* to panic.

correction:

S   V   ; S   V
The *crowd pushed* forward; *people began* to panic.

You need to memorize the seven coordinating conjunctions so that you can make a decision about punctuating your combined sentences. Remember these rules:

- If a coordinating conjunction joins the combined sentences, put a comma in front of the coordinating conjunction.

S   V   ,   S V
Tom had a barbecue in his back yard, and the *food was* delicious.

- If there is no coordinating conjunction, put a semicolon in front of the second independent clause.

S   V   ;   S V
Tom had a barbecue in his back yard; the *food was* delicious.

OPTION 3: USING A SEMICOLON AND A CONJUNCTIVE ADVERB

Sometimes you want to join two simple sentences (independent clauses) with a connecting word called a *conjunctive adverb*. Here is a list of some conjunctive adverbs.

Some Common Conjunctive Adverbs			
also	furthermore	likewise	otherwise
anyway	however	meanwhile	similarly
as a result	incidentally	moreover	still

ALONG THESE LINES/Prentice-Hall, Inc.

besides	in addition	nevertheless	then
certainly	in fact	next	therefore
consequently	indeed	now	thus
finally	instead	on the other hand	undoubtedly

You can use a conjunctive adverb (*c. a.*) to join simple sentences, but when you do, you still need a semicolon in front of the adverb.

two simple sentences:

    S   V   S V
My *parents checked* my homework every night. *I did* well in math.

two simple sentences joined by a conjunctive adverb and a semicolon:

    S   V   ; c.a. S V
My *parents checked* my homework every night; *thus I did* well in math.

  S   V   ;   c.a.   S   V
She gave me good advice; *moreover, she helped* me follow it.

Punctuating after a Conjunctive Adverb

Notice the comma *after* the conjunctive adverb in the preceding sentence. Here's the generally accepted rule: **Put a comma after the conjunctive adverb if the conjunctive adverb is more than one syllable long.** For example, if the conjunctive adverb is a word like *consequently, furthermore,* or *moreover,* you put a comma. If the conjunctive adverb is one syllable, you do not have to put a comma after the conjunctive adverb. One-syllable conjunctive adverbs are words like *then* or *thus*.

    I saw her cruelty to her staff; *then* I lost respect for her.
    We worked on the project all weekend; *consequently,* we finished a week
        ahead of the deadline.

▶ **EXERCISE 2: Correcting Run-on (Fused) Sentences**

Some of the following sentences are correctly punctuated. Some are run-on (fused) sentences, two simple sentences run together without any punctuation. If the sentence is correctly punctuated, put *OK* in the space provided. If it is a run-on sentence, put an *X* in the space provided and correct the sentence above the lines. To a correct a sentence, you do not have to add words; just add the necessary punctuation.

    a. _____   Susan gave Sam a clock radio for his birthday she wanted him to wake up on time for work.

    b. _____   I've never been to Florida but I hear it's got the most beautiful beaches in the world.

    c. _____   Among the wedding presents was a gift certificate for a hardware store they used it to buy a new bathtub.

    d. _____   Even the most careful people can't avoid accidents or protect themselves from every danger in life.

e. _____ The book was a real awakening it opened my eyes to the possibility of a nuclear disaster.

f. _____ Movies with lots of blood and gore make me sick and keep me awake at night.

g. _____ My brother has a car phone he is constantly worried about theft.

h. _____ Mr. Espinoza worked overtime at his laundry yet couldn't seem to make a profit.

i. _____ Jhoma went to driving school all summer yet she couldn't learn to parallel park.

j. _____ Some families seem to be very close but are putting on an act.

k. _____ Other families argue all the time then they support each other in a crisis.

l. _____ Outsiders can't judge a family's relationships only family members know the truth of the family's connections.

m. _____ Actors in television comedies and actors in action films have different schedules and job stresses.

n. _____ Basketball is the ideal sport for my cousin in Minnesota he can play it even in snowy January.

o. _____ Bernard treated the animal kindly thus the stray dog became a loyal and loving pet.

▶ EXERCISE 3: Correcting Comma Splices

Some of the following sentences are correctly punctuated. Some contain comma splices, errors which occur when two simple sentences are joined together with only a comma. If the sentence is correctly punctuated, put *OK* in the space provided. If it contains a comma splice, put an *X* in the space provided and correct the sentence above the lines. To correct a sentence, you do not need to add words, just correct the punctuation.

a. _____ The people in line for the movie pushed and crowded forward, some were already late for the show.

b. _____ Jamie has a pager in her purse, you can call her and leave a message.

c. _____ Our neighbors spent a fortune on the latest exercise equipment, then they got bored with it after a month.

d. _____ I bought the speakers at a huge sale, thus I saved nearly a hundred dollars on the list price.

e. _____ I was determined to learn conversational Spanish, but I didn't know what class to take.

f. _____ She sprained her ankle, nevertheless, she completed the gymnastics exercise.

g. _____ Our friends helped us move the furniture into our new house, otherwise, we would have had to rent a truck.

h. _____ The man had never taken an art class, yet his talent for drawing was obvious to us all.

i. _____ Davonia decided to bring her finger paints into the living room, then she decided to decorate the living room walls.

j. _____ Casita is the best Mexican restaurant in town, however, it isn't cheap.

k. _____ I hate to throw anything out, as a result, my closets are stuffed with junk.

l. _____ James never reminded me about the meeting, so I missed an important vote yesterday.

m. _____ You have to get there early, the place fills up fast.

n. _____ Air conditioning feels good on hot days, but I like to leave the windows open.

o. _____ One way to meet new people is to join a softball team, another is to do volunteer work.

▶ **E X E R C I S E   4 :** **Collaborative Exercise: Combining Simple Sentences Three Ways**

Add a comma, or a semicolon, or a semicolon and a comma to the following sentences. Don't add, change, or delete any words. Just add the correct punctuation.

a. The cat has been staring at the canary for an hour soon that cat will pounce.

b. All-terrain vehicles are fun to drive but they are not for children.

c. It was the best party of the summer moreover it was the best party of the year.

d. Jeans are popular in all countries American jeans cost a fortune in Europe.

e. Renovating a house is a big project furthermore it's an expensive undertaking.

f. The crowd in the stadium cheered wildly and the team felt enormously proud.

g. The crowd in the stadium cheered wildly the team felt enormously proud.

h. You can plan your future carefully however you can't avoid surprises.

i. The surfer got up at dawn then he checked the local weather report.

j. Bill forgot to pack his camera consequently he has no pictures of his trip.

k. Kim was disappointed at the turnout for she had expected a larger crowd at the last game of the season.

E X E R C I S E

l. We sat in front of the fireplace roasting chestnuts meanwhile the snow swirled against the windows.

m. He sat right next to me yet he ignored me all evening.

n. Driving across the country can be boring instead you can look for a cheap airfare.

o. First he showed us the basic scuba equipment next he stressed the importance of safety.

p. My father never spanked me nor did he threaten me with a spanking.

q. That restaurant used to be a firehouse now the antique fire equipment is used for decoration.

r. I am sick of eating fast food still it beats cooking for myself.

s. The doctor's office kept putting me on hold so I got angry and hung up.

t. The quarrel was partly his fault he could have been more tactful in asking for his money back.

▶ **E X E R C I S E 5 : Collaborative Exercise: Combining Simple Sentences**

Following are pairs of simple sentences. Working with a partner or partners, combine each pair into one sentence. Create two new sentences. Remember to combine them by using the three options: (1) a comma and a coordinating conjunction, (2) a semicolon, (3) a semicolon and a conjunctive adverb (with a comma, if it is needed). The first one has been done for you.

Pick the options that make the most sense for these sentences. When you've completed the exercise, be ready to share your sentences with the class.

a. Jim missed the beginning of the movie.

I had to explain the story to him.

combinations:

1. Jim missed the beginning of the movie, so I had to explain the story to him.

2. Jim missed the beginning of the movie; therefore I had to explain the story to him.

b. The meal was very expensive.

It was worth the price.

combinations:

1. _____

2. _____

ALONG THESE LINES/Prentice-Hall, Inc.

c. I opened the velvet box.

I saw a beautiful diamond ring.

combinations:

1. _____

_____

2. _____

_____

d. He forgot to check the oil regularly.

He had to pay for major car repairs.

combinations:

1. _____

_____

2. _____

_____

e. The bank was closed.

The automatic teller was available.

combinations:

1. _____

_____

2. _____

_____

MORE ON COMBINING SIMPLE SENTENCES

Before you go any further, look back. Review the following:

- A clause has a subject and a verb.
- An independent clause is a simple sentence; it is a group of words, with a subject and verb, that makes sense by itself.

There is another kind of clause called a *dependent clause*. It has a subject and a verb, but it doesn't make sense by itself. It can't stand alone. It isn't complete by itself. That is, it *depends* on the rest of the sentence to give it meaning. You can use a dependent clause in another option for combining simple sentences.

OPTION 4: USING A DEPENDENT CLAUSE TO BEGIN A SENTENCE

Often, you can **combine simple sentences by changing an independent clause from one sentence into a dependent clause** and placing it at the beginning of the new sentence.

two simple sentences:

S V   S   V
I was late for work. My *car had* a flat tire.

changing one simple sentence into a beginning dependent clause:

                    S   V   S   V
Because my *car had* a flat tire, *I was* late for work.

ALONG THESE LINES/Prentice-Hall, Inc.

OPTION 5: USING A DEPENDENT CLAUSE TO END A SENTENCE

You can also **combine simple sentences by changing an independent clause into a dependent clause and placing it at the end of the new sentence:**

S V   S V
I was late for work because my *car had* a flat tire.

Notice how one simple sentence can be changed into a dependent clause in two ways:

two simple sentences:

S   S   V   S V
Mother and *Dad* wrapped my presents. *I slept.*

changing one simple sentence into a dependent clause:

S   S   V   S V
Mother and *Dad wrapped* my presents while *I slept.*

or

S V   S   S   V
While *I slept, Mother* and *Dad wrapped* my presents.

Using a Subordinating Conjunction

Changing an independent clause to a dependent one is called *subordinating*. How do you do it? You add a certain word, called a *subordinating conjunction,* to an independent clause, which makes it dependent, less "important," or subordinate, in the new sentence.

Keep in mind that the subordinate clause is still a clause; it has a subject and a verb, but it doesn't make sense by itself. For example, here is an independent clause:

S   V
Caroline studies.

Somebody (Caroline) does something (studies). The statement makes sense by itself. But if you add a subordinating conjunction to the independent clause, the clause becomes dependent, incomplete, unfinished, like this:

When Caroline studies (When she studies, what happens?)
Unless Caroline studies (Unless she studies, what will happen?)
If Caroline studies (If Caroline studies, what will happen?)

Now, each dependent clause needs an independent clause to finish the idea:

dependent clause   independent clause
When Caroline studies, she gets good grades.

dependent clause   independent clause
Unless Caroline studies, she forgets key ideas.

dependent clause   independent clause
If Caroline studies, she will pass the course.

There are many subordinating conjunctions. *When you put any of these words in front of an independent clause, you make that clause dependent.* Here is a list of some common subordinating conjunctions.

Some Common Subordinating Conjunctions			
after	how	until	whether
although	if	what	which
as	in order that	whatever	whichever
because	since	when	while
before	that	whenever	who
even if	though	where	whoever
even though	unless	whereas	whose

If you pick the right subordinating conjunction, you can effectively combine simple sentences (independent clauses) into a more sophisticated sentence pattern. Such combining helps you add sentence variety to your writing and helps to explain relationships between ideas.

simple sentences:

   S   V   V   S   V
Leo could not *read* music. His *performance was* exciting.

new combination:

dependent clause   independent clause
Although Leo could not read music, his performance was exciting.

simple sentences:

S   V   S   V
I caught a bad cold last night. *I forgot* to bring a sweater to the baseball game.

new combination:

independent clause   dependent clause
I caught a bad cold last night because I forgot to bring a sweater to the baseball game.

The new combination, which has one independent clause and one (or more) dependent clause(s), is called a *complex sentence*. Complex sentences are very easy to punctuate. See if you can figure out the rule for punctuating by yourself. Look at the following examples. All are punctuated correctly.

Punctuating Complex Sentences

dependent clause   independent clause
Whenever the baby smiles, his mother is delighted.

ALONG THESE LINES/Prentice-Hall, Inc.

independent clause   dependent clause
His mother is delighted whenever the baby smiles.

dependent clause   independent clause
While you were away, I saved your mail for you.

independent clause   dependent clause
I saved your mail for you while you were away.

In the previous examples, look at the sentences that have a comma. Now look at the ones that don't have a comma. Both kinds of sentences are punctuated correctly. Do you see the rule?

When a dependent clause comes at the beginning of a sentence, the clause is followed by a comma. When a dependent clause comes at the end of a sentence, the clause does not need a comma.

Although we played well, we lost the game.
We lost the game although we played well.

Until he called, I had no date for the dance.
I had no date for the dance until he called.

▶ **EXERCISE 1: Punctuating Complex Sentences**

All of the following sentences are complex sentences; that means they have one independent and one (or more) dependent clause(s). Add a comma to the sentences that need one.

   a. Until I tried out for the team I was over-confident and arrogant.

   b. Be careful with that mirror when you take it off the wall.

   c. After he bought a microwave oven he stopped eating at fast-food restaurants.

   d. He stopped eating at fast-food restaurants after he bought a microwave oven.

   e. He hates to talk to anyone when he wakes up in the morning.

   f. Because I was saving money for a vacation I couldn't splurge on clothes.

   g. People will not trust you unless you do something to earn their trust.

   h. Carl works out at the gym every day while his brother lifts weights at home.

   i. If no one notices my new haircut I'll be disappointed.

   j. Before she goes to her office she takes her son to his day-care center.

Combining Sentences: A Review of Your Options

You've seen several ways to combine simple sentences. The following chart will help you to see them all, at a glance:

Five Options for Combining Sentences

Examples

Combine two simple sentences (two independent clauses) by *coordinating.*

Option 1: Using a comma preceding a coordinating conjunction (*and, but, or, nor, for, yet, so*).

The team won the game, *and* everybody cheered.

Option 2: Using a semicolon between independent clauses.

The team won the game; everybody cheered.

Option 3: Using a semicolon and a conjunctive adverb (*also, anyway, as a result, besides, certainly, consequently, finally, furthermore, however, incidentally, in addition, in fact, indeed, instead, likewise, meanwhile, moreover, nevertheless, next, now, on the other hand, otherwise, similarly, still, then, therefore, thus, undoubtedly*) between independent clauses.

The team won the game; *consequently,* everybody cheered.

Combine two simple sentences (two independent clauses) by *subordinating.*

Option 4: Using a comma and a dependent clause in front of an independent clause. (Words that begin dependent clauses are called subordinate adverbs: *after, although, as, because, before, even if, even though, how, if, in order that, since, that, though, unless, until, what, whatever, when, whenever, where, whereas, whether, which, whichever, while, who, whoever, whose.*)

When the team won the game, everybody cheered.

Option 5: Using a dependent clause following an independent clause (but no comma).

Everybody cheered *when* the team won the game.

▶ **EXERCISE 2: A Collaborative Exercise on Combining Sentences**

Do this exercise with a partner or with a group. Following are pairs of sentences. Combine each pair of sentences into one clear, smooth sentence. Create two new combinations for each pairing.

When you have completed your combinations, appoint one member of your group as reader. Have the reader read your combinations to another group, for comparison.

ALONG THESE LINES/Prentice-Hall, Inc.

a. I love the music store in the mall.
   The owners let me browse in it for hours.

combination 1: _____

_____

combination 2: _____

_____

b. I had never been to the Grand Canyon.
   I wasn't prepared for its beauty.

combination 1: _____

_____

combination 2: _____

_____

c. Jack was falling asleep at the wheel of his car.
   He ran a red light.

combination 1: _____

_____

combination 2: _____

_____

d. I fell on the icy sidewalk.
   I wasn't injured.

combination 1: _____

_____

combination 2: _____

_____

e. Several of my cousins are planning a family reunion.
   Not all family members are enthusiastic about the plan.

combination 1: _____

_____

combination 2: _____

_____

f. Mario needs a down payment for the house.
   He is saving money and working overtime.

combination 1: _____

_____

combination 2: _____

_____

E X E R C I S E

E X E R C I S E

g. The air gets damp and chilly in the winter.
   I can feel the change in my bones.

combination 1: _____

_____

combination 2: _____

_____

h. He loves the old *Star Trek* series.
   He's not impressed with *The Next Generation* of *Star Trek*.

combination 1: _____

_____

combination 2: _____

_____

i. My father and brother watch football together.
   They always argue about the fine points of the game.

combination 1: _____

_____

combination 2: _____

_____

j. I love Japanese food.
   I've never tried to cook it.

combination 1: _____

_____

combination 2: _____

_____

▶ **E X E R C I S E   3:   Collaborate and Review: Create Your Own Text on Combining Sentences**

One way to review the grammar you've just learned is to design your own examples for some of the rules. Following is a list of rules for coordinating and subordinating sentences. Working with a group, create your own examples of each rule and write those sentences on the lines provided.

   After your group has completed this exercise, share your examples with another group.

Option 1: You can join two simple sentences (two independent clauses) into a compound sentence with a coordinating conjunction and a comma in front of it.

The coordinating conjunctions are *and, but, or, nor, for, yet, so.*

   example 1: _____

_____

ALONG THESE LINES/Prentice-Hall, Inc.

example 2: _____

_____

Option 2: You can combine two simple sentences (two independent clauses) into a compound sentence with a semicolon between independent clauses.

example 1: _____

_____

example 2: _____

_____

Option 3: You can combine two simple sentences (two independent clauses) into a compound sentence with a semicolon and a conjunctive adverb between independent clauses.

Some conjunctive adverbs: *also, anyway, as a result, besides, certainly, consequently, finally, furthermore, however, incidentally, in addition, indeed, in fact, instead, likewise, meanwhile, moreover, nevertheless, next, now, on the other hand, otherwise, similarly, still, then, therefore, thus, undoubtedly.*

example 1: _____

_____

example 2: _____

_____

Option 4: You can combine two simple sentences (two independent clauses) into a complex sentence by making one clause dependent. The dependent clause starts with a subordinating conjunction. Then, if the dependent clause begins the sentence, the clause ends with a comma.

Some common subordinating conjunctions: *after, although, as, because, before, even if, even though, how, if, in order that, since, that, though, unless, until, what, whatever, when, whenever, where, whereas, whether, which, whichever, while, who, whoever, whose.*

example 1: _____

_____

example 2: _____

_____

Option 5: You can combine two simple sentences (two independent clauses) into a complex sentence by making one clause independent. Then, if the dependent clause comes after the independent clause, no comma is needed.

example 1: _____

_____

example 2: _____

_____

SECTION

4

Avoiding Sentence Fragments

A *sentence fragment* is a group of words that looks like a sentence, is punctuated like a sentence, but isn't a sentence. Writing a sentence fragment is a major error in grammar because it reveals that the writer isn't sure what a sentence is.

The following groups of words are all *fragments:*

> Because customers are often in a hurry and have little time to look for bargains.
> My job being very stressful and fast-paced.
> For example, the introduction of salad bars into fast-food restaurants.

There are *two* simple steps that can help you check your writing for sentence fragments.

Two Steps in Recognizing Sentence Fragments

Step 1: Check each group of words punctuated like a sentence; look for a subject and a verb.

Step 2: If you find a subject and a verb, check that the group of words makes a complete statement.

RECOGNIZING FRAGMENTS

Step 1: Check for a subject and a verb. Some groups of words that look like sentences may actually have a subject, but no verb, or they may have a verb, but no subject, or they may have no subject *or* verb.

> The puppy in the pet store window. (*Puppy* could be the subject of a sentence, but there's no verb.)
> Doesn't matter to me one way or the other. (There is a verb, *Does matter,* but there is no subject.)
> In the back of my mind. (There are two prepositional phrases, *In the back,* and *of my mind,* but there is no subject or verb.)

348

ALONG THESE LINES/Prentice-Hall, Inc.

Remember that an -*ing* verb by itself cannot be the main verb in a sentence. Therefore groups of words like the following ones may look like sentences but are missing a verb and are really fragments:

Your sister having all the skills required of a good salesperson.
The two top tennis players struggling with exhaustion and the stress of a highly competitive tournament.
Jack being the only one in the room with a piece of paper.

An infinitive (*to* plus a verb) can't be a main verb in a sentence, either. The following groups of words are also fragments:

The manager of the store to attend the meeting of regional managers next month in Philadelphia.
The purpose to explain the fine points of the game to new players.

Groups of words beginning with words like *also, especially, except, for example, in addition,* and *such as* need subjects and verbs, too. Without subjects and verbs, these groups can be fragments, like the ones below:

Also a good place to grow up.
Especially the youngest member of the family.
For example, a person without a high school diploma.

▶ **EXERCISE 1: Checking Groups of Words for Subjects and Verbs**

Check the following groups of words for subjects and verbs. Some have subjects and verbs and are sentences. Some are missing subjects or verbs or both. They are fragments. Put an *S* by the ones that are sentences; put an *F* by the ones that are fragments.

a. _____ For example, candy wrappers and soda cans litter the park.

b. _____ For instance, another tie for my father on his birthday.

c. _____ The rock musician strutting across the stage, rhythmically swinging the microphone towards the audience and back again.

d. _____ Can't possibly be the person with the best chance of getting the job.

e. _____ Especially a small child afraid of the water.

f. _____ The child was skipping across the sidewalk and trying hard not to step on a crack.

g. _____ In the darkest part of the forest with no flashlight.

h. _____ In addition, the pizza was stale and soggy.

i. _____ Spike being the brightest of the boys in the family.

j. _____ Across the street from her house was an empty lot.

k. _____ My best friend Jaime to go with me to the tournament.

l. _____ Someone without a hope of passing the driving exam.

m. _____ The reason being the lack of good schools in that area.

n. _____ My cousin Christina wanted to see a city with nightlife.

o. _____ Could have been an accident instead of a crime.

Step 2: If you find a subject and a verb, check that the group of words makes a complete statement. Many groups of words have both a subject and a verb, but they don't make sense by themselves. They are *dependent clauses.*

How can you tell if a clause is dependent? After you've checked each group of words for a subject and verb, check to see if it begins with one of the *subordinating conjunctions* that start dependent clauses. (Here again are some common subordinating conjunctions: *after, although, as, because, before, even if, even though, how, if, in order that, since, that, though, unless, until, what, whatever, when, whenever, where, whereas, whether, which, whichever, while, who, whoever, whose.*)

A clause that begins with a subordinating conjunction is a dependent clause. When you punctuate a dependent clause as if it were a sentence, you have a kind of fragment called a *dependent clause fragment.*

After I woke up this morning.
Because he liked football better than soccer.
Unless it stops raining by lunchtime.

It's important to remember both steps in checking for fragments:

Step 1: Check for a subject and a verb.

Step 2: If you find a subject and a verb, check that the group of words makes a complete statement.

▶ **EXERCISE 2:** **Checking for Dependent-Clause Fragments**

Some of the following groups of words are sentences; some are dependent clauses punctuated like sentences but are sentence fragments. Put an *S* by the sentences and an *F* by the fragments.

a. _____ As he carefully washed the outside of the car and polished the chrome trim with a special cloth.

b. _____ Commuters rushed past the ticket windows and slipped into the train at the last possible minute.

c. _____ Because no one in the class had been able to buy a copy of the required text in the campus bookstore.

d. _____ Even though many people expect to own their own home and to be able to meet the mortgage payments.

e. _____ Most of the movies were sequels to the popular movies of last summer.

f. _____ While I wanted to go to a place in the desert with dry air and bright sunshine.

g. _____ Although defendants in some countries are considered guilty until they prove their innocence.

h. _____ If people in our community were more serious about conserving water.

i. _____ Ever since Ron began taking martial arts classes.

j. _____ When women are afraid to leave their homes at night.

▶ **E X E R C I S E 3 : Using Two Steps to Recognize Sentence Fragments**

Some of the following are complete sentences; some are fragments. To recognize the fragments, check each group of words by using the two-step process: Step 1: Check for a subject and a verb; Step 2: If you find a subject and a verb, check that the group of words makes a complete statement.

After you've used both steps, put an *S* by the groups of words that are sentences, an *F* by the ones that are fragments.

a. _____ The reason being a computer error on the bill from the telephone company.

b. _____ As the graduates lined up for their march into the auditorium.

c. _____ Christopher was being very stubborn about apologizing to his uncle.

d. _____ Whenever it is cold and dreary outside and my bed seems warm and cozy.

e. _____ Without a single word of explanation for her rude behavior.

f. _____ Around the border of the yard was a hedge of thick, thorny bushes.

g. _____ Without a comfortable pair of shoes, you'll have trouble walking that distance.

h. _____ Because of their lack of education and inability to compete with others in the workforce.

i. _____ Expensive cars representing the height of success to him.

j. _____ Which was precisely the wrong thing to say to her.

k. _____ Armand feeling lost and alone without his family in Haiti.

l. _____ For example, a child with no self-esteem or confidence.

m. _____ Although I'd never thought much about it, one way or another.

n. _____ The expensive gift to be sent Federal Express to the girl from California.

o. _____ Oranges providing a good source of Vitamin C in the winter.

p. _____ While he did all the paperwork and paid all the bills.

q. _____ From the first day of school to the last, she enjoyed her math class.

r. _____ When I'd spent hours pleading with her to keep it a secret.

s. _____ The answer came to me all of a sudden.

t. _____ The reason being a resistance to facing the truth about herself.

CORRECTING FRAGMENTS

You can correct fragments easily if you follow the two steps for identifying them.

Step 1: Check for a subject and a verb. If a group of words is a fragment because it lacks a subject or a verb, or both, *add what's missing.*

> **fragment:** My father being a very strong person. (This fragment lacks a main verb.)
>
> **corrected:** My father is a very strong person. (The verb *is* replaces *being*, which is not a main verb.)
>
> **fragment:** Doesn't care about the party. (This fragment lacks a subject.)
> **corrected:** Alicia doesn't care about the party. (A subject, *Alicia*, is added.)
>
> **fragment:** Especially on dark winter days. (This fragment has neither a subject nor a verb.)
> **corrected:** I love a bonfire, especially on dark winter days. (A subject, *I*, and a verb, *love*, are added.)

Step 2: If you find a subject and a verb, check that the group of words makes a complete statement. To correct the fragment, you can turn a dependent clause into an independent one by removing the subordinating conjunction, *or* you can add an independent clause to the dependent one, to create something that makes sense by itself.

> **fragment:** When the rain beat against the windows. (The statement does not make sense by itself. The subordinating conjunction *when* leads the reader to ask, "What happened when the rain beat against the windows?" The subordinating conjunction makes this a dependent clause, not a sentence.)
> **corrected:** The rain beat against the windows. (Removing the subordinating conjunction makes this an independent clause, a sentence.)
> **corrected:** When the rain beat against the windows, I reconsidered my plans for the picnic. (Adding an independent clause turns this into something that makes sense by itself.)

Note: Sometimes you can correct a fragment by linking it to the sentence before it or after it.

> **fragment (underlined):** I have always enjoyed outdoor concerts. <u>Like the ones at Pioneer Park.</u>
> **corrected:** I have always enjoyed outdoor concerts *like the ones at Pioneer Park.*
>
> **fragment (underlined):** <u>Even if she apologizes for that nasty remark.</u> I will never trust her again.
> **corrected:** *Even if she apologizes for that nasty remark,* I will never trust her again.

You have several choices for correcting fragments: you can add words, phrases, or clauses; you can take words out or combine independent and dependent clauses; you can transform fragments into simple sentences or create compound or complex sentences. To punctuate your new sentences, use the rules for combining sentences.

▶ **E XERCISE 4 : Correcting Fragments**

All of the following groups of words contain sentence fragments. Correct them in the most appropriate way.

a. Once a year I brighten up my room with some inexpensive decoration. Such as new curtains, a plant, or fresh paint.

corrected: _____

_____

b. If Michael asks his boss for the day off. His boss will probably say yes.

corrected: _____

_____

c. Exploring the city without a map. We ended up walking in a circle.

corrected: _____

_____

d. Everyone was fascinated by the get-rich-quick scheme. Especially Ned.

corrected: _____

_____

e. The toddler learning to drink milk from a cup instead of a baby bottle.

corrected: _____

_____

f. Whoever borrowed my camera without my permission.

corrected: _____

_____

g. Because we ran out of staples. We were forced to use paper clips.

corrected: _____

_____

h. The dancers demanded more music. As the band packed up for the night.

corrected: _____

_____

i. He was eager to meet his co-workers. To get to know their habits and to learn their routines.

corrected: _____

_____

j. Anyone can learn to ski. If he or she is willing to keep trying.

corrected: _____

_____

▶ **EXERCISE 5: Collaborative Exercise on Correcting Fragments**

The following groups of words all contain fragments. With a partner or a group, construct two ways to eliminate the fragment. You can add words, phrases, or clauses, take out words, combine independent and dependent clauses, or attach a fragment to the sentence before or after it. One example has been done for you.

a. Whenever I am waiting for an important phone call.

corrected: I am waiting for an important phone call.

corrected: Whenever I am waiting for an important phone call, I am extremely impatient and nervous.

b. Christina took the customers' orders. While Robert worked in the kitchen.

corrected: _____

_____

corrected: _____

_____

c. When we get together on Sundays. We have an enormous dinner.

corrected: _____

_____

corrected: _____

_____

d. Jason being more talented than any of the professional hockey players.

corrected: _____

_____

corrected: _____

_____

e. With a great deal of enthusiasm for his subject. He began his lecture.

corrected: _____

_____

corrected: _____

_____

f. Although no one could tell him how to get to the mall.

corrected: _____

_____

corrected: _____

_____

ALONG THESE LINES/Prentice-Hall, Inc.

g. In the forest, where the fighting had originally broken out.

corrected: _____

_____

corrected: _____

_____

h. He'll never make friends. Unless he learns to control his temper.

corrected: _____

_____

corrected: _____

_____

i. I was beginning to feel sick. As the boat rocked from side to side.

corrected: _____

_____

corrected: _____

_____

j. Which is one place I'd like to visit.

corrected: _____

_____

corrected: _____

_____

k. Who takes his responsibilities seriously and expects his employees to do
   the same.

corrected: _____

_____

corrected: _____

_____

Parallelism means balance in a sentence. To create sentences with parallelism, remember this rule: *Similar points should get a similar structure.*

Often, you will include two or three (or more) related ideas, examples, or details in one sentence. If you express these ideas in a parallel structure, they will be clearer, smoother, and more convincing.

Here are some pairs of sentences with and without parallelism:

not parallel: Of all the sports I've played, I prefer tennis, handball, and playing golf.

parallel: Of all the sports I've played, I prefer *tennis, handball, and golf.* (Three words are parallel.)

not parallel: If you're looking for the car keys, you should look under the table, the kitchen counter, and behind the refrigerator.

parallel: If you're looking for the car keys, you should look *under the table, on the kitchen counter, and behind the refrigerator.* (Three prepositional phrases are parallel.)

not parallel: He is a good choice for manager because he works hard, he keeps calm, and well-liked.

parallel: He is a good choice for manager because *he works hard, he keeps calm, and he is well-liked.* (Three clauses are parallel.)

From these examples you can see that parallelism involves matching the structures of parts of your sentence. There are two steps that can help you check your writing for parallelism.

Two Steps in Checking a Sentence for Parallel Structure

Step 1: Look for the list in the sentence.

Step 2: Put the parts of the list into a similar structure.

(You may have to change or add something to get a parallel structure.)

ALONG THESE LINES/Prentice-Hall, Inc.

ACHIEVING PARALLELISM

Let's correct the parallelism of the following sentence:

sample sentence: The committee for neighborhood safety met to set up a schedule for patrols, coordinating teams of volunteers, and also for the purpose of creating new rules.

To correct this sentence, we'll follow the steps.

Step 1: Look for the list. The committee met to do three things. Here's the list:

1. to set up a schedule for patrols
2. coordinating teams of volunteers
3. for the purpose of creating new rules

Step 2: Put the parts of the list into a similar structure:

1. *to set up* a schedule for patrols
2. *to coordinate* teams of volunteers
3. *to create* new rules

Now revise to get a parallel sentence.

parallel: The committee for neighborhood safety met *to set up* a schedule for patrols, *to coordinate* teams of volunteers, and *to create* new rules.

If you follow Steps 1 and 2, you can also write the sentence like this:

parallel: The committee for neighborhood safety met to *set up* a schedule for patrols, *coordinate* teams of volunteers, and *create* new rules.

But you can't write a sentence like this:

not parallel: The committee for neighborhood safety met *to set up* a schedule for patrols, *coordinate* teams, and *to create* new rules.

Think of the list again. You can have

The committee met
    1. to set up
    2. to coordinate   }   parallel
    3. to create

Or you can have

The committee met to
    1. set up
    2. coordinate   }   parallel
    3. create

But your list can't be

The committee met to
    1. set up
    2. coordinate   }   not parallel
    3. to create

In other words, use the *to* once (if it fits every part of the list), or use it with every part of the list.

Caution: Sometimes making ideas parallel means adding something to a sentence because all the parts of the list can't match exactly.

sample sentence: In his pocket the little boy had a ruler, rubber band, baseball card, and apple.

Step 1: Look for the list. In his pocket the little boy had a

1. ruler
2. rubber band
3. baseball card
4. apple

As the sentence is written, the *a* goes with *a ruler, a rubber band, a baseball card, and a apple.* But *a* isn't the right word to put in front of apple. Words beginning with vowels (a, e, i, o, u,) need *an* in front of them: *an apple.* So to make the sentence parallel, you have to change something in the sentence.

Step 2: Put the parts of the list into a parallel structure.

parallel: In his pocket the little boy had *a ruler, a rubber band, a baseball card,* and *an apple.*

Here's another example:

sample sentence: She was amused and interested in the silly plot of the movie.

Step 1: Look for the list.
She was
   1. amused
   2. interested in
the silly plot of the movie.

Check the sense of this sentence by looking at each part of the list and how it is working in the sentence: "She was *interested in* the silly plot of the movie." That part of the list seems clear. But "She was *amused* the silly plot of the movie"? Or "She was *amused in* the silly plot of the movie"? Neither sentence is right. People are not *amused in.*

Step 2: The sentence needs a word added to make the structure parallel.

parallel: She was *amused by* and *interested in* the silly plot of the movie.

When you follow the two steps to check for parallelism, you can write clear sentences and improve your style.

▶ **EXERCISE 1: Revising Sentences for Parallelism**

Some of the following sentences need to be revised so they have parallel structures. Revise the ones that need parallelism.

a. The road begins at the beach; the city center is where it ends.

revised: _____

_____

b. The restaurant is very popular and has crowds.

revised: _____

_____

c. My work day is so crowded with activities that I have to shop for groceries, washing and ironing my clothes, and clean my room at night.

revised: _____

_____

d. You can get to the carnival by bus or by special train.

revised: _____

_____

e. He is a player with great energy and who is ambitious.

revised: _____

_____

f. When we meet tomorrow, I'd like to discuss your job description, explaining your health benefits, and describe the package of retirement options you will have also.

revised: _____

_____

g. The location of the house, its size, and how much it cost made it the best choice for the family.

revised: _____

_____

h. Going to college is not the same as when you go to high school.

revised: _____

_____

i. Jim was the friendliest person she met at school, also the most helpful person and the most funny.

revised: _____

_____

j. Ramona would rather sew her own wedding gown than paying a fortune to buy one.

revised: _____

_____

▶ **EXERCISE 2:** **Collaborative Exercise on Writing Sentences with Parallelism**

With a partner or with a group, complete each sentence. Begin by brainstorming a draft list; then revise the list for parallelism. Finally, complete the sentence in parallel structure. You may want to assign one task (brainstorming a draft list, revising it, etc.) to each group member, then switch tasks on the next sentence. Following is a sample of how to work through each question, from list to sentence.

Sample incomplete sentence: Three habits I'd like to break are

draft list	revised list
1. worry too much	1. worrying too much
2. talking on the phone for hours	2. talking on the phone for hours
3. lose my temper	3. losing my temper

sentence: Three habits I'd like to break are worrying too much, talking on the phone for hours, and losing my temper.

a. Three ways to spend a rainy Sunday are

draft list	revised list
1. _____	1. _____
2. _____	2. _____
3. _____	3. _____

sentence: _____

_____

b. Two reasons to stop smoking are

draft list	revised list
1. _____	1. _____
2. _____	2. _____

sentence: _____

_____

c. Three irritations in my daily life are

draft list	revised list
1. _____	1. _____
2. _____	2. _____
3. _____	3. _____

sentence: _____

_____

d. Exercise is good for you because (add three reasons)

draft list	revised list
1. _____	1. _____

2. _____   2. _____

3. _____   3. _____

sentence: _____

_____

▶ **E X E R C I S E   3 :   Collaborative Exercise on Combining Sentences and Creating a Parallel Structure**

Working with a group, combine each of the following clusters of sentences into one clear, smooth sentence. Each new sentence should include a parallel structure. Following is a sample of how the exercise should be done.

sample: Before you buy a used car, you should research what similar models are selling for.
It would be a good idea to have a mechanic examine the car.
Also, how much mileage it has racked up is a consideration.

combination: _Before you buy a used car, you should compare prices of similar_

models, get a mechanic to examine the car, and think carefully about the

mileage.

a. The dinner was delicious.
The dinner was full of nutritional value.
It was priced inexpensively.

combination: _____

_____

b. If you want to lose weight, you should limit the amount of fat in your diet.
Cutting back on junk food is also a good idea.
Regular exercise is important, too.

combination: _____

_____

c. Business people advertise by computer.
Children use computers to play video games.
Computers are used by teachers to teach basic skills.

combination: _____

_____

d. He was a dynamic salesman.
He had energy.
He had enthusiasm.

combination: _____

_____

e. As a friend, he was extremely loyal.
   As a friend, he also told the truth.
   He was also a compassionate friend.

combination: _____

_____

f. Richard joined the bicycle club.
   Richard rode with club members every weekend.
   Richard soon became a strong competitive cyclist.

combination: _____

_____

g. The demonstrators came from small towns.
   The demonstrators came from major cities.
   The demonstrators came from farms.
   The demonstrators came from factories.
   The demonstrators came to express their concern about the environment.

combination: _____

_____

h. People crowded the entrances to the department store.
   They hoped to be the first inside the store.
   Their goal was to find a bargain at the sale.

combination: _____

_____

i. The house was old.
   It had a spiral staircase.
   It had elaborately carved woodwork.
   It had bay windows.
   The house was beautiful.

combination: _____

_____

j. People don't swim at the lake any more.
   The shore is littered with garbage.
   Chemicals pollute the water.

combination: _____

_____

Modifiers are words, phrases, or clauses that describe (modify) something in a sentence. The following words, phrases, and clauses that appear in italics are modifiers.

the *blue* van (word)
the van *in the garage* (phrase)
the van *that she bought* (clause)

foreign tourists (word)
tourists *coming to Florida* (phrase)
tourists *who visit the state* (clause)

Sometimes modifiers limit another word. They make another word (or words) more specific.

the girl *in the corner* (tells exactly which girl)
fifty acres (tells exactly how many acres)
the movie *that I liked best* (tells which movie)
He *never* calls. (tells how often)

▶ **EXERCISE 1:** Recognizing Modifiers

In each of the following sentences, underline the modifiers (words, phrases, or clauses) that describe the italicized word or phrase.

a. *The kitten* with the gray and white stripes has the sweetest disposition.

b. I saw *a girl* driving a beautifully restored Corvette.

c. *The people* standing in the long lines showed great patience.

d. The fisherman reeled in *the fish*, fighting every inch of the way.

e. Julie and Kate always write thank-you *notes*.

f. I found my neighbor's lost *parakeet*.

g. Flashing its pink neon message, *the sign* attracted many new customers.

h. *The* little *boy* dressed in a sailor suit saluted the troops.

i. Jumping across the sidewalk, *the frog* startled me.

j. The battered old jean *jacket,* with its frayed sleeves and torn pocket, finally had to be thrown out.

CORRECTING MODIFIER PROBLEMS

Modifiers can make your writing more specific and more concrete. Used effectively and correctly, modifiers give the reader a clear, exact picture of what you want to say, and they help you to say it precisely. But modifiers have to be used correctly. You can *check for errors with modifiers as you revise your sentences.*

Three Steps in Checking for Sentence Errors with Modifiers

Step 1: Find the modifier.

Step 2: Ask, "Does the modifier have something to modify?"

Step 3: Ask, "Is the modifier in the right place, as close as possible to the word, phrase, or clause it modifies?"

If you answer *No* to either Step 2 or Step 3, you need to revise your sentence.

Let's use the steps in the following example.

sample sentence: I saw a girl driving a Porsche wearing a bikini.

Step 1: Find the modifier. The modifiers are *driving a Porsche, wearing a bikini.*

Step 2: Ask, "Does the modifier have something to modify?" The answer is "Yes." The girl is driving a Porsche. The girl is wearing a bikini. Both modifiers go with *a girl.*

Step 3: Ask, "Is the modifier in the right place?" The answer is *Yes,* and *No.* One modifier is in the right place:

> I saw *a girl driving a Porsche*

The other modifier is *not* in the right place

> *a Porsche wearing a bikini*

The Porsche is not wearing a bikini.

revised: I saw a girl *wearing a bikini* and *driving a Porsche.*

Let's work through the steps once more:

sample sentence: Scampering through the forest, the hunters saw two rabbits.

Step 1: Find the modifier. The modifiers are *scampering through the forest,* and *two.*

Step 2: Ask, "Does the modifier have something to modify?" The answer is *Yes*. There are *two rabbits*. The *rabbits* are *scampering through the forest*.

Step 3: Ask, "Is the modifier in the right place?" The answer is *Yes* and *No*. The word *two* is in the right place:

> *two* rabbits

But *Scampering through the forest* is in the wrong place:

> *Scampering through the forest,* the hunters

The hunters are not scampering through the forest. The rabbits are.

revised: The hunters saw two rabbits *scampering through the forest.*

Caution: Be sure to put words like *almost, even, exactly, hardly, just, merely, nearly, only, scarcely,* and *simply* as close as possible to what they modify. If you put them in the wrong place, you may write a confusing sentence.

> sample sentence: Etienne only wants to grow carrots and zucchini. (The modifier that creates confusion here is *only.* Does Etienne have only one goal in life—to grow carrots and zucchini? Or are these the only vegetables he wants to grow? To create a clearer sentence, move the modifier.)
> revised: Etienne wants to grow *only* carrots and zucchini.

The preceding examples show one common error in using modifiers. This error involves *misplaced modifiers,* words that describe something but are not where they should be in the sentence. Here is the rule to remember: **Put the modifier as close as possible to the word, phrase, or clause it modifies.**

▶ **E X E R C I S E 2 :** **Correcting Sentences with Misplaced Modifiers**

Some of the following sentences contain misplaced modifiers. Revise any sentence that has a misplaced modifier by putting the modifier as close as possible to whatever it modifies.

a. Falling from the top of my refrigerator, I saw my best glass dish.

revised: _____

_____

b. When we criticized her performance, the actress was ready to nearly cry.

revised: _____

_____

c. When she goes to the supermarket, she only wants to buy necessary items.

revised: _____

_____

d. Wrapped in shiny paper, I accepted the tiny gift.

revised: _____

_____

e. The doctor gave the prescription for sedatives to the nervous patient.

revised: _____

_____

f. When he starts college next fall, he wants to take only business courses.

revised: _____

_____

g. Cracked in two places, she was sure the window would have to be replaced.

revised: _____

_____

h. The team doesn't like the umpire that lost the game.

revised: _____

_____

i. Soaked in brandy, she tasted the fruitcake.

revised: _____

_____

j. Straining against the leash, Jim pulled back his bulldog.

revised: _____

_____

Correcting Dangling Modifiers

The three steps for correcting modifier problems can help you recognize another kind of error. For example, let's use the steps to check the following sentence.

sample sentence: Strolling through the tropical paradise, many colorful birds could be seen.

Step 1: Find the modifier. The modifiers are *Strolling through the tropical paradise,* and *many colorful.*

Step 2: Ask, "Does the modifier have something to modify?" The answer is *Yes* and *No.* The words *many* and *colorful* modify birds. But who or what is *Strolling through the tropical paradise?* There is no person mentioned in this sentence. The birds are not strolling.

This kind of error is called a *dangling modifier.* It means that the modifier doesn't have anything to modify; it just dangles in the sentence. To correct this kind of error, you can't just move the modifier:

still incorrect: Many colorful birds could be seen strolling through the tropical paradise. (There is still no person strolling.)

ALONG THESE LINES/Prentice-Hall, Inc.

The way to correct this kind of error is to add something to the sentence. If you gave the modifier something to modify, you might come up with several different revised sentences:

revised sentences: *As I strolled through the tropical paradise,* I saw many colorful birds.

or

Many colorful birds could be seen *when we were strolling through the tropical paradise.*

or

While the tourists strolled through the tropical paradise, they saw many colorful birds.

Try the process for correcting dangling modifiers once more:

sample sentence: Ascending in the glass elevator, the hotel lobby glittered in the light.

Step 1: Find the modifier. The modifiers are *Ascending in the glass elevator,* and *hotel.*

Step 2: Ask, "Does the modifier have anything to modify?" The answer is, *Yes, hotel* modifies lobby, and *No, Ascending in the glass elevator* doesn't modify anything. Who is ascending in the elevator? There is nobody mentioned in the sentence.

revised: Put somebody or something in the sentence, for the modifier to describe.

revised sentences: *As the guests ascended in the glass elevator,* the hotel lobby glittered in the light.

or

Ascending in the glass elevator, she saw the hotel lobby glitter in the light.

Remember that you can't correct a dangling modifier just by moving the modifier. You have to give the modifier something to modify; you have to add something to the sentence.

▶ **EXERCISE 3**: **Correcting Sentences with Dangling Modifiers**

Some of the following sentences use modifiers correctly. Some sentences have dangling modifiers. Revise the sentences with dangling modifiers. To revise, you will have to add words and change words.

a. Racing across the station, the train was reached before the doors closed.

revised: _____

_____

b. Breaking into the house at night, the homeowners lost their most valuable possessions.

revised: _____

_____

c. At the age of five, my family moved to Pennsylvania.

revised: _____

_____

d. Lost in the fog, the lighthouse could not be seen.

revised: _____

_____

e. Stumbling across the finish line, the runner gasped for breath.

revised: _____

_____

f. When taking the geometry exam, an argument between the teacher and a student began.

revised: _____

_____

g. While mowing the lawn, a wasp stung him.

revised: _____

_____

h. Tired and irritable, the work day seemed endless.

rrevised: _____

_____

i. Visiting Mexico for the first time, I thought the country was strange and exciting.

revised: _____

_____

j. To enter that contest, an entry fee of $50.00 is needed.

revised: _____

_____

REVIEWING THE STEPS AND THE SOLUTIONS

It's important to recognize problems with modifiers and to correct these problems. Modifier problems can result in confusing or even silly sentences. And when you confuse or unintentionally amuse your reader, you're not making your point.

Remember to check for modifier problems by using three steps, and to correct each kind of problem in the appropriate way.

A Summary of Modifier Problems

Checking for Modifier Problems

Step 1: Find the modifier.

Step 2: Ask, "Does the modifier have something to modify?"

Step 3: Ask, "Is the modifier in the right place?"

Correcting Modifier Problems

• If a modifier is in the wrong place (a misplaced modifier), put it as close as possible to the word, phrase, or clause it modifies.

• If a modifier has nothing to modify (a dangling modifier), add or change words so that it has something to modify.

▶ **E X E R C I S E 4 : A Collaborative Exercise on Revising Sentences with Modifier Problems**

Working with a partner or with a group, correct the following sentences. All of them have some kind of modifier problem. Write a new, correct sentence for each incorrect one. You can move words, add words, change words, or remove words. The first one is done for you.

a. Stopping suddenly, the box with the cake in it fell from the seat of the car.

revised: When I had to stop suddenly, the box with the cake in it fell from the seat of the car.

b. Without a trace of bitterness, the argument between the neighbors was settled.

revised: _____

_____

c. Staring into space, the teacher scolded the student.

revised: _____

_____

d. After considering the alternatives, a compromise was reached by the two sides.

revised: _____

_____

e. After drag racing down the street until 3 a.m., the neighbors decided to complain to the teenagers' parents.

revised: _____

_____

f. Inflated to huge dimensions, he dragged the inner tube across the stream.

revised: _____

_____

g. Susan nearly missed all the multiple-choice questions on the test.

revised: _____

_____

h. Covered in mud, I doubted if the shoes could ever be clean again.

revised: _____

_____

i. To make friends at school, an outgoing personality is necessary.

revised: _____

_____

j. When packing a suitcase for a trip, a little ingenuity and planning go a long way.

revised: _____

_____

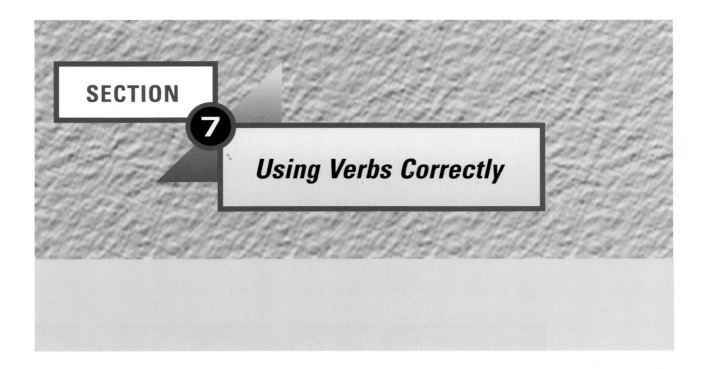

Verbs are words that show some kind of *action* or *being*.

> verb
> He *runs* to the park.

> verb
> Melanie *is* my best friend.

> verb
> The pizza *tastes* delicious.

Verbs also tell about *time*.

> He *will run* to the park. (The time is future.)
> Melanie *was* my best friend. (The time is past.)
> The pizza *tastes* delicious. (The time is present.)

The time of a verb is called its *tense*. You can say a verb is in the *present tense,* the *future tense,* or many other tenses.

Using verbs correctly involves knowing which form of the verb to use, choosing the right verb tense, and being consistent in verb tense.

USING STANDARD VERB FORMS

Many people use nonstandard verb forms in everyday conversation. But everyone who wants to write and speak effectively should know different levels of language, from the slang and dialect of everyday conversation to the standard English of college, business, and professional environments.

In everyday conversation, you might use nonstandard forms like

I goes	he don't	we was
you was	it don't	she smile
you be	I be	they walks

But *these are not correct forms in standard English.* Look at the standard verb forms for the present tense of *listen.*

The Present Tense

verb: listen

I listen	we listen
you listen	you listen
he, she, it listens	they listen

Take a closer look at the standard verb forms. Only one form is different:

he, she, it *listens*

This is the only form that ends in *s* in the present tense.

> In the present tense, use an *s* or *es* ending on the verb only when the subject is *he, she,* or *it,* or the equivalent of *he, she,* or *it.*

He calls his mother every day.
She chases the cat away from the bird cage.
It runs like a new car.
Jim calls his mother every day.
Samantha chases the cat away from the bird cage.
The jalopy runs like a new car.

Take another look at the present tense. If the verb is a standard verb, it will follow this form in the present tense.

I attend every lecture.
You care about the truth.
He visits his grandfather regularly.
She drives a new car.
The new *album sounds* great.
We follow that team.
You work well when you both compromise.
They buy the store brand of cereal.

▶ **EXERCISE 1: Picking the Right Verb in the Present Tense**

To familiarize yourself with standard verb forms in the present tense, underline the subject and circle the correct verb form in each of the following sentences.

a. The dress in the discount store look/looks better to me than the one in the boutique.

b. I work/works in a dirty part of the city.

c. Grocery shopping take/takes a good part of the morning.

d. The snake in the yard frighten/frightens my sister.

e. She sometimes travel/travels for three days without calling home.

f. Jimmie concentrate/concentrates better with the radio on.

g. Down the street by the bank stand/stands a statue of Thomas Jefferson.

h. With great determination, Carla and Leon exercise/exercises every day.

i. A meal in a restaurant cost/costs more than a meal at home.

j. It seem/seems like a good idea.

k. In cold weather, the pond freeze/freezes over for days at a time.

l. You want/wants more money than I can give you.

m. The vice president carry/carries a lot of weight in the club.

n. A rich dessert add/adds empty calories.

o. Behind the wall live/lives a tiny gray mouse.

THE PAST TENSE

The past tense of most verbs is formed by adding d *or* ed *to the verb.*

verb: listen

I listened	we listened
you listened	you listened
he, she, it listened	they listened

Add *ed* to *listen* to form the past tense. For some other verbs, you may add *d*.

The sun *faded* from the sky.
He *quaked* with fear.
She *crumpled* the paper into a ball.

▶ **EXERCISE 2: Writing the Correct Form of Past Tense**

To familiarize yourself with the past tense, write the correct past tense form of each verb in the blank space.

a. Last week, he and I _____ (remove) the stain

from the counter.

b. The coach in high school _____ (warn) some

players to pay attention to the game.

c. As a child, Lucille _____ (perform) in a chil-

dren's theater troupe.

d. After doing some research into the company, I _____

_____ (reject) its offer of a job.

e. Last night, we _____ (compromise) on the

issue of where to build the park.

f. Yesterday, Christine _____ (call) me about

driving to the party.

g. Reporters at the scene of last night's train accident _____

_____ (interview) a witness.

h. Ten years ago, Arnold and Bruce _____

(start) a climb to success in Hollywood.

i. The girl at the desk _____ (wave) at me.

j. You _____ (waste) too much time on it

yesterday.

THE FOUR MAIN FORMS OF A VERB

When you are deciding what form of a verb to use, you will probably rely on one of four forms: the present tense, the past tense, the present participle, or the past participle. Most of the time, you will use one of these forms or add a helping verb to it. As an example, look at the four main forms of the verb, *listen.*

Present	Past	Present Participle	Past Participle
listen	listened	listening	listened

You use the *four verb forms—present, past, present participle, past participle—alone or with helping verbs to express time (tense).* They are very easy to remember when a verb is a *regular verb,* like *listen.* Use the present form for the present tense:

We *listen* to the news on the radio.

The *past* form expresses past tense:

I *listened* to language tapes for three hours yesterday.

The *present participle,* or *-ing* form is used with helping verbs:

He *was listening* to me.
I *am listening* to you.
You *should have been listening* more carefully.

The *past participle* is the form used with the helping verbs *have, has,* or *had:*

I *have listened* for hours.
She *has listened* to the tape.
We *had listened* to the tape before we bought it.

Of course, you can add many helping verbs to the present tense:

present tense:

We *listen* to the news on the car radio.

add helping verbs:

We *will* listen to the news on the car radio.

ALONG THESE LINES/Prentice-Hall, Inc.

We *should* listen to the news on the car radio.
We *can* listen to the news on the car radio.

> When a verb is regular, the past form is created by adding *d* or *ed* to the present form. The present participle is formed by adding *ing* to the present form, and the past participle is the same as the past form.

IRREGULAR VERBS

Irregular verbs don't follow the same rules for creating verb forms that regular verbs do. Three verbs that we use all the time—*be, have, do*—are irregular verbs. You need to study them closely. Look at the present tense forms for all three, and compare the standard, present tense forms to the nonstandard ones. *Remember to use the standard forms for college or professional writing.*

verb: be

Nonstandard	Standard
~~I be~~ or ~~I is~~	I am
~~you be~~	you are
~~he, she, it be~~	he, she, it is
~~we be~~	we are
~~you be~~	you are
~~they be~~	they are

verb: have

Nonstandard	Standard
~~I has~~	I have
~~you has~~	you have
~~he, she, it have~~	he, she, it has
~~we has~~	we have
~~you has~~	you have
~~they has~~	they have

verb: do

Nonstandard	Standard
~~I does~~	I do
~~you does~~	you do
~~he, she, it do~~	he, she, it does
~~we does~~	we do
~~you does~~	you do
~~they does~~	they do

Caution: Be careful when you add *not* to *does*. If you're writing a contraction of *does not,* be sure you write *doesn't,* instead of *don't.*

not this: ~~The light don't work.~~
but this: The light doesn't work.

▶ **E X E R C I S E   3 : Choosing the Correct Form of** *be, have,* **or** *do*

To practice using *be, have,* and *do* correctly, circle the correct form of the verb in each of the following sentences.

    a. Two of the salesmen *is/are* meeting at the branch office.

    b. I am sure the dancers *has/have* the ability to reach the top.

    c. My mother *don't/doesn't* need another set of towels for her birthday.

    d. The winner of the contest *do/does* whatever he wants with the money.

    e. Without an excuse, he *has/have* no choice but to apologize.

    f. Every weekend, I *do/does* the laundry for the whole family.

    g. The musicians *has/have* a huge bus equipped for traveling long distances.

    h. I *is/am* very embarrassed.

    i. They know he *do/does* his exercises early in the morning.

    j. Rose and Lee *be/are* coming over in half an hour.

    k. Unfortunately, Lisa *has/have* no excuse for her behavior.

    l. Today I *be/am* the only one of the cousins still living at home.

    m. I told her it *has/have* nothing to do with her.

    n. Spelling is important; it *do/does* count in your grade.

    o. On Saturday mornings, you *do/does* the yard work too early for me to help.

The Past Tense of *be, have, do*

The past forms of these irregular verbs can be confusing. Again, compare the nonstandard forms to the standard forms. *Remember to use the standard forms for college or professional writing.*

verb: be

Nonstandard	Standard
~~I were~~	I was
~~you was~~	you were
~~he, she, it were~~	he, she, it was
~~we was~~	we were
~~you was~~	you were
~~they was~~	they were

verb: have

Nonstandard	Standard
~~I has~~	I had
~~you has~~	you had
~~he, she, it have~~	he, she, it had
~~we has~~	we had
~~you has~~	you had
~~they has~~	they had

ALONG THESE LINES/Prentice-Hall, Inc.

verb: do

Nonstandard	Standard
~~I done~~	I did
~~you done~~	you did
~~he, she, it done~~	he, she, it did
~~we done~~	we did
~~you done~~	you did
~~they done~~	they did

▶ **E X E R C I S E   4 :   Choosing the Correct Form of** *be, have,* **or** *do* **in the Past Tense**

To practice using *be, have,* and *do* correctly for past tense, circle the correct verb form in each sentence.

a. The people next door *was/were* mysterious in their habits.

b. Last night, Alonzo *done/did* the decorating for the Super Bowl party.

c. In spite of the rain, the club *had/have* a large turnout for the picnic.

d. Three hours after the deadline, we *was/were* still busy.

e. Yesterday, at that intersection, I *have/had* a minor car accident.

f. As a little girl, Dora *were/was* quiet and shy around strangers.

g. Believing in helping others, the volunteers *done/did* a good deed for two lost people.

h. I *was/were* unhappy with the grade on my math test.

i. Two years ago, you *were/was* the most valuable player on the team.

j. Her class in music appreciation *did/done* the most to interest her in music.

More Irregular Verb Forms

Be, have, and *do* are not the only verbs with irregular forms. There are many such verbs, and everybody who writes uses some form of an irregular verb. When you write and you are not certain if you are using the correct form of a verb, check the following list of irregular verbs.

For each irregular verb listed, the *present,* the *past,* and the *past participle* forms are given. The present participle isn't included because it is always formed by adding *ing* to the present form.

Irregular Verb Forms

Present	Past	Past Participle
(Today I *arise.*)	(Yesterday I *arose.*)	(I have/had *arisen.*)
arise	arose	arisen
awake	awoke, awaked	awoken, awaked
bear	bore	born, borne
beat	beat	beaten
become	became	become

Present	Past	Past Participle
begin	began	begun
bend	bent	bent
bite	bit	bitten
bleed	bled	bled
blow	blew	blown
break	broke	broken
bring	brought	brought
build	built	built
burst	burst	burst
buy	bought	bought
catch	caught	caught
choose	chose	chosen
come	came	come
cling	clung	clung
cost	cost	cost
creep	crept	crept
cut	cut	cut
deal	dealt	dealt
draw	drew	drawn
dream	dreamed	dreamed
drink	drank	drunk
drive	drove	driven
eat	ate	eaten
fall	fell	fallen
feed	fed	fed
feel	felt	felt
fight	fought	fought
find	found	found
fling	flung	flung
fly	flew	flown
freeze	froze	frozen
get	got	got, gotten
give	gave	given
go	went	gone
grow	grew	grown
hear	heard	heard
hide	hid	hidden
hit	hit	hit
hold	held	held
hurt	hurt	hurt
keep	kept	kept
know	knew	known
lay (means to put)	laid	laid
lead	led	led
leave	left	left
lend	lent	lent
let	let	let
lie (means to recline)	lay	lain
light	lit, lighted	lit, lighted
lose	lost	lost

Present	Past	Past Participle
make	made	made
mean	meant	meant
meet	met	met
pay	paid	paid
ride	rode	ridden
ring	rang	rung
rise	rose	risen
run	ran	run
say	said	said
see	saw	seen
sell	sold	sold
send	sent	sent
sew	sewed	sewn, sewed
shake	shook	shaken
shine	shone, shined	shone, shined
shrink	shrank	shrunk
shut	shut	shut
sing	sang	sung
sit	sat	sat
sleep	slept	slept
slide	slid	slid
sling	slung	slung
speak	spoke	spoken
spend	spent	spent
stand	stood	stood
steal	stole	stolen
stick	stuck	stuck
sting	stung	stung
stink	stank, stunk	stunk
string	strung	strung
swear	swore	sworn
swim	swam	swum
teach	taught	taught
tear	tore	torn
tell	told	told
think	thought	thought
throw	threw	thrown
wake	woke, waked	woken, waked
wear	wore	worn
win	won	won
write	wrote	written

▶ **E X E R C I S E   5 :   Choosing the Correct Form of Irregular Verbs**

To become more familiar with irregular verb forms, write the correct form of the verb in the following sentences. Be sure to check the list of irregular verbs.

   a. I bought a huge bag of potato chips last night, and by midnight, I had

   _____ (eat) the whole thing.

E X E R C I S E

b. Patty and Tom should have _____ (know) how to get to the store; they've been there before.

c. We separated the glass beads into three colorful piles and then _____ (string) the beads, alternating the colors.

d. I bought my five-year-old a new pair of blue jeans yesterday, but she has _____ (tear) them already.

e. I don't know what he _____ (mean) when he said, "I'm not interested."

f. Virginia asked Jack if he had ever _____ (lend) money to a friend.

g. I went to the beach yesterday, and I _____ (lie) in the sun too long.

h. For years, that pawnbroker has _____ (deal) in stolen merchandise, but now he is being investigated.

i. The children have _____ (drink) all the milk in the refrigerator.

j. The child was hoping to get toys for his birthday, but instead his uncle _____ (bring) a sweater.

▶ **EXERCISE 6:** **Collaborative Exercise on Writing Sentences with Correct Verb Forms**

With a partner or with a group, write two sentences that correctly use each of the following verb forms. In writing these sentences, you may add helping verbs to the verb forms, but you may *not* change the verb form itself. When your group has completed the exercise, be ready to share your answers with another group or with the class.

The first example shows how to do the exercise.

a. sent

1. *He sent her a dozen roses on Valentine's Day.* _____

2. *I have sent him all the information he needs.* _____

b. bitten

1. _____

2. _____

c. cost

1. _____

2. _____

d. drew

1. _____

2. _____

e. run

1. _____

2. _____

f. felt

1. _____

2. _____

g. hurt

1. _____

2. _____

h. driven

1. _____

2. _____

i. gotten

1. _____

2. _____

j. eaten

1. _____

2. _____

k. slid

1. _____

2. _____

More on Verbs: Consistency and Voice

Remember that your choice of verb form indicates the time (tense) of your statements. Be careful not to shift from one tense to another unless you have a reason to change the time.

CONSISTENT VERB TENSES

Staying in one tense (unless you have a reason to change tenses) is called *consistency of verb tense.*

incorrect shifts in tense:

The waitress *ran* to the kitchen with the order in her hand, *raced* back to her customers with glasses of water, and *smiles* calmly.

He *grins* at me from the ticket booth and *closed* the ticket window.

You can correct these errors by putting all the verbs in the same tense.

consistent present tense:

The waitress *runs* to the kitchen with the order in her hand, *races* back to her customers with glasses of water, and *smiles* calmly.

He *grins* at me from the ticket booth and *closes* the ticket window.

consistent past tense:

The waitress *ran* to the kitchen with the order in her hand, *raced* back to her customers with glasses of water, and *smiled* calmly.

He *grinned* at me from the ticket booth and *closed* the ticket window.

Whether you correct by changing all the verbs to the present tense, or by changing them to the past tense, you are making the tenses *consistent.* Consistency of tense is important in the events you are describing because it helps the reader understand what happened and *when it happened.*

ALONG THESE LINES/Prentice-Hall, Inc.

▶ **E X E R C I S E 1:** **Correcting Sentences That Are Inconsistent in Tense**

In each sentence following, one verb is inconsistent in tense. Cross it out and write the correct tense above. An example of how to do the exercise is given.

example:

We take the same algebra class, and we often meet in the cafeteria where

study
we ~~studied~~ our algebra notes.

a. Every month I stack all the household bills in a pile and get out my checkbook; then I paid all the bills at one time.

b. On the news, the reporter described the scene of the accident and interviewed a witness, but the reporter never explains how the accident happened.

c. When my father comes home from work, he sits in his recliner and turns on the television because he was too tired to talk.

d. Hundreds of pieces of junk mail come to our house every year and offered us magazine subscriptions, gifts, clothes, and fabulous prizes, but I throw all that junk mail in the garbage.

e. They were the top athletes in their class because they trained rigorously and follow a strict exercise routine.

f. In the kitchen, Adam struggled with the pipes under the sink and swore loudly; meanwhile, Jason calls a plumber.

g. Whenever she is depressed, she buys something chocolate and devoured it.

h. Because the parking lot at the supermarket is always crowded, people parked next door and walk the extra distance.

i. Working nights is hard for me because I had to get up early for classes and I have to find time for my family.

j. Although my friend says he's not afraid of heights, he shrank whenever he is at the edge of a balcony or apartment railing.

▶ **E X E R C I S E 2:** **Editing Paragraphs for Consistency of Tense**

Read the following paragraphs. Then cross out any verbs that are inconsistent in tense and write the correction above.

a. The rain came suddenly and pelted the holiday crowd with hail-sized nuggets. The storm transformed the scene. People grabbed their blankets and picnic baskets and run for cover. Several people congregated under nearby trees, but the lightning flashed nearby and worried them. Others sit under a picnic table while some raced to their cars. Everyone was soaking wet, and the picnic area becomes a scene of sopping paper plates and waterlogged barbecue grills.

b. The alarm clock blasted into my ear. I cringed, crawled out from under the covers, and reached my arm across the nightstand. I fling the stupid clock across the room and burrowed back under the covers. The bed felt warm and cozy. I tried to fall back into my dream. But soon my dog leaped into the room, jumped onto the bed, and plants kisses all over my face. In spite of all my attempts to go back to sleep, all the signs told me it was time to get up.

▶ **EXERCISE 3:** Collaborative Exercise on Writing
                     a Paragraph with Consistent Verb Tenses

The following paragraph has many inconsistencies in verb tense; it shifts between past and present tenses. Working with a group, write two versions of the paragraph: Write it once in the present tense, then a second time in the past tense. Split your activity; half the group can write it in one tense while the other half writes it in the other tense.

After both rewrites are complete, read the new paragraph aloud to both parts of the team, as a final check.

The day starts off well, but it doesn't end that way. At first, I am confident about taking my driving test and getting my driver's license. Then I got into the car with the examiner and wait for him to tell me to start. When he does, I turned the key in the ignition and slowly pull out of the parking lot. For some reason, I am sweating with fear, but I tried not to show it. I managed to drive without hitting another car. I remember to stop at a stop sign. But when it came to parallel parking, I knocked down all those orange markers! My driving examiner never cracks a smile or even talked to me. He just gives instructions. But I knew what he was thinking, and I know I won't get a license. I feel like the worst driver in the world.

Paragraph Revised for Consistent Tenses:

_____

_____

_____

_____

_____

_____

_____

_____

_____
_____
_____
_____
_____
_____
_____
_____
_____
_____
_____
_____

THE PRESENT PERFECT AND PAST PERFECT TENSES

In order to choose the right verb tense, you need to know about two verb tenses that can make your meaning clear: the *present perfect* and the *past perfect*.

The present perfect tense is made up of the past participle form of the verb plus have *or* has *as a helping verb.* It is used *to show an action that started in the past but is still going on in the present.*

> **past tense:** My father *drove* a truck for five months. (He doesn't drive a truck anymore, but he did drive one in the past.)
> **present perfect tense:** My father *has driven* a truck for five months. (He started driving a truck five months ago; he is still driving a truck.)
>
> **past tense:** For years, I *studied* ballet. (I don't study ballet now; I used to.)
> **present perfect tense:** For years, I *have studied* ballet. (I still study ballet.)

Remember, use the *present perfect tense to show that an action started in the past and is still going on.*

▶ **EXERCISE 1:** **Distinguishing Between the Past and the Present Perfect Tenses**

Circle the correct verb tense in each of the following sentences. Be sure to look carefully at the meaning of the sentences.

a. Jason *has borrowed/borrowed* a book from the library last night.

b. William *sang/has sung* in the choir for many years now.

c. The old car *was/has been* having mechanical problems, but no one wants to get rid of it.

E X E R C I S E

    d. I called the office and *have asked/asked* for the supervisor.

    e. The comedians *performed/have performed* together for two years and are now appearing at our campus theater.

    f. Two of my best friends *were/have been* musicians but gave music up for business careers.

    g. MTV *was/has been* influencing teenagers for years now.

    h. While he was in basic training, he *has written/wrote* many letters home.

    i. He *sent/has sent* his resume to fifty companies and accepted a job from the first company that responded.

    j. Melissa *lost/has lost* that bracelet three weeks ago.

THE PAST PERFECT TENSE

The past perfect tense is made up of the past participle form of the verb with had *as a helping verb.*

    You can use the past perfect tense to show more than one event in the past; that is, when more than one thing happened in the past but at different times.

past tense: He *washed* the dishes.
past perfect tense: He *had washed* the dishes by the time I came home. (He washed the dishes *before* I came home. Both actions happened in the past, but one happened earlier than the other.)

past tense: Susan *waited* for an hour.
past perfect tense: Susan *had waited* for an hour when she gave up on him. (Waiting came first; giving up came second. Both actions are in the past.)

The past perfect tense is especially useful because you write most of your essays in the past tense, and you often need to get further back into the past. Just remember to *use* had *with the past participle of the verb, and you'll have the past perfect tense.*

    ▶ **EXERCISE 2:** **Distinguishing Between the Past and the Past Perfect Tenses**

Circle the correct verb tense in the following sentences. Be sure to look carefully at the meaning of the sentence.

    a. The child *had hidden/hid* the shattered vase just minutes before his aunt entered the living room.

    b. My father drove a rental car last week because he *had wrecked/wrecked* his own car last month.

    c. Bernie bought a set of drums yesterday; he *had saved/saved* for that set for years.

   d. Every weekend, I *had run/ran* errands and ironed my clothes.

   e. The salesman asked whether we *had received/received* the merchandise yet.

   f. As I *had cut/cut* the pattern for another dress, I thought about becoming a dress designer.

   g. They *had left/left* for the party by the time we came to pick them up.

   h. She *threw/had thrown* the candy wrapper on the grass and ignored a nearby trash bin.

   i. I was not sure if he *had returned/returned* my tools earlier in the day.

   j. When the little boy screamed, the mother *had jumped/jumped* up with a worried look on her face.

PASSIVE AND ACTIVE VOICE

Verbs not only have tenses, they have voices. When the subject in the sentence is doing something, the verb is in the *active voice.* When something is done to the subject, when it receives the action of the verb, the verb is in the *passive voice.*

active voice:

I painted the house. (*I,* the subject, did it.)
The people on the corner made a donation to the emergency fund. (The *people,* the subject, did it.)

passive voice:

The house was painted by me. (The *house,* the subject, didn't do anything. It received the action—it was painted.)
A donation to the emergency fund was made by the people on the corner. (The *donation,* the subject, didn't do anything. It received the action—it was given.)

Notice what happens when you use the passive voice instead of the active:

active voice: I painted the house.
passive voice: The house was painted by me.

The sentence in the passive voice is two words longer than the one in the active voice. Yet the sentence that uses the passive voice doesn't say anything different, and it doesn't say it more clearly than the one in the active voice.

Using the passive voice can make your sentences wordy, it can slow them down, and it can make them boring. The passive voice can also confuse readers. When the subject of the sentence isn't doing anything, readers may have to look carefully to see who or what *is doing* something. Look at this sentence, for example:

A decision to fire you was reached.

Who decided to fire you? In this sentence, it's hard to find the answer to that question.

Of course, there will be times when you have to use the passive voice. For example, you may have to use it when you don't know who did something, as in these sentences:

Our house was broken into last night.
A leather jacket was left behind in the classroom.

But in general, you should avoid using the passive voice and rewrite sentences so they are in the active voice.

► **EXERCISE 3:** **Rewriting Sentences, Changing the Passive Voice to the Active Voice**

In the following sentences, change the passive voice to the active voice. If the original sentence doesn't tell you who or what performed the action, add words that tell who or what did it. An example is done for you.

example: He was appointed chief negotiator last night.

rewritten: *The union leaders appointed him chief negotiator last night.*

a. My favorite actor was arrested in Hollywood yesterday.

rewritten: _____

_____

b. A compromise has been reached by the lawyers on both sides.

rewritten: _____

_____

c. The wrong number was called several times.

rewritten: _____

_____

d. Finally, a restaurant was decided on by the hungry family.

rewritten: _____

_____

e. Great care was taken to protect the fragile package.

rewritten: _____

_____

f. The dolls were placed in a row by the little girl.

rewritten: _____

_____

g. Every day, the park is patrolled by a security guard.

rewritten: _____

_____

h. Last week, my car was hit by a careless driver.

rewritten: _____

_____

i. The real reason for his tardiness was not known by his teacher.

rewritten: _____

_____

j. The murder is being investigated by the police.

rewritten: _____

_____

Avoiding Unnecessary Shifts in Voice

Just as you should be consistent in the tense of verbs, you should be consistent in the voice of verbs. Don't shift from active voice to passive voice, or vice versa, without a good reason to do so.

　　　　　　active　　　　　　　　　　　　　　　　　passive
　　shift: *I designed* the decorations for the dance; *they were put up* by Chuck.

　　　　　　　　active　　　　　　　　　　　　　　　active
　　rewritten: *I designed* the decorations for the dance; *Chuck put* them *up*.

　　　　　　　　　　　passive
　　shift: Many *problems were discussed* by the council members, but

　　　active
　　they found no easy answers.

　　　　　　　　　　　　　　　active　　　　　　　　　active
　　rewritten: The council *members discussed* many problems, *they found*
　　no easy answers.

Being consistent in voice can help you to write clearly and smoothly.

▶ **E X E R C I S E　4 :** **Rewriting Sentences to Correct Shifts in Voice**

Rewrite the following sentences so that all the verbs are in the active voice. You may change the wording to make the sentences clear, smooth, and consistent in voice.

a. Christine called Jack yesterday, but I was called by Tom today.

rewritten: _____

_____

b. A revised set of rules is being written by the disciplinary committee; the committee is also writing a list of penalties.

rewritten: _____

_____

c. That girl can be helped by your advice because you know her problems.

rewritten: _____

_____

d. The windows were opened by the office workers as the temperature soared above ninety degrees.

rewritten: _____

_____

e. It was decided by a team of experts that the water contains harmful bacteria.

rewritten: _____

_____

f. My sister has been chosen by the senior class to speak at graduation; she will deliver the welcoming address.

rewritten: _____

_____

g. Some people worship celebrities; musicians, actors, and athletes are regarded as superhuman.

rewritten: _____

_____

h. Michael showed his dismay when his brother Chris was rejected by the admissions committee.

rewritten: _____

_____

i. If a deal was made by the officers, I never knew about it.

rewritten: _____

_____

j. People didn't worry about protecting their homes until South Florida was hit by a monster hurricane.

rewritten: _____

_____

Small Reminders about Verbs

There are a few errors that people tend to make with verbs. If you are aware of these errors, you'll be on the lookout for them as you edit your writing.

Used to　Be careful when you write that someone *used to* do, say, or feel something. It is incorrect to write *use to*.

not this: Janine ~~use to~~ visit her mother every week.
　　　　　They ~~use to~~ like Thai food.

but this: Janine use*d* to visit her mother every week.
     They use*d* to like Thai food.

Could Have, Should Have, Would Have Using *of* instead of *have* is another error with verbs.

not this: I ~~could of~~ done better on the test.
but this: I *could have* done better on the test.

not this: He ~~should of~~ been paying attention.
but this: He *should have* been paying attention.

not this: The girls ~~would of~~ liked to visit Washington.
but this: The girls *would have* liked to visit Washington.

Would Have/Had If you are writing about something that might have been possible, but that did not happen, use *had* as the helping verb.

not this: If I ~~would have~~ taken a foreign language in high school, I
     wouldn't have to take one now.
but this: If I *had* taken a foreign language in high school, I wouldn't have
     to take one now.

not this: I wish they ~~would have~~ won the game.
but this: I wish they *had* won the game.

not this: If she ~~would have~~ been smart, she would have called a plumber.
but this: If she *had* been smart, she would have called a plumber.

▶ **E X E R C I S E   5 :   Collaborative Exercise on Writing Sentences
               with the Correct Verb Forms**

Do this exercise with a partner or with a group. Write or complete each of the following sentences. When you have finished the exercise, be ready to share your answers with another group or with the class.

a. Complete this sentence and add a verb in the correct tense: I had cleaned the whole house by the time

_____

_____

_____

b. Write a sentence that is more than six words long and that uses the words *has studied karate* in the middle of the sentence.

_____

_____

_____

c. Write a sentence that uses the past tense form of both these words: *run, stumble.*

_____

_____

_____

d. Write a sentence in the passive voice.

_____

_____

_____

e. Write a sentence in the active voice.

_____

_____

_____

Making Subjects and Verbs Agree

Subjects and verbs have to agree in number. That means a singular subject must be matched with a singular verb form; a plural subject must be matched with a plural verb form.

singular subject, singular verb
My *sister walks* to work every morning.

plural subject,   plural verb
Mary, David, and Sam believe in ghosts.

singular subject, singular verb
That *movie is* too violent for me.

plural subject, plural verb
Bulky *packages are* difficult to carry.

Caution: Remember that a regular verb has an s ending in one singular form in the present tense—the form that goes with *he, she, it,* or their equivalents.

He makes me feel confident.
She appreciates intelligent conversation.
It seems like a good buy.
Bo runs every day.
That girl swims well.
That machine breaks down too often.

▶ **EXERCISE 1:** **Correcting Errors in Subject-Verb Agreement in a Paragraph**

There are errors in subject-verb agreement in the following paragraph. If a verb does not agree with its subject, change the verb form. Cross out the incorrect verb form and write the correct one above. There are four errors in agreement in the paragraph.

Every night, my sister follows the same routine. She pours a big glass of diet cola, sit down in an old easy chair, and settles down for a night on the telephone. My sister always call the same person, her best friend Irene. She and Irene talks for hours about the most trivial subjects. The two girls gossip

E X E R C I S E

about their friends, about their enemies, about what happened that day, and about what will happen the next day. My brother says men never spend as much time on the phone. But he always say that while he is trying to get the phone from my sister so he can make his evening calls!

PRONOUNS AS SUBJECTS

Pronouns can be used as subjects. Pronouns are words that take the place of nouns. *When pronouns are used as subjects, they must agree, in number, with verbs.*

Here is a list of the subject pronouns and the regular verb forms that agree with them, in the present tense.

pronoun	verb	
I	listen	
you	listen	all singular forms
he, she, it	listens	
we	listen	
you	listen	all plural forms
they	listen	

In all of the following sentences, the pronoun used as the subject of the sentence agrees with the verb, in number.

singular pronoun, singular verb
I make the best omelet in town.

singular pronoun, singular verb
You dance very well.

singular pronoun, singular verb
She performs like a trained athlete.

plural pronoun, plural verb
We need a new refrigerator.

plural pronoun, plural verb
They understand the situation.

SPECIAL PROBLEMS WITH AGREEMENT

Agreement seems fairly simple, doesn't it? If a subject is singular, use a singular verb form. If a subject is plural, use a plural verb form. However, there are special problems with agreement that will come up in your writing. Sometimes it's hard to find the subject of a sentence; at other times, it's hard to determine if a subject is singular or plural.

Finding the Subject

When you are checking for subject-verb agreement, you can find the real subject of the sentence by first eliminating the prepositional phrases. To find the real

ALONG THESE LINES/Prentice-Hall, Inc.

subject, put parentheses around the prepositional phrases. Then it's easy to find the subject because nothing in a prepositional phrase is the subject of a sentence.

prepositional phrases in parentheses:

S   V
One (of my oldest friends) *is* a social worker.

  S   V
A *student* (from one)(of the nearby school districts) *is* the winner.

   S   V
The *store* (across the street) (from my house) *is* open all night.

 S   V
Jim, (with all his silly jokes), *is* a nice person.

▶ **E X E R C I S E 2 :** **Finding the Real Subject by Recognizing Prepositional Phrases**

Put parentheses around all the prepositional phrases in the following sentences, and identify the subject and verb by writing *S* or *V* above them.

 a. Two of my favorite television shows are comedies with African-American stars.

 b. The toothpaste with fluoride in it is the best choice.

 c. One of the three people on the decorations committee is a professional artist.

 d. The clerk behind the counter at the bakery is a new employee.

 e. A representative of the company from the proposed site has presented a convincing proposal.

 f. The cat behind the curtains is my sister's pet.

 g. The middle school with the modern architecture is down the road from my house.

 h. With a great deal of poise, she took the termination notice from her employer's hand.

 i. The coat in the downstairs closet is the one with the keys in it.

 j. The field of cornflowers is a vision in the springtime.

▶ **E X E R C I S E 3 :** **Selecting the Correct Verb Form by Identifying Prepositional Phrases**

In the following sentences, put parentheses around all the prepositional phrases; then circle the verb that agrees with the subject.

 a. A speaker from The Council of Cities *is/are* lecturing in our anthropology class today.

 b. Several of the biggest bargains in the shop *is/are* stashed in the back room.

c. One of the contestants from the semifinal rounds *face/faces* the winner of this round.

d. The consequences of her argument with her father *seem/seems* severe.

e. A salesman with a background in communications *has/have* a competitive advantage.

f. With a velvet ribbon in her hair, the little girl in the cereal advertisements *look/looks* like a little angel.

g. A friend of mine from the boondocks *is/are* dazzled by the big mall at the edge of town.

h. A change of plans *is/are* no reason for a change in your attitude.

i. An honest statement of the facts *is/are* behind the mayor's popularity in this city.

j. A person with energy, intelligence, and drive *is/are* needed for this job.

Changed Word Order

You are probably used to looking for the subject of a sentence in front of the verb, but not all sentences follow this pattern. Questions, sentences beginning with words like *here* or *there*, and other sentences change the word order. So you have to look carefully to check for subject-verb agreement.

>   V   S
> Where *are* my *friends?*

>   V S   V
> When *is he going* to work?

>   V   S
> Behind the courthouse *stands* a huge *statue.*

>   V   S
> There *are potholes* in the road.

>   V   S
> There *is* a *reason* for his impatience.

▶ **EXERCISE 4:** **Making Subjects and Verbs Agree in Sentences with Changed Word Order**

In each of the following sentences, underline the subject; then circle the correct verb form.

a. Included in the package of coupons *was/were* a coupon for a free breakfast.

b. Among my happiest memories *is/are* the memory of a day at the beach.

ALONG THESE LINES/Prentice-Hall, Inc.

   c. Along the side of the road *is/are* a flower stand and an old-fashioned diner.

   d. There *is/are* several explanations for his tantrum.

   e. There *was/were* my brother and sister, in the midst of an argument about my birthday party.

   f. Behind the fence *lurk/lurks* a fierce and evil dog.

   g. There *was/were* a sudden increase in the price of groceries.

   h. Under the porch *sit/sits* an enormous frog.

   i. Where *is/are* the photographs of your trip to Mexico?

   j. Here *is/are* the insurance policy for the car.

COMPOUND SUBJECTS

A *compound subject* is two or more subjects joined by *and, or,* or *nor.*

   When subjects are joined by *and,* they are usually plural.

       S   S   V
   Jermaine and *Lisa are* bargain hunters.

         S   S   V
   The *house* and the *garden need* attention.

      S   S   V
   A *bakery* and a *pharmacy are* down the street.

Caution: Be careful to check for a compound subject when the word order changes.

         V   S   S
   There *are* a *bakery* and a *pharmacy* down the street. (Two things, a *bakery* and a *pharmacy, are* down the street.)

       V   S   S
   Here *are* a *picture* of your father and a *copy* of his birth certificate (A *picture* and a *copy,* two things, *are* here.)

When subjects are joined by or, either . . . or, neither . . . nor, not only . . . but also, *the verb form agrees with the subject closer to the verb.*

               singular S   plural S, plural V
   Not only the restaurant *manager* but also the *waiters were* pleased with the new policy.

             plural S   singular S, singular V
   Not only the *waiters* but also the restaurant *manager was* pleased with the new policy.

          plural S   singular S, singular V
   Either the *parents* or the *boy walks* the dog every morning.

        singular S   plural S, plural V
   Either the *boy* or the *parents walk* the dog every morning.

▶ **E X E R C I S E 5 :** Making Subjects and Verbs Agree—
Compound Subjects

Circle the correct form of the verb in each of the following sentences.

   a. Neither my sister nor my cousin *is/are* good at sports.

   b. When they came to this country, Stephen and Richard *was/were* eager to find employment.

   c. Here *is/are* the guest of honor and her husband.

   d. Either Jaime or his sisters *is/are* supposed to take out the garbage on Saturdays.

   e. Either his sisters or Jaime *is/are* supposed to take out the garbage on Saturdays.

   f. Doughnuts and a coffee cake *was/were* in the bag.

   g. Under the sofa there *is/are* an old ragged slipper and a shriveled apple.

   h. Either Christopher or Ted *is/are* going to play first base.

   i. Not only the teacher but also the students *like/likes* the new classroom.

   j. Hanging out with my friends and complaining about my parents *was/were* my principal activities in high school.

INDEFINITE PRONOUNS

Certain pronouns, called indefinite pronouns, always take a singular verb.

Indefinite Pronouns

one	nobody	nothing	each
anyone	anybody	anything	either
someone	somebody	something	neither
everyone	everybody	everything	

If you want to write clearly and correctly, you must memorize these words and remember that they always take a singular verb. Using your common sense isn't enough because some of these words seem plural: for example, *everybody* seems to mean more than one person, but in grammatically correct English, it takes a singular verb. Here are some examples of the pronouns used with singular verbs:

singular S   singular V
Everyone in town *is talking* about the scandal.

singular S   singular V
Each of the boys *is* talented.

singular S   singular V
One of their biggest concerns *is* crime in the streets.

singular S   singular V
Neither of the cats *is* mine.

Hint: You can memorize the indefinite pronouns as the *-one*, *-thing*, and *-body* words—every*one*, every*thing*, every*body*, and so forth—plus *each*, *either*, and *neither*.

▶ **E X E R C I S E   6 :   Making Subjects and Verbs Agree—Using Indefinite Pronouns**

Circle the correct verb in the following sentences.

   a. Anybody in the suburbs *know/knows* the way to that turnpike exit.

   b. Nothing in the sales racks *is/are* sufficiently marked down.

   c. Somebody *has/have* painted graffiti all over the walls.

   d. Everything in the closet and in the hallways *is/are* neatly packed in cardboard boxes.

   e. *Is/Are* anyone coming over for birthday cake?

   f. Everybody in both schools *listen/listens* to the same radio station.

   g. Nobody from the service clubs *was/were* interested in volunteering for this project.

   h. Anything in shades of pink or green *match/matches* my new dress.

   i. One of my most foolish decisions *was/were* to call in sick last week.

   j. Here *is/are* someone to see you.

   k. *Has/Have* anybody seen my car keys?

   l. Either of the restaurants *is/are* a fine place for lunch.

   m. Someone *leaves/leave* trash in the empty lot every weekend.

   n. Each of my aunts *visits/visit* Jamaica at least once a year.

   o. Neither of the cars *has/have* anti-lock brakes.

COLLECTIVE NOUNS

Collective nouns refer to more than one person or thing, such as

team	company	council
class	corporation	government
committee	family	group
audience	jury	crowd

Most of the time, collective nouns take a singular verb.

singular S   singular V
The *committee is sponsoring* a fundraiser.

singular S singular V
The *audience was* impatient.

singular S singular V
The *jury has reached* a verdict.

The singular verb is used because the group is sponsoring, or getting impatient, or reaching a verdict, *as one unit. Collective nouns take a plural verb only when the members of the group are acting individually, not as a unit.*

The sophomore *class are fighting* among themselves. (The phrase among themselves shows that the class is not acting as one unit.)

▶ **EXERCISE 7:** **Making Subjects and Verbs Agree—Using Collective Nouns**

Circle the correct verb in each of the following sentences.

  a. My family *is/are* moving to another state next month.

  b. The company with the safest work environment *is/are* receiving an award tomorrow.

  c. Our class *has/have* less school spirit than other classes.

  d. The Student Council *meet/meets* every Tuesday afternoon.

  e. My group of friends *is/are* as close as friends can be.

  f. A team from the Phillipines *was/were* competing in the international contest.

  g. After Labor Day, the crowd at the beach *isn't/aren't* so large.

  h. A truly enthusiastic audience *help/helps* the performers.

  i. The governing board *vote/votes* on the annual budget tomorrow night.

  j. The men's club *has/have* never endorsed candidates for political office.

MAKING SUBJECTS AND VERBS AGREE: THE BOTTOM LINE

As you've probably realized, making subjects and verbs agree is not as simple as it first appears. But if you can remember the basic ideas in this section, you will be able to apply them automatically as you edit your own writing. Following is a quick summary of subject-verb agreement.

Making Subjects and Verbs Agree: A Summary

1. Subjects and verbs should agree in number: singular subjects get singular verb forms; plural subjects get plural verb forms.

2. When pronouns are used as subjects, they must agree, in number, with verbs.

3. Nothing in a prepositional phrase can be the subject of the sentence.

4. Questions, sentences beginning with *here* or *there,* and other sentences can change word order, so look carefully for the subject.

5. Compound subjects joined by *and* are usually plural.

6. When subjects are joined by *or, either . . . or, neither . . . nor, not only . . . but also,* the verb form agrees with the subject closest to the verb.

7. Indefinite pronouns always take singular verbs.

8. Most of the time, collective nouns take singular verbs.

▶ **EXERCISE 8: A Comprehensive Exercise on Subject-Verb Agreement**

This exercise covers all the rules on subject-verb agreement. Circle the correct verb form in the following sentences.

a. One of the cooks at the restaurant *was/were* in my math class last year.

b. Anybody from Arizona *know/knows* how to stay cool in the summer.

c. When *was/were* the packages delivered?

d. Each of the cars on the showroom floor *was/were* polished to a dazzling brightness.

e. Within the circle of diamonds *was/were* a deep red stone.

f. Neither my cousin nor his parents ever *think/thinks* about home security.

g. Every day, apathy and pessimism *grow/grows* stronger in the city.

h. Nothing in ten years *has/have* pleased her more than that party.

i. The candidate with a strong background in liberal arts and good leadership skills *remain/remains* my first choice for the position.

j. Behind the refrigerator *sit/sits* a giant cockroach.

k. Everything in the Botanical Gardens *is/are* rare and exotic.

l. Down the street from the bank there *is/are* a Chinese restaurant and an Italian deli.

m. Because of the lateness of the hour, the jury *is/are* adjourning until tomorrow.

n. The company *was/were* not eager to recruit college graduates.

o. Clearly defined steps and a realistic schedule *help/helps* you complete a difficult project.

p. If the city doesn't fix that road soon, someone *is/are* going to have an accident.

q. Last year there *was/were* a shooting and two muggings in the parking lot by the club.

r. Neither of my parents *is/are* anxious about my decision.

s. The most popular nightclubs *look/looks* shabby in daylight.

t. Here *is/are* the letters from your girlfriend.

▶ **EXERCISE 9: A Collaborative Exercise on Subject-Verb Agreement**

With a partner or with a group, write two sentences for each of the following phrases. Use a verb that fits and put it in the present tense. Be sure that the verb agrees with the subject.

When your group has completed the exercise, be ready to share your answers with another group or with the whole class.

a. A crate of oranges _____

_____

A crate of oranges _____

_____

b. Either Superman or Batman _____

_____

Either Superman or Batman _____

_____

c. The committee _____

_____

The committee

_____

d. Thelma and Louise_____

_____

Thelma and Louise_____

_____

e. Everything in my closet _____

_____

Everything in my closet _____

_____

f. Someone from the suburbs _____

_____

Someone from the suburbs _____

_____

g. Not only the child but also his parents _____

_____

Not only the child but also his parents _____

_____

h. Anybody in town _____

_____

Anybody in town _____

_____

i. One of my greatest fears _____

_____

One of my greatest fears _____

_____

j. Everyone in the office _____

_____

Everyone in the office _____

_____

► **E X E R C I S E   1 0 :   Collaborate in Creating Your Own Text
on Subject-Verb Agreement**

Work with a partner or with a group to create your own grammar handbook.
Following is a list of rules on subject-verb agreement. Write two sentences that
are examples of each rule. (The first one is done for you, as a sample.)

After you've completed this exercise, share your group's answers with another
group.

Rule 1: Subjects and verbs should agree in number: singular subjects get singular verb forms; plural subjects get plural verb forms.

examples: _A battered old car stands in the front yard._____

_Country roads look pretty in the autumn._____

Rule 2: When pronouns are used as subjects, they must agree, in number,
with verbs.

examples: _____

_____

Rule 3: Nothing in a prepositional phrase can be the subject of the
sentence.

examples: _____

_____

Rule 4: Questions, sentences beginning with *here* or *there,* and other sentences can change word order, so look carefully for the subject.

examples: _____

_____

Rule 5: When subjects are joined by *and,* they are usually plural.

examples: _____

_____

Rule 6: When subjects are joined by *or, either . . . or, neither . . . nor,* or *not only . . . but also,* the verb form agrees with the subject closest to the verb.

examples: _____

_____

Rule 7: Indefinite pronouns always take singular verbs.

examples: _____

_____

Rule 8: Most of the time, collective nouns take singular verbs.

examples: _____

_____

Pronouns are words that substitute for nouns. The word or words a pronoun replaces is its *antecedent*.

antecedent   pronoun
Jack is a good friend; *he* is very loyal.

        antecedent   pronoun
I hated *the movie* because *it* was too violent.

    antecedent   pronoun
Playing tennis was fun, but *it* started to take up too much of my time.

        antecedent   pronoun
Mike and Michelle are sure *they* are in love.

antecedent   pronoun
Sharon gave away *her* old clothes.

antecedent   pronoun
The dog rattled *its* dish, begging for dinner.

► **EXERCISE 1: Identifying the Antecedents of Pronouns**

In each of the following sentences, a pronoun is underlined. Underline the word or words that are the antecedent of the underlined pronoun.

a. Kim and I are quitting tomorrow because <u>we</u> can't make enough money at the job.

b. Riding a stationary bike is good exercise because <u>it</u> strengthens leg muscles.

c. My parents said <u>they</u> couldn't afford to send me to college.

d. The museum presented <u>its</u> best collection last week.

e. David, can <u>you</u> ever forgive me?

f. A small boy learns a great deal by observing <u>his</u> father.

g. Alan loves swimming, but I am not fond of <u>it</u>.

h. We told the security guard we had lost our tickets, but <u>he</u> wouldn't let us in.

i. The musicians at the club play <u>their</u> last set at midnight.

j. Constant criticism is dangerous; in fact, <u>it</u> can destroy a person's confidence.

AGREEMENT OF A PRONOUN AND ITS ANTECEDENT

A pronoun must agree in number with its antecedent. If the antecedent is singular; the pronoun must be singular. If the antecedent is plural, then the pronoun must be plural.

singular antecedent   singular pronoun
Susan tried to arrive on time, but *she* got caught in traffic.

plural antecedent   plural pronoun
Susan and Ray tried to arrive on time, but *they* got caught in traffic.

plural antecedent   plural pronoun
The visitors tried to arrive on time, but *they* got caught in traffic.

Agreement of pronoun and antecedent seems fairly simple. If an antecedent is singular, use a singular pronoun. If an antecedent is plural, use a plural pronoun. There are, however, some special problems with agreement of pronouns, and these problems will come up in your writing. If you become familiar with the explanations, examples, and exercises that follow, you'll be ready to handle the special problems.

INDEFINITE PRONOUNS

Certain words, called *indefinite pronouns, are always singular.* Therefore, if an indefinite pronoun is the *antecedent,* the pronoun that replaces it must be singular. Here are the indefinite pronouns:

Indefinite Pronouns

one	nobody	nothing	each
anyone	anybody	anything	either
someone	somebody	something	neither
everyone	everybody	everything	

You may think that *everybody* is plural, but in grammatically correct English, it is a singular word. Therefore, if you want to write clearly and correctly, memorize these words as the *-one, -thing,* and *-body* words: every*one*, every*thing*, every*body,* and so forth, plus *each, either, neither.* If any of these words is an antecedent, the pronoun that refers to it must be singular.

singular antecedent 　　　　singular pronoun
Each of the Boy Scouts received *his* merit badge.

singular antecedent 　　　　　singular pronoun
Everyone in the sorority donated *her* time to the project.

Avoiding Sexism

Consider this sentence:

Everybody in the math class brought _____ own calculator.

How do you choose the correct pronoun to fill in the blank? You can write

Everybody in the math class brought *his* own calculator.

if everybody in the class is male. Or you can write

Everybody in the math class brought *her* own calculator.

if everybody in the class is female. Or you can write

Everybody in the math class brought *his or her* own calculator.

if the class has students of both sexes.

In the past, most writers used the pronoun *his* to refer to both men and women. Today, many writers try to use *his or her* to avoid sexual bias. If you find using *his or her* is getting awkward or repetitive, you can rewrite the sentence and *make the antecedent plural:*

The students in the math class brought their own calculators.

But you can't shift from singular to plural. You *can't write*

~~Everybody in the math class brought their own calculators.~~

▶ **E X E R C I S E 2:** Making Pronouns and Antecedents Agree

In each of the following sentences, write the appropriate pronoun in the blank space. Look carefully for the antecedent before you choose the pronoun.

a. The hall closet is disorganized and messy; I really should clean

_____ .

b. Years ago, most people were careful with their cash; _____ were taught to save money, not to spend it.

c. I noticed that a woman was advertising a reward for the return of

_____engagement ring.

d. Some of the customers at the store use _____ credit cards whenever there is a sale.

e. When the little girl had a birthday party, _____ wanted to invite the whole neighborhood.

f. A boy with nothing to do all summer may wind up getting into trouble with _____ friends because he's bored.

g. Neither of the men chosen to lead the campaign wanted to devote _____ time to fund-raising.

h. Everyone named an Outstanding Mother of the Year had _____ own opinion about the ceremony.

i. Each of the brothers has won an athletic scholarship to the college of _____ choice.

j. I am beginning to enjoy my exercise class; _____ helps me relax.

COLLECTIVE NOUNS

Collective nouns refer to more than one person or thing.

some collective nouns:

team	company	council
class	corporation	government
committee	family	group
audience	jury	crowd

Most of the time, collective nouns take a singular pronoun.

      collective noun   singular pronoun
      The *team* that was ahead in the playoffs lost *its* home game.

      collective noun   singular pronoun
      The *corporation* changed *its* policy on parental leave.

Collective nouns are usually singular because the group is losing a game or chang-ing a policy as one, as a unit. *Collective nouns take a plural pronoun only when the members of the group are acting individually, not as a unit.*

   The class picked up their class rings this morning. (The members of the class pick up their rings, individually.)

▶ **E X E R C I S E   3 :   Making Pronouns and Antecedents Agree: Collective Nouns**

Circle the correct pronoun in each of the following sentences.

a. The computer company has a reputation for being extremely generous to *their/its* employees.

b. Skyward Airlines was involved in a campaign to change *their/its* image.

c. The hiring committee deliberated for hours and then told the applicant *their/its* decision.

d. After the singer left the stage, the audience expressed *their/its* disappoint-ment with boos and shouts.

e. Two of the teams were selling candy to raise money for *their/its* equip-ment.

f. The family lost *their/its* home in a fire last week.

g. I loved working at The Castle Company because *it/they* gave me such a generous package of benefits.

h. The club divided the responsibilities among *itself/themselves*.

i. The general was worried that the army would not be able to hold *their/its* position.

j. The gang began to fall apart when the members quarreled among *them-selves/itself*.

▶ **E X E R C I S E   4 :   Correcting Errors of Pronoun-Antecedent Agreement within a Paragraph**

Read the following paragraph carefully, looking for errors in agreement of pro-nouns and their antecedents. Cross out any pronouns that do not agree with their antecedents and write the correct pronoun above. There are five pronouns that need correcting.

The Paper Company is a great place to work. The managers are firm but friendly in their relations with the employees, and working conditions are pleasant. The company has designed their policies to motivate employees, not to intimidate them. Everybody in the workplace knows they will be treated fairly. The Paper Company is not only considerate of workers; it is concerned for the environment. All the products are made of recycled paper. Thus, each of the items made for sale contributes their part to conservation. Workers and managers can feel good, knowing that he or she can help the planet. I wish everyone in this country would do their part, just as The Paper Com-pany does.

▶ **E X E R C I S E   5 :   Collaborative Exercise on Writing Sentences with Pronoun-Antecedent Agreement**

With a partner or with a group, write a sentence for each of the following pairs of words, using each pair as a pronoun and its antecedent. The first pair is done for you, as an example. After you've completed the exercise, be ready to share your sentences with another group or with the class.

a. women . . . their

sentence: Women who work outside the home have to plan their time carefully.

b. council . . . its

sentence:_____

_____

c. anyone . . . his or her

sentence:_____

_____

d. celebrities . . . they

sentence:_____

_____

e. complaining . . . it

sentence:_____

_____

f. neither . . . her

sentence:_____

_____

PRONOUNS AND THEIR ANTECEDENTS: BEING CLEAR

Remember that pronouns are words that replace or refer to other words, and those *other words* that are replaced or referred to are called antecedents.

Make sure that a pronoun has one clear antecedent. Your writing will be vague and confusing if a pronoun appears to refer to more than one antecedent or if it doesn't have any specific antecedent to refer to. In grammar, such confusing language is called a problem with *reference of pronouns.*

When the *pronoun refers to more than one thing,* the sentence can become confusing or silly. The following are examples of unclear reference.

Jim told his father that his bike had been stolen. (Whose bike was stolen? Jim's? His father's?)

She put the cake on the table, took off her apron, pulled up a chair, and began to eat it. (What did she eat? The cake? the table? Her apron? The chair?)

If there is no one clear antecedent, you must rewrite the sentence to make the reference clear. Sometimes the rewritten sentence may seem repetitive, but a little repetition is better than a lot of confusion.

unclear: Jim told his father that his bike had been stolen.
clear: Jim told his father that Jim's bike had been stolen.
clear: Jim told his father that his father's bike had been stolen.
clear: Jim told his father, "My bike has been stolen."

unclear: She put the cake on the table, took off her apron, pulled up a chair, and began to eat it.

ALONG THESE LINES/Prentice-Hall, Inc.

clear: She put the cake on the table, took off her apron, pulled up a chair, and began to eat the cake.

Sometimes the problem is a little more tricky. Can you spot what's wrong with this sentence?

unclear: Bill decided to take a part-time job, which worried his parents. (What worried Bill's parents? His decision to work part time? Or the job itself?)

Be very careful with the pronoun *which*. If there is any chance that using *which* will confuse the reader, rewrite the sentence and get rid of *which*.

clear: Bill's parents were worried about the kind of part-time job he chose.
clear: Bill's decision to work part time worried his parents.

Sometimes, a pronoun has nothing to refer to; it has no antecedent.

When Bill got to the train station, they said the train was going to be late. (Who said the train was going to be late? The ticket agents? The strangers that Bill met on the tracks?)
Maria has always loved medicine and has decided that's what she wants to be. (What does "that" refer to? The only word it could refer to is "medicine," but Maria certainly doesn't want to be a medicine. She doesn't want to be an aspirin or a cough drop.)

If a pronoun lacks an antecedent, add an antecedent or eliminate the pronoun.

add an antecedent: When Bill got to the train station and asked the ticket agents about the schedule, they said the train was going to be late.
eliminate the pronoun: Maria has always loved medicine and has decided she wants to be a physician.

Note: To check for clear reference of pronouns, underline any pronoun that may not be clear. Then try to draw a line from that pronoun to its antecedent. Are there two or more possible antecedents? Is there no antecedent? In either case, you need to rewrite.

▶ **E X E R C I S E 6 : Rewriting Sentences for Clear Reference of Pronouns**

Rewrite the following sentences so that the pronouns have clear references. You can add, take out, or change words.

a. Ashley told Laura she had the messiest room in the dormitory.

b. Every time I go to Quick Mart, they are too busy gossiping on the phone to help me.

c. I was offered a position at Express Service which pleased me.

d. I loved my visit to Mexico City; they are so friendly and warm.

e. My father is a successful salesman, but I am not interested in it.

f. Parents often fight with adolescent children because they are stubborn and inflexible.

g. The supervisor told the assistant that his office would be moved to a new location.

h. The car crossed the median and hit a truck, but it wasn't badly damaged.

i. They never told me about the fine print when I signed a lease for my apartment.

j. Ray accused Diane of starting the argument, which was silly.

Using Pronouns Correctly: Consistency and Case

When you write, you write from a point of view, and each point of view gets its own form. If you write from the first person point of view, your pronouns are in the *I* (singular) or *we* (plural) forms. If you write from the second person point of view, your pronouns are in the *you* form, whether they are singular or plural. If you write from the third person point of view, your pronouns are in the *he, she,* or *it* (singular) or *they* (plural) forms.

Different kinds of writing may require different points of view. When you are writing a set of directions, for example, you might use the second person (*you*) point of view. For an essay about your childhood, you might use the first person (*I*) point of view.

Whatever point of view you use, be consistent in using pronouns. That is, you shouldn't shift the form of your pronouns without some good reason.

> **not consistent:** Every time *I* go to that mall, the parking lot is so crowded *you* have to drive around for hours, looking for a parking space.
> **consistent:** Every time *I* go to that mall, the parking lot is so crowded *I* have to drive around for hours, looking for a parking space.

▶ **EXERCISE 1: Consistency in Pronouns**

Correct any inconsistency in point of view in the following sentences. Cross out the incorrect pronoun and write the correct one above it.

a. Birthdays, for me, are times when I can look back at what I've accomplished and plan your goals for the year ahead.

b. When passengers enter the plane, the flight attendant greets you with a friendly smile.

c. Beginners should be careful when they cook souffles; if you open the oven at the wrong time, they will destroy the souffle.

d. At my doctor's office, patients can wait for an hour before the doctor is ready to see you.

e. The law students filed into the auditorium, nervously waiting for the proctors to enter and give you the three-hour exam.

EXERCISE

413

f. They were irritated by his conversation because you couldn't get a word into his endless chatter.

g. Although we have our tires checked before a trip, you have to remember to have the belts checked also.

h. As she drove her jeep through the valley, the fog was so thick you couldn't see the lights of the village.

i. Every time I visit my sister's house, you know she's been cleaning and polishing all day.

j. The last time I ate at Billy's Barbecue, I thought the staff was so rude to you that I swore I'd never eat there again.

► **EXERCISE 2: Collaborate in Correcting Sentences with Consistency Problems**

Do this exercise with a partner or with a group. Rewrite the following sentences, correcting any errors with consistency of pronouns. To make the corrections, you may have to change, add, or take out words. After you've corrected the sentences, share your answers with another group or with the entire class.

a. You could smell autumn in the air when we walked through the woods.

rewrite: _____

_____

b. My grandmother's house was a favorite with all the grandchildren; you knew you would always have fun there.

rewrite: _____

_____

c. A supervisor can gain respect if you treat all the workers fairly and show them respect.

rewrite: _____

_____

d. Students who are just starting college can be overwhelmed by the reading assignments; you are not used to reading so much so quickly.

rewrite: _____

_____

e. Public Speaking was my favorite course; I enjoyed planning my presentation, the audience responding to you, and the feedback from my peers.

rewrite: _____

_____

ALONG THESE LINES/Prentice-Hall, Inc.

f. I can't ask Miguel to help me because he'll talk your ear off about self-reliance.

rewrite: _____

_____

g. It doesn't matter how politely I try to explain my situation; she'll get angry with you every time.

rewrite: _____

_____

h. Students who miss the test can take a make-up test only after the instructor decides you have a valid excuse.

rewrite: _____

_____

i. The worst thing about my job at the market is that you have to spend hours on your feet.

rewrite: _____

_____

j. If a worker genuinely cares about a pleasant work environment, you shouldn't gossip with co-workers.

rewrite: _____

_____

CHOOSING THE CASE OF PRONOUNS

Pronouns have forms that show number and person, and they also have forms that show *case*. Following is a list of three cases of pronouns.

singular pronouns

	subjective case	objective case	possessive case
1st person	I	me	my
2nd person	you	you	your
3rd person	he, she, it	him, her, it	his, her, its

plural pronouns

	subjective case	objective case	possessive case
1st person	we	us	our
2nd person	you	you	your
3rd person	they	them	their

The rules for choosing the case of pronouns are simple:
1. *When a pronoun is used as a subject, use the subjective case,*
2. *When a pronoun is used as the object of a verb or the object of a preposition, use the objective case,*
3. *When a pronoun is used to show ownership, use the possessive case.*

pronouns used as subjects:

He practices his pitching every day.
Bill painted the walls, and *we* polished the floors.

pronouns used as objects:

Ernestine called *him* yesterday.
He gave all his money to *me*.

pronouns used to show possession:

I'm worried about *my* grade in Spanish.
The nightclub has lost *its* popularity.

Problems Choosing Pronoun Case

One time when you need to be careful in choosing case is when the pronoun is part of a related group of words. *If the pronoun is part of a related group of words, isolate the pronoun.* Next, try out the pronoun choices. Then decide which pronoun is correct and write the correct sentence. For example, which of these sentences is correct?

Aunt Sophie planned a big dinner for Tom and *I*.

or

Aunt Sophie planned a big dinner for Tom and *me*.

Step 1: Isolate the pronoun. Eliminate the related words *Tom and*.

Step 2: Try each case:

Aunt Sophie planned a big dinner for *I*.

or

Aunt Sophie planned a big dinner for *me*.

Step 3: The correct sentence is

Aunt Sophie planned a big dinner for Tom and me.

The pronoun acts as an object, so it takes the objective case.
Try working through the steps once more, to be sure that you understand this principle. Which of the following sentences is correct?
Last week, *me* and my friend took a ride on the new commuter train.

or

Last week, *I* and my friend took a ride on the new commuter train.

Step 1: Isolate the pronoun. Eliminate the related words *and my friend*.

Step 2: Try each case:

Last week, *me* took a ride on the new commuter train.

or

Last week, *I* took a ride on the new commuter train.

Step 3: The correct sentence is

Last week, I and my friend took a ride on the new commuter train.

The pronoun acts as a subject, so it takes the subjective case.
Note: You can also write it this way:

Last week my friend and I took a ride on the new commuter train.

COMMON ERRORS WITH CASE OF PRONOUNS

Be careful to avoid these common errors:

1. *Between* **is a preposition. The pronouns that follow it are objects of the preposition:** between *us,* between *them,* between *you and me.* It is *never correct* to write *between you and I.*

   examples:

   not this: ~~The plans for the surprise party must be kept secret between you and I.~~

   but this: The plans for the surprise party must be kept secret between you and me.

2. **Never use** *myself* **as a replacement for** *I* **or** *me.*

   examples:

   not this: ~~My father and myself want to thank you for this honor.~~
   but this: My father and I want to thank you for this honor.

   not this: ~~She thought the prize should be awarded to Arthur and myself.~~
   but this: She thought the prize should be awarded to Arthur and me.

3. **The possessive pronoun** *its* **has no apostrophe.**

   example:

   not this: ~~The car held it's value.~~
   but this: The car held its value.

▶ **EXERCISE 1: Choosing the Right Case of Pronoun**

Circle the correct pronoun in each of the following sentences.

a. The elephant escaped when the trainer left *its/it's* cage open.

b. My co-workers and *I/myself* would like to arrange a formal meeting with the management.

c. When the neighbor couldn't get an answer, he kept calling Carla and *they/them* all night.

d. Without a guidebook, Mr. Martinez and *she/her* were lost in the big city.

e. I promise not to mention what we discussed; our conversation will be strictly between you and *I/me.*

f. The nominating committee selected two applicants from out of town and *me/myself* as finalists for the position.

g. My pickup truck is twelve years old; it's on *it's/its* last legs.

h. His comments about the proposal were unfairly critical of my staff and *myself/me.*

i. The security officer and *we/us* looked all over for the missing car.

j. The job was a wonderful opportunity; it was a new beginning for *me/I* and him.

▶ **EXERCISE 2:** **Collaborate in Writing Your Own Text on Pronoun Case**

With a partner or with a group, write two sentences that could be used as examples for each of the following rules. The first is done for you. When you've completed the exercise, share your examples with another group or with the whole class.

Rule 1: When a pronoun is used as a subject, use the subjective case.

examples: He complained about the noise in the street.

Tired and hungry, they stopped for lunch.

Rule 2: When a pronoun is used as the object of a verb or the object of a preposition, use the objective case.

examples: _____

_____

Rule 3: When a pronoun is used to show ownership, use the possessive case.

examples: _____

_____

Rule 4: When a pronoun is part of a related group of words, isolate the pronoun to choose the case. (For examples, write two sentences in which the pronoun is part of a related group of words.)

examples: _____

_____

You probably know a good deal about punctuation. In fact, you probably know most of the rules so well that you punctuate your writing automatically, without having to think about the rules. Nevertheless, there are times when every writer has to stop and think, "Do I put a comma here?" or "Should I capitalize this word?" The following review of the basic rules of punctuation can help you answer such questions.

THE PERIOD

Periods are used two ways.

    1. Use a period to mark the end of a sentence that makes a statement.

       We invited him to dinner at our house.
       When Richard spoke, no one paid attention.

    2. Use a period after abbreviations.

       Mr. Ryan
       James Wing, Sr.
       ten p.m.

THE QUESTION MARK

Use a question mark after a direct question.

       Isn't she adorable?
       Do you have car insurance?

If a question is not a direct question, it does not get a question mark.

       They asked if I thought their grandchild was adorable.
       She questioned whether I had car insurance.

THE SEMICOLON

There are two ways to use semicolons.

    1. Use a semicolon to join two independent clauses.

       Michael loved his old Camaro; he worked on it every weekend.

The situation was hopeless; I couldn't do anything.

> **Note:** If the independent clauses are joined by a conjunctive adverb, you still need a semicolon. You will also need a comma after the conjunctive adverb, if the conjunctive adverb is more than one syllable long.

He was fluent in Spanish; consequently, he was the perfect companion for our trip to Venezuela.
I called the hotline for twenty minutes; then I called another number.

> Independent clauses joined by coordinating conjunctions (the words *and, but, or, nor, for, yet, so*) do not get semicolons. They get a comma in front of the coordinating conjunction.

Michael loved his old Camaro, and he worked on it every weekend.
He was fluent in Spanish, so he was the perfect companion for our trip to Venezuela.

2. If a list contains commas and needs to be clarified, use a semicolon to separate the items on a list.

examples:

The contestants came from Rochester, New York; Pittsburgh, Pennsylvania; Trenton, New Jersey; and Boston, Massachusetts.
The new officers of the club will be Althea Bethell, president; Francois Riviere, vice-president; Ricardo Perez, secretary; and Lou Phillips, treasurer.

▶ **EXERCISE 1: Punctuating with Periods, Question Marks, and Semicolons**

Add any necessary periods, question marks, and semicolons to the following sentences. Do not change or take out any existing punctuation marks; do not change small letters to capital letters. Some sentences do not need any additional punctuation.

a. The house needed cleaning and repair, and the back yard needed work, too.

b. Has John ever told you about his college days

c. Linda asked me to stay with her she was afraid to be alone in the house.

d. I am sure Dr Welch is a reasonable man.

e. I don't know whether they are arriving tomorrow

f. The day was cloudy and cool nevertheless, we had a wonderful time at the beach.

g. Are they arriving tomorrow

h. Sarah thinks they are coming in at around four p m, but I'm not sure.

i. You can have that dress it doesn't fit me anymore.

j. Julia asked me if I was going to the festival

THE COMMA

There are four main ways to use a comma, and there are other, less important ways. Memorize the four main ways. If you can learn and understand these four rules, you will be more confident and correct in your punctuation. That is, you will *use a comma only when you have a reason to do so;* you will not be scattering commas in your sentences simply because you think a comma might fit, as many writers do.

The four main ways to use a comma are as a *lister,* a *linker,* an *introducer,* or an *inserter* (use two commas).

1. Use a comma as a lister. Commas support items in a series. These items can be words, phrases, or clauses.

> **comma between words in a list:** Her bedroom was decorated in shades of blue, green, and gold.
> **comma between phrases in a list:** I looked for my ring under the coffee table, between the sofa cushions, and behind the chairs.
> **comma between clauses in a list:** Last week he graduated from college, he found the woman of his dreams, and he won the lottery.

Note: In a list, the comma before *and* is optional, but most writers use it.

2. Use a comma as a linker. A comma and a coordinating conjunction link two independent clauses. The coordinating conjunctions are *and, but, or, nor, for, yet, so.* The comma goes in front of the coordinating conjunction.

> I have to get to work on time, or I'll get into trouble with my boss.
> My mother gave me a beautiful card, and she wrote a note on it.

3. Use a comma as an introducer. Put a comma after introductory words, phrases, or clauses in a sentence.

> Yes, I agree with you on that issue.
> In the long run, you'll be better off without him.
> If you call home, your parents will be pleased.

4. Use a comma as an inserter. When words or phrases that are *not* necessary are inserted into a sentence, put a comma on *both* sides of the inserted material.

> The game, unfortunately, was rained out.
> My test score, believe it or not, was the highest in the class.
> Potato chips, my favorite snack food, are better tasting when they're fresh.
> James, caught in the middle of the argument, tried to keep the peace.

Using commas as inserters requires that you decide what is essential to the meaning of the sentence and what is nonessential.

> **If you do not need material in a sentence, put commas around the material.**
> **If you need material in a sentence, do not put commas around the material.**

For example, consider this sentence:

> The girl who called me was selling magazine subscriptions.

Do you need the words "who called me" to understand the meaning of the sentence? To answer this question, write the sentence without these words:

> The girl was selling magazine subscriptions.

Reading the shorter sentence, you might ask, "Which girl?" The words *who called me* are essential to the sentence. Therefore you *do not put commas around them.*

correct: The girl who called me was selling magazine subscriptions.

Remember that the proper name of a person, place, or thing is always sufficient to identify it. Therefore any information that follows a proper name is inserted material; it gets commas on both sides.

Video Views, which is nearby, has the best prices for video rentals.
Sam Harris, the man who won the marathon, lives on my block.

Remember the *four main ways to use a comma—as a lister, linker, introducer, or inserter*—and you'll solve many of your problems with punctuation.

▶ **EXERCISE 2: Punctuating with Commas:
                    The Four Main Ways**

Put commas wherever they are needed in the following sentences. Do not add any other punctuation, and do not change any existing punctuation. Just add the necessary commas. *Note:* Some of the sentences do not need commas.

a. Whether you like it or not you have to get up early tomorrow.

b. Nancy and I decorated our dorm room with pillows curtains posters and rugs.

c. I was forced to call the emergency towing service and wait two hours for help.

d. The two-story house by the lake is the most attractive one in the neighborhood.

e. Chicken Delights the only restaurant in my neighborhood is always crowded on a Saturday night.

f. No you can't get a bus to the city on Saturdays unless you are prepared to leave early.

g. Dripping wet and miserable I crouched under a huge tree until the rain stopped.

h. Nick got a job right after college for he had spent his senior year making contacts and sending applications.

i. I wanted to look professional for my job interview so I wore a conservative suit.

j. Cleaning the kitchen is a chore because I have to scrub the sink wipe the counters empty the trash and wash the floor.

Other Ways to Use a Comma

There are other places to use a comma. Reviewing these uses will help you feel more confident as a writer.

1. *Use commas with quotations.* Use a comma to set off direct quotations from the rest of the sentence.

> My father told me, "Money doesn't grow on trees."
> "Let's split the bill," Raymond said.

Note the comma that introduces the quotation goes before the quotation marks. But once the quotation has begun, commas or periods go inside the quotation marks.

2. *Use commas with dates and addresses.* Put commas between the items in dates and addresses.

> August 5, 1950, is Chip's date of birth.
> We lived at 133 Emerson Road, Lake Park, Pennsylvania, before we moved to Florida.

Notice the comma after the year in the date, and the comma after the state in the address. These commas are needed when you write a date or address within a sentence.

3. *Use commas in numbers.* Put commas in numbers of one thousand or larger.

> The price of equipment was $1,293.

4. *Use commas for clarity. Put a comma when you need it to make something clear.*

> Whoever it is, is about to be punished.
> While hunting, the eagle is swift and strong.
> I don't like to dress up, but in this job I have to, to get ahead.

▶ **EXERCISE 3: Punctuation: Other Ways to Use a Comma**

Put commas wherever they are needed in the following sentences. Do not add any other punctuation, and do not change any existing punctuation. Just add the necessary commas.

a. Mr. Chen used to say "Every cloud has a silver lining."

b. My best friend was born on January 29 1976 in Philadelphia Pennsylvania.

c. "I would never borrow your car without asking first" my little brother asserted.

d. She bit into the apple and mumbled "This is the best apple I've ever tasted."

e. I graduated from Deerfield High School on June 19 1995 and started my first real job on June 19 1996 in the same town.

f. The repairs on my truck cost me $2392.

g. The Reilly mansion across town is selling for $359000.

h. The first graders dressed as trees danced in leotards covered with paper leaves.

i. On April 14 1996 my father warned me "Don't forget to mail your income tax forms."

j. "Nothing exciting ever happens around here" my cousin complained.

▶ **EXERCISE 4:** **Punctuating with Commas:**
A Comprehensive Exercise

Put commas wherever they are needed in the following sentences. Do not add any other punctuation, and do not change any existing punctuation. Just add the necessary commas. *Note:* some of the sentences do not need commas.

a. I wanted a fabric with gray white and navy in it but I had to settle for one with gray and white.

b. He was born on July 15 1970 in a small town in Ohio.

c. I am sure Jeffrey that you are not telling me the whole story.

d. The family wanted to spend a quiet weekend at home but wound up doing errands all over town.

e. My miniature poodle a truly crazy dog is afraid of the vacuum cleaner.

f. She devoted an entire day to cleaning the kitchen cabinets reorganizing the pantry shelves and scrubbing the hall floor.

g. The man who wrote you is a friend of mine.

h. Whether David likes it or not he has to work overtime again.

i. "Get out your notebooks" the teacher said.

j. Honestly I can't say which is a better buy.

k. I tried to reason with her I tried to warn her I even tried to frighten her but she was determined to proceed with her plans.

l. Pizza Pronto my favorite restaurant is going out of business.

m. We can call him tomorrow or stop by his house.

n. For the third time the child whispered "Mommy I want to go home now."

o. People who have never seen the ocean are not prepared for its beauty.

p. My sister is in two important ways the opposite of my mother.

q. In two important ways my sister is the opposite of my mother.

r. The visitors were friendly and polite yet they seemed a little shy.

s. If you lose lose with style and class.

t. The car in the garage doesn't belong to me nor do I have permission to borrow it.

THE APOSTROPHE

Use the apostrophe two ways.

1. Use an apostrophe in contractions to show that letters have been omitted.

do not	=	don't
I will	=	I'll
is not	=	isn't
she would	=	she'd
will not	=	won't

2. Use an apostrophe to show possession. If a word does not end in *s*, show ownership by adding an apostrophe and *s*.

the ring belongs to Jill	=	Jill's ring
the wallet belongs to somebody	=	somebody's wallet
the books are owned by my father	=	my father's books
Ann and Mike own a house	=	Ann and Mike's house

If a word already ends in *s* and you want to show ownership, just add an apostrophe.

the ring belongs to Frances	=	Frances' ring
two boys own a dog	=	the boys' dog
the house belongs to Ms. Jones	=	Ms. Jones' house

Caution: Be careful with apostrophes. These words, the possessive pronouns, do not take apostrophes: his, hers, theirs, ours, yours, its.

not this: ~~The pencils were their's.~~
but this: The pencils were theirs.

not this: ~~The steak lost it's flavor.~~
but this: The steak lost its flavor.

Do not add an apostrophe to a simple plural.

not this: ~~He lost three suitcase's.~~
but this: He lost three suitcases.

▶ **EXERCISE 5: Punctuating with Apostrophes**

Add apostrophes where they are needed in the following sentences. Some sentences do not need apostrophes.

a. I'm sure Morris intentions were good.

b. That movie sure doesnt live up to its reputation.

c. I love my cousins, but I disagree with their political views.

d. I was sure that the items recovered in the police raid would turn out to be ours.

e. I was surprised by Dallas glass buildings and its network of highways.

f. Professor Lyons is an expert in the field of childrens rights.

g. She had lost the womens tickets.

   h. I know shes not interested in aerobics.

   i. Theyll take the train to Jim and Davids house.

   j. I can give the boys advice, but the problem is still theirs.

THE COLON

A colon is used at the end of a complete statement. It introduces a list or an explanation.

> **colon introduces a list:** When I went grocery shopping, I picked up a few things: milk, eggs, and coffee.
>
> **colon introduces an explanation:** The room was a mess: dirty clothes were piled on the chairs, wet towels were thrown on the floor, and an empty pizza box was tossed in the closet.

Remember that the colon comes after a complete statement. What comes after the colon explains or describes what came before the colon. Look once more at the two examples, and you'll see the point.

> When I went grocery shopping, I picked up a few things: milk, eggs, and coffee. (The words after the colon, *milk, eggs, and coffee,* explain what few things I picked up.)

> The room was a mess: dirty clothes were piled on the chairs, wet towels were thrown on the floor, and an empty pizza box was tossed in the closet. (In this sentence, all the words after the colon describe what the mess was like.)

Some people use a colon every time they put a list in a sentence, but this is not a good rule to follow. Instead, remember that a colon, even one that introduces a list, must come after a complete statement.

> **not this:** ~~When I go to the beach, I always bring: suntan lotion, a big towel, and a cooler with iced tea.~~
>
> **but this:** When I go to the beach, I always bring my supplies: suntan lotion, a big towel, and a cooler with iced tea.

A colon may also introduce long quotations.

> In a letter to a woman who had lost several sons in the Civil War, Abraham Lincoln said: "I feel how weak and fruitless must be any words of mine which should attempt to beguile you from the grief of a loss so overwhelming. But I cannot refrain from tendering to you the consolation that may be found in the thanks of the Republic they died to save."

THE EXCLAMATION MARK

The exclamation mark is used at the end of sentences that express strong emotion.

> **appropriate:** You've won the lottery!
>
> **inappropriate:** We had a great time! ("Great" already implies excitement.)

ALONG THESE LINES/Prentice-Hall, Inc.

Be careful not to overuse the exclamation mark. If your choice of words is descriptive, you should not have to rely on the exclamation point for emphasis. Use it sparingly, for it is easy to rely on exclamations instead of using better vocabulary.

THE DASH

Use a dash to interrupt a sentence; use two to set off words in a sentence. The dash is somewhat dramatic, so be careful not to overuse it.

> This is my last chance to warn him—and he'd better listen to my warning.
> That silly show—believe it or not—is number one in the ratings.

PARENTHESES

Use parentheses to set off words in a sentence.

> I was sure that Ridgefield (the town I'd just visited) was not the place for me.

Note: Commas in pairs, dashes in pairs, and parentheses are all used as inserters. They set off material that interrupts the flow of the sentence. The least dramatic and smoothest way to insert material is to use commas.

THE HYPHEN

A hyphen joins two or more descriptive words that act as a single word.

> The old car had a souped-up engine.
> Bill was a smooth-talking charmer.

▶ **EXERCISE 6: Punctuating with Colons, Exclamation Marks, Dashes, Parentheses, and Hyphens**

In the following sentences, add any of the punctuation listed above that is needed. Answers may vary, because some writers may use dashes instead of parentheses.

   a. His plan for making a million dollars was the most lame brained scheme I'd ever heard.

   b. The Carlton Gallery of Fine Art the place where I had my first job is located east of the river.

   c. My nephew can't go anywhere without his collection of animals two panda bears, a purple dinosaur, and a pink alligator.

   d. Rosa could tell that the speaker was nervous he fidgeted with his notes, stumbled over his words, and blushed beet red.

   e. There's a dinosaur at the window

   f. Bring a raincoat, sweaters, thermal underwear, heavy socks it's going to be freezing cold out there.

g. Cocoa Forest the smallest town in Midland County is best known for its Victorian houses and restored town square.

h. Don't you ever speak to me like that again

i. There are two kinds of desserts desserts that are good for you, and desserts that taste good.

QUOTATION MARKS

Use quotation marks for direct quotes, for the titles of short works, and for other, special uses.

1. Put quotation marks around direct quotes, a speaker or writer's exact words.

> My mother told me, "There are plenty of fish in the sea."
> "I'm never going there again," said Irene.
> "I'd like to buy you dinner," Peter said, "but I'm out of cash."
> My best friend warned me, "Stay away from that guy. He will break your heart."

Look carefully at the preceding examples. Notice that a comma is used to introduce a direct quote, and that, at the end of the quotation, the comma or period goes inside the quotation marks.

> My mother told me, "There are plenty of fish in the sea."

Notice how direct quotes of more than one sentence are punctuated. If the quote is written in one unit, quotation marks go before the first quoted word and after the last quoted word.

> My best friend warned me, "Stay away from that guy. He will break your heart."

But if the quote is not written as one unit, the punctuation changes.

> "Stay away from that guy," my best friend warned me. "He will break your heart."

Caution: Do *not* put quotation marks around indirect quotations.

indirect quotation: He asked if he could come with us.
direct quotation: He asked, "Can I come with you?"

indirect quotation: She said that she wanted more time.
direct quotation: "I want more time," she said.

2. Put quotation marks around the titles of short works. If you are writing the title of a short work like a short story, an essay, a newspaper or magazine article, a poem, or a song, put quotation marks around the title.

> In middle school, we read Robert Frost's poem "The Road Not Taken."
> My little sister has learned to sing "Itsy Bitsy Spider."

However, if you are writing the title of a longer work like a book, movie, magazine, play, television show, or record album, underline the title.

> Last night I saw an old movie, <u>Stand By Me.</u>

ALONG THESE LINES/Prentice-Hall, Inc.

I read an article called "Campus Crime" in <u>Newsweek</u> magazine.

In printed publications such as books or magazines, titles of long works are put in italics. But when you are handwriting, typing, or using a word processor, underline the titles of long works.

3. There are other, special uses of quotation marks. You use quotation marks around special words in a sentence.

When you said "never," did you mean it?
People from the Midwest pronounce "water" differently than I do.

If you are using a quote within a quote, use single quotation marks.

My brother complained, "Every time we get in trouble, Mom has to say 'I told you so.' "
Kyle said, "Linda has a way of saying 'Excuse me' that is really very rude."

CAPITAL LETTERS

There are ten main situations where you capitalize.

1. Capitalize the first word of every sentence.

Yesterday we saw our first soccer game.

2. Capitalize the first word in a direct quotation if the word begins a sentence:

My aunt said, "This is a gift for your birthday."
"Have some birthday cake," my aunt said, "and have some more ice cream." (Notice that the second section of this quote does not begin with a capital letter because it does not begin a sentence.)

3. Capitalize the names of persons.

Nancy Perez and Frank Murray came to see me at the store.
I asked Mother to feed my cat.

Do not capitalize words like "mother," "father," or "aunt" if you put a possessive in front of them.

I asked my mother to feed my cat.

4. Capitalize the titles of persons.

I was a patient of Dr. Wilson.
He has to see Dean Johnston.

Don't capitalize when the title is not connected to a name.

I was a patient of that doctor.
He has to see the dean.

5. Always capitalize nationalities, religions, races, months, days of the week, documents, organizations, holidays, and historical events or periods.

In high school, we never studied the Vietnam War, just the Civil War.
The Polish-American Club will hold a picnic on Labor Day.

Use small letters for the seasons.

I love fall because I love to watch the leaves change color.

6. Capitalize the names of particular places.

We used to hold our annual meetings at Northside Auditorium in Springfield, Iowa, but this year we are meeting at Riverview Theater in Langton, Missouri.

Use small letters if a particular place is not given.

We are looking for an auditorium we can rent for our meeting.

7. Use capital letters for geographic locations.

Jim was determined to find a good job in the West.

But use small letters for geographic directions.

To get to my house, you have to drive west on the turnpike.

8. Capitalize the names of specific products.

I always drink Diet Pepsi for breakfast.

But use small letters for a general type of product.

I always drink a diet cola for breakfast.

9. Capitalize the names of specific school courses.

I have to take Child Psychology next term.

But use small letters for a general academic subject.

My advisor told me to take a psychology course.

10. Capitalize the first and last words in the titles of long or short works, and capitalize all other significant words in the titles:

I've always wanted to read <u>The Old Man and the Sea.</u>
Whenever we go to see the team play, my uncle sings "Take Me Out to the Ballgame."

(Remember that the titles of long works, like books, should be underlined; the titles of short ones, like songs, are quoted.)

▶ **E X E R C I S E 7 : Punctuating with Quotation Marks, Underlining, and Capital Letters**

In the following sentences, add any punctuation listed above that is needed.

a. Don't ever call me again, the repairman said, unless it's an emergency.

b. No one expected Home Alone to be such a popular movie, but it broke all box office records at the Sunset mall theater.

c. James, you should be careful what you wish for, my aunt said, because you may get it.

d. That old word jock is mistakenly applied to anyone who likes sports.

e. My sisters all attended Broward Community college, but I'm going to a community college in the midwest.

f. When I was a growing up, my favorite television show was Charles in Charge, but now I love to watch old movies like Rocky or The breakfast club.

g. Yesterday I tried to buy tickets for the concert at the coral beach amphitheater, but the man at the ticket office said, we're sold out.

h. You always say I'm sorry when you never mean it, my boyfriend complained.

i. I told uncle Phil to be on time, but my uncle is a procrastinator.

j. Next semester I'm taking courses in speech, business, and economics.

NUMBERS

Spell out numbers that take one or two words to spell out.

> Alice mailed two hundred brochures.
> I spent ninety dollars on car repairs.

Use the numbers themselves if it takes more than two words to spell them out.

> We looked through 243 old photographs.
> The sticker price was $10,397.99.

Also use numbers to write dates, times, and addresses.

> We live at 24 Cambridge Street.
> They were married on April 3, 1993.

ABBREVIATIONS

Although you should spell out most words rather than abbreviate them, you may use common abbreviations like *Mr., Mrs., Ms., Jr., Sr., Dr.* when they are used with a proper name. Abbreviations may also be used for references to time, and for organizations widely known by initials.

> The moderator asked Ms. Steinem to comment.
> The bus left at 5 p.m., and the trip took two hours.
> He works for the FBI.

You should spell out the names of places, months, days of the week, courses of study, and words referring to parts of a book.

> **not this:** I missed the last class, so I never got the notes for Chap. Three.
> **but this:** I missed the last class, so I never got the notes for Chapter Three.

> **not this:** He lives on Chestnut Street in Boston, Mass.
> **but this:** He lives on Chestnut Street in Boston, Massachusetts.

> **not this:** Pete missed his trig. test.
> **but this:** Pete missed his trigonometry test.

▶ **EXERCISE 8: A Comprehensive Exercise on Punctuation**

To assess how well you've learned all the rules of punctuation, complete the following exercise. Add all the necessary punctuation to the following sentences.

a. My sister had a hard time meeting her three boys demands for attention but she did her best.

b. The people at the store were extremely helpful furthermore they were willing to handle special orders.

c. Turquoise blue which is my favorite color is being used to decorate many restaurants.

d. Every time I study with you she said I get good grades on my tests.

e. Parents should be willing to listen children should be willing to talk and both groups should be open to new ideas if families are going to live in harmony.

f. Repairing the damages caused by the fire cost three hundred and fifty-seven dollars.

g. Most people have trouble hitting the high notes in The Star-Spangled banner.

h. Dont forget to pick up the food we need for the picnic hamburgers hot dogs potato salad and corn.

i. No one told Jose about the job opening so he didn't apply for the position.

j. Leo was born in Philadelphia, Penn. on June 3 1968 and he grew up in a nearby town.

k. Christina Ruggiero who always sends me a birthday card is a considerate and thoughtful person.

l. We were sure that rain or shine he would be there.

m. I'm sorry dad that I was late for James farewell dinner.

n. Unless you replace those worn out tires you cant drive safely on rain slicked roads.

o. Philip asked Is there a shortcut to the warehouse

p. Philip asked if there was a shortcut to the warehouse

q. When he was in high school he took english courses but at Jackson college he is taking communications courses.

r. The girl running across the ice slipped and fell then she grabbed at a fence post and pulled herself up.

s. Bolton Furniture has kept its reputation for quality merchandise at a reasonable price thus its been able to survive in hard times.

t. I'm thinking of writing a book called how to manage your time but I never seem to have time to write it.

Acknowledgments

Edna Buchanan, "Rocky Rowf" from *The Corpse Had a Familiar Face*. Copyright © 1987 by Edna Buchanan. Reprinted with the permission of Random House, Inc.

Sandra Cisneros, "Eleven" from *Woman Hollering Creek and Other Stories* (New York: Random House, 1991). Copyright © 1991 by Sandra Cisneros. Reprinted with the permission of Susan Bergholz Literary Services, New York. All rights reserved.

Dennis Hevesi, "Parental Discretion" from the *New York Times* (April 8, 1990), Educational Supplement. Copyright © 1990 by The New York Times Company. Reprinted with the permission of the *New York Times*.

John Holt, "Three Disciplines for Children" from *Freedom and Beyond* (New York: E. P. Dutton, 1972). Copyright © 1972 by John Holt. Reprinted with the permission of Boynton/Cook Publishers, Inc., a subsidiary of Reed Elsevier, Inc., Portsmouth, New Hampshire.

John Kellmayer, "Students in Shock" from David I. Daniels, Janet M. Goldstein, and Christopher G. Hayes, *A Basic Reader for College Writers*. Reprinted with the permission of Townsend Publications.

Julianne Malveaux, "Afrocentric Education Pointless if Girls Are Excluded" (1991). Reprinted with the permission of King Features Syndicate. All rights reserved.

Davidyne Mayleas, "How to Land the Job You Want" from *Reader's Digest* (June 1976). Copyright © 1976 by Reader's Digest Association. Reprinted by permission.

Douglas Noble, "The Myth of Computer Literacy" from "The Underside of Computer Literacy" from *Raritan* (Spring 1984). Copyright © 1984 by Douglas Noble. Reprinted with the permission of the author.

Gwinn Owens, "A Ridiculous Addiction" from *Newsweek* (December 4, 1989). Copyright © 1989 by Gwinn Owens. Reprinted with the permission of the author.

Brent Staples, "Just Walk on By: A Black Man Ponders His Power to Alter Public Space" from *Ms. Magazine* (September 1986). Copyright © 1986 by Brent Staples. Reprinted with the permission of the author.

Brad Wackerlin, "Against All Odds, I'm Just Fine" from *Newsweek* 65, no. 27 (June 1990). Copyright © 1990 by Brad Wackerlin. Reprinted with the permission of the author.

Elizabeth Wong, "A Present for Popo" from the *Los Angeles Times* (December 30, 1992). Copyright © 1992 by Elizabeth Wong. Reprinted with the permission of the author.

Photo Credits

Page 94, photograph A, Junebug Clark/Photo Researchers, Inc.; page 94, photograph B, Jay Ullal/Stern/Black Star; page 124, photograph A, Larry Fleming/Simon & Schuster/PH College; page 124, photograph B, Steve McCurry/Magnum Photos, Inc.

Index

Abbreviations, 431
Action verbs, 315, 327, 371
Active voice, 387–90
Adverbs, 323, 328
  conjunctive, 344
    commonly used, 334–35
    punctuation after, 335
  subordinate, 344
"Afrocentric Education Pointless
    if Girls Are Excluded"
    (Malveaux), 260–62
"Against All Odds, I'm Just
    Fine" (Wackerlin),
    187–88
Always, 323, 328
And, 330–33
Announcements, turning into
    topic sentences, 18–19
Apostrophes, 425–26
Argument. *See also* Argument
    paragraphs
  definition of, 237
  examples, 258–63
Argument paragraphs, 237–63
  final lines, 253–54
  hints for writing, 237–39
  outlines, 245–49, 253
  peer review form, 257
  roughlines, 249–54
  thoughtlines, 241–45
  topic sentences, 237–41, 243
  transitions, 250, 252
Attitude toward writing from
    reading, 40–41
Audience, 3

Be
  past tense, 376–77
  present tense, 375
Being verbs, 315, 327, 371
Between, 417
Body of essay, 282–85
-*body* words, 399, 406
Brainstorming, 4–5, 20
  for argument, 241–43
  basis for classification,
    194–95
  for cause or effect, 216
  creating questions for, 8–9
  for description, 75–76

for illustration, 4–7
for narrative, 107–8
for reaction to a reading,
    57–58
for sense details, 72–73
Buchanan, Edna, 126–29
But, 330–33

Capital letters, 295, 429–30
Case, 415–18
Cause and effect. *See also* Cause
    or effect paragraphs
  definition of, 212
  example, 234–36
Cause or effect paragraphs,
    212–36
  final lines, 229–31
  hints for writing, 212–13
  order, 221, 223
  outlines, 220–24, 229
  peer review form, 233
  roughlines, 224–30
  thoughtlines, 215–20
  topics, 212–14, 218–19
  topic sentences, 214, 217,
    219–20, 222–23
  transitions, 225–26
Cisneros, Sandra, 304–6
Classification. *See also*
    Classification paragraphs
  definition of, 189
  example, 209–11
Classification paragraphs,
    189–211
  basis for classifying, 190–94
  details for, 196–97
  final lines, 203–6
  hints for writing, 189–90
  outlines, 197–200, 203–4
  peer review form, 208
  roughlines, 200–202, 204
  thoughtlines, 194–97
  topic sentences, 195, 197,
    199–200
  transitions, 202–3
Clause, definition of, 315, 329
Coherence, definition of, 2–3
Collective nouns, 399–400,
    408–9
Colons, 426

Commas
  with coordinating
    conjunctions, 331–33
  with quotation marks, 105
  use of, 421–24
Comma splices
  correcting, 336–37
  definition of, 334
Comparison. *See also*
    Comparison and contrast
    paragraphs
  definition of, 155
  example, 187–88
Comparison and contrast
    paragraphs, 155–88
  final lines, 177, 179–80, 183
  hints for writing, 155–56
  irrelevant details, 173
  outlines, 170–74, 177–78,
    180–81
  peer review form, 186
  point-by-point pattern, 156,
    158–60, 162–63, 170–71,
    177–80
  roughlines, 175–79, 181–82
  subject-by-subject pattern,
    156–58, 163–64, 174,
    180–83
  thoughtlines, 165–70
  topic sentences, 156, 161,
    169–70
  transitions, 162–65, 175,
    181–82
Complex sentences
  definition of, 342
  punctuating, 342–43
Compound sentences
  comma and coordinating
    conjunctions, 330–33
  definition of, 332
  semicolon and conjunctive
    adverb, 334–35
  semicolon between
    independent clauses,
    333–34
Compound subjects, 397–98
Conclusion of essay, 285–86
Conjunctions
  coordinating, 330–33, 346
  subordinating, 341–42, 347,
    350

Conjunctive adverbs, 344
   commonly used, 334–35
   punctuation after, 335
Consistency
   in pronouns, 413–15
   of verb tense, 382–85
Contractions, 323, 375
Contrast. *See also* Comparison
      and contrast paragraphs
   definition of, 155
Contrast paragraphs. *See*
      Comparison and contrast
      paragraphs
Coordinating conjunctions,
      330–33, 344, 346, 420
Coordination. *See* Sentence
      variety
Could have, 391

Dangling modifiers, 366–68,
      369
Dash, 427
Dependent clause
   definition of, 340
   fragments, 350–51
Description
   definition of, 68
   example, 95–97
   See also Descriptive
      paragraphs
Descriptive paragraphs, 68–97
   dominant impression, 76–79
   final lines, 88–91
   hints for writing, 68–75
   order of details, 80–84
   outlines, 78–84, 89
   peer review form, 94
   roughlines, 84–88, 90
   specific words and phrases,
      68–72
   thoughtlines, 75–78
   topic sentences, 79, 81–84
   transitions, 87–88
Details
   adding, 20, 25–26, 30–31
      to dominant impression,
         77–78
      to ideas, 6–7
   checking, 19–20
   creating dominant impression
      from list of, 78
   distinguishing between
      reasons and, 243–44
   eliminating, 20–21, 26
   finding specific, 9–10

grouping related items in lists,
      15–16
irrelevant
   in comparison and contrast
      paragraphs, 173
   in illustration paragraphs,
      20
   in narrative paragraphs,
      112–14
   order of, 23–24, 27, 80–84,
      104, 111–12
   writing topic sentences from
      lists of, 16–17, 109–10
Directional process, 130, 141
Do
   past tense, 376–77
   present tense, 375
Dominant impression, 76
   adding details to, 77–78
   creating from list of details,
      78
Drafts. *See* Roughlines

Each, 398, 399, 406, 407
Editing, 28
Effects. *See* Cause or effect
      paragraphs
Either, 399, 406, 407
"Eleven" (Cisneros), 304–6
Emphatic order, 23, 221, 245
Essays, 264–310
   body of, 282–85
   compared to single
      paragraphs, 264–66
   conclusion of, 285–86
   definition of, 264
   examples, 304–10
   final lines, 295, 298–300
   introduction of, 279–82
   organizing, 266
   outlines, 273–79, 295–96
   peer review form, 303
   proofreading, 299–300
   roughlines, 279–94, 296–97
   synonyms and repetition, 289,
      294
   thesis
      characteristics of, 266–67
      good sentences, 267–68
      hints for writing, 267
      placement of, 279–80
      relating to subpoints, 268
      restating, 285–87
   thoughtlines, 269–73
   titles of, 295

topic sentences, 274, 282–85
   transitions, 288–90, 292–93
Ever, 323, 328
Everybody, 398, 406
Examples, 22
Exclamation marks, 426–27

Final lines, 2
   definition of, 32
   essays, 295, 298–300
   paragraphs, 3, 28–32, 34
      argument, 253–54
      cause or effect, 229–31
      classification, 203–6
      comparison and contrast,
         177, 179–80, 183
      descriptive, 88–91
      illustration, 34
      narrative, 120–23
      process, 145, 147–48
   writing from reading
      reaction to a reading,
         59–60
      summary, 55–56
      writing reaction to a
         reading, 59–60
First draft. *See* Roughlines
First person, 141, 413
For, 330–33
Formal outline of essay, 273
Framing essay, 286
Freewriting, 4, 20
   for cause or effect paragraphs,
      215
   for descriptive paragraphs, 75
   for essay topics, 269
   finding specific details, 9–10
   finding topics, 11–12
   for illustration paragraphs, 4
   for narrative paragraphs, 107
   for process paragraphs,
      134–36
   for reaction to a reading,
      56–57
Fused sentences. *See* Run-on
      (fused) sentences
Fuzzy description, 85

General ideas, 5
General sentences, 72
General words, 68–70
Grammar. *See* Modifiers;
      Pronouns; Punctuation;
      Sentences; Verbs

Have
  past tense, 376–77
  present tense, 375
Helping verbs, 316–17, 374
Here is/are, Here was/were,
      322–23
Hevesi, Dennis, 63–66
Holt, John, 209–11
"How to Land the Job You
      Want" (Mayleas), 151–54
Hyphens, 427

Ideas. *See also* Thoughtlines
  adding details to, 6–7
  brainstorming and, 4–5
  clustering, 270, 272–73
  freewriting and, 4
  general and specific, 5–6
  grouping related, 13
  journals and, 4, 5
  listing related, 12
  listing for reaction to a
      reading, 57
  mapping, 13
  marking list of, 50–52,
      269–70, 272–73
  related, 12–13
  selecting main, 52
Illustration, definition of, 22
Illustration paragraphs, 3–39
  adding details, 6–8
  eliminating details, 6–8
  finding ideas, 31–32, 34
  order of details, 23
  outlines, 19–23, 33
  peer review form, 39
  roughlines, 28–30, 33
  thoughtlines, 3–8, 12–13, 15
  topic sentences, 13–15
  transitions, 29–30
Indefinite pronouns, 398–99,
      406–7
Independent clause, 329
  definition of, 340
Infinitives, 328, 349
  commonly used, 324
  correcting problems with,
      325–26
Informational process, 130, 141
-ing verbs, 324–26, 328, 349
Interviewing, 36–37
  for process paragraphs, 149
  for specific answers, 70
Introduction of essay, 279–82
Irregular verbs, 375–80

Irrelevant details
  in comparison and contrast
      paragraphs, 173
  in narrative paragraphs,
      112–14
Italics, 429
Its, 417

Journals, 4, 5, 20
"Just Walk on By: A Black Man
      Ponders His Power to
      Alter Public Space"
      (Staples), 306–10

Kellmayer, John, 234–36
Key phrases, 21–22

Logical order, 221
"Lots of" phrases, 88–89

Malveaux, Julianne, 260–62
Mapping ideas, 13
Mayleas, Davidyne, 151–54
Misplaced modifiers, 365–66,
      369
Modifiers
  correcting problems,
      364–70
  dangling, 366–68, 369
  definition of, 363
  misplaced, 365–66, 369
  recognizing, 363–64
Myself/I/me, 417
"Myth of Computer Literacy,
      The" (Noble), 258–60

Narration. *See also* Narrative
      paragraphs
  definition of, 98
  example, 126–29
Narrative paragraphs, 98–129
  clarity in, 103–4
  dull, 104
  final lines, 120–23
  irrelevant details, 112–14
  order of details, 104, 111–12
  outlines, 110–14
  peer review form, 125
  roughlines, 114–22
  speaker's exact words, 105
  thoughtlines, 105–10

  topic sentences, 98–103,
      108–10, 116–18
  transitions, 118–20
Nearly, 323
Neither, 399, 406, 407
Never, 323, 324, 328
Noble, Douglas, 258–60
Nor, 330–33
Not, 323, 324, 328
Nouns, collective, 399–400,
      408–9
Numbers, 431

Objections. *See* Argument
      paragraphs
Objective case, 415, 416, 418
Often, 323, 328
-one words, 399, 406
Or, 330–33
Order
  of details, 23–24, 27, 80–84,
      104, 111–12
  emphatic, 23, 221, 245
  of reasons in argument,
      245–47
  space, 23
  time, 23, 104, 111–12,
      130–31, 134, 138–39,
      221
Outlines, 1
  definition of, 21, 32
  essays, 273–79, 295–96
  paragraphs
    adding details, 20
    argument, 245–49, 253
    cause or effect, 220–24,
        229
    checking details, 19–20
    classification, 197–200,
        203–4
    comparison and contrast,
        170–74, 177–78,
        180–81
    descriptive, 78–84, 89
    eliminating details, 20–21
    illustration, 21–23
    narrative, 110–14
    order of details, 23–24
    process, 136–40, 145–46
    unity of details, 23
  writing from reading
    reaction to a reading, 58
    summary, 53–54
    writing reaction to a
        reading, 58

Owens, Gwinn, 42, 46–50,
53–61

Paragraphs
  argument, 237–63
    final lines, 253–54
    hints for writing, 237–39
    outlines, 245–49, 253
    peer review form, 257
    roughlines, 249–54
    thoughtlines, 241–45
    topic sentences, 237–41,
      243
    transitions, 250, 252
  audience for, 3
  cause or effect, 212–36
    final lines, 229–31
    hints for writing, 212–13
    order, 221, 223
    outlines, 220–24, 229
    peer review form, 233
    roughlines, 224–30
    thoughtlines, 215–20
    topics, 212–14, 218–19
    topic sentences, 214, 217,
      219–20, 222–23
    transitions, 225–26
  classification, 189–211
    basis for classifying, 190–94
    details for, 196–97
    final lines, 203–6
    hints for writing, 189–90
    outlines, 197–200, 203–4
    peer review form, 208
    roughlines, 200–202, 204
    thoughtlines, 194–97
    topic sentences, 195, 197,
      199–200
    transitions, 202–3
  comparison and contrast,
    155–88
    final lines, 177, 179–80,
      183
    hints for writing, 155–56
    irrelevant details, 173
    outlines, 170–74, 177–78,
      180–81
    peer review form, 186
    point-by-point pattern, 156,
      158–60, 162–63, 170–71,
      177–80
    roughlines, 175–79, 181–82
    subject-by-subject pattern,
      156–58, 163–64, 174,
      180–83

    thoughtlines, 165–70
    topic sentences, 156, 161,
      169–70
    transitions, 162–65, 175,
      181–82
  consistency of verb tense in,
    383–85
  definition of, 3
  descriptive, 68–97
    dominant impression,
      76–79
    final lines, 88–91
    hints for writing, 68–75
    order of details, 80–84
    outlines, 78–84, 89
    peer review form, 94
    roughlines, 84–88, 90
    specific words and phrases,
      68–72
    thoughtlines, 75–78
    topic sentences, 79, 81–84
    transitions, 87–88
  essays compared to, 264–66
  illustration, 3–39
    adding details, 6–8
    eliminating details, 6–8
    finding ideas, 31–32, 34
    order of details, 23
    outlines, 19–23, 33
    peer review form, 39
    roughlines, 28–30, 33
    thoughtlines, 3–8, 12–13,
      15
    topic sentences, 13–15
    transitions, 29–30
  length of, 3
  narrative, 98–129
    clarity in, 103–4
    dull, 104
    final lines, 120–23
    irrelevant details, 112–14
    order of details, 104,
      111–12
    outlines, 110–14
    peer review form, 125
    roughlines, 114–22
    speaker's exact words, 105
    thoughtlines, 105–10
    topic sentences, 98–103,
      108–10, 116–18
    transitions, 118–20
  process, 130–54
    final lines, 145, 147–48
    hints for writing, 131–32
    outlines, 136–40, 145–46
    peer review form, 150

    roughlines, 140–47
    thoughtlines, 133–36
    topic sentences, 131–34,
      137–38, 145
    transitions, 142–44
  purpose of, 3
  title of, 32
  unity in, 3, 23
  writing process, 3–39
    final lines, 31–32, 34
    outlines, 19–24, 33
    peer review form, 39
    roughlines, 28–31, 33
    thoughtlines, 3–19
Parallelism in sentences, 356–62
"Parental Discretion" (Hevesi),
  63–66
Parentheses, 427
Passive voice, 387–89
Past participle, 374, 375,
  377–79
Past perfect tense, 385–87
Past tense, 373–79, 385–87
Peer review form
  for argument paragraphs, 257
  for cause or effect paragraphs,
    233
  for classification paragraphs,
    208
  for comparison and contrast
    paragraphs, 186
  for descriptive paragraphs, 94
  for essays, 303
  for illustration paragraphs, 39
  for narrative paragraphs, 125
  for paragraph, 39
  for process paragraphs, 150
  for writing from reading, 62
Periods, 419, 420
Phrases
  definition of, 315
  key, 21–22
  prepositional, 319–22, 327,
    348
    subject-verb agreement and,
      394–96
  specific, 68–72
  transitions, 87–88
Plural, 141. See also Pronouns;
  Subject- verb agreement
Point-by-point comparisons,
  156, 158–60, 162–63,
  170–71, 177–80
Possessive case, 415, 417, 418
Prepositional phrases, 319–22,
  327, 348

subject-verb agreement and, 394–96
Prepositions, commonly used, 319
Prereading, 40
    checklist, 41
    example, 42–44
    reasons for, 41–42
"Present for Popo, A" (Wong), 95–97
Present participle, 374, 375
Present perfect tense, 385
Present tense, 371–75, 377–79
Process. *See also* Process paragraphs
    definition of, 130
    example, 151–54
Process paragraphs, 130–54
    final lines, 145, 147–48
    hints for writing, 131–32
    outlines, 136–40, 145–46
    peer review form, 150
    roughlines, 140–47
    shift in persons, 141–43
    thoughtlines, 133–36
    topic sentences, 131–34, 137–38, 145
    transitions, 142–44
Pronouns, 405–18
    antecedent agreement, 406–10
    antecedents of, 405–6
    avoiding sexism, 407
    case of, 415–18
    consistency in, 413–15
    indefinite, 398–99, 406–7
    as objects, 415, 416, 418
    possessive, 415–18
    reference of, 410–12
    as subjects, 394, 415–18
Pronoun test, 324
Proofreading, 2, 122–23, 148, 255, 299–300. *See also* Final lines
Punctuation, 329, 419–33
    abbreviations, 431
Purpose, 3
    after conjunctive adverbs, 335
    apostrophes, 425–26
    capital letters, 295, 429–30
    colons, 426
    commas
        with coordinating conjunctions, 331–33
        with quotation marks, 105
        use of, 421–24

for complex sentences, 342–43
    dash, 427
    exclamation marks, 426–27
    hyphens, 427
    numbers, 431
    parentheses, 427
    periods, 419, 420
    question marks, 419, 420
    quotation marks, 105, 428–29
    semicolons
        and conjunctive adverbs, 334–35, 344, 347
        between independent clauses, 333–34, 344, 347
        use of, 419–20

Question marks, 419, 420
Questions
    forming before reading, 42
    word order in, 323
Quotation marks, 105, 428–29

Rarely, 323
Reading
    with questions in mind, 44
    speed, 45
    writing from. *See* Writing from reading
Reasons. *See* Argument paragraphs
Reference of pronouns, 410–12
Regular verbs, 372, 374, 375
Related ideas, 12–13
Repetition, 289, 294
Rereading with pen or pencil, 40, 45–49
Revising. *See* Roughlines
"Ridiculous Addiction, A" (Owens), 42–44, 46–50
"Rocky Rowf" (Buchanan), 126–29
Roughlines, 2
    definition of, 32
    essays, 279–94, 296–97
    paragraphs, 28–31
        argument, 249–54
        cause or effect, 224–30
        classification, 200–202, 204
        comparison and contrast, 175–79, 181–82
        illustration, 28–30, 33
        descriptive, 84–88, 90

narrative, 114–22
    process, 140–47
    writing from reading
        reaction to a reading, 59
        summary, 54–55
        writing reaction to a reading, 59
Run-on (fused) sentences, 332
    correcting, 335–36

Second person, 141, 413
Semicolons
    and conjunctive adverbs, 334–35, 344, 347
    between independent clauses, 333–34, 344, 347
    use of, 419–20
Sense words, 72–75, 85
Sentences, 315–62. *See also* Sentence variety; Verbs
    complex
        definition of, 342
        punctuating, 342–43
    compound
        comma and coordinating conjunctions, 330–33, 344, 346
        definition of, 332
        semicolon and conjunctive adverb, 334–35
        semicolon between independent clauses, 333–34
    definition of, 315
    fragments
        correcting, 352–55
        definition of, 348
        recognizing, 348–51
    general, 72
    modifiers
        correcting problems, 364–70
        dangling, 366–68, 369
        definition of, 363
        misplaced, 365–66, 369
        recognizing, 363–64
    parallelism in, 356–62
    prepositional phrases in, 319–22, 327, 348
    run-on (fused), 332
        correcting, 335–36
    subjects of
        compound, 397–98
        recognizing, 317–18, 320, 394–95

Sentences *(cont.)*
  sentence fragments and, 348–52
  word order and, 322–23, 327
  subject-verb agreement, 323
    collective nouns, 399–400
    compound subjects, 397–98
    indefinite pronouns, 398–99
    pronouns as subjects, 394
    special problems, 394–97
  topic. *See* Topic sentences
  word order, 322–23
Sentence variety, 30, 329–47
  comma and coordinating conjunction, 330–33, 344, 346
  dependent clauses, 340–42, 344, 347
  semicolon and conjunctive adverb, 334–35, 344, 347
  semicolon between independent clauses, 333–34, 344, 347
Sexism, avoidance of, 407
Shift in persons, 141–43
Should have, 391
Simple sentences
  combining. *See* Sentence variety
  definition of, 329
Singular, 141. *See also* Pronouns; Subject-verb agreement
So, 330–33
Space order, 23
Specific ideas, 5–6
Specific words and phrases, 68–72
Staples, Brent, 306–10
"Students in Shock" (Kellmayer), 234–36
Subject-by-subject comparisons, 156–58, 163–64, 174, 180–83
Subjective case, 415, 417, 418
Subjects (of sentence)
  compound, 397–98
  recognizing, 317–18, 320, 394–95
  sentence fragments and, 348–52
  word order and, 322–23, 327
Subject-verb agreement, 323
  collective nouns, 399–400
  compound subjects, 397–98

indefinite pronouns, 398–99
pronouns as subjects, 394
special problems, 394–97
Subordinate adverbs, 344
Subordinating conjunctions, 341–42
  commonly used, 342, 347, 350
Subordination. *See* Sentence variety
Summary of reading
  final lines, 55–56
  outlines, 53–54
  roughlines, 54–55
  thoughtlines, 50–53
Support, definition of, 23
Synonyms, 289, 294

There is/are, There was/were, 322–23
Thesis
  characteristics of, 266–67
  good sentences, 267–68
  hints for writing, 267
  placement of, 279–80
  relating to subpoints, 268
  restating, 285–87
-thing words, 399, 406
Third person, 141, 413
Thoughtlines, 1
  beginning, 3–12
  definition of, 32
  essays, 269–73
  focusing, 12–19
    forming topic sentence, 13–15
    listing related ideas, 12–13
    mapping, 13
  paragraphs
    argument, 241–45
    cause or effect, 215–20
    classification, 194–97
    comparison and contrast, 165–70
    descriptive, 75–78
    illustration, 3–8, 12–13
    narrative, 105–10
    process, 133–36
  writing from reading
    marking list of ideas, 50–52
    reaction to a reading, 56–58
    selecting main idea, 52
    summary, 50–53

"Three Disciplines for Children" (Holt), 209–11
Time order, 23, 104, 111–12, 130–31, 134, 138–39, 221
Titles
  of essays, 295
  of paragraphs, 32
  quotation marks and, 428–29
  underlining and, 428–30
Topics. *See also* Thoughtlines
  for cause or effect paragraphs, 212–14, 218–19
  definition of, 14
  narrowing, 269, 271
  turning into topic sentences, 17
Topic sentences, 19–24
  adding details to support, 25–26
  broad and narrow, 14–15
  definition of, 14
  essays, 274, 282–85
  forming, 13–15
  paragraphs
    argument, 237–41, 243
    at beginning, 23–24, 99
    cause or effect, 214, 217, 219–20, 222–23
    classification, 195, 197, 199–200
    comparison and contrast, 156, 161, 169–70
    descriptive, 79, 81–84
    at end, 24, 100
    illustration, 13–15
    in middle, 24, 100
    narrative, 98–103, 108–10, 116–18
    process, 131–34, 137–38, 145
  revising broad, 17–18
  revising narrow, 19
  turning announcements into, 18–19
Transitions
  adding, 28
  for essays, 288–90, 292–93
  for paragraphs
    argument, 250, 252
    cause and effect, 225–26
    classification, 202–3
    comparison and contrast, 162–65, 175, 181–82
    descriptive, 87–88

narrative, 118–20
process, 142–44

Underlining, 428–30
Unity, definition of, 23
Used to, 390–91

Vague description, 85
Verbs, 371–404
    action, 315, 327, 371
    active voice, 387–90
    being, 315, 327, 371
    definition of, 315
    forms of
        consistency of tense,
            382–85
        past participle, 374, 375,
            377–79
        past perfect tense, 385–87
        past tense, 373–79, 385–87
        present participle, 374, 375
        present perfect tense, 385
        present tense, 371–75,
            377–79
    helping, 316–17, 374
    infinitives, 324–26, 328, 349
    -ing , 324–26, 328, 349
    irregular, 375–80
    main, 324
    passive voice, 387–89

pronoun test, 324
    recognizing, 316, 320, 324
    regular, 372, 374, 375
    sentence fragments and,
        348–52
    subject-verb agreement, 323
        collective nouns, 399–400
        compound subjects, 397–98
        indefinite pronouns, 398–99
        pronouns as subjects, 394
        special problems, 394–97
    word order and, 322–23

Wackerlin, Brad, 187–88
Walk-through assignments
    argument paragraphs, 255–56
    cause or effect paragraphs,
        231
    classification paragraphs, 206
    comparison and contrast
        paragraphs, 183–84
    descriptive paragraphs, 91
    essays, 300–301
    narrative paragraphs, 123
    process paragraphs, 148–49
    writing a paragraph, 35–36
    writing from reading, 60
Wong, Elizabeth, 95–97
Word order, 322–23, 327
    subject-verb agreement and,
        396–97

Words. *See also* Transitions
    definition of, 315
    general, 68–70
    sense, 72–75, 85
    specific, 68–72
Would have/had, 391
Writing from reading, 40–67
    attitude towards, 40–41
    definition of, 40
    peer review form, 62
    prereading
        checklist, 41
        example, 42–44
        reasons for, 41–42
    reading step
        with questions in mind, 44
        speed, 45
    rereading with pen or pencil,
        45–49
    summary
        final lines, 55–56
        outlines, 53–54
        roughlines, 54–55
        thoughtlines, 50–53
    writing reaction to a reading
        final lines, 59–60
        outlines, 58
        roughlines, 59
        thoughtlines, 56–58

Yet, 330–33